NO TIME TO GRIEVE...

ALSO BY HELENE ISWOLSKY

As Author:
La Jeunesse rouge d'Inna
La Vie de Bakounine
L'Homme 1936 en Russie soviétique
Femmes soviétiques
Light before Dusk
The Soul of Russia Today
Christ in Russia

As Co-Author:
Les Rois aveugles
    (with Joseph Kessel)

As Editor:
Mémoires d'Alexandre Iswolsky, ancien ambassadeur de Russie à Paris, 1906–1910
    (Alexandre Iswolsky)
Au service de la Russie: Alexandre Iswolsky; correspondance diplomatique, 1911, V. 1-2
    (Alexandre Iswolsky)

NO TIME TO GRIEVE...

An Autobiographical Journey

HELENE ISWOLSKY

The Winchell Company • Philadelphia

Copyright © 1985 by Our Lady of the Resurrection Monastery

All rights reserved, including the rights to reproduce this book or portions thereof in any form.

For information, address: The Winchell Company
1315 Cherry Street, Philadelphia, PA 19107.

Distributed in the United States and Canada by
Hippocrene Books, Inc., 171 Madison Avenue, New York, NY 10016.

Printed in the United States of America.

Library of Congress Cataloging in Publication Data

Iswolsky, Helene
  No time to grieve....

  Includes index.
  1. Iswolsky, Helene.   2. United States—Biography.   3. Russian Americans—Biography.   I. Title.
CT275.I75A35   1985   973'.04917102   85-9530
ISBN 0-87052-204-3 (Winchell)

We have no time to grieve...
T.S. Eliot, "Murder in the Cathedral"

To
Dorothy Day

a dear friend in all seasons

Acknowledgments

To fulfill Helene Iswolsky's fondest wish, and to coincide with the tenth anniversary of her death, a few of her dedicated friends, colleagues and students gathered together to bring about the publication of her drafted memoirs, *No Time to Grieve...*

To this end, an editorial committee contributed its time, effort and expertise. The following members of the committee should be singled out with special acknowledgments and grateful thanks. They are, alphabetically:

BROTHER VICTOR-A. D'AVILA-LATOURRETTE, a monk from Our Lady of the Resurrection Monastery, who assisted Helene the last five years of her life, and became her executor. In this capacity, he relentlessly pursued the realization of this undertaking.

MARGUERITE TJADER — herself an author of note — contributed the foreword and epilogue, edited the text and organized Helene's manuscript. Miss Tjader, a longtime friend of Helene Iswolsky, journeyed with her on her first return trip to Russia after the Revolution, in 1961.

MARGARET MUDD, a devoted student, met Helene Iswolsky through the Catholic Worker Movement headed by Dorothy Day. When Helene settled at Cold Spring-on-the-Hudson, Margaret Mudd helped her re-establish her Center for Russian Studies and *The Third Hour*. She studied Russian language and literature under Helene's guidance, and after her death, determined to work for the publication of her autobiography.

HELENE OBOLENSKY coordinated and arranged the book's illustrations from Helene Iswolsky's archives.

CARL SHAIFER, President of The Winchell Company, in charge of the technical aspects of the publication, tirelessly provided his professional expertise.

Additional thanks to:

PRINCE JEAN-LOUIS DE FAUCIGNY-LUCINGE and DR. ALEXANDER P. OBOLENSKY for their first-hand introductory remarks.

Special thanks to:

THE LEBENSBURGER FOUNDATION for initial funding to underwrite printing costs.

Contents

Acknowledgments		vii
Foreword *Marguerite Tjader*		xi
Her Early Years *J. L. de Faucigny-Lucinge*		xiii
Her Last Years *Alexander Obolensky*		xv
Family Coat of Arms		xxii
Chapter I	Family Saga	1
Chapter II	Journey Through Siberia to Japan	9
Chapter III	Copenhagen "La Chère Villa" Palace Square	25
Chapter IV	The Fateful Years	37
Chapter V	The Russian Years—Petersburg to Paris	53
Chapter VI	I Am a Debutante	73
Chapter VII	End of a Golden Age	89
Chapter VIII	War—The "Hôpital Russe"	103
Chapter IX	Endings and Beginnings	123
Chapter X	New Horizons	137
Chapter XI	Writer's Progress	159
Chapter XII	The 1930s: Time of Decision	183
Chapter XIII	Farewell to France	205
Chapter XIV	America—The Grand Tour	229
Chapter XV	Wartime and Peacetime	245
Chapter XVI	From Noon Till Twilight	263
Epilogue		285
Index		289

Illustrations

Family Album (from 1890 to 1914)	*following page*	24
Souvenirs from the Growing Up Period	*following page*	88
In France	*following page*	136
In the United States	*following page*	204

Foreword

WHO CAN ESTIMATE the value and influence of Helene Iswolsky's great life? The luxury and prestige of her youth as an ambassador's daughter, the glamour of her debut at the court of the Tsar in St. Petersburg make a staggering contrast to her plight as a young student in Paris, suddenly bereft of position, money and many friends. Then followed her brave struggle to forge a career, to write, to finish her education and support her mother and herself. In spite of setbacks, the richness of her life could only increase because of her brilliant mind, her strong will and her Russian temperament that would not be defeated.

During the First World War, she worked as a nurse at the Russian Hospital in Paris. By the Second World War, she had become an accomplished journalist and worked for the Voice of America in New York. In between, lay a literary involvement with groups of the Catholic revival and, in Paris, contacts with Russian Orthodox circles and the Russian philosopher Nicholas Berdiaev. The Catholic Jacques Maritain and Emmanuel Mounier were also prominent figures in Helene's development. The sophisticated circle of the Bassiano's at Versailles offered her new friends in the world of art, music and poetry.

Emotions surged around her because of her talented, unusual friends. If she did not have the obvious fulfillments of a husband and children, so many other relationships came to her, changing affections, affinities with great artists, thinkers, poets, rare souls to whom she was drawn, as they were to her. Later, as she matured, taught, lectured, she found many spiritual children who loved her and spread her influence. To hear her speak of her beloved Russian authors was a transmutation of their characters into living people.

Helene was a true child of Dostoevsky because of a certain mystery and inscrutability in her nature. Also, because of her strong sense of the reality of spiritual things and her so typically Russian thirst for God.

In her remarkable book *Christ in Russia,* Helene shows the deep cultural and spiritual heritage of her past, and her love of her country and the Russian people. Her pioneer work in the ecumenical movement had finally won her recognition and praise because of her basic love of people and belief in the essential unity of all mankind under God.

Marguerite Tjader

Her Early Years

THE FIRST TIME I met Helene Iswolsky was in 1917. I was still a very young boy, and she was already a mature young woman. My mother, then a young widow with three children, had married her only brother, Gregory (Grisha) Iswolsky. Their parents were, on the paternal side, Alexander Iswolsky, who was the son of a distinguished Russian family with a long tradition of public service, and on the other side, Marguerite Iswolsky, who was born Countess Toll, of a Russian-Baltic family, her own mother born a Bavarian. Among her direct ancestors was Marshal Count Toll, one of Kutuzov's lieutenants in the Napoleonic Wars.

Alexander Iswolsky had had a very brilliant diplomatic career, having held posts in Italy, Bavaria, Japan, Denmark. Finally, in Russia he was Minister of Foreign Affairs and, later, was Russia's Ambassador to France. His close friendship with President Poincaré enabled him to create the Franco-Russian Alliance shortly before the First World War. He was a man of superior intelligence and always struck me, at my early age, as a rather stern personality. Madame Iswolsky, on the other hand, was a person of infinite charm, very feminine and lovely.

Helene and her brother, though devoted to each other, were different in character. He was gifted, witty, a wonderful storyteller, and bubbling with gaiety. He had inherited his mother's natural charm, whereas Helene had much of her father's intellect, seriousness and dedication. I would say that one had more feminine qualities and the other more virile ones.

Grisha's success, at the beginning of their lives, may have given Helene an inferiority complex. Of course, as a member of the aristocracy, she had to go through the usual process of being presented at the Tsar's Court, attending many balls and parties to which her nature was not attuned. Her brother, however, handsome and brilliant, enjoyed the best of things.

Her experience as a nurse in Paris during the First World War encouraged Helene to turn all her energies to serious matters. It was then that we met, just after her brother's marriage to my mother, shortly after the Russian Revolution broke out. Alexander Iswolsky, who had followed with misgiving the errors of the Court, had already witnessed the assassination of Stolypin, the Prime Minister, and must have often feared for his own life for he had written to the Tsar, and also to the dowager Empress, asking them to look after his family if something should happen to him. Immediately after the Tsar's abdication, Iswolsky resigned his post in Paris, packed up, and with his wife and daughter settled in a small Basque villa in Biarritz, where he transferred his few possessions and papers.

Meanwhile, Grisha and my mother left for Washington, where he had been sent as an attaché-secretary to the Russian Embassy.

My sisters and I were left to the supervision of the Ambassador and his wife in a flat next to their house, with Miss McCulloch, Helene's former English governess, in charge.

It was then that we got to know Helene. After Alexander Iswolsky's death, she and her mother moved back to Paris. My mother, stepfather and sisters were still living in the United States. I, being older, was pursuing my studies in Paris, and for a time lived with Madame Iswolsky and Helene. I was a young man full of intellectual curiosity, and there is no doubt that Helene did much to satisfy it and to guide me. Both ladies were popular with the large colony of Russian émigrés, and Helene, who had assumed the responsibility for her mother, always helped her to entertain. Her heart, nevertheless, was already on other matters; but since this is all in her autobiography, I shall stop here.

Let me say, however, that except for the last two years of World War II, when communications between the United States and occupied France were virtually nonexistent, we never lost touch. My mother, who was in New York, always saw a good deal of Helene and, as for me, on my yearly visits I was able to follow the progress and evolution of this great person.

Helene Iswolsky was a woman of infinite courage. She was a person of spontaneous and passionate nature. All those who knew her, who worked and prayed with her, can testify to the nobility of her spirit.

I can only add this modest tribute of one who was her friend from early years.

J. L. de Faucigny-Lucinge

Her Last Years

MY FIRST VIVID recollection of Helene Iswolsky takes me back to a hot day in July of 1947, when, as a young man emigrating from Paris to the United States, I stepped directly from my Liberty transport to land — so to speak — right on her doorstep, in New York. My wife's uncle, a longtime friend of Helene's and her family, was also her neighbor in a modest rooming house located at 120 East 76th Street, a converted brownstone. This became my haven as well. In that boiling hot summer, when I was deprived of even elementary facilities, the only relief was provided by Helene's sense of humor and her providential ice-cooler, which she eventually let me share, and which, in my capacity of absent-minded weekend custodian, I invariably allowed to flood her floor.

At first, I was so preoccupied with my daily mundane problems of finding a job and adapting myself to this new existence that I had little opportunity to take advantage of the informal visits to Helene's "salon" of such prominent thinkers as Jacques Maritain, Jean Danielou and the exiled Russian statesman Alexander Kerensky. These and others were entertained by Helene in a haphazard manner on a shaky card table, where many a talk on religious and philosophical matters took place. There were also interesting discussions of a political nature, which sometimes became quite animated, since I did not share Helene's political outlook.

Her cheerful and always good-natured ways helped me, at this stage of my life, to make the transition less brutal, through the good humor, the wit, the warmth and the *entrain* with which she made the best of our camp-like life together, in this third-floor walk-up. She also shared news from abroad, and we marveled at the earthly preoccupations of the formidable Berdiaev, who, as I recall from his letters to her, addressed himself to requesting basic foodstuffs, such as flour, sugar, buckwheat groats, shortening and the like, from our "land of plenty." To postwar Europeans, America could be no less than bountiful, and overflowing with whatever they craved in Clamart![1]

---

1. A Paris suburb

In the close and familiar circle where I first took part in the causeries, so dear to Helene's heart, her highly intellectual and cultural upbringing, which was reflected in her organization of the Third Hour group, was brilliantly exemplified. In 1946, a small group of friends belonging to various Christian churches — Roman Catholic, Russian Orthodox and Protestant — pledged themselves to promote a sincere and informal exchange of ideas in order to work together in the spirit of Christian unity. Together, they founded the religious-philosophical series, entitled *The Third Hour*. The publication of *The Third Hour* was due to personal contacts established by this group of friends. At its very beginning, it was an intercourse shared by a few Orthodox, Catholics and Protestants who were seeking a better understanding, trying to discover all that could bring them closer together. Only when this personal friendly contact was achieved did *The Third Hour* start being published, offering its message for a wider exchange of views, in the social, philosophical and religious fields, attempting to solve the spiritual crisis of our time.

The issues of *The Third Hour* were not periodical, they appeared at such times as were most convenient and in the language which best fitted the moment: Russian, French, English. The Third Hour group invited their friends, known and unknown, to take part in their intercourse; it called upon all those who were working and seeking in the same direction and who knew that the souls of men in their diversity are inhabited and moved by the Spirit Who is One.

Let us recall that the name "Third Hour" was chosen in commemoration of that Third Hour of the Pentecost, when, according to the words of an ancient Eastern hymn (as quoted in the journal's Introduction, Vol. V.i.), the Holy Spirit was sent to "unsnare the world" and to "call everyone to Unity."

Among all the recollections of times spent with Helene, a moment which flashes clearly through my mind now was our "month in the country" spent together in Connecticut in the early 60's in a small country house among the woods, where I took refuge in order to write my doctoral dissertation on Constantine Leontiev. However, the most lasting and meaningful memories of my almost 30-year-long friendship with her relate to that period, too short, alas, when she lived in Cold Spring, New York, where she founded the Saint Benedict and Saint Sergius Ecumenical Center. Because I find this to be the culmination of her lifelong effort, and because to me this ecumenical center seems to have been the natural outcome and continuation of the Third Hour movement, I should like to address myself more specifically to this aspect of Helene's activities.

Helene did not choose the names of Saint Benedict and Saint Sergius of Radonezh at random to symbolize her intentions; somehow, she put herself and her endeavor under the patronage of these two saints, who, although far apart in time and space, pursued their quest in a similar spirit, during the most critical moments in the life of their respective countries and eras. It is remarkable that the very selection and juxtaposition of the names of Saint Benedict and Saint Sergius inspired the fellowship not only to pray together in the name of this fellowship, but also to act in unison for the common goal of unity. Both saints eschew all theological or dogmatic quarrels. From the depths of time they would seem to have blessed Helene's worthy striving for religious unity.

The Benedictine ideal as proclaimed in the rule of Saint Benedict is based upon Christ and Christ only. The "instructions" as established in his rule have endured, and are applied, unchanged to date from their original formulation in the sixth century.

Conversely, Saint Sergius did not leave any written precepts to convey his beliefs. There is only scant information about his life. Nevertheless, as the initiator of monastic life in northern Russia in the fourteenth century, he seems to have perceived through contemplation one of the most mysterious of all Christian dogmas, that of the Holy Trinity, particularly difficult to define in terms of concrete terminology. To it he dedicated his church and his monastery, which subsequently became a theological center, known as the "Holy Trinity Monastery of Zagorsk." The trinitarian dogma became for Saint Sergius a direct Christian experience — the inner vision of God in his Trinitarian manifestation. The spiritual experience resulting from this inner vision is, in my judgement, best expressed by the word *sobornost'*. Its initial formulation is to be found in the writings of the first Slavophiles. The definition of *sobornost'* presupposes a sort of spiritual ecumenism stemming from the concept of *ecclesia* of believers' unity, and not necessarily originating from or submitted to hierarchical power and authority. As the concept of *sobornost'* is based on mutual love, it might be also extended to underline a joint communion of Catholics, Orthodox and Protestants with the Spirit of God. One cannot avoid being stuck by the relevance of the *sobornost'* concept to the ecumenical spirit as it was understood by the members of the Third Hour.

Helene had already set out on her ecumenical mission while in Europe. Over the years she shared her views with many prominent thinkers and writers. Among the latter, Julien Green, in 1960, refers to their exchanges as follows:

> Had a visit from Helene Iswolsky whom I used to see in America, and for whom I have a true affection. She speaks to me about the rapprochement of the Catholic and Orthodox churches. Soon, she believes, that thanks to the efforts of Monsignor DuMont, we can attend Mass and take communion at the Russian church, rue Daru [Paris] if we so desire, and that the [Russian] Orthodox, in turn, will be able to attend Mass at our church. It will be a great achievement. I wish with all my heart she would be proven right.[2]

---

2. Julien Green: "Vers l'Invisible," *Journal 1958-1966*, Plon, Paris, 1967, Trans. A. Obolensky, p. 206.

At the outset, the term "ecumenical" was interpreted in some circles as suggesting something bordering on the illegal, as some kind of religious dilettantism, libertinism or, at best, religious syncretism. To be a partisan of the ecumenical movement was (and in some instances still is) construed as being a reformer, a radical, an extremist, in any case a liberal. But let me say that in truth the situation is quite the reverse; I submit that it means rather to be a retrograde, a conservative. In fact, the ecumenical movement appeals and reverts to the past, to the single, individual Christian faith and the unrestricted jurisdictional freedom which, in times of yore, the Holy Apostles preached throughout the world to men of good will. Indeed, as Paul Ricoeur so rightly observed, "hope and reminiscence are one and the same."

The ecumenical problem rests on the question of whether or not this original Christian faith has been replaced in some manner by Catholic, Eastern Orthodox or Protestant jurisdictions. Each one of these confessions affirms itself to be the representative of true Christianity, and cannot do otherwise. However, in the economy of human assessment, three cannot replace one, they can only share in it. And for that reason, at least at present, the ecumenical spirit cannot be integrated *de facto* into the external organization of the Churches, although it overflows and transcends their boundaries.

The question of unity among the different church denominations in their respective canonical aspects had little impact on the participants of our Third Hour meetings. We were looking for an answer not in a set of rules of a doctrinal theology but rather in the living process which belongs to all God's people as they attempt to express God's interaction with them. Therefore, first, we had to get to know and to understand each other. The emphasis on "authenticity" seemed to many of the participants of secondary importance. We were brought together by the same ideals, the same hope to achieve unity among men of different religious denominations. That feeling of spiritual unity at meetings testified more to a high level of spiritual oneness than to any factual disposition of dogmatic differences and variants of intellectual approach. We believed that spiritual unity might be achieved without theological uniformity. No union will turn into communion until that day when people will gather and find a way to restore that initial communion of love. Vladimir Soloviev was perhaps the only man who rose above the historic creeds toward an all-inclusive Christianity. But, as Berdiaev put it, "the formal agreements by which he sought to attain a unity of the Orthodox and Catholic Churches . . . has been drowned in them." Until the heads of Churches recognize that unity cannot be achieved by signing papers or making statements it seems that ecumenism is possible only among lay individuals of different religious denominations, as well as those jurisdictional dropouts who are eager to discard the grief and anguish prompted by theological and jurisdictional separations.

Helene Iswolsky was born Russian Orthodox but became Catholic. However, she never ceased to belong to the truly Russian spiritual culture. As a Catholic, she continued to propagate the Christian teachings of Khomiakov, Dostoevsky, Soloviev and Fedorov. Herein she is unique, for she remained deeply and spiritually Russian and Catholic at the same time. She never indulged in any religious polemics; on the contrary, she unremittingly advocated religious nonproselytism. Toward the end of her life, Helene lived not within herself or for herself, but in others and for others. She leaves us an outstanding example of a profoundly devoted Christian who achieved within herself the much coveted religious harmony, and in so doing became one of those of whom it has been said: "Blessed are the pure in heart, for they will see God."

Alexander P. Obolensky

No Time to Grieve...

COAT OF ARMS OF THE ISWOLSKY FAMILY

A golden moon crescent, with downward pointed tips, appears on the red background of the shield. The ringbolt of the silver anchor atop hangs directly above the crescent. A nobleman's crowned helmet towers over the shield. Two outstretched arms rise at the edge of the crown. Blue and gold hues are reflected throughout the crest.

CHAPTER I

Family Saga

WHERE DID the Russian Land come from? So begins Russia's most ancient chronicle. I am part of this land, though torn away from it for more than fifty years. I still have my roots in it, and I, too, might ask: Where do I come from?

Actually, as in the case of many of my compatriots, my ancestry is mixed. Although the Iswolskys have lived in Moscow and, later, in Petersburg for some five hundred years, the first one mentioned in our family history, Vasily Dimitrievich Iswolsky, came from Poland and was probably of Lithuanian origin. His arms, which we preserved, bore the shield and helmet of the Crusaders.

Like many Lithuanian and Polish gentlemen of that time, Vasily Iswolsky emigrated to Moscow in 1462 with his armed retinue, and was granted land in the province of Tula; we still held the remnants of this estate up to the time of the Revolution. Tolstoy's famous country home, Yasnaya Polyana, was located in this area. It has now become a national shrine and museum, while ours, as far as I could make out, is part of a network of collective farms.

These Tula estates were about 600 miles south of Moscow, and Iswolsky, with his retinue, was to defend the capital against the last Mongol hordes which were still raiding the country, though the massive Mongol forces were already drawing away far into Asia, after some two hundred years of occupation.

The ruling sovereign of Moscow, Ivan III, still known as Grand Prince, had married Sophia Paleologos, the daughter of the last Byzantine Emperor, and was soon to acquire the title of Tsar (Caesar), together with the cultural and religious heritage of Constantinople. Moscow was to be known as the Third Rome, the pillar of Orthodoxy. The Tsar's gentlemen-at-arms from Catholic Poland or Lithuania were received into the Orthodox Church, married Russian gentlewomen and were soon absorbed as part of the Tula landed gentry.

From then on, this untitled gentry was in the service of the Tsar, as soldiers, judges, court officials and bureaucrats, up to the time that my grandfather became governor of Irkutsk in Siberia and my father, a diplomat and statesman.

Russia is a melting pot; grandmother Iswolsky was of Georgian origin, and there is still a poet, Yashvili, in the Caucasus, who bears my great-grandmother's maiden name. My maternal grandfather was from the Baltic province of Estonia; his family came from Sweden and he was a Lutheran, while his wife was half-Baltic, half-Polish and a Catholic. Thus I was formed in the tradition of three religions, which perhaps explains my interest in ecumenism, though I was brought up strictly as a Russian Orthodox.

From this melting pot, families like mine emerged and were molded into three principal categories: landed gentry, the bureaucracy or the military. We were mostly of the bureaucracy; only one of my uncles served in the army and my father was never in military uniform. As to the lands granted to us by the Grand Prince, they had dwindled in our time to something like Chekov's *Cherry Orchard*. We rarely set foot in them, and let them go without regret.

When I am asked what part of Russia I come from, I hesitate to answer. Do I come from Moscow, where my father was born, or from Petersburg, where he served? My best answer is that I am Russian born, although as a diplomat's daughter I spent a number of years abroad, including those of my early childhood; I was actually born in Bavaria.

Of those first years of my life there is much that I can remember. Not because I have such a good memory, but because my first impressions were so vivid, with so many changes of scenes and faces, and because at least four languages were spoken around me.

Even so, I must fill up certain blanks, going back to the days before Grisha and I were born, to complete what I call the "family saga."

Most interesting to me were my father's stories about Rome. When he was in his thirties, he was appointed unofficial envoy to the Vatican. He was entrusted with a negotiation with the Holy See, with which Russia had broken diplomatic relations in 1863. Pope Leo XIV was in his nineties when Iswolsky crossed the threshold of his apartment. An unofficial agent was not a member of the diplomatic corps and could not be admitted through the Vatican's main gates. Instead, Iswolsky was "let in" through a private entrance — so the saga tells us — when no other visitors were around. It was six o'clock, when the bells were ringing for the Angelus. This must have lent to these meetings (for there were a number of encounters) an atmosphere of mystery. The Pope and my father conversed in Latin, which both men spoke fluently. Later, my father also learned Italian.

During these secret talks, many sharp edges were smoothed out. It seemed that the aged Pope and Iswolsky really liked each other. Till the end of his life, my father spoke of Leo with sincere admiration. . . . As for the Pontiff, he manifested the most friendly feelings toward his visitor of the Angelus hour. The very nature of their conversations, always peaceful and constructive, was proof of excellent contacts; the Pope's final gift to my father was his portrait with the inscription: *Alexandro Iswolsky, vir prudens et fidelis.*

In 1890, while an agent in Rome, my father was sent as a courier with a diplomatic "pouch" to Copenhagen. Why a diplomat was to carry such a "pouch," which meant "top secret," to Denmark's capital can be explained by the fact that this small city was at that time the center of many events connected to international affairs. It was the meeting place of a few very important persons, among them Alexander III, Tsar of Russia, who had married Princess Dagmar, the daughter of Christian IX of Denmark, and Edward, Prince of Wales, who had married Alexandra, another daughter of King Christian.

The Court of Denmark was in those days, and still remains, extremely democratic. Queen Louise, who was called the "mother-in-law of Europe," received her daughters and their husbands in all simplicity. Protocol was a mere token. King Christian, too, liked simple family life. He would take the Queen and his two daughters for long drives in the country, the young women perched on folding seats opposite their parents.

The Russian Legation also participated in this happy way of life. It was a cozy, hospitable home, presided over by Count Toll; his handsome wife, Helen, and his two young daughters, Olga and Marguerite, played hostesses.

When my father arrived in Copenhagen, he took his "pouch" to the Russian Legation, reported to the minister and was invited to dinner. He met young Marguerite Toll, admired her candid manner, her pretty face, her charming smile. He returned the next day, saw Marguerite, and on the following day asked her to marry him. Almost breathless with surprise, the young girl accepted and Charles Toll good-naturedly gave his consent.

The young diplomat from Rome seemed eligible as far as his career and reputation were concerned. As to financial means, they did not have any misgivings, though neither the Tolls nor the Iswolskys were wealthy. My father's salary seemed good enough for a young couple to start a life together, with promotions likely in the future.

Olga, Toll's elder daughter, was exceptionally beautiful; she also married a diplomat, Prince John Kudashev. He came from a wealthy family but had made a less promising debut in the service. However, he filled various important posts, ending up as Ambassador to Madrid. "Uncle Vania," as we called him, became our satellite for many years, the most devoted friend of our family. Although of a far narrower intellectual and political view than my father, he enjoyed immense popularity and social esteem. His wedding in Copenhagen was attended by Tsar Alexander and Tsarina Maria Fedorovna (the former Princess Dagmar). The Tsar brought his two small daughters, Olga and Xenia, to the ceremony, which was celebrated in the Russian Orthodox church of Copenhagen, especially built for King Christian's son-in-law. The children became somewhat boisterous, and the Tsar remarked that it was more difficult to keep them quiet than to govern his empire. He still felt pretty sure of keeping his country in hand, but he did not communicate this assurance to his son, the Tsarevich Nicholas. The Tsarevich also came to Copenhagen; a timid youth, he met my mother, still a very young girl, and remembered her long afterwards, as I shall relate further on. As to the Tsarina, Maria Fedorovna, she remained on most friendly terms with my mother and father, whose career she promoted, sharing his liberal ideas.

My father's love at first sight had not been a mistake, as I can truly say that my mother became his perfect mate and companion. She came from solid, Baltic stock, combining the Protestant tradition and sense of duty with a selfless love of my father and of Russia, with faith in their destinies.

I never knew Grandfather Toll, who died before I was born. There is little more that I can say about him, except that he was the son of General Charles Toll, who was a veteran of Russia's wars against Napoleon. Tolstoy presents him in several episodes of his *War and Peace* with the irony he usually shows for "the brass." Toll's portrait still hangs in the Hermitage Gallery of Leningrad in the section dedicated to Russian generals who fought Napoleon in 1819. We also had a large painting of the general, my great-great-grandfather, in full dress uniform standing on a hill, probably a battleground, with his Cossack orderly, also smartly uniformed, holding his horse.

Grandmother Toll survived her husband by many years, retiring to a house in Bavaria. Before World War I, we used to spend our vacations with her. She died in her late seventies, still preserving the traces of her rare beauty when she had been one of the handsomest and best dressed women of the diplomatic corps.

Helen Toll's daughters inherited her good looks, poise and elegance, and also a certain worldliness which served them well when they became diplomats' wives. My mother had made her debut in Copenhagen and was popular in Danish society. She danced at the balls with King Christian's sons, George, who became King of Greece and was later assassinated, and Waldemar, who became Admiral of the Danish navy. She sang in a musical comedy with Prince John, another member of the royal family, and with her own father, all wearing fancy costumes. I have a photo of her impersonating a young lady at a hunt; she holds a gun which she balances as delicately as if it were a parasol, never having fired a shot in her life!

My mother's happy girlhood ended in tragedy when she fell seriously in love, for the first time, with a young Russian officer whom she met at a summer resort. He was the Prince Charming of her dreams. Tall and handsome, he courted her assiduously and finally proposed. They were engaged to be married, when the young man was suddenly stricken with paralysis. He survived the crisis, but remained an invalid condemned to a wheelchair. My mother was broken-hearted when told that she could never marry her fiancé. She kept her suffering to herself, and, after the first shock, never spoke of it again. When my father appeared on the scene, she quite simply, and with blind confidence, accepted him as her inevitable destiny.

As for the tragedy she had experienced, I could only piece together a few fragments of the sad story. Years later, we went to the summer resort where they first met, and where her Prince Charming subsequently had built himself a home. There he lived with a middle-aged nurse who took care of him, for he was completely helpless. She used to take him on long drives. We saw him one day, seated in an open carriage, a tall, erect, almost motionless old man still handsome in spite of his long illness, riding in state, as if at his own funeral. My mother must have seen him too and turned away in silence.

I think this breaking up of her initial happiness explains a great deal in my mother's character as it appeared in her married life—the forced serenity of her manner and the reserve she maintained, even in the most trying or dramatic moments. Her resignation when misfortune struck us, her strict dedication to her family duties, her patience and self-control, all were useful factors of her successful marriage, which sailed through many rough seas.

I must say a few words about the reasons which prompted my father's sudden decision to get married.

Before he was sent to Europe and even during his secret mission to the Vatican, he had been something of a playboy, fancying beautiful young women, especially the Italian ladies, going to parties and over-indulging in drinking, smoking, hunting and galloping over the Roman countryside. His younger brother, Gregory, was also a "gay blade," who had spent his own and his wife's fortune living lavishly until he was suddenly stricken with tuberculosis. When he died, my father's life was badly shaken, as he had been devoted to his young brother. It caused my father to size up his own physical and moral condition. Warned by his doctor, he gave up smoking and drinking and, after recuperating in Switzerland, began to put his life in order. He longed for a home, a wife and children. When he arrived in Copenhagen with his diplomatic "pouch," he was in a mood for serious and drastic reform. Thus, both he and my mother were ready to build a new life, without looking back.

As I have said, their marriage was successful. We had a happy home in which we found love and security until the storm of the Revolution brought destruction, and even then we were strong enough to stand on our feet.

To go back to the saga of our life in Rome, my parents loved to talk about their home on the Spanish Steps and about the Pincio Park where we were taken for airings, I in my baby carriage and my brother, Grisha, named after his Uncle Gregory, holding the hand of our Italian nurse.

Now that the agreement between the Vatican and Russia had been achieved, my parents shared the social life of the diplomatic corps. However, there were certain restrictions. In those days, Roman society was divided into two camps: the "white" set and the "black." The former sided with the King of Italy and his secular power. The other, took up the defense of the Pope, whose vast domains had dwindled to a mere token. He refused, as did his two predecessors, to issue forth from his self-imposed prison, the Vatican Palace. Being accredited to the Holy See, my father and mother could not, without breach of an unwritten law, go to "white" parties which could have been fun. But the "black" parties offered compensation. The men and women of the papal *beau monde* belonged to Italy's most ancient families: the Sermonettas, the Guicciolis, the Colonnas, the Aldobrandinis, the Somaglies, the Ruspolis. The women were beautiful and elegant, the men no less handsome and chivalrous. Perhaps too chivalrous for my very correct and somewhat prudish mother, who had to be constantly on her guard, for they all admired the *Signora Russa* and wanted her to know it. Once when one of the gentlemen who had pressed his attentions on her and been rebuffed was leaving, he sighed and whispered: "Never mind, I shall return—later."

But that day never came. My father received another appointment. He was named Russian minister to Bavaria, a post he accepted with regret after the delightful years in Rome. Most Russians love the "Eternal City," its art treasures, its fountains and blue skies, which present such a contrast with the austere and sometimes melancholy landscapes of their own country. Mother, on the contrary, was quite pleased, not because she disliked Italy, but because her own mother had built a house in Bavaria (it was here that I was born). It was not far from Munich, where we were to reside. We packed our belongings, put our furniture in a moving van and entrained *en famille* to our new destination.

Diplomats are like gypsies; every four or five years they are back on the road. They have no stable home, no permanent connections, no constant friends, only friends they acquire for a short time and then lose, without being allowed to feel too much regret. There is a sense of sadness, almost of doom, about these brief encounters. And yet there is also the excitement of the open road, of ever-new horizons and lands and people. And every land and its people must be understood and loved, be it only for a short time. Scarcely had we settled in Munich and become acquainted with Bavaria, that Father got a new appointment; this time it was Tokyo, Japan.

Such was the world, or rather the many worlds, of my childhood. I still retain, after all these years, some traits of a diplomat's daughter: the awareness of many lands, many nationalities and languages, the remembrance of many friends long lost and the joy of making new ones, the capacity of adapting myself easily to unfamiliar environments and the instinctive search for a permanent home never to be found, the dread of being uprooted and the readiness to start all over again. There will always be, for me, a wanderlust. As I begin this journey into the past, I am thrilled to be on the road again, that road that sometimes brought joy and sometimes grief, but never time to grieve.

CHAPTER II

Journey Through Siberia to Japan

IT HAPPENED one day in the spring of 1900, while we were still in Munich, that Father called us together in his study and told us that we were going to Japan. He had been transferred as Russian envoy in Munich to the same post in Tokyo. The news could scarcely have impressed me, age four, nor was Grisha surprised. At age seven, his interest was playing games, and he could go on playing them wherever we might go. It was my mother who was disturbed and made us aware that going to Japan was something portentous. The idea of a far, exotic country filled her with anxiety; and when Father told her that she would have to undertake a long sea voyage, she was particularly frightened. I remember the expression of fear on her face, and the outcry of our German nurse, Bertha, who declared that the "ocean was full of monsters." This stayed in my mind like a bad dream. But the spell of fear was soon broken when Father offered us another itinerary. The journey could be undertaken by land, through Siberia, where a great railroad was under construction. This would reduce the sea voyage to the short crossing by ship from Port Arthur to Yokohama.

Mother was reassured and accepted this plan without further complaint. From that time on, I never heard her object to any of the many changes that life was to hold for her. So we left Munich for Saint Petersburg, which was the first step of our long journey.

Here we spent a few days visiting my godmother, Princess Helen of Saxe-Altenburg, who invited us to her beautiful palace on the Kamenny Ostrov. Some fourteen years later, I was to return to Kamenny Ostrov (Stone Island) and shall describe in detail my godmother, who was a very exceptional woman, and her home, which is now a historical monument. I remember almost nothing of this first visit except that we played with the Princess' two daughters and their cousins, who were older than Grisha and myself but kind and gentle with smaller children. We played all sorts of exciting games; one led us up a spiral staircase in one of the turrets of the palace. When I saw this staircase again as an adult, I recognized it immediately as something secret and romantic, out of a fairytale. My memory of the children I played with also retained a romantic note; they seemed like tall, young giants. By the time I met them again, they were no taller than Grisha and I; time had leveled us all to the same size.

We soon left for Moscow, where we stayed at a luxury hotel called the Slavonic Bazaar, which seemed to us as magnificent as Kamenny Ostrov and full of wonders. There were colonnades and galleries running all around and above the main dining room, which had a mirrored ceiling, there was a huge tank of live fish, fat starlets and bream, the Russian gourmet's delight. They were fished right out of the tank and cooked to order, which amazed me.

It was April when our family boarded the "wagon-salon" or private car which had been assigned to us by the railroad administration, and now five thousand miles of rail stretched ahead. We were accompanied by a governess, Miss Nadezhda Vladimirovna Mukhanova, whom Father had especially engaged to take care of us children, an able educator who lived up to her reputation all the years she remained with us. Her immediate duty was to teach us to speak Russian.

Father had little time for us and Mother spoke hardly any Russian, since my parents communicated mostly in French. Grisha and I had picked up some of Bertha's German, which we had to relearn in our teens. Our "mother tongue" was a complete jumble until Nadezhda Vladimirovna gave us large doses of excellent and highly refined Russian. Bertha, terrified of sea monsters, had stayed home but our German valet, Jacob, and his wife, Johanna, my mother's maid, followed us without hesitation to Japan. They were devoted to our family. But the most exciting member of our party was Daban, our Cossack bodyguard. He was loaned to us for the duration of our rail journey, together with the "wagon-salon." Part of our trip was to pass through the Manchurian area, rampant with unrest and banditry. Daban was a Cherkess, a typical Caucasian mountaineer wearing the picturesque homespun tunic, with silver cartridges decorating his chest, the Persian lamb cap tilted jauntily on his head, soft, leather boots and a long dagger with a silver-inlaid sheath slipped under his embroidered belt. You can still see the handsome, manly Cherkess in their native garb appearing in Soviet dance festivals. Daban was not particularly handsome nor could he dance like the stars of a Moiseev Company, but he was an authentic tribesman, sprightly and fierce-looking. We children looked upon him with awe and admiration. He turned out to be quite friendly and became our playmate and something of a male nurse.

Thanks to Miss Mukhanova, Jacob, Johanna and Daban, my mother did not have much trouble running her new home on wheels. Like all Russian railroads, the Trans-Siberian was double-gauged and our private car, divided into several compartments, was roomy and comfortably furnished with folding beds and tables, washrooms and a diner all to ourselves. We had brought with us a variety of conveniences: portable rubber bathtubs made in England, alcohol burners, silver saucepans with ivory handles, traveling cups, goblets, flasks and all kinds of other containers, packed in the typical British wicker picnic baskets. Indeed, my parents had arranged our trip as some sort of a long picnic.

We had company, too; the adjoining car was occupied by another party: Prince Dolgoruky, a government official on an inspection tour, and Father's colleague in the diplomatic service, Elim Demidov, who was vacationing and on his way to Kamchatka for a hunting expedition. He had brought his wife, the beautiful and charming Sophie Demidov, who was my mother's age so they had many tastes and interests in common.

Elim Demidov was an immensely wealthy man, the owner of a vast empire in the Ural mountains where gold, platinum and precious stones were mined. He had inherited his empire from his father who had lived in Italy, where he had acquired the estate of San Donato, near Florence. The title of Prince of San Donato went with it. His son, Elim, did not use this title officially nor was he interested in his Ural domains, but put his ambitions in a diplomatic career and in Kamchatka safaris.

I shall add a footnote to the Demidov story; most readers of Pasternak's story *Doctor Zhivago* are unaware that his hero's journey to Siberia brought him into the mining country which formerly had belonged to the Prince of San Donato. Zhivago's caretaker was an offspring of the famous nobleman from Florence, his name, *Samdevyatov,* distorted and Russified.

During the first part of our journey, my parents and the "grownups" settled down to a routine certainly more comfortable than that of Dr. Zhivago in his boxcar. Grisha and I played in our compartment or gazed at the constantly changing scenes unfolding before us. The train crossed the mighty Volga, chugged through great forests of oak and cedar, then emerged into the rolling plains and ran between endless wheat and rye fields, and villages with their log houses and thatched roofs. Horses and colts grazed peacefully in the meadows; when we came near and the engine blew its whistle, the animals scattered and galloped wildly along the tracks.

One day, we reached a mountain range, the Urals, and Miss Mukhanova, who was watching the panorama with us, said, "Look, children, we are entering Asia." Sure enough, we had arrived at a deep gorge marked by a tall signpost, which said "Europe" on one side and "Asia" on the other. I could not read, but Grisha spelled the words out for me and with them came the realization that this was a solemn moment in our lives. Nadezhda Vladimirovna then explained that we were in Siberia. What better way to learn geography?

Our train moved on without any particular haste, into the depths of Russia's Asian empire. We stopped several times a day to refuel; like all Russian locomotives, our engine burned wood, plentiful in these regions and piled up at every station. The arrival of the Trans-Siberian was a great event for the population, especially at the smaller stops where very little happened between trains. They brought the mail, newspapers and packages from Europe to the wasteland. They brought interesting people, officials in uniform, young engineers and prospectors, wealthy businessmen in search of bargains in Chinese tea, furs and timber. There were even actors and actresses on these trains, touring to perform in Irkutsk, the Siberian capital. The ladies displayed the latest fashions, never seen before, not even in their magazines which were outdated and scarce. As the passengers descended from their coaches, having reached their destination, or merely to take exercise, the local "intelligentsia" or townsfolk watched them eagerly. In fact the arrival of each train was the occasion for a social gathering, people parading up and down the platform or greeting each other. There would be a buffet with vodka and sandwiches, where Europeans and Siberian Russians mingled for a short time, never to meet again. The peasants from neighboring villages came to see the train. They offered cottage cheese, pickled cucumbers, mushrooms, honey and preserved berries and nuts, which relieved the monotony of the dinner menu. They also sold objects of rustic art, and handicraft, embroideries, toys, baskets and delicately woven homespuns. These were my first contacts with the Russian land and its people. I remember many details of these stops and of the animated crowds that made up these vivid experiences.

We children thoroughly enjoyed ourselves during these brief relaxations from our shut-in existence. Accompanied by Daban, we rushed out of our car and into the backyard of the station, which usually opened into a garden or a meadow, which especially attracted us. We ran as fast as we could, Daban chasing us, and only returned to our car at the sound of the third bell that called the passengers to the final "All aboard."

When we stopped at the stations of larger towns, the atmosphere was more formal. The mayor, governor, commander of the local garrison and chief of police, wearing full dress uniforms, came to pay their respects to my parents. Father, too, had to don his uniform of an official of the Ministry of Foreign Affairs, although, as a traveler he did not wear full dress, but a short coat with golden epaulettes and buttons stamped with the Russian eagle, and a peaked hat to match. As the weather grew warmer, the black material was changed for white drill.

About half way on our journey, we reached Irkutsk, the commercial and political center of Siberia. My paternal grandfather had been Governor of this city in the eighteen-fifties. My father had a dim recollection of it from his own youth, but he often told of an event which marked grandfather Iswolsky's career. He had given a pass to the anarchist Michael Bakunin, who had been exiled there. Bakunin asked permission to cross the town's boundary on important business, promising to return in a few days. Instead, he fled to Japan and from there to the United States; finally, he got to Switzerland.

It was announced that we must stay a few days in Irkutsk before our train was ready to proceed. Mother was rather apprehensive of this city: a considerable part of its male population was made up of ex-convicts allowed to stay on after ending their prison terms for various crimes, some political but mostly antisocial. Many of these were still considered exiles and were not allowed to return to European Russia. Others had volunteered to stay and held various jobs from cabdrivers to businessmen. There was a former army officer who had been punished for insulting his superior. After his prison term, he went into the fur business. He took French lessons and paid his teacher with the finest sable pelts, worth hundreds of rubles. But all were not as lucky as this tradesman. Many we observed were probably former burglars or murderers who found a meager subsistence.

But we did not have the opportunity to meet them, for we were met immediately at the station and driven in an elegant carriage to the home of the "great Vtorov," as he was known in Irkutsk and in Moscow. Today this name is forgotten but in the early nineteen hundreds, Vtorov was a most influential Russian businessman. He was one of those powerful merchants who stimulated Russian industry and commerce, as well as progress and culture, from the capital to the most remote corners of the country. Actually, the story of this class has never been fully written; it was a caste apart which rarely mingled with the aristocracy, but was a society in its own right. These dynamic men were absorbed in deals on a grand scale, directing textile, lumber, china and mining enterprises. Some of them were highly educated, patrons of art and literature, the theater and the opera. They poured millions into cultural experiments and more millions into their own pioneering. They were regarded with favor and respect by the Tsarist government but not admitted at court. This boycott turned many of them against the monarchy and incited some of them to put their money into leftist and even revolutionary movements. And it was the Revolution that wiped out this class almost entirely. Only a few of them survive, and even fewer remember the Vtorov empire.

Vtorov himself was away on a business trip, but left us to enjoy his hospitality, with a whole staff of servants, cooks and parlor maids. As far as I can remember, the house was luxuriously furnished. There were many rooms and foyers and a large dining room, all heavily curtained and carpeted with oriental rugs. The greatest attraction for us children was a man-sized mechanical doll representing a Negro seated cross-legged, with a banjo on his knee, striped pants, red jacket and a tall collar. He held a cigar in his mouth. If you pressed a button, he would roll his eyes and the tip of his cigar would light up.

The next day, we were taken by our parents for a look at the town. We drove again in Vtorov's carriage through the wide streets and boulevards of Irkutsk. We visited a large department store built by the English firm of Muir and Merrilies. These enterprising Britishers were the first to introduce the department store to Russia. They built an emporium in Moscow, which is now GUM, as state department stores are now called in Russia. A few years ago, I came across the names of Messrs. Muir and Merrilies in Lewis Carroll's *Russian Journal*. The author of *Alice in Wonderland* visited St. Petersburg, Moscow and other Russian cities in 1867 in the company of these businessmen who were very intent on their department store projects. They were very helpful to their compatriot. Lewis Carroll (Rev. Charles Dodgson) was especially interested in Russian Orthodox churches and their services, as well as museums and historic sites. The "indefatigable Mr. Merrilies," as he calls him, was his guide in St. Petersburg and they had dinner with "Mr. and Mrs. Muir and some charming little children." Thus "Alice," whom I have always loved, is somehow connected to the Irkutsk emporium.

After a few restful days at the Vtorov home, we continued our journey through Siberia. Reaching the shores of Lake Baikal, our train was loaded, with all its passengers, onto the icebreaker which was to take us to the opposite side. Although it was spring, the lake was solidly frozen. We crowded on deck watching the ironclad bow of our boat make a wide channel in the dazzling white sheet of ice. Lake Baikal is the largest freshwater lake in Eurasia. When we reached the Eastern shore of the lake, our train was put back on its tracks.

Only those who have crossed Siberia can realize the immensity of this land. Chita, where we made a stop, is the center of a gold-mining district bigger than California. Then came Sretensk and Blagovestchensk. Here we had to leave our train because the tracks of the Trans-Siberian had not been laid beyond that point. We were to cover the remaining part of our journey by steamship, down the Amur River to Khabarovsk, where we could take the South Chinese railroad to Port Arthur.

The ship which took us down the Amur was neither large nor comfortable and as we sat on deck or ate in the uninviting salon a feeling of gloom hung over us. There were no lounges, no formal reception at the captain's quarters. In fact we never saw the captain during the entire passage. He kept to his cabin and the ship was piloted by a boorish mate. There were no other passengers on board.

As we watched the mighty river flowing past, our faithful mentor, Nadezhda Vladimirovna, pointed to the opposite bank with her parasol, saying: "There, children, lies Manchuria and the people who live here are called the Manchus."

We could see the Manchus standing on the shore, their Mongol features and narrow eyes tense and full of suspicion. The land of these people was the center of a dispute between Russia, China and Japan. There was defiance in the air, rebellion brewing in the *fanzas*, the poor Manchu villages scattered along the Amur.

Today, the Russian bank of the Amur, which, in those days was almost a wilderness, is now a series of public beaches, where young Siberian boys and girls swim and sunbathe in trunks or bikinis.

Our boat would stop from time to time for fresh water and fuel and we were allowed to go ashore, but only escorted by Daban, who strode up and down the quay fingering his dagger. Father was somber and silent.

As I learned later, he felt grave concern over Russia's growing attempts at expansion in these regions. This was particularly resented by Japan, but viewed favorably by our European neighbors. In Germany, Kaiser Wilhelm was obsessed by the idea of the "yellow peril" and encouraged his cousin, the Tsar, to invest millions of rubles in "peaceful conquest." This was the main cause of Father's anxiety at the time, as he saw war looming up on the horizon. Playing and running on the decks or walking in the dusty Manchu villages, Grisha and I, and even our mother, were unaware of these dark forebodings.

One day, halfway on our river cruise, we were leaning over the rail, admiring the picturesque wooded slopes of the Amur banks, which at that point were reflected in the quiet, shining water. Suddenly, there was a violent jolt; the little boat shuddered and seemed to rise in midair. The crew rushed out on deck. One of the men sounded the depths with a long pole. Others went to the engine room. Whistles blew, bells rang, the engine pulsated madly. Then it stopped.

The mate stood on the bridge, looking more boorish than ever. Father and Demidov climbed to the bridge to ask him what had happened. He answered in a blank voice: "We are stranded on a sand bank. The engine broke down. We cannot move. We have sent a man ashore in a dinghy to telegraph for help."

"But where is the captain," asked Father.

"The captain is in his cabin, dead drunk," was the curt reply.

We sat for two days on that sand bank. The accident had occurred in a wild, deserted area with no *fanzas* in sight. There were some supplies left, but they were running low.

On the third day, Demidov sighted a deer swimming in the river and, being an excellent shot, he bagged it for our next meal. We shared it with the mate and the crew. The captain was still invisible.

Finally, we were picked up by another steamer, and as we were ready to be transferred to it we saw the captain emerge from a hatch. He was put under arrest for drunkenness and neglect of his duties and led out by two men in uniform. He was marched away with bowed head, handcuffed and shackled so that he could scarcely walk. It was a horrible and humiliating sight. The picture of this man whom I had never seen before and who was in chains filled me with a wild and terrible dismay. Do children feel pity at a tender age? I cannot say, but they can experience something like horror. I remember the captain with extraordinary clarity; no doubt this is why I have ever since retained a horror of violence, of punishment of any kind, of chains and prisons.

It was the end of May when we reached Khabarovsk and proceeded on the South Chinese railroad to Port Arthur, the Russian military and naval base. All along the line, danger lurked. Periodically this line was attacked by wild Hung hu-tzu tribesmen and other guerrilla bands in liaison with the Chinese Boxer rebels. We were not harassed, however, and reached Kharbin and then passed safely through Mukden, where a decisive battle was to be fought four years later in which Russia's defeat by Japan was sealed. At Port Arthur, the Russian cruiser *Ryurik* was waiting to take us to Japan.

Little could anyone foresee that this elegant, freshly painted and refurbished ship, glistening in the Asian sun, would go down with its entire crew at Tsushima, where the Russian fleet of the Pacific was destroyed by Admiral Togo.

When the *Ryurik* anchored in the Bay of Yokohama, June 11, 1900, members of the Russian Legation from Tokyo arrived to meet us. The chargé d'affaires, Mr. Paklevsky, and the naval attaché, Captain Rusin, headed the committee of welcome. We all went ashore and looked around us with astonishment, for everything in this Far Eastern port was unlike anything we had ever seen before. In those days, Japan had scarcely been touched by the European way of life. There were few stone buildings, the streets were lined with bright and colorful stores and the people wore kimonos. As we drove to the station, Miss Mukhanova duly announced: "Now, children, we are in Japan and the people here are the Japanese."

My father had a special respect for the Japanese nation and its culture, even before setting foot in the country. Unfortunately this feeling was not always shared by his colleagues. Diplomats in the East usually remained proud and isolated, entrenched in their compounds, looking down at the native population as "an inferior race."

Arriving at the Tokyo station, we were met by an open carriage; the coachman and footman wearing coolie dress, the dark-blue, short kimono, marked by a Japanese crest, the Russian Legation emblem, and large, mushroom-like hats. Two men, in similar attire, ran on each side of our carriage, at a swift, elastic pace.

We were driven through the residential quarter to Ichi-Ban (No. 1), the Legation's main building, where we were to reside. Next to it was

Ni-Ban (No. 2), assigned to the legation staff. Both houses were strictly European style, built of stone and plaster. They stood in the center of a European garden with a sprawling lawn and flower beds; only a bamboo grove in the corner lent it an oriental look.

Beyond the Legation grounds stretched the great Japanese city, the almost aerial wooden houses with their rice-paper sliding doors and windows, the beautiful, miniature gardens and fish ponds, the stepping stones, lanterns and dwarf trees and clusters of peonies in full bloom. Still further on loomed the pagodas and tall white walls of the Imperial Palace.

The first day in Tokyo, Grisha fell off a swing and broke his collarbone. The doctor who took care of the diplomatic corps was summoned. He was an elderly Englishman who was most courteous but somewhat absent-minded. He set the broken bone and Grisha was soon able to play with me again in the garden. But this incident upset my mother, at the beginning of this new life. She could never be drawn, as Father was, into the mores of Japanese life. She missed her mother, the house in Munich which she had grown to love and her summer vacation in the Bavarian Alps — the security she had always known. She never complained, but we felt that she was not happy.

For Grisha and me, on the contrary, the three years spent in Japan were the happiest of our entire childhood. We loved Ichi-Ban and its spacious set-up. There were so many things to observe, so many people to get acquainted with, all of them friendly and many of them exciting. I remember quite clearly the Legation's staff, and since I was to see some of them again in later years, I will describe them briefly.

Mr. Poklevsky-Kozell, first secretary, was of Polish descent, an expert and intelligent young diplomat who later occupied important posts. One of his great assets in Tokyo was his knowledge of the language and of the Japanese people's psychology and traditions. His experience in these matters and fine sense of diplomacy were of great help to my father.

The second secretary was Prince Nicholas Kudashev, brother of my "Uncle Vania" (who had married my mother's sister, Olga). He was a confirmed bachelor and was accompanied by his maiden sister, Princess Catherine or "Aunt Kitty." The two were inseparable. He was a gentle soul, blue-eyed and soft-voiced, but an able diplomat. She was quite a character, her blue eyes sparkled with wit and humor, or sometimes flashed with anger. She wore stiffly starched blouses, a man's collar and black bow tie and a dark suit with deep pockets containing a silver cigarette case and match box. She smoked incessantly, which was quite unusual for a woman in those days. She was passionately devoted to her brother and watched over him with jealousy. But she was also very fond of children. She spent hours telling us stories, playing games, drawing pictures.

Like all members of her family, she was a devout Russian Orthodox believer, but secretive about her faith. One day as I stood by Aunt Kitty's door, ready to visit her, I heard that she was reciting the prayers from the Slavonic prayer book in a solemn, resonant voice, which made a deep impression on me.

The consul general was a Prince Gagarin. I recall him only vaguely, but his wife, Nina, was to become my mother's lifelong friend. She was a very good-looking and cultured young woman with an interest in the arts and literature. Thirty years after our first meeting in Tokyo we saw her again in Paris, where she was conducting a correspondence with the poet Rainer Maria Rilke.

We were on friendly terms with the family of the military attaché, Colonel Vanovsky. But Vanovsky himself rarely appeared in our intimate circle. He was a source of constant vexation for my father who was trying to improve Russia's relations with Japan. The Colonel had, on the contrary, adopted a belligerent and contemptuous attitude toward that country and was, moreover, completely misinformed as to its growing military strength.

Father's preoccupation with the threat of Russian expansion in the Far East continued to develop. His predecessor, Rosen, had signed a convention with the Japanese premier according to which Russia and Japan bound themselves to preserve the independence and integrity of Korea. But both powers were seeking to establish their spheres of influence as far as they could reach. The timber on the Yalu River in North Korea was of special interest to a group of unscrupulous St. Petersburg businessmen connected with court circles. They had obtained concessions in this area, to Japan's great annoyance. Manchuria had been occupied by Russian troops during the Boxer Rebellion and they were withdrawn only on the insistence of America, England and Japan. The latter signed a treaty with Great Britain in 1902 and started actively to prepare for war. Russia pursued its policy of provocation by naming Admiral Alexeev, a supporter of the Yalu project and of aggressive policy, to the post of High Commissioner of the newly established Russian Far Eastern zone. It included the Kwantung Province in South Manchuria. Observing Japan's bellicose reaction to this move, but aware that Tokyo was still inclined to negotiate, Father sent dispatch after dispatch to his chief, the Minister of Foreign Affairs, Count Lamsdorf, warning him of growing Japanese military power. But Colonel Vanovsky also sent his own reports, belittling the danger of the situation. These reassuring reports gave the Yalu people a completely false sense of security. *Shapkami zakidayem* was their slogan, meaning "We shall destroy them by throwing our caps at them"—a popular Russian expression for an easy victory.

To return to our own life at the Legation, it was well-run and comfortable. With the exception of our faithful Jacob and Johanna, our servant staff was Japanese. There was the old majordomo, Maida-San, very formal in his dark kimono, who had several assistants. Our Japanese cook gave us only strictly European food, except for a few "colonial curries." The children's nurse was Kiva-San, who had been baptized at a Russian Orthodox mission and spoke a little Russian. She was very gentle, and, at the same time, alert and intelligent. Grisha and I grew very fond of her and I will always remember that small figure in a brown kimono, the wide, dark *obi* neatly bound around her waist, her black, oiled hair pulled tightly into a bun, and the white socks and sandals on her nimble feet. It was unfortunate that we could never learn Japanese for she was fluent in our tongue, but she gave us much of the Japanese flavor; she told us native fairy tales, explained the meaning of native toys, songs and festivals. She showed me how to celebrate the feast of little girls, with an array of beautifully dressed dolls, while Grisha had a collection of bows and arrows, samurai swords and helmets, for the feast of boys. She taught us how to fly fantastically shaped kites and make delicate rice-paper lanterns.

Father encouraged our initiation by Kiva-San into these little things that pertained to Japanese culture, which he loved. In fact, his criticism of his own country's blundering in the East was due in part to his deep esteem for the spiritual force, traditions and arts of Asia. He would take us to see Japanese art treasures and we went with him to Kyoto, and to Nara, the sacred city of ancient temples. The tame deer on the Nara grounds looked at us with gentle brown eyes and followed us into the temples. This enchanted me and years later, when I returned to Japan and revisited Nara, I recognized the details of this truly Franciscan scene.

At the time that we were living in the Tokyo Legation, Japan was being discovered and eulogized by Lafcadio Hearn and Chamberlain. Father had read their books attentively and we even met Mr. Chamberlain dressed in a kimono, having gone completely native but still looking very British; these authors were very useful in introducing us to Japan, but Father also wished us to develop contacts directly with the Japanese. It was arranged that we should be invited to play with the young princes Shimadzu, who were related to the Mikado. We would go over to the princes' residence and engage in various sports with the youngest children. The Shimadzu family was one of the most progressive and democratic members of this strictly feudal aristocracy. Contacts with these lively but very polite little boys was good for our own training.

For the rest, our education was in the hands of Miss Mukhanova; I cannot explain the secret of her power over us. I was a quiet little girl but Grisha was a most vivacious and stubborn boy. She never punished him or raised her voice, but she made him obey her. One of her methods was to tell him about her own brothers Vitya and Borya who, when they were Grisha's age, always did the right thing. The *right thing* in her mind was to be "real boys," courageous, straightforward, athletic, religious and patriotic. Many years later, when Grisha's stormy and dramatic life would carry him away from Miss Mukhanova's lofty ideals, he would say sadly to me: "She wanted me to be a real boy, like Vitya and Borya." Only we two knew what these words meant, and would laugh a little, but always gratefully, for we never ceased loving our governess long after she left us.

Father rarely intervened in our education. The maternal presence was scarcely felt, except that Mother gave us a sense of security which would never fail. For Grisha especially, she was the one to be relied upon. Of the two of us, he was the most important, the first-born, the one most like herself, for he had inherited her good looks and her charm. I, too, considered him the center of our world and imitated him in most of the things he did, without any sense of jealousy or frustration. Somehow, Grisha was number one, and I was number two; not a good way of developing a child's identity, which I had to work out later for myself. Thus it was that while Grisha was studying regularly if not assiduously, I found myself behind. One day he copied a poem and illustrated it in watercolor. I still retain this "masterpiece" in my papers. My brother never cared for literary works in later years, but on that memorable day, watching him busy with his poem, I realized that I could not read it. I marched into my father's study and stood on tiptoes before his desk. "Now what is it, Helene darling," he said, putting his pen down. Then, holding my breath a moment, I burst out: "I want to learn to read and write!"

"Why, of course," he exclaimed, "how very absent-minded of me not to have thought of it. Tell Miss Mukhanova to start you immediately."

And so I learned the Russian letters, tracing them on foolscap. This was sheer bliss. Not only did I catch up with Grisha, but I discovered the power of words, printed, written or read. All this I had gained through my own determination. I became an avid reader, and later, a writer.

I had a schoolmate in the first year of my study. She was Kiva-San, who learned to write and read Russian with me. Kiva was a primitive soul with a deep sense of the Christian faith. Before she learned to read the Gospels, she knew them almost by heart. There was a chapel at Ichi-Ban where a missionary monk said Mass every Sunday and we attended this service regularly. Grisha and I sang in the choir mostly made up of Japanese converts, and I enjoyed being part of this mystery, which I dimly recognized as being something beautiful. According to Russian Orthodox custom, I had received communion when a small baby in my nurse's arms; then, as soon as I could walk, I was led to the priest, who bent down and gave me bread and wine on a little golden spoon, as he did to adults. But now that I had passed the age of seven, Miss Mukhanova told me that I had reached the age of reason and that I must go to confession before receiving communion. It is given most solemnly during the Lenten season and it was during that time that I stood in front of the priest for confession. He was a man full of understanding and I do not remember any fear in the telling of my sins but rather a sense of concern that I might forget some of them and their need to be forgiven. What a joy it was to be "absolved" and to approach the chalice with the hope of being worthy of the joy in the Kingdom to come.

Kiva-San was among the faithful who attended Mass in our chapel but she told me that there was a much bigger and more beautiful church where she had been baptized by Vladyka himself. This was the title of the Russian Bishop, Nicholas Kasatkin, the great missionary who had built the cathedral and who had spent many years evangelizing the people of Japan at a time when Christianity was still persecuted in that country. We betook ourselves to the cathedral and were astonished by its size and beauty; Vladyka was celebrating High Mass. Many Japanese voices made the responses; the church was ablaze with candles and enveloped in clouds of incense. In front of the shining altar, wearing a miter and golden robes, loomed the tall, majestic figure with flowing gray beard of Vladyka Nicholas Kasatkin.

When the people in the cathedral at last dispersed, Vladyka Nicholas took us to his own apartments. He talked with us children for a while, blessed us and gave us each a brightly colored picture. Mine represented Noah's ark landing on a steep slope after the flood. It was an awesome scene with gray skies overhead and stormy waves receding from a devastated world. But high above in the cloud there was a rainbow spanning the horizon. As I looked at its bright colors I suddenly felt reassured and happy. This feeling of joyful peace comes over me whenever I see a rainbow.

Seven decades after this meeting of a small child with the Bishop (who afterwards became Archbishop) he was canonized by the Russian Orthodox Church. I learned that Vladyka Nicholas Kasatkin was known not only for his great charity and love of his people, but also as a healer. After his death, many miracles were attributed to him. Even during his lifetime, an unusual occurrence proved his prestige among the Japanese. After the defeat of Russia by Japan, in 1905, there was a victory march along the streets of Tokyo. The Commander ordered his troops to make a detour, so as not to pass before the Russian cathedral of Vladyka Nicholas.

A festive social occasion was the visit of the Grand Duke Boris, the Tsar's youngest and most unruly cousin. His constant revelries were widely known as the *tournées du Grand Duc*. He chose an unfortunate time to visit Japan, where anti-Russian feelings were already running high. The slightest faux pas could offend the Mikado and further damage international relations. So Father and his staff kept this "important person" under constant surveillance. He was given a gala dinner at the Legation, and appeared in full military dress, a jovial, rather plump man in his forties. Since he was discretely told to be on his best behavior, there were no "incidents" during his stay. The members of his retinue were young officers who shared his carefree life. Among them was my mother's cousin from the Baltic provinces, Nicholas Strandtmann, whom we called "Uncle Kodosha." He was the Grand Duke's aide-de-camp, a lieutenant in the *Streltsy*, one of the Tsar's elite regiments. He wore a picturesque blue tunic over a dark red silk shirt which resembled the dress of a young boyar rather than a uniform. "Uncle Kodosha" was extremely handsome, tall, fair-haired with regular features and large blue eyes. Grisha and I fell in love with him and followed him around like enchanted children.

Our uncle was one of the most reckless of the Grand Duke's companions. None of us could have foreseen that he was to have a complete change of heart some fifteen years later during the Revolution. This brilliant officer suffered much (some said he had killed a man in combat). He escaped death by fleeing from Russia and after many tribulations landed in Greece. Turning to long-abandoned religious practices, he went to make a retreat at the Monastery of Mt. Athos, the great center of Russian and Greek Orthodoxy. Here he decided to stay and become a monk. For seven years, Nicholas Strandtmann lived in a remote cave, speaking only to his spiritual director.

I had the occasion of seeing him again, wearing a threadbare, black habit and a leather belt, when he came out of his silence to collect funds for his brethren who were cut off from all support. He was as charming and vivacious as usual, even making jokes in French, which he spoke with great elegance. But when he spoke of his life on Mt. Athos, his eyes grew serious, almost austere. He slept on a board, fasting the entire year, eating only a few vegetables that he raised around his hut, and a little fish on feast days. His name in religious life was Father Nikon. When he had been ordained a priest, he spent some time in his community, where life was less severe. But he longed to retire again to his solitary hut, and finally did so. I was amazed at his faith and confidence in his vocation. When I asked how he could bear such a rigorous life, he answered: "It is enough for me to behold the view stretching below at the feet of Mt. Athos, the blue sea, the rocks glistening in the sun — the beauty of it all!"

I could never see Father Nikon again for he did not leave his monastery again, and women are not allowed on Mt. Athos, but several friends, laymen and priests, sought him out. When they mentioned my name he smiled graciously but seemed aloof, as if he did not wish to talk, though he seemed to enjoy some French and Russian magazines they brought him. I heard that Father Nikon died in the late sixties, at the age of ninety. For half a century he had led a life so different from his *tournées du Grand Duc*.

However much we enjoyed Japanese life, there were some things that were rather terrifying—the earthquakes and typhoons which are a constant threat to the islands. We saw cracks in our house which had been caused by an earthquake before we arrived, but except for a few tremors we never experienced a dangerous shock. However, a typhoon overtook us once when we were vacationing on Lake Chuzenji, a mountain resort where various members of the diplomatic corps had summer homes.

The handsome Princess Gagarin and other young couples would join us for our beach parties. But half of the fun was getting to Chuzenji. The train from Tokyo stopped at Nikko and from there we would be carried in litters by coolies, or walk up a steep, winding path through deep volcanic gorges, some of them bubbling with hot springs.

One afternoon, we were assembled at our villa when heavy clouds began to gather; then it began to rain and a strong wind blowing through the woods around us became a hurricane. Maida-San came running into the living room to tell us we were in great danger. We must leave the house immediately and escape to the hinterland. Father took command, got a few papers and valuables together, and we started down the road. He told us to run as fast as we could; I remember following my elders, Grisha, Maida-San and Kiva, clutching my only treasure, my rag doll. As we looked back, I saw hundreds of pine trees rolling down the hill, their bark entirely peeled off their trunks, torn by the rocks as they were plunged down muddy torrents.

We found refuge in a hotel a few miles below the lake. The next day we returned to get our belongings. The house had been preserved; Maida-San had had enough presence of mind to unboard the basement, so the torrents descending upon the house had passed under it. The rest of the flourishing village had disappeared, together with a Buddhist priest. Fishermen with long poles were looking for bodies of drowned villagers.

We tried to get back to Tokyo as soon as possible. But the typhoon had wrought havoc as far as Nikko, destroying its great temples. We came to a mountain torrent which had lost its bridge and Father was concerned, because he had an important message to send to Petersburg. A Japanese escort suggested that we tie the dispatch to an arrow and shoot it to the other side of the torrent, where it would be picked up by messengers along the road. Sure enough, the dispatch reached its destination. This was one of Father's last reports from Japan. Soon afterward he was transferred to Copenhagen.

Family Album (from 1890 to 1914)

The last Ambassador to France of Imperial Russia at his working desk at the Russian Embassy in Paris, 1913 (Photo Manuel)

Alexander Iswolsky (1856-1919), Helene's father

General Count Charles Toll
Helene Iswolsky's maternal great-grandfather (mentioned in Tolstoy's War and Peace*)*

Count and Countess Toll, Helene's grandparents

Alexander Iswolsky with Maguerite Toll (Helene's parents, as fiancés)

Prince ("Uncle Vania") and Princess Kudashev

Father Nikon; Helene's uncle Nicholas Strandtmann, a monk of Mt. Athos

Father Peter Iswolsky, Helene's other uncle (her father's brother)

Helene and brother, Grisha (Gregory) with their father aboard the Ryurik

Helene and Grisha in sailor suits

Helene's father on board ship

In front of their Bavarian house at Tegernsee

Father and son in Tyrolian costumes

Helene

Grisha (1905?)

Grisha Iswolsky with student friends, left to right: Grisha, Count N. Musin-Pushkin, Prince Victor Kochubey, Count A. Musin-Pushkin

With the Faucigny-Lucinge Family
Helene Iswolsky, center, with Jean-Louis de Faucigny-Lucinge's sisters:
Charlotte (Lolotte), left, and Aymone (the latter married Françoise de Brantes)

Princess Guy de Faucigny-
Lucinge et Coligny (Natty)
mother of Jean-Louis, and later
wife of Grisha Iswolsky

Prince Jean-Louis de
Faucigny-Lucinge as a youth

Helene Iswolsky as a debutante in 1914

CHAPTER III

Copenhagen
"La Chère Villa"
Palace Square

Our long journey home was very like our first experience, except that the Trans-Siberian railroad was now finished and we did not have to sail up the Amur. Our only misfortune was that Grisha caught scarlet fever and was obliged to stay in a hospital in Irkutsk. Miss Mukhanova stayed with him, in quarantine, and Mother and I were given rooms in a comfortable *dacha*, or country house, outside the city. Father stayed in a dreary hotel, as Mr. Vtorov was out of town and his house was closed. Finally, our quarantine was over and we were able to continue our journey to Copenhagen.

Why was my father transferred from the Far East to Denmark? He is quite frank about it in his *Mémoires*: "I had been resolutely opposed to the 'strong' policy adopted by Russia towards Japan and inspired by an irresponsible coterie which had gained great influence over the Emperor. The attempts made to facilitate a rapprochement between the two countries had been turned down by the Russian government, and so convinced from that moment that the policy adopted by my sovereign . . . was leading to war, I asked leave to return to Europe."[1] His request was duly granted and the appointment to Copenhagen followed.

This could have been considered a minor diplomatic post, not a promotion. It was, however, an important step in a diplomat's career because of the close ties which bound the Danish royal family to other courts of Europe. As we have seen, Alexandra, the wife of King Edward VII of England, and Maria Fedorovna, widow of Alexander III, were daughters of the Danish King Christian IX. Their mother, Queen Louise, was called the "Mother-in-law" of Europe. The English royal couple, as well as the dowager Empress, Maria Fedorovna, often visited the king, as did Kaiser Wilhelm, cousin to both Edward and the reigning Tsar, Nicholas. The German Emperor made sudden and dramatic appearances at Copenhagen, unwelcome though he was, because of his annexation of the two Danish provinces of Schleswig-Holstein.

Because of these royal visits, Denmark's capital was considered a good observation post for diplomats. By deference to the dowager, the

---
1. Alexandre Iswolsky: *Mémoires*.

Russian minister's post in Copenhagen was filled only with her approval. The dowager welcomed my father for he had the reputation of being a liberal who wanted Russia to adopt a constitutional regime, limiting the Tsar's absolute power. Paradoxically enough, the Tsar's own mother entertained these liberal ideas.

In spite of the dowager's sympathy, Nicholas II disapproved of Father, both in the diplomatic and political positions he had adopted. Before assuming his new post, he had reported to the Tsar and had been received with marked coldness and scarcely disguised resentment. He was clearly in disfavor.

In some respects Copenhagen could have seemed to us somewhat anticlimatic after our colorful life in Japan, but Denmark had its own charm, the peculiarly invigorating and friendly atmosphere of Scandinavia.

Grisha and I spent a quiet year, continuing our education with Miss Mukhanova. Because of the language barrier, we could not attend schools in Denmark, but she piloted us safely through grammar school, and Father took care of the examination period, giving us tests for which we diligently prepared. Our playmates were, as usual, the children of other diplomats as well as some Danish friends who spoke French or English. We went to dancing lessons with them. One boy took a snapshot of me, a little girl of eight with straggling hair and knitted brow. This boy grew up to be a distinguished diplomat and was Danish ambassador to Washington in the 1940's when I arrived in America. He heard of me, and to my great surprise, sent me this photo! Alas, I did not see him, for he left his post with an incurable disease.

Among the children in dancing school were the sons and a daughter of Prince Waldemar, brother of the dowager Empress. He had married a French princess of the house of Bourbon. Just as with the Shimadzu boys in Japan, Father wanted us to meet the Danes in their own country. Grisha, who was now eleven, replaced his sailor suits with teenagers' clothes made in London. (Father was decidedly Anglophile!) For gala occasions, he had a short, black Eton jacket, long trousers, and a bowler hat which came with the outfit. The other boys got hold of the hat and played football with it and crushed it, which made Grisha very sad. One evening he got dressed up for Father, with crushed bowler hat, and performed a wild dance for us. He had a comic gift of imitation, and even Father laughed though he did not always approve of Grisha's performances. We applauded and laughed so hard that tears ran down our cheeks.

Our Legation was right across from the residence of King Christian, Amalienborg. Queen Louise had died, and as he was advanced in age, he felt lonely in spite of his great popularity and used to come over to the Russian Legation on the long winter afternoons for a visit and a game of cards. When we children saw his heavy topcoat and large galoshes in our hall, a big umbrella in the corner, we knew the King was in the house. He came unannounced and unescorted — a very tall, slightly bent old gentleman with a benign smile and charming simplicity of manner.

While we were in Denmark, Scandinavian history was made before our eyes. After years of tension and diplomatic conflict, Norway, which belonged to Sweden, broke her ties and, after a referendum, Sweden gave Norway its independence without a struggle. Prince Charles, Christian's son, accepted the title of King, under the name of Haakon; his wife, Maud, King Edward's youngest daughter, became Queen. They sailed for Norway in November. Grisha and I, with Miss Mukhanova, walked to the pier, where a crowd had assembled in perfect order, to see the new sovereign board his ship with his wife and son, Olaf, now heir apparent. Obviously in those days separatists had a better chance to achieve their goal without violence than is the case in our day.

The yearly visits of the Russian dowager Empress to her father in Copenhagen always brought excitement to the quiet city. She arrived with her ladies- and gentlemen-in-waiting and was accompanied by her bodyguard, a huge Cossack in dazzling uniform. The very appearance of this bearded giant was a sensation.

Maria Fedorovna was a very gracious person, short and rather plain, but spirited, with a friendly smile for everyone. During her visits she attended the services of the Russian Orthodox church which had been built especially for her and Alexander III in Copenhagen. A curious crowd assembled at the doors of the church to see the dowager and to admire her magnificient Cossack bodyguard. We closed the procession and took our place behind Maria Fedorovna. But in spite of protocol, we children looked upon her as a friendly old lady. Since this was no official visit, Father did not have to entertain her with lavish dinners and receptions, but she held long consultations with him which were to bring about important changes in his career.

Thus our life flowed along quite pleasantly until disaster struck our country. Though far away, we could not fail to feel its tragic repercussions. On January 27th, 1904, Japanese destroyers attacked Russian warships anchored outside Port Arthur, heavily damaging several of them. On the same day, other units of the Russian navy were sunk off the Korean coast. Admiral Makarov, commander of the Pacific fleet, was blown up with his battleship, the *Petropavlovsk*.

With the crippling of her fleet, Russia went on suffering defeat after defeat; the Japanese landed in Korea, invaded Manchuria and besieged Port Arthur. The Pacific fleet was destroyed and the Russian army was forced to retreat from its positions in Liao-Tung. Father's somber predictions concerning the Japanese armed superiority were fully justified.

The heavy sacrifices which Russia had had to pay in human lives were not easily forgotten. There were demonstrations, strikes and protests throughout Russia. The climax came on "Bloody Sunday" when police and army units fired on a crowd of peaceful demonstrators who had marched to the Winter Palace bearing a petition to the Tsar. There were more than a hundred killed and several hundred wounded. On that day, January 9th, 1905, one may truly say that the curtain rose on the Russian Revolution.

As the disastrous war was drawing to an end and the country was in the grip of political unrest, it would have been unsafe for Mother to go to Russia and take her children. Instead we spent the winter months in Copenhagen, and then for our vacation period we went to Tegernsee, the Bavarian mountain resort where I was born and where Grandmother Toll had built her villa. She had planned it for her daughters as well as herself; it was spacious and pleasant for family reunions. Father and Uncle John, busy with their diplomatic concerns, could seldom come to be with us; but for the other members of the family, it had become routine to spend three or four months in the Bavarian Alps.

Life at the Villa Toll was geared to an unfailing routine to which the obedient family cheerfully complied. It consisted of hearty meals cooked and served by devoted Bavarian servants, various tedious parties with a few distinguished neighbors, and long drives taken every afternoon in an open carriage. Motorcars had not yet entered our lives and if one or two appeared on the roads our horses would shy and our coachman would pull up his reins dramatically. It was, however, the age of the bicycle and as soon as we learned how to ride, we escaped and went on our own excursions, Miss Mukhanova dutifully pedaling along with us. We rode through a most beautiful countryside, the wooded slopes of the Alps rising around us. Happy days, indeed, until Miss Mukhanova decided to leave us.

I now salute for the last time Nadezhda Vladimirovna Mukhanova, who on one of those summer days at Tegernsee vanished from our lives as suddenly as she had entered. My parents had decided that Grisha should have a tutor who could speak Russian with me as well, and Miss Mukhanova did not wish to share her young pupils with a stranger. Her mind was made up and she left us, quietly but resolutely. She was destined for a higher post, that of a director on the staff of the Smolny Institute, the school of higher education for young girls of the Petersburg aristocracy. This was the finest girl's college in Russia. Nothing could suit our admirable mentor better.

Grisha took her departure philosophically but I was deeply grieved. Soon I was entrusted to an English governess and I had to get used to a completely new personality and to a language and culture of which I knew only the rudiments. Later, however, I was grateful to my English educators — for several of them succeeded each other as I grew up. I owe them not only my knowledge of English and of English literature, but I also found them warmhearted and devoted friends.

My mother, in particular, was happy at Tegernsee. Among the photographs I found after her death was one of our spacious mountain home; it was inscribed in French, in her fine, elegant handwriting: *Ma Chère Villa*. Yes, this was the house beloved by all of us; not a luxurious mansion but a picturesque cottage in the style of a chalet, with brightly painted shutters and geraniums on every balcony.

So it was that even around this small mountain village, history was spinning its intricate web. Looking back at the scenes of my childhood vacations, I can pick up the thread of events that were happening in Germany, Denmark, France and Russia, and of which I had little knowledge at the time.

One of these events, which took place in October, 1905, had a decisive influence on my father's life and was to bring changes for us all. On one of the dowager's long visits to Denmark she had a long and earnest consultation with my father. During the preceding months there had been intense political and social unrest in Petersburg as well as in other cities of Russia; demonstrations, strikes, student rebellions, acts of violence, tempestuous meetings — these had broken out all over the country. The most dramatic episode was the mutiny of the sailors on the battleship *Potemkin* (which was the subject of a famous film by the Soviet director Eisenstein). Soldiers, the police and the navy were called in but repression only fanned the flames. Deeply alarmed and grieved, the dowager Empress was convinced that only the granting of a constitution by the Tsar, the limitation of his absolute power, and a new liberal cabinet could bring relief to the country. She asked Father to go to Petersburg to obtain an audience with the Tsar, and to bring him her personal message imploring him to give Russia a freely elected parliament.

Father accepted the challenge but encountered great difficulties. Transportation was crippled by strikes so the dowager arranged passage on the East Asiatic Line. He reached Petersburg after a stormy voyage and delivered Maria Fedorovna's message to her son, adding his own support.

During the three weeks he spent in the capital, he had frequent meetings with the Tsar and with the men engaged in the preliminary draft of a new order. On October 30th, an Imperial Manifesto was published announcing the creation of the Duma, the first Russian elected chamber, to which an upper house, the Council of Empire, was adjoined.

The October Manifesto brought about a brief détente followed by further unrest, the radical parties not being satisfied with the new setup. A list of tentative nominees for the Ministerial Cabinet was prepared, and to my father's surprise, he was informed that he was on the list as Foreign Minister. The liberalization of Russian political life had led to the removal of Count Lamsdorf, whose diplomatic methods were considered out-dated. A new man was needed at this post of international relations, a man with friendly relations with France and England and who was in sympathy with the moderate liberals who were building up the new regime. Father did not feel himself ready for the task offered to him and suggested another candidate. But when the latter refused the post, there was nothing my father could do but accept it, for better or worse.[2]

The opening of the Duma took place in April, 1906, and Father attended it. His appointment had not yet been confirmed nor made official, so he came as a "roving diplomat"; his political ideas had now reached at least the first step toward realization. But there was still a long way to go.

Soon after the opening ceremony, the names of the newly appointed ministers were announced. We were told that our stay in Denmark was at an end.

* * *

My father was appointed Minister of Foreign Affairs when I was ten years old. I remember this time of my life very vividly. I was anxious to return to Russia, and in spite of so many travels I felt that somehow this should be my real habitat.

However, my first impressions after stepping out of the station were something of a disappointment. My mother, Grisha and myself arrived in Petersburg alone, Father having been at the Ministry since the month of May, deeply engrossed in Russian foreign and interior affairs. November is not the best time to arrive in a northern city, wreathed in dark clouds and swept by chilling winds. The station square had a gloomy look as if frowning at newcomers. The small, shabby houses with narrow facades were painted yellow, brown or dark red; the colors did not glow but formed dull patches against the autumn sky.

We all got into an open carriage, known as a landau, drawn by two coal black *rysaks* (the Russian pacemakers) with flowing uncut manes and long black tails. The bearded coachman wore a long dark blue coat reaching to the heels of his high boots. This attire was completed by a lozenge-shaped hat and a bright sash with a fine, arabesque design. The French historian Jacques Bainville once told me that when he visited Russia the coachman's bright sash was the first sign for him that he was nearing the Orient.

Our smart vehicle, sent by the Ministry, dispelled the first depressing atmosphere. The coachman drove us at a swift pace, shouting to other vehicles to keep to the right. Of course, there were no cars in those days, but many horse-drawn cabs, carts and even buses—all made way—with a few oaths and much grumbling.

Small, cheap-looking stores displayed huge, painted signs for the illiterate, no lettering, only symbols; giant pretzels, sugarloaves, ironing

---

2. *Recollections of a Foreign Minister* —pp. 15–21. From *Mémoires* of Alexandre Iswolsky.

boards, clocks and watches, fruits and vegetables, scissors and tools, some realistic pictures that would be a pop artist's delight.

Then the streets grew wider, the buildings taller, resembling those of West European cities. There were no more crude paintings but gold lettering over plate-glass windows. Soon we reached the residential quarters, with their glamorous mansions built in baroque or neoclassic style — delicately designed iron gates and balconies, tall white columns, supporting marble canopies, stuccoed or sculptured decorations, with the monumental domes of two cathedrals looming in the background. This was the northern metropolis, a combination of Rome, Washington and Versailles.

Our landau passed under a tall arch and we emerged into a huge square framed by many official-looking buildings, one of them with a richly decorated facade and a monumental porch. This was the Winter Palace, the Tsar's residence.

In the middle of the square was a very tall, granite column surmounted by an angel holding a cross. Our horses trotted briskly on until our driver's firm hand pulled them to a halt in front of one of the uniform large buildings opposite the palace. A liveried porter helped us out of the carriage and ushered us into a vast hall. There was a marble stairway with Father peering over the balustrade. We were in the Ministry of Foreign Affairs, our new home on Palace Square.

The Ministry's long block, with its rows and rows of windows and many entrances, was located between Palace Square and the Winter Canal, one of Petersburg's numerous waterways which make this city resemble a Venice of the north. A small bridge connected our block with the Palace. It was called the "Chorister's Bridge" (Le Pont des Chantres in French diplomatic language) because members of the Imperial Court Choir, who lived in nearby houses, used to cross over it when they went to sing in the Palace chapel. Our "back door," so to speak, was on the canal and so the Ministry was often called *Le Pont des Chantres*, just as the London foreign ministry is called "Downing Street."

Our private apartments were only a small part of the Chorister's Bridge, the rest of the block being taken up with ballrooms, reception rooms, dining halls and a multitude of offices for the various departments of the ministry — Far East, Near East and European. My father's office was the center of this complex. His undersecretary of state, Mr. Sazonav (who was later to take his place) also had an office here, as did other department directors, and also Mr. Savinsky, chief of the chancellery.

There also were the "officers for special assignments," the Ministry's closest aides and trusted agents: Count Peter Pahlen, my mother's cousin, a handsome, white-haired man, and Mr. Gulkevich, who was always kind and attentive to children. I think I have never known a better man, as was proved after the Revolution when he was the last ambassador of the old regime in Stockholm and helped many refugees who fled Russia via Scandinavia. Both these officers were experienced, intelligent men who stood by my father at the time of his most severe trials, which were not far ahead.

Our living quarters were comfortable but not luxurious. Below were the servants' quarters where a large staff lived with their families. They had a courtyard used as a playground for their children. A long, red-carpeted corridor led from the schoolroom to a glass door which we were forbidden to unlock. It led to the "inner sanctum" of the Ministry. The walls of the corridor were hung with the portraits of all the foreign ministers, from the time of the boyars, in their Byzantine attire, and the eighteenth-century diplomats in powdered wigs, to Count Lamsdorf, my father's predecessor, with frock coat and whiskers. During the Revolution, I was once told, a Red sailor had amused himself by setting up a machine gun at one end of this corridor and shooting at a target at the other end—perhaps one of these portraits!

In the Ministry, my father worked in close cooperation with Mr. Sazonav, his undersecretary, or as he was called in Russian official circles, "comrade of the minister"—(no connection with Communist terminology!). Sazonav was an old friend of my father's and at that time saw eye to eye with him; later, he disagreed quite sharply with him, especially on the questions of the Straits when he, in turn, became Foreign Minister. In spite of disagreement, however, my parents always remained on friendly terms with Sazonav. Not all the Ministry's officials were as friendly. Many were cold and diffident, and some definitely hostile. There were several reasons for this. The new "man at the wheel" was much younger—more dynamic—and he stirred up matters which had been safely tucked away by bureaucratic inertia. He was impatient with the Asiatic department and its aggressive spirit. There were minor grievances as, for instance, when young diplomats wanted to make their debuts as attaché in Paris or London, and instead were appointed to the Far East or some distant South American capital. Father believed that this was the best way to acquire experience. There were unpleasant incidents such as recalling heads of legations and even embassies for mistakes which they thought would pass unnoticed.

He rebuked chiefs of departments, perhaps too sharply, wounding their feelings irrevocably. His liberal ideas were distasteful to many of his older subordinates, who frowned on Russia's new parliamentary regime. Last but not least, he was seeking a rapprochement with England while many Russian officials mistrusted the wiles of "deceitful Albion." They criticized my father's so-called Anglomania; reactionary papers showed cartoons of the Foreign Minister in tweeds. It was true that he ordered his clothes from England, from a tailor named Hill. But as to the more serious matter of ending the old feud between Russia and England, he had a plan nearing realization.

The various currents of open or secret hostility made my father's work extremely difficult. He had few friends and his drastic methods of attacking inertia and *laisser-faire* did not make matters easier. If he had few friends, it was because he found few people sharing his ideas, especially during these critical years on Palace Square when Russian policy was being tested. Grisha told me that when he was a young student in London, he saw Father dining alone in a London restaurant, while all the other tables were filled with animated patrons. Father knew many people in London, but he chose to eat alone, rather than to enter into futile or indiscreet conversations. My brother, who had no such fears, felt badly about my father's aloneness but hesitated to disturb him. The *maître d'hôtel*, noticing his hesitation, murmured: "There is Mr. Iswolsky dining alone as usual, and such a brilliant gentleman!"

Long after the Revolution had swept us all out of service, I still met Russian diplomats in exile who bore a grudge toward their ex-chief. They accused him of a mistaken policy; Russia, they argued, would have done better to side with Germany instead of with England. Others accused him of haughtiness and excessive ambition, forgetting that he had twice offered his resignation to the Tsar. Many of my father's enemies wrote their memoirs and mentioned his name with irony or bitterness. It is difficult for a daughter to restore his true image, for I will always be accused or suspected of partiality. All I can do is to write my own story showing him as he was during those dramatic years and letting the reader draw his own conclusions.

I should say here that my mother did a great deal to smooth tensions inside and outside of the Ministry. She was unaware of the deeper causes of these tensions, but was prompted by her womanly intuition. Her personal charm as well as her finesse and tact averted many scenes and conversations that might have been painful due to Father's inadvertent bluntness. She also had a sense of humor which he shared with her, a humor which helped us all to weather the storms arising around us. Her husband took an almost exaggerated care of her, when he was not too preoccupied with outside matters. But in spite of his pampering, she was not spoiled but always kind and considerate of others. The story of her coachman Mikhail is quite typical.

Mother had her own carriage and horses driven by Mikhail, a tall, black-bearded, cheerful fellow who had twelve children of his own and had adopted another. When Mother went to the theater or a dinner party, Mikhail, like all Petersburg coachmen, had to wait with his vehicle, sometimes until late at night in the bitter subzero winter weather. This was a great hardship in spite of the coachman's padded garments and the *braseros* burning in the streets to keep them warm. Mother was always worried about Mikhail and sent him home, figuring with remarkable exactness when he should return to fetch her. It may seem unbelievable, but after the Revolution when we were émigrés in France, a message "came through" to us from a person who had recently left Petersburg. The message was from Mikhail, who sent his greetings to my mother, remembering her concern about him when he was a coachman. He had become the president of a local soviet, an important post in the newly formed revolutionary government.

In the solidly structured world in which we lived it would have been quite impossible to foresee Mikhail's career. It seemed as if life would go on indefinitely in this beehive of diplomatic activity. As in all Petersburg government offices, work started late at the Chorister's Bridge — around 11 A.M. This was not due to sleeping late; we all had breakfast long before office hours. But winter mornings are dark and gloomy in northern lands. Lamps were still lit at noon and energies began to waken around that time, if not later. Luncheon was a dreary affair and early afternoon was scarcely enlivened by the pale Nordic sun, reluctantly shining in a misty sky. Soon darkness descended once more, the lamps were lit under their green glass shades, and everybody became alert and business-like. Then work really started and continued, sometimes until deep into the small hours of the morning. Nobody thought that two or three o'clock was late for a conference or a cabinet meeting. In spring, of course, it was different. This was the time of the famous "white nights" of Petersburg, when it was almost impossible to go to sleep. A strange, eerie mood and excitement came over the most sober-minded people and nobody bothered whether it was day or night.

In spite of this unusual schedule, things were efficiently taken care of at the Ministry, although office equipment was primitive compared to modern methods. Typewriters were being introduced, but slowly. At the Ministry, many papers and letters were written or copied by hand. My father wrote his own reports and all his letters. He had no secretary and conducted an almost daily correspondence with the Russian ambassadors abroad — Count Benkendorf in London, Prince Urusov in Berlin, Mr. Nelidov in Paris. To these he wrote in French, though he preferred to write in Russian to his contemporaries. His affairs were conducted in a bilingual style but the tendency was to use Russian, though a small part of the French terminology was preserved, having acquired an international meaning, such as *triplice*, or *triple entente*.

As I have said earlier, my brother and I were taught that Russian was our native tongue. Grisha was enrolled in school as soon as we arrived in Petersburg. To our friends' and relatives' surprise, Father decided to send his son to a *gymnasia*. This was a public school modeled after the German educational system, from which it got its name. Most families of Petersburg society enrolled their sons in the exclusive schools which admitted only the sons of aristocrats — the Imperial Lycée, the School of Law, the *Corps des Pages* — to prepare young men for civil service, the Court, or military careers. The *gymnasias* were open to almost everyone. Jews were admitted under two conditions: that their parents had special permission to reside in Petersburg, in other words, beyond the borderline drawn in the southwest of Russia, which Jews were hardly allowed to cross, and, as for the student, he had to conform to a quota accorded to a certain number of young Jews whose marks were above average. This anti-Semitic law defeated itself; Jewish boys maintained the highest marks in the school and were often far better educated than the Christian students. Thus a strong intelligentsia was formed.

In spite of their limitations, the *gymnasias* were no doubt in closer contact with the reality of life in Russia than were the institutions catering to the elite. My father himself, had graduated *cum laudae* from the Imperial Lycée. But he believed that the time had come to widen and stimulate a young boy's experience and make him rub shoulders with students of another class. Petersburg society was shocked by this move and again Father was branded a dangerous liberal.

CHAPTER IV

The Fateful Years

AT THE TIME when my father was put in charge of the Ministry of Foreign Affairs, grave political events were taking place in Russia as an aftermath of the 1905 Revolution. As he watched their development he wrote to Count Benkendorf, our Ambassador in London: "The interior situation dominates everything."[1]

Only a few months earlier, he had welcomed the establishment of the Duma, the first Russian parliament. He now realized that this new machinery, so carefully contrived, was facing many obstacles. Actually, though important international problems were being broached abroad, father had to turn away from them to confront interior troubles. He was keenly aware that constructive negotiations could not be conducted in the world capitals while Russia was directed by an ultrareactionary government. These matters were rarely discussed in the presence of children but I could not help overhear some of the hints and allusions exchanged by my father with Count Pahlen and Mr. Gulkevich, who had lunch with us daily. Later, when I grew older, many things were clarified and explained to me so that I can reconstruct the dramatic happenings of 1905 as they were reflected in our own home.

The spring and summer of that year was a period of intense political ferment. The majority of the Duma was socialist; the nonsocialist left wing was also strong, aggressive. Urgent reforms were on the agenda, from moderate land adjustments to expropriation of certain estates with or without compensation. These projects, even the most conservative ones, were systematically ignored by the Tsar and by the reactionary head of the Cabinet, Mr. Goremykin. In fact, the Duma was unable to process any bills though provision had been made for this in the new constitution.

In the previous chapter, I have told of my father's report to the Tsar in 1905, a year before his appointment to the Ministry. He was among the men who sought and succeeded in persuading the Tsar to grant Russia a constitutional body. Now he made an attempt to liberalize it.

---

1. See A. Iswolsky, *Au service de la Russie: Alexandre Iswolsky; correspondance diplomatique*, 1911, V. 1-2, Diplomatic Correspondence published in Paris, 1937.

Goremykin's obstinate boycott of the Duma's projects was to lead to another and more dangerous revolutionary crisis than that of the previous years. The only solution could be to remove the aging president and reshuffle his Cabinet. My father, who belonged to the progressive but moderate party known as the Octobrists, and his colleague Minister of the Interior Stolypin were the most active and farseeing of the Cabinet. In their opinion, the members of the nonsocialist left wing should be included in the Cabinet in order to restore the confidence of the people. Their advice to the Tsar being to no avail, they decided to enter into private conversations with the leftist leaders who seemed inclined to accept a portfolio in a coalition government.

The meetings of the active ministers and of the prospective candidates were veiled in deep secrecy; in fact, they had a conspiratorial character which was, on one occasion, not devoid of a humorous aspect. My father had an appointment with Mr. Miliukov, the powerful leader of the Constitutional-Democratic Party (known as "the Cadets"). The meeting was to take place outside the city limits on one of the islands of the Neva River. These islands with their private mansions and public parks and gardens made up Petersburg's most picturesque area. It was also famous for its restaurants and nightclubs. The "conspirators" met in a summer home where they could better escape the vigilant eye of the secret police. The conversation went on until daybreak and as it ended on a most friendly note, my father offered to drive the "Cadet" party leader home in his open carriage. On their way they saw, with dismay, that other vehicles were about to overtake them. They were filled with the patrons of the nightclubs with their ladies of doubtful reputation. Some saluted them ironically after their gay night with the Gypsies; others turned discreetly away. The two politicians could not help smiling at the thought that they were also suspected of all-night reveling.

Mr. Miliukov did not become a member of the Cabinet at that time, but he was appointed Minister of Foreign Affairs in the short-lived Cabinet of the Provisional Government under Kerensky. He was later exiled by the Bolsheviks and settled in Paris, where I met him again. I never dared to remind him of his excursion to the islands and its comic aspect.

On July 8th, 1906, my father boarded the small yacht put at his disposal for official trips and sailed down the Neva into the Gulf of Finland to Peterhof, the Imperial country home. It was the day of his monthly report to the Tsar, and having placed it in his hand, he urgently pleaded with him to read it. As usual, he listened attentively to his Foreign Minister and promised to read the memorandum. A few days later, he called my father for a further discussion; again the little yacht sailed down the Neva.

Its brasses were neatly polished and glistening in the July sun and its sailors were in their immaculate white summer uniforms. At Peterhof Park, the beautiful fountains laid out in imitation of Versailles were playing surrounded by bright flowerbeds, velvet lawns, and clipped box hedges: this was the Imperial Palace, built by Peter the Great in 1720, and enlarged by Rastrelli in 1746 and the years following.

But my father, hurrying through the garden and into the mirrored hall, escorted by court officials and liveried footmen, paid little attention to this glamorous décor, anxious as he was to present his memorandum. Then a master of ceremonies opened the door of the Tsar's study and the two men were once more face-to-face.

Remembering my father as he was in those days, I can picture him there, respectfully bowing in his formal frock coat with golden buttons and epaulettes, the uniform worn by ministers on such occasions. He was a broad-shouldered, rather thick-set man with a blond moustache and wavy, blond hair. His blue eyes were serious and attentive; when he put his monocle in his right eye, it gave him a rather fierce expression. When he suddenly dropped it, he seemed as if he were playing a joke on his interlocutor. Of course, he could indulge in no such joke in His Majesty's presence. He did not even dangle his monocle on its thick, black silk cord, as he was wont to do.

Short and bearded, wearing the white field uniform of his favorite infantry regiment, the Tsar rose to greet his visitor. He turned upon his Minister his candid, pale eyes which had a radiance but, at the same time, hid his intimate thoughts in a sad, strange mist.

Again, the two men discussed the memorandum and the Tsar agreed that preliminary talks should be held secretly with prospective candidates for a coalition Cabinet. These consultations were started immediately, but the Duma was impatient and would not wait any longer. The radical parties composed their own dramatic appeal. It was not addressed to the Tsar but to the entire nation, expressing its long-desired reforms. Goremykin did not hesitate to consider this an open act of rebellion. He, too, steamed down the Neva in the little white yacht to present his own report to the Tsar. He returned in no time, triumphantly carrying with him the Imperial decree, ordering the dissolution of the Duma and a new election.

This decision, coming so soon after two encouraging talks at Peterhof, had a stunning effect on my father. His first thought was that the dissolution, as soon as it was known, would cause serious disturbances and perhaps riots. He sent a circular letter to all the foreign ambassadors warning them that troops would have to be stationed around their homes. He did not reveal the reason for this measure, since the dissolution of the Duma was still a secret. After sending out these letters, my father cleared his desk and wrote instructions to his chiefs of departments to be followed after he left. He had resolved to offer his resignation to the Tsar.

That night he dined at the British Embassy. One of the guests was Sir Donald McKensie Wallace, who had been sent to Petersburg as an advisor to the newly appointed Ambassador, Sir Arthur Nicholson. McKensie Wallace was a London *Times* correspondent and was known as an expert on Russian affairs. He had often lived in Petersburg and visited many other towns and even villages. He spoke the language fluently and was aware of all the political tensions. In fact, one of his private assignments had been to persuade the Tsar to liberalize the Cabinet. He, too, had failed in his endeavor.

After dinner, Sir Donald and my father stepped out on the balcony. Both were preoccupied, but since the fate of the Duma was still unknown to the Englishman the conversation touched only on general subjects. Both men admired the view which lay at their feet. It was one of the most beautiful of the wide river, for the Embassy lay on the "English quai," further on was the "French quai," named after the French Embassy, and then the Palace quai, all lined with St. Petersburg's most elegant mansions. The Neva flowed peacefully between the granite embankments. The little yacht which had carried the conflicting statesmen to Peterhof was moored not far away.

I conjure up this scene from my father's own story, but it reminded me of other scenes and conversations conducted in similar fashion. Grisha and I were observant children and we noticed that Father had a way of drawing guests away to an open window or balcony so he could talk to them of grave matters in a low voice. We called it "talking by the window." But as far as we could tell, it did not avert the catastrophes which they saw approaching—we had not as yet read Tolstoy's *War and Peace*, which describes the fruitless efforts made by statesmen and military men to control events of destiny beyond their power.

It was on July 8th that an Imperial manifesto dissolved the Duma, and Father offered his resignation. In the struggle around the Duma, Goremykin seemed to be the winner. But not entirely, because the discontent that had been awakened in political circles was too obvious to be ignored, even by the Tsar. Goremykin was removed and Stolypin appointed in his place as president of the new Cabinet. As for my father, his resignation was not accepted. He wrote to Count Benkendorf, our Ambassador to London and one of his trusted friends:

> Some day, I will tell you *viva voce* the agitation which I have personally suffered during the last two weeks, and the efforts I made to have certain resolutions adopted . . . Nothing helped, so I saw no alternative except to offer my resignation, which I demanded with insistence . . . if I have ceased to insist, it is because I believe that the hour of danger is nearer than others think, and that since we could not prevent it, the only thing to do is to wait at my post.

It took no excess of pessimism to forsee these dangers. Though revolution was avoided for the time being, violence broke out on the left and on the right.

At this period, there were many terrorist activities and attempted assassinations. My father escaped disaster, but only by mere chance. During one of his travels, a bomb was discovered in his railroad compartment just before the train left the station. It had been planted there to kill a grand duke who had changed his mind at the last moment and taken another train. Father had been offered the vacant compartment. Another time, he witnessed the shooting of a high official strolling through a park in the vicinity of Peterhof.

Threatening letters were sent to all Cabinet members and they were advised to seek police protection. Father refused, saying that the police itself was infiltrated with double agents. He was anonymously informed that he would be killed by a young woman terrorist, which seemed quite romantic and made him smile. However, he remained on the alert. One day as he was crossing Palace Square, a stranger approached him. It was not a woman but a beggar asking for a coin. Father gave a few coins and the beggar seized his hand. *"This is it"* was the thought that ran through Father's mind. But the man only kissed his hand and ran away.

In 1906, each Cabinet meeting was a hazard, especially if it was presided over by Stolypin. Since the latter was very severe with terrorists, they had already condemned him to death. His assassination could be expected any moment. It would suffice to plant a bomb in the hall where the meetings took place and everybody present could be destroyed. Since these meetings took place at night and lasted until early morning, Mother would sit up or lie awake in bed waiting for her husband to return, never quite sure if he was still alive.

There were some scares which did not materialize, as when Grisha and a schoolmate who was interested in chemistry obtained a substance which could be detonated by water. They hurled this explosive from a window of Grisha's room and it fell into the canal right near the Chorister's Bridge and only a block away from the Winter Palace. A thundering explosion followed and the police came racing toward the embankment. Our building was searched from top to bottom until the two young red-faced "scientists" confessed their prank.

Real tragedy was soon to follow. On August 12th, Father was informed by phone that Stolypin's home had been blown up. He rushed to the scene and found many dead and wounded and the house in shambles. A bomb had been hurled into the entrance hall when the waiting room was filled with visitors who had business appointments or had brought petitions. Some thirty people were killed, including the terrorist. Stolypin was not hurt,[2] but one of his daughters was crippled

---
2. Stolypin escaped several other attempts on his life. He was killed in 1911, by a double agent while attending a gala performance at the Kiev Opera.

for life. Father found the Premier in a small summerhouse in the garden with his small son whom he had extracted from the ruins. All around, trees had been uprooted by the explosion.

Returning from this tragic scene, Father shut himself up in his study and wrote two letters. One was addressed to Tsar Nicholas, and the other to the dowager Empress, Maria Fedorovna. They were to be delivered in case of his death. The letter to the Tsar read as follows:

> Sire, knowing that, like many of Your Majesty's servants, I am threatened by almost inescapable death, I implore Your Majesty, in case of my demise, not to abandon my wife and children who are completely deprived of means.
>
> Firmly hoping that Your Majesty will not refuse this merciful protection, it will be easier for me to meet my death and to fulfill, up to the last moment, my duty to Your Majesty and to my native land.
>
> May God preserve Your Majesty, your family, and Russia.
>   Your Majesty's faithful servant,
>   Iswolsky.

The letter to the dowager Empress was written in French and contained the same request. The two letters were never sent. Father was not assassinated by terrorists, but died in Paris in 1919. The letters were found in my father's strongbox. They vividly brought back the anxious atmosphere in which we lived during those far-away fateful years. They also made me realize, once more, our father's concern for us and our future.

Looking over the records of the dramatic events which marked these years, I try to recall the mood which prevailed at our home. My parents must have lived under a severe strain, yet our daily life flowed on, as far as I can remember, quite normally, thanks to Father's restraint of his emotions and Mother's smiling serenity. They must have found support at least in the encouragement and sympathy offered by a few, sincere friends; Grand Duke Nicholas had mentioned in his letter to Father those friends who dared to approve openly and formed a not-so-silent minority.

These sympathizers belonged to various circles of Petersburg society, from members of the Duma and the Council of State (the elected ones) to high officials and even people nearest to the Court, who, as the Grand Duke put it, lived "in the shadow of inactivity" because they were *persona non grata*.

Since I was in my early teens, I did not have the opportunity of observing these friends of my parents at close range, for they came and went quietly when we were in our schoolroom. There was however, nothing particularly secret about their visits and outspokenness, for those who "dared" give their support were protected either by their former distinguished careers, by their powerful relatives, or by the historic names they bore, some of them more ancient or more brilliant than that of the Romanovs — the Tsar's dynasty. But they did not merely represent the power of bureaucracy or aristocracy, they enjoyed a reputation of the highest integrity in public affairs and in private life which remained undisputed even in the eyes of their enemies.

I was fortunate to see at least one of these men, living in the shadow of disfavor, but nevertheless respected and even feared. He was Count Constantine Ivanovich Pahlen, former Minister of Justice and Grand Marshal of the Imperial Court under two Tsars. Incidentally, he was the descendant of the nobleman who bore his name and in 1801 led the conspiracy against Emperor Paul I and engineered the latter's assassination.

A photograph taken at the coronation of Tsar Nicholas II shows Count Constantine Ivanovich immediately preceding the cortege of the senior grand dukes, leading the high-ranking Russian Orthodox clergy and opening the way with his grand-marshal's staff for the monarch to pass in regalia and jeweled crown.

Indeed it is paradoxical that the man with the name of a famous regicide should thus appear laden with honors in the Kremlin's most solemn procession. No less paradoxical is the fact that the Count, who was a confirmed Lutheran, as were most of the gentlemen from the Baltic, was "shepherding" the princes of the Orthodox Church in their gold vestments and miters.

At the time when we lived on Palace Square, Constantine Ivanovich lived in retirement after many years of active service in which he had manifested remarkable civic courage and a spirit of bold liberalism. Now, though officially inactive, he was still a formidable presence and often an angry voice. I quite frequently had the occasion of informally visiting this unusual old man, whom we called Uncle Constantine, for he was married to my maternal grandmother's sister, Helen Toll.

Uncle Constantine, his wife, and his unmarried daughter, Marussia, lived only a few blocks away from our home in a quiet street which for some reason which I never found out was called Millionnaya (Million Street) and has now been renamed in honor of a famous revolutionary. On one side of Millionnaya were apartment houses, on the other side loomed the monumental porch of the Hermitage Museum, one of Petersburg's historic landmarks.

The Pahlen's apartment was comfortable and attractive, but in no way luxurious. Like the people who lived in it, the setting had an air of noble but severe dignity. I always entered it with a sense of awe, though I knew only the rather vague outline of Uncle Constantine's life and could only dimly realize its meaning in Russian society and politics.

Count Constantine Ivanovich was born in Petersburg in 1833; he was graduated from the Petersburg University Law School and was in charge of the wounded during the Crimean War, spending three months in besieged Sebastopol. His first years were served as a young official of the Council of State and of the Ministry of the Interior. From then on his career proceeded by leaps and bounds, thanks to his brilliant intellectual gifts and moral strength. He was Secretary of State and Minister of Justice in the 1860s, at the time when Emperor Alexander II planned and put into immediate practice his liberal reforms: the emancipation of the serfs, the revision of the Russian judicial system, and other profound changes in the structure of the Russian Empire. These reforms, their legal and political aspects, were worked out through Count Pahlen's ministry and under his direct supervision. He was deeply convinced of the necessity of Russia's liberalization, and completely involved in it as he was, he would have gone further had he been permitted to do so. He had, in fact, sought to obtain from the Tsar a proclamation of freedom of conscience for all Russia but was not permitted to pursue his plan. He continued to be deeply concerned with the discrimination against religious minorities, Protestant, Catholic, and Jewish.

After the assassination of Alexander II, his successor, Alexander III switched from his father's liberal policy to extreme reactionary trends supported by his advisor on religious and political affairs, the Procurator of the Holy Synod, whose name was also Constantine and who was Alexander's *éminence grise*, the formidable Pobedonostsev. In spite of all the growing obstacles, Count Pahlen persisted in his liberalization projects. He was president of a special commission which was to work out a more tolerant status for the Jews, aiming at a complete abolition of the severe restrictions imposed upon them. The commission met during five years and was closed in 1886 without having been able to introduce even minor reforms.

Were the honors bestowed on Uncle Constantine, of which his appointment as Grand Marshal was no doubt the most dazzling, a "consolation prize" for all the frustrations he had suffered in the field of political reforms? In any case, honors meant little for this champion of human rights who was known "as the conscience of Petersburg."

My mother often visited the Pahlens and took me along with her. Aunt Helen and her daughter, Marussia, served tea in the drawing room, which was conventional, but devoid of the Victorian trimmings usually found in Petersburg salons: the innumerable pictures on the walls, love seats, "cozy corners," embroidered lamp shades and cushions, and the trinkets and statuettes in glass cases. Everything was sober and, as I said, severe in this room; its main feature was, however, quite imposing; two shiny black grand pianos stood side by side in the middle of the room, awaiting the deft fingers of mother and daughter, both of them devoted musicians.

As soon as tea was over, Aunt Helen and Marussia sat down at their respective instruments to give us a recital of Bach and Hayden.

Sitting on the edge of my chair and pulling down my skirt as far as it could go (Aunt Helen had pronounced it too short), I listened respectfully to the concert. Alas, it was far beyond my appreciation, my own piano lessons having been one of my childhood's worst disasters. It was only much later that I developed my love of music. The two ladies played on for what seemed to me an interminable time. The mysterious winter twilight would slowly descend upon the snow-covered Millionnaya Street outside, while curtains were drawn and lamps were lit in the rooms filled with the sound of music; it floated in the air, carrying away the two pianists into the world of pure joy and harmony, far from the bloody Sundays and threats of violence and war.

When the recital was over there was a hush, as if all were now awaiting something important to happen, to which the music was a prelude; and sure enough, the door of an adjacent room was flung open and Uncle Constantine appeared. He was then in his late seventies, a tall, wiry man who must have walked erect, carrying his head high in the days of his glory; even now he bore himself proudly, though slightly bent by age and the long years of service and struggle.

His ruddy complexion, thick, silver and somewhat tousled hair — he had just awakened from a nap — white, bushy eyebrows and long, white sideburns, made him look like a Norse skipper, or rather an old Viking. He reminded me of Wagner's "Flying Dutchman," for the old man had weathered many storms. A light, plaid shawl was thrown over his stooping shoulders and he held an amber cigarette holder in his hand with a lighted cigarette. I could feel the gaze of his deep, greenish blue eyes on me, almost childlike in their candor. He greeted me with great gentleness; he did not notice whether my skirt was long or short or if I sat straight on my chair. He seemed to be asking us all one question: "How honest are you with yourselves?"

Like many Baltic officials of his generation, Uncle Constantine spoke Russian with a pronounced German accent. He made quite a few grammatical mistakes or used the wrong expressions; lapses in his speeches or conversations were repeated in Petersburg as amusing anecdotes. But he was profoundly Russian in his culture, political concern and philosophy. Although a Protestant, he had a sincere respect for Russian spiritual tradition, far removed from the fanatical *bureaucratie* — the clerical establishment of Pobedonostsev — which he drastically opposed.

His wife, Helena Karlovna Pahlen, was as liberal-minded as her husband. She was devoted to philanthropic and educational work and for her services she was awarded the Order of St. Catherine, the highest honor given to women by the Tsar. Many a court lady could have envied this Order, but Countess Pahlen was too modest to exhibit it. She was more interested in Bach or in her Lutheran hymns than in St. Catherine's diamond-studded badge and Grand Cordon. Besides Marussia, the Pahlens had two other daughters, both of them married, and three sons; one of them, Peter Pahlen, I have mentioned as my father's special aide at the Ministry.

In the 1950s, I discovered one of Uncle Constantine's granddaughters living in the United States and married to a protestant pastor of Philadelphia, the Rev. Wooly. Together, we recalled her grandfather, that most remarkable character of bygone days. She gave me some biographical notes concerning Constantine Ivanovich, and a photograph showing him in the cortege of the Tsar's coronation.

On my paternal side, I had few relatives. I did not know my grandfather, Peter Alexandrovich, who died before I was born. But his role in the escape of Bakunin, the father of Russian anarchism, and his story as included in the "family saga" and often told me by my father seemed to me highly romantic.

Grandfather Iswolsky, if not a radical himself, was inclined to sympathize with the revolutionaries of that period. As governor of the town, he had been in touch with other political exiles even before Bakunin's arrival in Irkutsk. They were the conspirators who had attempted to overthrow the Tsar, Nicholas I, in December, 1825. Therefore, they were known as the "Decembrists." Their leaders had been executed and the other members of the group had been sent to labor camps in Siberia. After a number of years, they were allowed to live with their families in forced exile in Irkutsk. Though even in those days a center of trade in Siberia, it was a dull, provincial town. The Decembrists, most of them members of the aristocracy, were highly educated men and women who contributed a new cultural and intellectual element to Irkutsk society. My grandfather and his wife, Eudoxie Grigorievna, opened their home to these exiles. Among his visitors was Prince Volkonsky, who was one of the inspirers of the December revolt. His wife had followed him into exile, and while the Prince was imprisoned she had settled down with Princess Trubetskoy, the wife of another condemned Decembrist.

When the Volkonsky's were allowed to live in Irkutsk, they became close friends of my grandparents. This friendship linked the two families for three generations. My grandfather's concern for the Decembrists was keen because, as a young man, he had lived and studied in Moscow at the time that this city had become a center of intensive literary life where every aspect of religion, philosophy, social and political ideas was ardently discussed. My grandfather had known the ideological leaders, literary critics and writers who met at Madame Elagin's, the famous literary salon of Moscow where liberalism and humanism were predominant trends. His wife, Eudoxie Grigorievna, shared his aspirations; the Decembrists were always made welcome in their home, and when Bakunin appeared on the scene he was no less cordially greeted.

This fierce-looking giant of a man, who preached violence and destruction to build a better world, was in his private life a gentle soul and even a charmer. He was a brilliant conversationalist, played duets on the piano with the ladies and made himself attractive to everyone. So when he asked my grandfather for a permit to attend to some business out of town, he easily obtained it. He fled to America via Japan. Bakunin's defection cost my grandfather his post as governor of Irkutsk; he was transferred to a minor governorship in Kursk. But far from bearing a grudge against Bakunin, he seemed proud to include him in the "family saga."

Grandmother Eudoxie survived her husband and came to live on Palace Square where she stayed with her younger son, Peter and his family. She was a very quiet, benevolent old lady, very different from my dictatorial Grandmother Toll. I remember her with a round, wrinkled face and sparse white hair, tucked under a lace bonnet. But she had a personality of her own, a good mother, ambitious for her sons' education and careers.

This was why, no doubt, both my father and my Uncle Peter were given a thorough intellectual and linguistic formation, quite beyond the "cultural style" of that period and so, in later life, they showed independence and originality in the development of their careers.

I cannot say how this elaborate education had benefited my father's youngest brother, Gregory. He had an entirely different temperament and in spite of his early waywardness, he was a great favorite in our family.

Grandfather Iswolsky died in 1907 and was buried in our family vault. One of my nephews who visited Leningrad in the 1960s was told by an official in that city that the Iswolsky tombs are well cared for in a cemetery near a monastery. My nephew could not remember the name but it must be the Andronikov Lavra, where Turgenev is buried (Alexander Nevsky Lavra). I was surprised to hear that attention was paid to our family memorial, but have learned that my father's name is well-known and respected in the Soviet land, even though he himself died and was buried in a foreign land (France).

On the occasion of Eudoxie Grigorievna's death, Tsar Nicholas wrote a penciled note of condolence to my father, the only sign of sympathy he showed us, and as the years went by, his coldness was more and more accentuated. It coincided with the general "freeze" in his relationships with all his officials and his gradual withdrawal from all of Petersburg society, including even the military who, though loyal to him, opposed his views. He began to live almost exclusively at Tsarskoe Selo or in Peterhof during the summer months. He made but few appearances in the capital because of the continual threat of a terrorist attack on his person. There were, of course, good reasons for this fear, but the sovereign's almost constant absence from the Winter Palace reflected upon his popularity. The public was warned at the last minute by the cry "The Tsar is coming!"; streets were cleared, traffic halted, pedestrians lined the broad sidewalks behind police cordons. There were shouts of "Long live the Tsar!" But they died out as the imperial carriage drove by so fast that the people could barely catch a glimpse of the small figure sitting in it, saluting and waving timidly, and quickly disappearing from view.

There were other sights in Petersburg which attracted public interest or curiosity and even a certain silent sympathy, more spontaneous than the loud acclamation of the imperial visits. These were the student protests and demonstrations which had been spreading to become a feature of Petersburg academic life. These demonstrations were mainly protesting the control of the Ministry of Justice over the administration and faculty of Petersburg University. The great Russian poet Ossip Mandelstam, gives in one of his autobiographical sketches an ironic picture of the students' protests on the square of Our Lady of Kazan Cathedral, where they were usually held. Though apparently innocuous, they were considered dangerous by the police because some workers joined the students. The demonstrations were therefore known as "riots":

> Student riots near Kazan Cathedral were always known beforehand. There was always a student informer in every family. So that quite a mass of people gathered to watch the riots, true — at a respectable distance: children with their nurses, mummies and aunties who could not keep their rebels home, aged officials and various idlers. On the day of the riot, the sidewalks of Nevsky Prospect were swaying with a crowd of spectators from Sadovaya Street to Anichkov Bridge. All this crowd was afraid to come near Kazan Cathedral. The police were hidden in the backyards, for instance behind St. Catherine's Catholic Church. Kazan Square was relatively empty, small groups of students and real workers walked up and down, and the latter were pointed out by the spectators. Suddenly there arose from Kazan Square a long drawn-out ever-increasing wail, something like an unceasing *ooh* or *yooh* which swelled into a menacing howl, coming nearer and nearer. The crowd dashed aside and was trampled by horses; "the Cossacks, the Cossacks!" The cry flew like lightning, faster than the Cossacks. Actually the riot was encircled and directed to the Mikhailovsky Military Riding School, while Nevsky Prospect was deserted, as if swept clean with a broom.

Tensions in the universities continued to grow, and the administration refused to make any concessions, relying on Cossack protection. So the peaceful demonstrations did become riots.

My Uncle Peter had to face one of the most dramatic student protests as a member of "the establishment;" so, with him I will conclude my gallery of family portraits. The reshuffling of the Cabinet under Stolypin in 1907, my uncle's appointment as Procurator of the Holy Synod, and his election to the Council of State brought into the political arena a man who, in spite of his modesty, almost self-effacement, was known for his high moral character.

For many years the post of Procurator of the Russian Orthodox Synod was occupied by extreme reactionaries who faithfully followed in the footsteps of Pobedonostsev. They not only restricted the rights of religious minorities, but restrained secular education for all. With the 1906 proclamation of religious freedom, the reactionary forces receded reluctantly, but there was still a considerable task to be accomplished in the field of church affairs and education.

This task was undertaken by Uncle Peter Petrovich, but it was short-lived and, while it lasted, extremely complex. He seemed, however, well-prepared for his assignment. Though in many ways different from my father in temperament and many of his convictions, the two brothers had in common a concern for their country's best traditions and a seriousness of purpose in the fulfillment of their duties. I would say that these traits were even sharper in Uncle Peter's character, for he did not have the diplomatic veneer acquired by my father.

Peter Petrovich Iswolsky was a graduate of Petersburg University and had later studied abroad, mostly in Italy, and spoke Italian fluently. He had chosen for himself the career of educator and was successively Inspector of Schools in Kiev, Riga, and Petersburg. He was quite popular in these respective posts, for his academic judgements combined with an understanding of youth and of student problems. He shared my father's political ideas and became a member of the same party, the moderate liberal Octobrists. But he was more reserved in his views and did not go as far as his brother in his criticism of the Tsarist regime.

While holding the Inspector's office in Petersburg, he met the challenge of a particularly violent student strike at Petersburg University. The rebellious youths occupied an auditorium, throwing books and furniture out of the windows. The terrified rector of the university fled and locked himself up in the lavatories. Arriving on the scene, Peter Petrovich entered the auditorium fearlessly, though he had been warned that the students could be armed, and calmly addressed the turbulent crowd. Upon his request, the students dispersed and the incident was closed. He thus gained a reputation of firmness, and the university youth respected him, though he spoke to them quite sternly and had even donned for this occasion his full dress Inspector's uniform.

Peter Petrovich was a fervent Russian Orthodox and a man well-acquainted with the inner, truly spiritual life of his church, irrespective of the administrative chains which bound her. His piety was extreme and somewhat sanctimonious, but profoundly sincere. His devotion and attachment to ritual made him *persona grata* in high ecclesiastical circles. But his liberalism and open mind were welcomed by the younger clergy, which awaited from him the long expected church renewal. If this renewal was stalled, it was not because of lack of good will on my uncle's part, but due to the gradual slowdown in all matters of reform.

I remember Uncle Peter as a tall, rather lean man, with a delicate profile, hair and beard, and an austere, even ascetic expression and manner, which somewhat intimidated me. He was handsomer and more distinguished than my father, but there was something stiff, almost wooden in his figure due to his long association with bureaucracy. His four children, two boys and two girls, also had some of the conventionality of their father. Though a gentle and kindly man who never scolded nor punished, he observed certain strict standards of behavior at home, which appeared to me somewhat provincial. My four cousins considered Grisha and myself a little "foreign" and therefore somewhat permissive because of our long sojourns abroad, and our frequent association with other diplomat's children rather than with their own kind.

Because of his new post, Uncle Peter and his family, had moved from their private, modest apartment to the Holy Synod Procurator's residence, which had an official, ecclesiastical air. Memories of its former bigoted occupants still seemed to float in its halls. One of my cousins even assured me that the ghost of the late *éminence grise*, Pobedonostsev, roamed in these halls at night, and that the shuffling of his slippered feet could be distinctly heard.

Though our two families seemed to belong to two different worlds, diplomacy and the interior establishment, the ice was soon broken; I enjoyed visiting my cousins, overcoming the fear of Pobedonostsev's ghost, and growing quite fond of my newly discovered relatives. In fact, they were most lovable people.

Uncle Peter was married to Princess Mary Golitsyn, who had known misfortune and had been threatened with dire poverty in her childhood. Paradoxically, Aunt Masha, as we called her, was the daughter of one of Russia's wealthiest landowners. Prince Serge Golitsyn, who had a palatial home in Moscow's environs (today a museum), owned one million acres of land, scattered across Russia. He had linked his main residence with Moscow by building a private highway which nobody else was allowed to use. He must have had millions of rubles in the bank and was known as a *viveur* and an eccentric. He had been married four times, and one of his wives was a young and beautiful girl from a *tabor*, a Gypsy camp of singers and dancers who performed in the Moscow nightclubs. Golitsyn had several children by the Gypsy girl, whom he later abandoned with her brood, including Masha. She was raised by one of the Prince's cousins, the other children were cared for by other relatives. As to their mother, she too had to be provided for, without any help from her husband. Aunt Masha was carefully raised by her guardians, but they tried to obliterate, and partly succeeded, her Gypsy heritage. She had, however, her mother's large dark eyes, a slightly tanned skin and the narrow, beautiful hand and long fingers so characteristic of the *tabor* people. For the rest, she was a highly accomplished young lady, a devout Russian Orthodox, and morally almost pedantic.

Uncle Peter's position as an official close to ecclesiastical affairs brought him face-to-face with an unexpected aspect of his church: her inability to cope with certain mysterious happenings at the Tsar's Court — the growing influence exercised over the Imperial couple, especially over the Tsarina, by the pseudomonk Gregory Rasputin.

This influence was to develop as the years went by, but for a long time, Peter Petrovich refused to believe the rumors spread in Petersburg about Gregory's debauchery and wild nights in the Gypsy nightclubs, contrasting with the role of healer and "Holy Man" which he played in the Palace. Neither would Peter Petrovich listen to his liberal friends pointing to Rasputin's interference in political affairs. My cousins told me that one day at a luncheon someone mentioned these dark rumors. Their father denied them vehemently and as the gossipers continued, he threw down his napkin and left the table. Soon after this incident, Uncle Peter learned that the proctor of the Petersburg Theological Academy, a bishop of impeccable reputation, had been removed upon Rasputin's demand. Peter Petrovich did not need any further proof of the true situation he had previously ignored, and resigned without hesitation.

When the 1917 Revolution broke out, Uncle Peter fled with his family to Yalta in the Crimea. They lived in hiding for some time. The situation grew more dangerous, as their friend Princess B., who was wanted by the Bolsheviks, asked them to take her in. They did so, at their own risk, but were finally able to escape with her to Belgium. There, Uncle Peter began a new life and was able to fulfill a dream he had long cherished—to become a priest. Since Russian Orthodox priests may be married, he was able to be appointed rector of Saint Nicholas Church in Brussels, where he served until his death in 1929.

To return to the "fateful years," there was, as I have tried to show, a not-so-silent minority who backed my father's liberal ideas and who were working continually to find a broad base for positive political action. The older members remembered the time of the great reforms of Alexander II and hoped for their return. The younger members sought an active role in bringing about social and political change. However divided Russia was at that time, there was a general agreement that all must work for greater freedom at home and to improve Russia's reputation abroad, damaged as a result of the dark events, pogroms and repressions that had occurred.

This unanimity of feeling was brought out at the time of Tolstoy's death, in November 1910. I remember well this day of shock and mourning. It had been known that there were tragic tensions in Tolstoy's private life. The famous novelist, then 82, had suddenly left his home and boarded a crowded train, and sitting in a smoke-filled compartment had been unable to breathe. He was obliged to leave the train, and, in a tiny village, he lay dying in the stationmaster's house. The dramatic events were followed by the whole of Russia and by the European press as well. His wife came to make vain attempts at reconciliation. An abbot from a nearby monastery came to try to reconcile him with the Orthodox Church from which he had broken away, but the dying man would not even admit him. When death came to the old prophet, it was like a thunderbolt, followed by an uncanny silence.

In our secluded habitat I, too, felt the impact of what was going on. In the capital all shops were closed; people assembled in small groups in the streets to discuss the sad news. They spoke in hushed voices. There were no demonstrations, but rather spontaneous public mourning more impressive than if it had been organized. Some devoted souls asked for services in the churches but were strictly reminded that Tolstoy had rejected the dogmas of the Church and died unrepentant. Then his friends found a priest who was unaware of the situation (or seemed to be only half-aware) and he agreed to pray simply for the soul of the "deceased servant of God, Leo" a form prescribed by the Byzantine ritual, and no further questions were asked. Surely, he had been a champion of the common man.

CHAPTER V

The Russian Years – Petersburg to Paris

ALTHOUGH out of my long life, only five consecutive years were spent in Russia, they were, I believe, the most formative years of my youth. This was the time of my adolescence when my emotions and the consciousness of my own country were wakening in a city that has an extraordinary hold on its people.

The beauty of its architecture and the interest of its historical monuments have so often been described that I will not dwell on them. But there is something more that Petersburg evokes: a mystery, a magic which has been expressed by the great Russian poets from Pushkin to Blok and Mandelstam, who is known as the "poet of Petersburg." And what exactly is its charm? In winter, it is the snow-clad vistas of the boulevards and squares, the frozen whiteness of the Neva and of the canals that seem lost in a dream. As early night descends on them, the tall, shining street lamps come to life, only to vanish suddenly in swirling mists of fog or snow, which make the buildings, vehicles and every passerby look ghostly.

In spring, it is the greening of the islands which are so much a part of the city, so close to its heart that you can almost sense the fragrance of the lilacs bursting into bloom just across the river.

Here, shutters were opened up in the summer homes and nightingales trilled until dawn; lovers picked jasmine blossoms and lilies-of-the-valley or rode around the lakes in small boats between patches of water lilies. There was also something unreal or dreamlike about this atmosphere which hardly harmonized with the tensions and unrest of the city.

Then it was vacation time, and we moved to a house on the islands.

Our summer residence was called *Freylinskaya Dacha* (Ladies-in-Waiting's Cottage) for it was merely an annex to the nearby Elagin Palace, which had formerly been the abode of grand dukes with their families, while the ladies of their suite were lodged in the *Dacha*. It was a modest frame house, but comfortable and attractive. While the Palace, one of Petersburg's finest suburban buildings, had assumed an almost foreboding look, it had become the home of Prime Minister Stolypin, who had lost his former home in a bombing. He was heavily guarded since the attempt on his life and the Palace was protected by an armed police force. In spite of the menace that hung over all Cabinet ministers, our cottage did not need such formidable protection. We felt carefree during these spring and early summer days, and the boys and girls who had become our playmates in the city were invited to picnics and boating expeditions, at which Grisha and I enjoyed ourselves immensely. The islands are studded with ponds, cut through by inlets from the Neva, on which our small craft could glide for hours, as through a magic labyrinth.

Though Father went to the city for his regular office hours, for us it was vacation. Schools were closed until fall and my home tutoring was over for the season. I was doing a good deal of reading on my own. Father gave me *War and Peace* and it was one of the great experiences of my early teens. The world was never the same again after the first reading, it acquired a new dimension. It was both profoundly human, beautiful and rather terrifying. And this dimension widened through the years each time I reread this book and even today, it startles me anew, as something I had never read before.

It was during this Petersburg period that I became aware of a previously unsuspected world of joys, poetic dreams and suffering. And I discovered it not only through literature, but through my own youthful experience. It was first love, and love at first sight. It happened after our summer vacation was over and we had returned to Palace Square for another winter of serious studies—Grisha at the *gymnasia* where he was a senior, and I in my classroom at home with the highly-cultured English governess, Miss Maybury, and Grisha's Russian tutor, who taught me Russian composition, German and math, all that was needed for my education.

This severity of school work was relieved on Sundays and we eagerly awaited the evening when we had dancing lessons. These were not the rigid, formal lessons of our Copenhagen days. Though we had to learn the ballroom steps and postures prescribed by protocol, this indispensable training was followed by much youthful entertainment, when we could dance at our leisure without any curriculum.

These Sunday night sessions were held at the home of Count Z., whose youngest son was Grisha's classmate. Other boys were from the Lycée, the Law School and the *Corps des Pages,* in their tight little uniforms and silver or gold-embroidered collars. The girls were approximately my age and like myself, tutored at home. Only a few noble families sent their daughters to the *gymnasia* for girls. They were considered "middle class" and even private schools were frowned upon as too avant-garde and even subversive.

Count Z. was a wealthy but enlightened landowner, a liberal at heart; most of his relatives belonged to the strictly conservative camp.

When I think of the wealth, prestige and moral tradition represented by men like Count Z. and others of *liberal bent*, I feel that they could have been able to give their country a fair chance of survival as a democracy. As they lacked the civic courage to do so, they failed to repair the traces of decay which were appearing in the walls soon to crumble under their very eyes.

To us children, they were the good-natured parents who would be present at our Sunday evenings as chaperones or friends of our host. More formidable was the older generation; the grandfathers and grandmothers who gathered at the Count's home for their own weekly reunion. Seated in deep armchairs or cushioned sofas and leaning on their canes to watch us more closely, they were a strict and demanding audience, aligned in the adjacent drawing room with wide open doors, they could watch our every movement. They had seen us since our childhood and knew our family histories and antecedents, i.e., our pedigrees, and could foresee our futures. If marriages are made in heaven, Petersburg's patriarchs and matriarchs usually had a lot to do with them. Our Sunday evenings were something like entrance examinations.

Our dancing master was Mr. Aistov, a word originating from the Russian name for *stork*, and I always associated him with a tall, dignified and ceremonious-looking bird. He had neatly brushed hair, and a white moustache set off his handsome features. He wore evening dress, patent-leather shoes on his long, narrow feet, and a fixed smile which was a constant "invitation to the dance." He had trained many generations of boys and girls with that Olympian grace which was both friendly and distant. He taught us the formal dances: the polonaise, the quadrille, and the waltz, and also some fancy steps which were in fashion: the *pas de patineur*, a gliding motion resembling ice-skating, and the *Tonkinoise*, danced to a lively tune and imported from France. These dances seem quite silly today, but they meant fun and an opportunity of holding hands. This was all the "dating" we were allowed.

The best time began when the lesson was over. Mr. Aistov retired with a formal bow but the pianist remained and we could dance on without the master for another hour or two. We were served lemonade and cake in the dining room with crystal glassware and shining silver on snow-white tablecloths and starched napkins. The girls wore their prettiest frocks and the boys, their parade uniforms. It was all quite festive and yet informal, so we thoroughly enjoyed ourselves. Grisha soon became quite a favorite at these parties. He was a round-faced, fair-haired youth, quite handsome in his tight-fitting blue uniform. He was a good dancer, and having learned all he could from Mr. Aistov, he could imitate him in the most comic way. He made the boys laugh and all the girls eagerly awaited his invitation to dance. Soon Grisha fell head-over-heels in love with a graceful, serious young girl, whom I shall call Lisa. She had a mysterious charm and never lost her reserved manner, even when dancing the silly *Tonkinoise* with Grisha. Even though many tragic events separated them in later years, Grisha never forgot her.

All the boys and girls began to pair off on Sunday evenings but I alone had no constant partner. At home, I began to write poetry and dream of deep feelings, but I was not prepared for them.

Then, on one of those Sunday evenings, HE appeared and my life, my very being was changed. He had attentive, hazel eyes which rested on me with a smile. He was slim, of medium height, but somehow he seemed much more mature than the other boys. He wore a university student uniform, a long, blue coat of a more elaborate style than that of the *gymnasia* model. It was not the coat that impressed me, but the fact that I was with a man "from the university." Students were my heroes; there was something noble and dedicated about them. And I knew that they were mostly radicals, and even quite dangerous revolutionaries. By that time I had become quite inclined toward the radical myself. I had heard, of course, about strikes and demonstrations, about the people's unrest and the role of the intelligentsia in various protests. I knew that the majority of students was in the revolutionary camp, not necessarily violent but active in antagonizing the regime. Only a small group of university men did not participate in these activities. They were called "white-lined coats" which meant that they were affiliated with the reactionary parties. With a beating heart, I sensed that the "beautiful young man" who had appeared at our Sunday evening dance was not a "white-lined coat" and Grisha, who immediately made friends with him, proudly confided to me that Dimitri was a "revolutionary." Thus I learned his name and that he was a relative of Count Z.

The "revolutionary" tag attached to Dimitri was more or less imaginary. In spite of certain radical ideas and a reluctance to join the "white-lined coats" he still very much belonged to his set (as I was soon to discover). But he seemed different from others I had met at our dances. There was in him the breath of a new era, of the strange, new culture and of the gathering storm which threatened to destroy old values. Dimitri was "out of bounds" in his own family. He was misunderstood at home, but neither could he mix easily with the democratic intelligentsia. In short, he was a lonely young man and I believe that is why he sought my friendship.

Soon after my first meeting with Dimitri we became dancing partners at the Sunday evenings, but often we sat out the dances to talk about books, poetry and art. He told me about the symbolist movement and the poems and essays appearing in avant-garde reviews. He was a subscriber to these periodicals: *Apollon*, *Zolotoe Runo* (The Golden Fleece) and *Musaget* and recited to me Alexander Blok's latest poem: *Neznakomka*

(The Stranger), which brought new mystery and fascination to Russian lyrics. Dimitri's taste was fine and sophisticated and yet he was indulgent enough to take an interest in my own poetry, a poor but sincere imitation of our nineteenth-century classics. He encouraged me to persevere.

The miracle had happened. I fell deeply in love. Dimitri was constantly in my thoughts. I met him every Sunday at our dancing sessions and only wished that the week would pass more quickly and then once more, the hazel eyes would rest on me with gentle earnestness. Once Dimitri invited Grisha and me to a party at his parents' home. The entire dancing class came, too, and we played hide-and-seek in the various rooms and passageways of his large residence. Running along I discovered myself in Dimitri's study. The room was in darkness except for the faint glow of street lamps behind the windows. The curtains were not drawn and the lights outside were reflected on the white snow, filling the room with ghostly patches of pale lights and shadows. I stood there motionless — for I was supposed to be hiding but I was actually taking in every detail of Dimitri's den or *inner sanctum*. After many years, when much of my Petersburg period was forgotten, I clearly remember this room and the emotions it aroused in me.

It was a typical room of a studious young man with little taste for luxury but an insatiable appetite for books and magazines. The bookcases were full of them and they were piled up on the large writing desk and on the *takhta*, the low divan covered with Turkish rugs, an indispensable part of a manly setting, as was another large Oriental tapestry covering the wall behind the divan. On it were several pieces of Oriental arms, mostly Caucasian, covered with silver, in colorful array.

When I left the mystery den, nothing could betray the emotions I had just experienced and Dimitri never guessed them; he continued to offer me his calm and gentle camaraderie. Thoughts of love for the lanky, clumsy girl I was at that time never entered his mind. Alas, I was soon to see him infatuated with other young maidens and eating his heart out on their behalf. In spite of his charm and brilliant mind, his love affairs were unhappy. I alone loved him without even thinking that he would love me in return. Besides the dancing lessons and an occasional party, our youthful crowd had few other amusements. But we did meet for ice-skating in the gardens of the Tauride Palace. This is the beautiful mansion built by Catherine the Great for her favorite, Prince Potemkin, colonizer of the Crimea (poetically known by its Greek name: Tauride). In 1906, the Palace had been converted to house the Duma, the first Russian parliament. While we were happily skating on the frozen pond of the gardens, historic sessions were being held inside the Palace. My father made several speeches which appeared the following day in the Petersburg paper, so I could read them *in extenso*. But my main interest, I must confess, in those days, was directed to my idol, Dimitri.

He came almost daily to the Tauride gardens and so did I, under the not-too-strict chaperoning of Miss Maybury, who could not skate. I can still see my student-friend as he came gliding toward me in his winter attire, a snow-white lambskin jacket and a white fur cap. The ice of the pond, entirely cleared of snow, was a peculiar, peppermint green. At the far side of the pond were the "ice hills," tall, wooden constructions with a sharp incline; the slopes, some fifty feet long, were packed with ice, forming a smooth toboggan track, and we raced down them breathlessly on small steel sleds; this was an exciting winter sport, requiring no special skill. There were spills, of course, and during one of them I sprained my knee so badly that I had to be taken home in an ambulance. I was carried on a stretcher up the main staircase of the Ministry just as one of the officials was hurrying down, but he was too absorbed in some diplomatic tangle and paid no attention to me. I was put into my bed and Father was alerted. He rushed into my room and gave me a terrible scolding. It was no fault of mine but Father was really scared out of his wits. I recall this scene because it revealed his emotional temperament which he was always trying to control, and his almost dramatic concern for us. Mother remained calm and reassuring as usual. The doctor was summoned and said that only a few ligaments had been torn. I must simply rest in bed.

This was a happy time for me. I was surrounded by tender love. After his wrathful outburst, Father was once more the kindest, most stimulating parent. Many friends came to visit me, among them Dimitri. He read all the poems I had written and offered to type them out for me. After a few days, he presented me with a neatly typed and bound copy of my "complete works." He even decorated the cover with a hand-painting of his own. It represented a Russian bard in medieval attire, playing a harp. It was a copy of a well-known painting by the famous artist Vasnetsov, who had stimulated a fresh interest in the style of ancient Russian art; his frescoes in St. Vladimir's Cathedral in Kiev are particularly noteworthy. They have been preserved and survived the Revolution. Dimitri's little picture has also survived as well as the neat copy of my poems, a reminder of those happy days.

I recovered just in time for the carnival festivities which were held in Petersburg the week before Lent. There was an animated fair along a vast esplanade with booths, shops, puppet shows, music and folk dancing. Stravinsky's ballet *Petrushka* has captured the atmosphere of those Petersburg carnivals in which there is so much enchantment and magic —a creation of the primitive imagination of the peasant, and the sophisticated artistry of city people.

My first experience in the realm of deep emotions ended as abruptly as it had begun, and in a strange way. I had never hoped to win Dimitri's love, but I felt sure of his friendship. And I believe that he felt for me something deeper than a "big brother" condescension. Then when the summer came, we left Petersburg for *La Chère Villa* and our ties were severed. I did not venture to write to Dimitri, but I corresponded with his sister and sent greetings to him. Shortly afterwards, I got a letter from his sister, with a message from him. Dimitri informed me that he would have nothing to do with me any longer nor did he wish me to communicate with him. I read this message over and over, seeking desperately for the reason for such an unmerited rebuff. I even thought his sister might have played a trick on me, for she was an embittered, unhappy girl. Yet I doubted that she could have been so unkind.

When I returned to Petersburg, we did not resume our dancing sessions; Dimitri had left the university and enrolled in the army. It was years before we had occasion to meet again. And then we had become strangers. But for a long time I pondered over Dimitri's strange behavior. I did eventually find the key to this enigma. One day Grisha and I were recalling our Sunday evening dances and Grisha talked of Dimitri, with whom he had had much in common. But to his amazement, Dimitri told Grisha that their friendship was over, that they had nothing in common anymore and should go their separate ways. He had chosen his career in one of the crack regiments of the Tsar. His revolutionary "wild oats" had been sown. He would now serve as a loyal member of the aristocracy.

Dimitri fulfilled his promise. He was commissioned in a regiment of the Guards. At the outbreak of the war with Germany, he was sent to the front, and was killed in one of the most tragic battles of the initial operations, the Tannenberg defeat. Most of his unit was decimated and destroyed. He remains for me the first man I loved, and lost, and the symbol of a society that planned for a great future, and was doomed.

Let me conclude my Petersburg, or Russian, period on a brighter note. During one of our summer vacations, Grisha and I persuaded our parents to let us visit our old country estate, instead of going to *La Chère Villa*. We gladly departed to our homestead, Lipetsy, accompanied by my companion, Miss Maybury.

The 250-acre tract inherited by my father from Grandmother Iswolsky was in poor shape, as were many small estates at that time, due to neglect of previous landlords, too busy in the city to attend to the problems of rural life. Father was unable to cope with this inheritance, and had turned it over to his sister, Olga Vitaly, who was a widow with no children and willing to restore what property could be saved.

Lipetsy was in the heart of Russia, south of Moscow and about a hundred miles from Tula, an industrial center. From Tula, a train took us to the picturesque hinterland, so often described by Tolstoy and Turgenev, for they both came from this region. Tolstoy's estate, Yasnaya Polyana (bright field) was not far away, and I will always regret that I did not see him, as he died just before our trip to Lipetsy. We got off the train in Chern, a small town some thirty miles from our estate. Awaiting the carriage that was to take us there, we had lunch in the station buffet; the setting was unattractive, drab, the food mediocre, but through the open windows came the fragrant air of the countryside, the freshness of woods and meadows. We were just finishing lunch when our carriage arrived; it was an open landau, drawn by four horses harnessed abreast; foursomes were as common in the Russian countryside as the picturesque troikas, and more practical for long trips. The coachman wore the classic livery in these parts, a bright-red silk Russian shirt with buttoned collar, a black velvet, sleeveless coat and a velvet cap with peacock feathers. In fact, it looked more like fancy dress than a livery. He drove in smartly and the little bells attached to the harness jingled gaily as he pulled up to the station. We mounted our vehicle and our luggage was loaded onto a small cart which had followed the foursome. Off we drove, along the main street of Chern, in a cloud of dust, the bells jingling, and dogs, roaming the street, accompanied our departure with loud, excited barks.

We all wore dustcoats and looked like automobilists of the early 1900s. In Russia there were no autos, except for a few purchased in France by the wealthy elite. Driving was done along dirt roads. Even main highways were not asphalted, but were thick with dust in dry weather, swamped in mud at rainy seasons, and in winter, covered with snow, when only sleighs could make communications possible. Since this was a hot, dry summer, we were covered with layers of dust, like the young people in the beginning of Turgenev's *Fathers and Sons*. This dust had a peculiar, dark color, for the Tula region lies in the black-earth belt that stretches from the "bread basket" of the Ukraine and far beyond — soil of a rich, dark chocolate color which yields many crops and fruits and forage, clover and alfalfa. We rode between long rows of ripening wheat, billowing in the wind like golden waves, over bridges, spanning streams where children were fishing or swimming. We passed through villages incredibly poor and primitive, with log walls and thatched roofs, and rustic wells from which women were drawing water, carrying it in pails attached to a yoke over their stooping shoulders. Here more children played in the mud, their feet bare and stomachs swollen from malnutrition. Wild-looking dogs followed us for a while, and then fell back, growling. It was a somber picture, relieved now and then by a better house, with wood carving on the window frames and geraniums and small gardens. Every village was dominated by the bell tower and onion-shaped cupola of its parish church. There was a cemetery with humble, wooden crosses and the villages were usually named after the saint or feast day to which it was dedicated— Ascension, Trinity, Transfiguration, St. Nicholas, St. John, St. Michael. Though today, under Soviet rule, many of these parishes do not exist, the cemeteries are still there, and the names of saints or Biblical events still designate the villages.

Accustomed as I was to the flourishing Bavarian countryside, I was appalled by the misery of Russian peasant life; I could not help wondering whether the agrarian reforms planned by political leaders in Petersburg could ever solve the problems laid bare for the first time, before my eyes. I was not old enough to find an answer, but I realized the seriousness of the problems which beset Russia. Yet I was fascinated by the beauty of this land; the golden wheat fields, the meadows and streams, the tall oaks and birch trees on the hillsides, and over all, the sky like an immense cupola with its white, billowy clouds, arching over more meadows and fields, as far as the eye could see.

We drove through one last village called Spasskoe (Savior) and entered a long oak and acacia-lined *allée,* which led to the Lipetsy estate. In the midst of a very overgrown park stood our "ancestral mansion." It was a building of noble proportions. A fine terrace and a portico decorated its front, and the wide steps of its stoop descended into a rose garden. But as we neared the mansion, it became obvious, alas, that the entire structure was crumbling. The pillars of the portico were leaning like the "tower of Pisa"; boards of the terrace had been torn away, windows were broken or hidden behind broken shutters. It was as if a hurricane had swept over this once-proud house. "Where is everybody?" I asked anxiously. The coachman pointed with his whip to a small white cottage standing at some distance from the mansion, and said, "Olga Petrovna is awaiting you in the new wing."

He further explained that Aunt Olga had long since moved to the cottage; she had planned to replace the old living quarters. He drove smartly up to the "new wing" and stopped at the front steps where a group of people was waiting for us. Aunt Olga rushed to embrace us; she was followed by my four cousins, Sergei, Peter, Marussia and Olga. There were other people of various ages; they looked like the cast of a Chekov play, and there was something like the *Cherry Orchard* drama going on at Lipetsy, with its disintegrating homestead in a day-dreaming atmosphere.

Not that Aunt Olga was an unwise, unskilled administrator. She was doing her best to bring order to the estate, but things had gone too far due to an unscrupulous manager who was running the place behind its owner's back. All my aunt could do was to live on the budget that he allowed her, after retaining most of the crops and dairy products for himself. The only bright spot in the dark picture was the "new wing" which reflected the spirit of its builder.

Aunt Olga was one of the most excellent people I have known. Although not very attractive—short, stodgy, with a wrinkled face—she had an intelligent, animated look in her gray eyes. She was extremely good-natured and kind to children, well-educated and fluent in several languages. The "new wing" was conceived and furnished in perfect if simple good taste. It had modern furniture, chintz curtains, colorful Indian bedspreads which rendered every room cozy and inviting. This is probably why there were so many guests at Lipetsy. Some sixteen of them took their meals daily with her, some of them staying for months; others dropped in for a day or two. Almost every day the jingling bells of the troika or the foursome announced some new guest. Though the cottage looked small there was always a room available. There were five meals a day, starting with a copious breakfast and ending with a late supper. Most delicious was afternoon tea, with fresh strawberries and heavy cream, homemade bread, homemade butter — unless you preferred cold sour milk or cottage cheese. All this was no luxury, since all these products came from the land. But such broad hospitality did stretch the household's reserves to their limits. And there were mortgages to pay as well as other bills. They were forgotten in the euphoria of summer days and forgotten, alas, were all the good intentions of improving the life of the villages crying for reform.

Aunt Olga was a romantic, a daydreamer from her girlhood days. When living with her parents at Lipetsy, she had met a rather eccentric but fascinating neighbor. He was young Modeste Tchaikovsky, brother of the famous composer, and himself a fine musician. His family owned a neighboring estate and they were often brought together. I do not know whether Olga ever met Peter Ilich, but there must have been music in the background. She and Modeste fell in love and roamed in the fields and woods, or sat on the moonlit veranda of the old mansion, which was then in its prime. They were about to become engaged when my father arrived on the scene. He protested against Modeste's eccentricities and insisted that Olga give him up. A few years later, Olga married a dull, local bureaucrat, who was a good husband to her, but no one seemed too sorry when he died at a relatively early age.

So Aunt Olga went on daydreaming, which was part of her attraction for us. But the impractical side of her character sometimes created surprising results. Thus, when she had chosen the architect for her "new wing," she had chosen the wrong contractor. One day, we were all out on a picnic. When we came home, we found the whole cottage in a shambles. The roof had collapsed and the living and dining rooms were full of rubble. So were most of the adjoining living quarters. All that remained of the house was so unsafe that all the house guests left, and it was decided that Grisha, Miss Maybury and I should move to Golun, the estate of my Uncle Peter Iswolsky, which was only a short distance away. My four cousins were due, anyway, to return to their own home. So we all journeyed together, and we formed a cheerful party. As to Aunt Olga, she waved us a smiling goodbye; nothing could defeat her optimism. The cottage would soon be rebuilt and would look even better than before. This optimism or faith in life's opportunities was to serve her well during the Revolution when she was exposed to far greater dangers than a crumbling cottage.

Golun was a handsome estate; it was much larger than Lipetsy and was a belated gift from Uncle Peter's father-in-law, Prince Golitsyn, who had married a Gypsy. After thirty years, he had remembered his half-Gypsy daughter, Masha, and cut out a piece of his immense domains for her, a small piece compared to his own land, but pleasant enough to satisfy any amateur of old-fashioned Russian country life.

The main building was white and shiny, with a porch supported by Doric columns; it had a stuccoed hall and a rotunda, high French windows overlooking a terrace, a well-kept lawn and a lovely flower garden. There were two minor wings for house guests, a stable for troikas and foursomes, a cow shed and all the other outbuildings needed for a productive and well-kept farm. It had vegetable gardens as well, fruit trees, strawberries and raspberries. If Golun lacked Lipetsy's carefree charm, it reflected a serious and disciplined mood which had its own beauty.

Seriousness and discipline were the distinctive traits of Uncle Peter and Aunt Masha. Although Prince Golitsyn's gift had brought them more comfort and security than they had ever had, the family never knew luxury, nor did they want it. Besides his duties as Inspector of Schools and, later, Procurator of the Holy Synod, Uncle Peter gave a great deal of attention to his estate. He was a good manager and quite an expert in farming. He gave considerable thought to the welfare of the peasants who lived in the surrounding villages, for I remember his concern to improve their living conditions, and Aunt Masha went along with him. They founded a school, a child-care center, a free clinic with a maternity ward, and a dispensary for outpatients. The local doctors and teachers and priests cooperated with them. It was an expression of the new spirit which stimulated progressive landowners, but unfortunately these were few and the problems set before them difficult to solve.

My youngest cousin, Olga, was later to join her parents in these activities. When I visited Golun, she was in her teens and had already considerable experience in rural life. She spent several winters with her mother in the country, for it was her father's wish to take them away from the troubled city. The winter months in the Tula region were severe, the roads were snowbound, the rail station, post and telegraph far away. They were cut off for weeks at a time from any civilized contact; the small villages all around were also hibernating. Olga had no objection to this life, she grew to love it. It was relieved at Christmas time when the boys came home for their vacation (road conditions permitting). The great attraction was the wolf hunts in which Olga participated, being herself an excellent horsewoman.

But amusements were few. Olga grew up a lonely child, withdrawn and often silent. From her Gypsy grandmother she had inherited a lovely mezzo-soprano voice and sang the *tabor* songs which are so closely related to Hungarian- and Spanish-Gypsy melodies and hold a common, mysterious origin. Uncle Peter and Aunt Masha tried to discourage Olga's singing, which reminded them of the *tabor* from which Prince Golitsyn had taken his bride. Perhaps they did not understand her, but they loved her and took care of her for the rest of her life. She died of tuberculosis.

While I was staying at Golun my eldest cousin, Marussia, became engaged to the owner of a nearby estate and we gaily celebrated this event. We had many visits from friends and neighbors and often drove out to picnic in the woods. Yet my most vivid memories are related to my first close contacts with the villagers, so typical of the Russian peasantry of prerevolutionary days.

I could see them at work in the fields, sowing or harvesting or in the barns where the wheat stalks were threshed and the grain winnowed, or driving cattle to the pastures: strong, young, sunburned boys and girls and older peasants, bent by age and constant labor. All had the quiet dignity long lost by city people.

On Sundays and feast days, the little Holy Savior Church was crowded. Watching the peasant men and women fervently praying and crossing themselves and teaching the smallest children to attend the service devoutly, I understood, for the first time, what the liturgy really meant for the Russian country folk. There was deep respect and veneration, but there was also a sort of intimacy, a familiarity with the sacred. Young men would think nothing of leaving the church in the middle of the service, to sit for a breath of air, on the tombs or graves of the nearby cemetery, and then return to the service.

Such simple, almost family relations of the people with God or Christ and the Blessed Mother of God filled my own heart with a new confidence and trust in things divine. In Petersburg, we attended the Ministry church, which held services only for officials and our servant staff. Here, it was truly a "people's Mass," a term so often used today by leaders of religious renewal in the West, where such spontaniety is not often attained.

Sundays and feast days were also the occasion for folk dances and music in the village square. The peasants wore their festive attire, white blouses of homespun cloth with red embroidery or ancient Slavic needlework. The singing was mostly in chorus with a leader, but songs were also heard all day long, at work, coming home from work, and in the evenings. These were the joyful aspects of rural life. But it had another side which was dark and grim; scenes of debauchery and drunken brawls around the *kabaks*, taverns of evil fame, where vodka, a government monopoly, was sold without restraint. And there were peasant feuds which broke out suddenly with frightening intensity.

One evening when we were sitting on the terrace of Golun mansion, we saw the sky light up, all of a sudden, with a red glow. Many houses were burning in Spasskoe, their thatched roofs turning into mounting flames. "This is the Red Cock," my uncle said, using a popular term for that kind of arson, inspired by hatred and revenge. I watched the blaze with a sense of fear and sorrow for the poor souls destroying each other.

Uncle Peter and the boys ran to the rescue and joined the long line of villagers, passing buckets of water to extinguish the fires. I will never forget this scene, symbolic of these poor people's conflicting characteristics. A capacity of hating and also of loving, of destruction and cooperation. And it was like an omen of the great conflagration which was soon to fill the Russian sky.

That night, when the fires were put out, we sat once more on the terrace. None of us spoke and I believe that we all dimly felt that the conflagration to come was very near.

My visit to our homestead and to Golun was a turning point in my youthful years. It gave me my first real close-up of the Russian rural population even though there might not have been more than some seventy of them here, but it was a typical cross-secton, in the very heart of the back country. It was not only a formative experience, but it awakened in me a deep love of my native land—not a chauvinistic blind infatuation but what I might call a tender concern for it and a recognition of its suffering, and of its cultural and spiritual values.

* * *

In September, 1911, the Petersburg period of my life was ended and I had to prepare for an entirely new experience, for my father was relieved of his duties as Minister of Foreign Affairs and was appointed Russian Ambassador to France. His new appointment seemed to please him, after the difficulties and persecution he had suffered from the ultraconservatives around the Tsar.

So we were once more on the move. Once more I would have to leave the friends I had made. This was nothing new and the idea of seeing another country could not trouble me, but this time, it did seem harder to have my roots pulled out, for the soil in which I had taken root was my own native land, and the friends I had made were dearer to me than those I had left in other countries. But there was no time to grieve; I began to pack and say goodbye, if not cheerfully, at least with youthful good humor. Father went to Paris ahead of us, to prepare our new home, the Russian Embassy. It was his continual concern to make Mother happy and comfortable and spare her any worry or fatigue in every new surrounding. However great his kindness and solicitude, it had the effect of increasing her feeling of helplessness; she had grown accustomed to rely entirely on her husband's assistance and initiative in all matters, great and small. This had made her very unrealistic in many ways. Her life was secure, even in the midst of dramatic circumstances, as long as father lived. After his death, she could not pick up the broken threads, but depended entirely on the only person left to her—myself.

So she came to Paris where a perfectly organized residence was waiting for her. She was very pleased with the setup, as, I must admit, I was myself, in spite of my regret at leaving Petersburg. Compared to the monumental proportions of the Ministry on Palace Square, the Embassy on the rue de Grenelle seemed like an elegant but relatively small private mansion. It had been built in the eighteenth century and had initially belonged to one of Queen Marie-Antoinette's ladies-in-waiting. Like all Paris houses of that period built for the aristocracy, it stood *entre cour et jardin* —between the entrance court and a garden. The large courtyard on the street was guarded by an impressive iron gate and watched over by a *concierge*, looking out of the small, doorkeeper's window. In the rear was a charming French garden, complete with terrace, flowerbeds and neatly clipped boxtrees, a Greek vase and ivy. There was a story to the effect that the little Dauphin, who would have been Louis XVII, came to play in this garden, as the lady-in-waiting was his governess.

The house was hardly big enough to accommodate all the offices needed for the embassy, the large staff which had to work day and night, the various attachés, press agents, etc., but no one complained, for Paris, in spite of these minor discomforts, was the most desired and envied post for career diplomats.

My own life was resumed in surroundings more relaxed than those of Palace Square. Rue de Grenelle was a quiet street on the Left Bank where no bombs nor demonstrations threatened. I did feel a certain emptiness, for one of our family circle was missing. Father had decided to let Grisha enroll in the Petersburg University Law School; he was now on his own. The idea of having my brother spend his student years in his native land was a good one. The Law School was known for its high standards due to its two famous teachers, Petrozhitsky and Vinogradov. The latter taught in England and was knighted for his contribution to the studies of old English legal traditions. Both these scholars were leaders in the Russian humanist and liberal movement. Their courses offered Grisha an opportunity of studying on the highest academic and moral level. But his off-campus life did not correspond to this high level. He was left very much to himself, suffered from loneliness and found nothing better to do than sow his wild oats at an accelerated tempo. My parents seemed completely unaware of the strain of weakness that had inadvertently developed in their son's character. While at home he had been a quiet, cheerful, trustful boy. He was always first in his class at school, passed his exams brilliantly wherever he went. I do not know whether we had been spoiling him, satisfying his every wish and admiring him too much for his charm and talent, or whether some trauma had occurred in his adolescence, or perhaps later on, when he was far from us. But it must have been a deep and lasting one, for he remained immature, unarmed for life.

Two members of our former household were also missing. My mother's maid, Johanna, had died in Petersburg and we all felt we had lost a member of the family. The faithful Jacob remained with Father until we came to Paris. Then he returned to Germany and was replaced by a French butler who, by strange coincidence, was also called Jacob. My dear Miss Maybury faded out of the picture because of ill health and went back to England. My new governess was Scottish and proud of her name, MacCulloch. She belonged to a well-known clan and displayed her plaid. We called her Miss Mac; she was quite an extraordinary little person, not as intellectual or high strung as my former mentor, but warm, understanding and generous, a woman of decision, who ceased to be a governess to me but became a wonderful companion and friend.

As usual, my father carefully attended to my schooling. I brushed up my French with a Parisian teacher and had some other private lessons at home. More fruitful were the studies I followed at the Cours de Jeunes Filles, which offered courses in French literature and history, but I studied nothing that would prepare me for an academic career.

It seemed strange that with my father's liberal ideas and his concern for Grisha's thorough education, this concern was not extended to me. My curriculum was based on quite conventional and even reactionary principles. He would take great interest in my horseback riding, supervised the tailoring of my riding clothes (I could no longer ride astride, but on a sidesaddle). He took me out riding in the Bois de Boulogne. He also took me to the Louvre and other galleries, showing himself to be a great art connoisseur and excellent guide, but he kept a close eye on my reading. There was a row of "forbidden books" on our library shelves, to which I helped myself discretely. They were mostly classics to which any girl of my age would have access; I never understood my father's objections to these books, while he would let me read others that seemed "more advanced." I learned the "facts of life" from Shakespeare. All and all, my education was well-rounded when I was sixteen or seventeen, and my future seemed to hold no surprises. My parents hinted that if I did not get married, I would be appointed a "lady-in-waiting" to one of the grand duchesses, as my grandmother Countess Toll had been as a young girl. I resented such a solution and declared that I would rather find a job, a thing unheard of for young ladies in my position.

There was quite a large Russian colony in Paris. Some were permanent residents, *boulevardiers* and *bons vivants,* lovers of life like the old Prince Trubetskoy, who at the age of seventy was still officially an attaché of the Russian Embassy and arrived every day at the offices of the rue de Grenelle, in a four-in-hand vehicle which he drove himself. By then, all the other members of the staff had their cars or arrived in taxis, but the Prince never gave up his horses.

Grand Duke Paul Alexandrovich, uncle of the Tsar, had his residence in the outskirts of Paris. He lived outside of Russia because of his morganatic marriage to Countess Pistolkors, a divorcée. She was granted the title of Princess Paley, which was also given to her children, but she was not invited back to Russia until many years later. In fact she had sought this invitation with great insistence and was finally to receive it on the eve of the Revolution. It caused her husband's tragic death. He was executed by the Bolsheviks with several other grand dukes, including Father's friend Nikolai Mikhailovich.

At the time we lived in Paris, Grand Duke Paul and his wife were still banned from Russia but very much a part of French society. They frequented the same circles as my parents and were entertained at the embassy. But this created endless problems of protocol and precedence.

Even in the Russian Orthodox cathedral, built especially for the embassy, these questions arose. Was it Father, as the official representative of the Tsar, who should lead the religious processions, or these Imperial relatives? When other grand dukes and their families visited Paris, as often happened, the situation grew even more tense. It required my parents' tact and prudence to solve these problems. I remember in particular one dramatic incidence during a Holy Week service when this question of precedence in a solemn procession was raised. Father S., our kindly and wise pastor, found some way out of the dilemma, but it did not help to create a recollected spirit among the congregation, for opinions were divided.

Father attended the liturgy every Sunday at the cathedral dedicated to Saint Alexander Nevsky. He felt it his duty to appear and afterwards to visit the rector when the service was over. I accompanied him, standing at his side in the place reserved for us, and followed the service attentively. Ever since my early childhood in Tokyo, I had loved the Byzantine liturgy, and knowing every word of it, I was penetrated by its beauty. This was all I actually knew about religion. Father had no special love for the Church, having seen only her negative aspects as a reactionary force in his country and as an instrument of diplomacy and intrigue. He respected Mother's strict, sincere Calvinist faith. A special car drove her every Sunday to her Protestant church, *Le Temple* as it was called in Paris, and he made sure that Miss Mac had a ride to her own Anglican church at the British Embassy. Thus all religions were honored in my home, which developed my ecumenical spirit, even though the word "ecumenism" was unknown in those days. On the other hand, no one talked about faith in our family, the religious and mystical aspects of life. They were as remote for me, as though I had been an agnostic, although I cannot say that I ever lost my faith; it went on illuminating my life, but only with a faint, dim light of which I was scarcely aware, except during Holy Week, when, according to the Russian Orthodox custom, I attended daily services, went to confession and communion and prepared myself devoutly for the "Feast of Feasts" and the great Easter night Vigil which climaxed these days of intensive prayer.

Easter midnight service followed by a Mass are the highest point of the Byzantine liturgy. In all countries where the oriental rite is observed it is the celebration in which all the people participate. In our Embassy church it was a formal affair, with father, the members of the staff, the military and naval attachés and even the visiting grand dukes, arrayed in their respective uniforms and the ladies wearing their most elegant evening dresses. There was the joy, the exaltation of the *paskha*. The cathedral was crowded, the people standing shoulder to shoulder, holding lighted candles, and each time the priest came out of the sanctuary and exclaimed "Christ is risen," we all answered: "In truth, He is risen." After the Mass, we had a reception at the Embassy, or rather an Easter breakfast for the numerous members of the Russian colony. We called them "the night birds" as we saw them only on that Easter night; most of them were elderly retired people but the afterglow of the paschal joy shone in their wrinkled faces.

There were hundreds of Russians living in Paris who were not on our invitation list and of whose presence we were scarcely aware. These were the Jewish garment workers who had escaped pogroms and famines in Poland and the Ukraine, and had migrated to France. Many found work in the shops of the Paris garment district but others were not so fortunate and were reduced to great poverty. Since they were still considered Russian citizens, the French relief services did not take care of them. They held Russian passports which had either expired or never been properly legalized and they appealed in vain to our consulate. Finally, Mother heard about their plight and founded a charitable society to aid them. She raised funds through appeals, benefits, concerts and bazaars. She had an immense correspondence, and in those days no one dreamed of having a secretary to type and keep files. Her personal, handwritten letters were always warm and obtained good responses. I have a number of these answers signed by famous people, in my autograph collection. Mother also founded a home for Russian women.

There was another group of Russians of whom we saw nothing at the embassy. They were the political exiles; socialists or anarchists who somehow, managed to have their papers in order. I believe that every

Russian revolutionary of that period who had escaped police surveillance at home had either lived in Paris or briefly visited there. They managed to avoid the dragnet of the Russian and French intelligence and led secluded lives, but met quite openly in certain cafés, such as the Closerie des Lilas, which their patronage made famous. Among them was a short, bearded man with resolute features and an air of quiet obstinacy. He spent hours studying philosophy at the Bibliothèque Nationale, the Paris public library, or took long, solitary bicycle rides in the suburbs of the city. His name was Vladimir Ilich Lenin, who had been since 1903 the leader of the Bolshevik party. I suppose his name was not unknown to my father, nor his presence in Paris ignored, but I do not remember any mention of him. He must have been considered a "minor hazard" compared to the more spectacular and romantic terrorists.

I was now eagerly absorbing the stimulating and sophisticated atmosphere around me. Almost daily, interesting people came to our luncheon or dinner table. At first, I was extremely shy, so one day my mother said to me, "You absolutely must talk to the people next to you and make them feel at home." I tried hard, and surprisingly enough soon succeeded in playing hostess. I was rewarded for my efforts; one of my luncheon neighbors whom I dutifully entertained was a most remarkable man who became my lifelong friend.

He was Prince Vladimir Nikolaevich Argutinsky-Dolgoruky of ancient Armenian stock, a distinguished art connoisseur and one of the sponsors of Diaghilev's Ballets Russes which was making its triumphant tours throughout Europe. He was not only a personal friend of Diaghilev but also of his entire company and its stars as well as of the composers, choreographers and painters who worked with him. The Prince was also known as a man of absolute taste and artistic intuition who gave Diaghilev unerring advice for his productions. This little man with large brown eyes which shone behind his round glasses, had a soft, dreamy voice which lent him a mysterious charm. He opened the wonderful world of the Ballets Russes to me and my shyness was soon dispelled. I eagerly listened to him and was longing to see these new productions.

But alas, my parents did not take me to the Ballets Russes. They had become a subject of violent controversy after the two premieres of *L'Après-midi d'un Faune,* and that of the *Sacre du Printemps.* In the former, Nijinsky's gestures had been judged obscene, to say nothing of his costume, which was "all spotted," said my mother, with candid surprise, meaning Nijinsky's tights which were made to look like the body of the young faun, half-goat and half-man. Father kept a shocked silence about the whole affair. The following year, an even greater demonstration took place in the Paris Champs Elysées theater when Diaghilev produced the *Sacre du Printemps* with the Stravinsky score. The first night was marked by pandemonium and even fighting in the parterre and gallery. The violence displayed by the French public shocked Stravinsky himself and the newspapers started a campaign of unbridled hostility. This time, Father took the side of the Ballets and complained that the campaign was not anti-Stravinsky but anti-Russian. Diaghilev took his production to London where it was enthusiastically acclaimed. But I did not see the Ballets Russes till years later when the famous company, like ourselves, became exiles, driven out of Russia by the Revolution.

During the seasons 1912-1913, when the Ballets caused such trouble, Diaghilev triumphed in his operatic productions. *Boris Godunov* with its great music, its beautiful sets and the admirable basso Fedor Chaliapin in the title role, was unanimously recognized as a masterpiece. Mother asked Chaliapin to sing at the Embassy for her charity benefit and he graciously accepted. He was photographed in our garden, a giant of a man, towering over all our guests and not too comfortable in his formal cutaway and top hat. He looked much more at ease on stage, in the golden robes and crown of the Tsar Boris.

I was now seventeen, my schooling was over but I still attended many lectures on literature, art and drama criticism, and some on bacteriology at the Paris School of Medicine. Secretly, I dreamed of a medical career, but not being able to prepare for it, I enrolled in a class offered by the French Red Cross. I studied diligently and obtained a diploma as an auxiliary medical nurse. I had the intuition that my services might soon be needed; there was so much talk of wars and revolutions going on around me. But little did I suspect that I had really guessed right.

These were busy days for me, but there were also pleasant times of relaxation. My former schoolroom was transformed into a "den" where we served tea to the members of the Embassy staff. They enjoyed leaving their offices for this short break and thanks to their friendliness I lost the remains of my shyness. Miss Maybury and later, Miss Mac were also popular at these tea parties.

One day a strange visitor appeared in my den. He had been invited by Miss Maybury who had met him at the British Embassy church. (This was shortly before she left us.) He was a short, bearded, middle-aged man and there was something shrewd and owlish about his face as he sat very quietly sipping his tea. He had been introduced as Dr. Dillon, correspondent of the London *Daily Telegraph*. He seemed to be waiting for something and after a brief chat with me, he rose at Miss Maybury's signal and followed her to an old-fashioned elevator which served our three floors. I never saw Dr. Dillon again, but I later learned that he was one of the most influential columnists of the British press. He had disagreed with my father on a serious, diplomatic issue and was not *persona grata* in our home. But he was now very eager to "make it up" with Father and to obtain an interview with him. So an invitation to my den was the only possible strategy he could think of to attain his aim. Miss Maybury tactfully guided him to my father. She admired the doctor greatly and was glad to help him in this way. As it turned out, she had acted wisely. Thanks to her, a reconciliation took place. Not only was Dr. Dillon an outstanding expert on international affairs, but an extremely fair and loyal man. In his book *The Eclipse of Russia* he pays a tribute to my father, which not many other political historians have done.

I often heard my father say: "It is difficult to deal with journalists: if you do not see them, they write fantastic things about you. And if you see them, well, you just have to take a chance." So my little "tea parties" were, in a small way, something like my initiation into the political game.

CHAPTER VI

I Am a Debutante

I HAD LIVED four years in Paris and the period had been a happy and exciting one. Now in January, 1914, had come the time for my "debut." This meant going to St. Petersburg again. I was to be presented to the Tsarina Alexandra Fedorovna and make my bow to the high society of the Russian capital. Only then would I be permitted to attend the grand social activities of the coming Paris spring season.

Preparations for the great event were started well ahead of time. My mother was, of course, to accompany me and we had to order a complete new wardrobe of formal and semiformal gowns, as well as the warm clothes indispensable in the northern city. Mother had to have her jewelry reset: the small diamond tiara, the fine pearl choker and the sapphire brooch, the three main pieces in her jewelry box. The famous couturier Worth, agreed to make our formal gowns at a reduced price since to cater to the embassy was good publicity. The minor items were done by the *petites couturières* of Paris, the little seamstresses expert in their art.

I was provided with a sealskin coat, muff and hat, while Mother could boast of a *breitschwanz* ensemble, the priceless fur of unborn Persian lambs, as smooth as silk, The skins had been presented to Mother by the Emir of Bokhara when, in 1913, he visited the Tsar. The Emir's puppet kingdom was a protectorate of Russia and he brought gifts to the entire imperial family, and to the ministers and high officials.

At last our preparations were over and we started off on our great expedition. Father and Grisha saw us off. My brother was on vacation from the university and I was sorry he was not going back to Petersburg for another few weeks. We boarded the Nord Express with our maid and a considerable amount of baggage. We stopped at the border station of Verzhbolovo, where we were transferred to the Russian double-gauged sleeping cars. This transfer took a couple of hours, during which I inhaled the familiar Russian odors: the whiffs of *makhorka*, the strong pungent peasants' tobacco, the smell of tar, used to smear their heavy high boots, the smell of sheepskins and the smoke of huge, wood-burning stoves. Clouds of engine steam hung over the wide tracks and fur-clad railroad workers were silhouetted like black ants against the snowcovered fields. Yes, this was Russia, the Russian winter. I eagerly inhaled the frozen air.

A colonel of the *gendarmes* hurried forward to meet us, saluting and clicking his heels. He ushered us into an ornate waiting room reserved for high officials. It was furnished in grand style with gilded sofas and armchairs, upholstered in heavy brocade which looked completely out of place in this dingy frontier station. The colonel spoke to us in French, took a quick glance at our diplomatic passports and ordered lunch for us. It was soon brought to us on silver platters by an obsequious waiter. Everything was gloomy and musty in these drawing rooms. I looked enviously through the glass partition at the public first class buffet where everything seemed warm, animated and gay. There were tables with spotless linen and white aproned waiters bustling around. A counter held rows and rows of bottles: wines, vodka and liqueurs. In the eastern corner of the room was a large ikon with a vigil light burning in front of it. This was Saint Nicholas, patron saint of travelers.

Soon the buffet was filled with well-clad, good-looking men and women, in smart fur-lined coats. This was Russia's affluent society. But when I returned to our sleeper, I passed the third class waiting room, which offered quite another picture. It was unswept, crowded; ragged peasants in sheepskins sat or lay on wooden benches. The room was filled with *makhorka* smoke; weak tea and bagels were dispensed at the canteen. These were the farmers who were licensed to cross the border to sell their products in nearby German towns. Some of them drove their geese to German markets; they smeared the birds' feet with tar to protect them on the long, wintry roads.

Gendarmes entered the waiting room to check the peasants' passports. They handled them roughly, pushed them around and arrested some of them for not carrying their identity papers; they were led away to be tried for major misdemeanor, while those who had been cleared, climbed into their carts drawn by skinny horses.

I looked at these men trying in vain to understand their lives, their fate. Close as we were in this railroad station, we were miles apart. Their world was entirely different and unknown to me — a sad, frustrated world, full of fear, brutality and suspicion. An impenetrable wall separated them from the diplomat's daughter who was going to become a "debutante."

Our journey came to an end on a cold, wintry afternoon; the street lamps were already lighted in St. Petersburg, it was snowing and the lemon-colored sky hung low over the frozen Neva River. Once more we drove along the granite embankment, but did not turn toward Palace Square. We crossed the river and rode out to one of the islands, the Kamenny Ostrov to the residence of my godmother, Princess Helen of

Altenburg. It was here we had stayed years earlier on our way to Japan. Now the Princess had invited us to stay in her home during the "coming out" season. Kamenny Ostrov, named after the island on which it was located, was a fine piece of early eighteenth-century Russian architecture. The high, stuccoed ceiling of the vestibule, its colonnades and galleries were decorated with one large gilt letter, the initial of Emperor Paul I, who had lived in this palace and of whom our hostess was a direct descendant. A majordomo in livery met us at the door and solemnly announced that Her Highness would expect us for supper. He then directed us to our apartments.

We were led through vast drawing rooms, halls, libraries, loggias, corridors and lobbies of a miniature Versailles. Then up a grand marble staircase, and the smaller, spiral one which had scared me in my childhood. How well I remembered it! Now, once more, it stirred my imagination, for it was full of shadows and strange echoes and seemed to lead to some haunted passage. As we went along, I caught glimpses of many rooms and nooks, with shaded lamps and candelabras burning in the afternoon dusk. Finally, we entered our apartments; two large bedrooms and a sitting room furnished in antiques—Russian birch and mahogany. The bathroom had added fixtures of the Napoleonic era such as we had seen in the bathroom of the grand waiting room at Verzhbolovo, at the border; the Imperial trademark was everywhere the same!

A silver tea urn and fine china cups with an array of delicate pastry had been prepared for us. After finishing our tea, we stretched out on our beds for a short nap. We were surprised to find that our beds were narrow and extremely hard. On further investigation, we discovered that the mattresses were made of beautifully tooled but nonresilient Morocco leather, an old tradition in Russian palaces.

The curtains were drawn and the antique bronze lamps were lit in Princess Helen's sitting room when we entered at the appointed hour. She rose to greet us rather stiffly, leaning on a cane due to some infirmity —or was it the burden of sadness and anxiety which weighed on her? For as I was soon to learn, my godmother was the one of all the Tsar's relatives most keenly aware of the tragedy developing behind the scenes of the court.

Princess Helen of Altenburg was then a middle-aged woman whose air of nobility was not merely due to her birth but to her deeply honest, highly moral and courageous character. Her graying hair was tied in a tight knot at the back of her small head which made her resemble an old-fashioned schoolmistress more than the descendant of a proud aristocrat. She wore a dark dress of almost monastic cut. Not a single jewel adorned her austere attire, though the Altenburg coffers contained many pieces of gold and precious stones. In fact, the Princess was immensely rich and possessed, besides Kamenny Ostrov, the historic Palace of

Oranienburg in the outskirts of Petersburg. She dispensed her wealth in cultural and charitable activities. In her private life, she seemed almost ashamed of her privileged position. Her thoughts seldom turned to the mundane aspects of life. Having lost her husband and married off her two daughters, she could retire to her *inner sanctum*, receiving only a few intimate friends dedicated to art, culture, and especially to music. She piously preserved and cultivated the heritage of her grandmother, who also bore the name of Helen and who was a famous patroness of music of the previous century.

The Grand Duchess Helen, née Princess of Altenburg, was the wife of Grand Duke Michael, the Tsar's great-granduncle. The story of this remarkable woman has not been written but I often heard about her from my own Grandmother Toll, who, before her marriage, had been a lady-in-waiting at the Grand Duchess' court.

To be more exact, Mademoiselle Strandtmann, which was my grandmother's maiden name, had waited on the Grand Duchess' daughter, Princess Catherine, as a companion, the two girls being of the same age. Grand Duke Michael and his family lived in one of the monumental palaces along the Neva embankment, which my grandmother always referred to in French, as the *Palais Michel*. The Grand Duchess, imbued with the Wurzburg's love of music, imported it to her new adopted land. Franz Liszt gave recitals at the *Palais Michel* and Tchaikovsky became her protégé, as were also the brothers Anton and Nicholas Rubinstein who were to found the Petersburg and the Moscow *conservatoires*, the two main Russian music schools. Anton dedicated to the Duchess his romantic suite *Kamenny Ostrov,* for Kamenny Ostrov had been inherited by her husband from Emperor Paul (hence the initial Π [P] decorating the palace.) The Grand Duchess also founded the Petersburg Imperial Music Society, which was directed by Anton.

This great period in Russian music was passed at the time we were guests at Kamenny Ostrov. I felt a mysterious doom hanging over the palace. My godmother seemed to be the prisoner of a bewitched world. It followed the routine of all other imperial residences. The members of the Princess' household wore the red and gold livery, decorated with double-headed eagles, of the Tsar's court. Everybody obeyed an invariable schedule, something like the strict rules of a convent. Things were managed according to century-old traditions which the Princess could neither break nor change. She had long since given up such duties as ordering meals, supervising the kitchen, the stables, or the hothouses —all run by silent, human machinery.

The great lady kept mostly to her private apartments and we rarely saw her except for a few occasions when we were invited to her table. Mother and I took our meals apart, served by a staff especially assigned to us. The food was, of course, delicious but quite unpretentious. One of the rules of palace life was to "cut down" on daily luxuries and be lavish only on special gala dinners. There was none of that continual abundance in which Russian high officials, wealthy landowners and big businessmen indulged.

Soon after our arrival, Mother and I started on a round of visits which were to prepare my "coming out." I was introduced to a few important hostesses who were to invite me to their parties. Many balls were scheduled in close succession, for we had only a few weeks before Lent when all social activities would be stopped and not resumed until the following winter. Invitations began to pour in as soon as our arrival was known.

We duly reported to the Grand Marshal of the Court and the Court Ministry and were advised that the Tsarina Alexandra Fedorovna would receive us in audience. We were to await Her Majesty's pleasure, as she was not in the best of health and the debutantes were presented to her in small groups when it was convenient to her.

Meanwhile, our engagement book was filled and scarcely had we unpacked our new wardrobe and grown accustomed to our new environment, when our social life began. Mother hired a motorcar, one of the few available for rent. Cars were still but rarely seen on Petersburg streets and only wealthy people and the Imperial Court owned them privately. Our rented vehicle was not as good as our Paris Renault but it served its purpose as Kamenny Ostrov was quite a distance from the residential quarters in the city.

My first ball was at the home of General Count Nostitz, and his American wife; she was later to publish her memoirs under the title: *A Countess from Iowa*. The General was military attaché at our embassy in Paris but had a house in Petersburg where he came with the Countess for the winter season and the ball was a very good headstart for me because the parties given by the Nostitzes were known for their gay, relaxed atmosphere, not as rigid as the grand affairs I was soon to attend.

Tolstoy admirably described the coming out of his charming young heroine Natasha Rostova in *War and Peace:* "The excitement of getting ready, of wearing the new gown, of being driven to the great mansion; then the shyness, almost the terror inspired by this brilliant pageant, and the annoyance of not being immediately noticed and admired. And finally the joy, the delight as she joined the fun and finally met the man of her destiny."

There was no such romance in my debut. But I did experience some of Natasha's joys and torments. A ball in the twentieth century was very much like the ones held a hundred years ago. In Russia, the grand balls and *folles journées* (the days of folly), which lasted from the early afternoon til the next morning, were held in magnificent residences, famous for their architecture and furnishings. One of these historic homes belonged to Countess Elizabeth (Betsie) Shuvalov, whose sister, Marie, had married my Uncle Gregory. She considered us part of the family and often invited us. She was a very popular hostess, known for her excellent taste. She had had the best architects and decorators remodel her home, or rather, bring it back to its original eighteenth century style. Her dazzling white ballroom and grand marble staircase made a perfect setting for gala occasions. After the Revolution, Countess Shuvalov was an *émigrée* in Paris and died there. Her mansion was used by Soviet movie directors to shoot scenes of historic interest.

The English writer Maurice Baring was often a guest at the Shuvalov home. He was a member of the famous banking family the Baring Brothers, who had many dealings with Russia. The oldest brother, Lord Revelstoke, was a friend and frequent visitor at our Embassy in Paris. He was the classic type of highly polished English gentleman, gracious but aloof. Maurice, on the other hand, was a bohemian; he fell in love with Russia and spent many months in Petersburg every year. At night he often vanished and would appear at daybreak much to the disapproval of the Shuvalov's servants who suspected him of being an incurable night-reveler. The truth was that Baring made the rounds of Petersburg taverns and of the city's poorest districts to study the lives and *mores* of the Russian people. He was the first writer and literary critic to introduce Russian literature to the English. His books, devoted to this subject, still make excellent reading.

If Maurice Baring, Sir Donald McKensie and the extraordinary Dr. Dillon of the *Daily Telegraph* (who later had come to my Paris "den"), could see the serious, dramatic side of Russian life, the world I was shown was highly static, with little drama visible. It was a world formal, regimented, entirely governed by tradition. It was something like a parade or general inspection of lovely girls and brides-to-be. But it had, also, the freshness and glow of youth, set in an antique frame. The whole had a glitter and elegance which I was never to see again.

The scene was enhanced by the number and variety of the men's military dress; some twenty cavalry and infantry regiments of the Tsar's elite guards were stationed in or around Petersburg (supposedly to protect the capital in case revolution broke out again). There were also units of the elite Baltic fleet. The uniforms ranged from conservative dark blue and black, smartly tailored tunics with gold and silver epaulettes and high collars to the Hussars' flaming reds and the scarlet of His Majesty's own Cossack bodyguards. The latter wore the native dress of Caucasian tribes, displaying rows of silver cartridges on their chests and silver belts and daggers in silver sheaths. Their soft, pointed high boots made them look like ballet dancers. Then there were officers of the *Streltsy* regiment, a remnant of ancient Muscovy, their bright blue coats slipped over typical silk Russian blouses of a deep raspberry color. They all looked as though they were part of some costume ball, lovely but not real. There were only a few white ties and tails in this motley crowd and they were mostly foreign diplomats. Everybody in Russia seemed to be in uniform. Several junior grand dukes, all of them officers of guards' regiments attended these balls.

Some of the older grand dukes were also often present. They were generals, admirals, commanding huge units of ships and many thousands of officers and men. The junior grand dukes stood in awe of their seniors who inflicted strict military discipline on them in parades and maneuvers. Here in the ballroom they still observed distances.

The young girls, of course, were no less strictly held by their parents and elderly relatives who chaperoned them. They had to sit around for hours while the young people danced. Chaperones had special sitting rooms assigned to them where they could play bridge, gossip and try to stay awake until suppertime when they were relieved of their duties.

Here you could see all the great titled aristocracy of Russia: the Trubetskoys, the Obolenskys, the Gagarins, the Sheremetevs, the Tolstoys, the Dolgorukys, and so many others who in their youth had danced at the same balls to which they were now bringing their daughters.

Among the ladies I remember most distinctly two sisters who presented a striking contrast: the rather stocky Princess Ella Kochubey, the mother of my two best friends, and the tall, racy Princess Olga Orlov, the most elegant woman in Petersburg. Her husband, Prince Vladimir Orlov, supervised the Tsar's fleet of automobiles. And there were two American-born women: the lovely Princess Beloselsky and Princess Cantacuzene, a descendant of President Grant.

To my regret, my former boyfriends from the dancing class were not at the balls. They were doing their military service and had not as yet received their commissions. No enlisted man could be invited to these formal affairs, neither were students or any pupils of the elite schools admitted. The only exception was made for the senior class of the *Corps des Pages* who were commissioned before graduation. They waited on the Tsar at various court affairs and at the balls they wore their full-dress uniforms which were stiff, heavily braided with gold, and had high collars which made them look like puppets.

We danced strictly traditional dances: the quadrilles, similar to American square dances, with a master of ceremony calling out the various figures in French; the polonaise, a slow processional march which opened the ball; and the old-fashioned, slow waltzes. And there was the gay, dynamic mazurka in which our Polish partners were most brilliant. Though wearing Russian uniforms, their hearts beat to Polish rhythms.

The mazurka climaxed the ball. It was usually assumed that the young man who asked a girl for the mazurka, would propose at the end of the season. Young people were somehow paired off in advance. Matchmaking was easy because both parties were wealthy and titled. There was no fortune-hunting, no title-hunting, with only a few exceptions which were always frowned upon.

One of the crucial moments of the ball was the *cotillon*, when colored favors, fancy pins and fresh corsages were given out. Roses, carnations and parma violets were shipped to Petersburg from the Riviera in refrigerated cars brought out for these occasions.

The traditional young ballroom set had its fringe of "rebellion." These were a few young married women who were branded as "fast." They danced with the civilians and sent in requests for the "one-step" and the tango, strictly prohibited in our milieu. They wore bold evening gowns and high turbans and feathers and smoked perfumed cigarettes in long, jade holders. If the orchestra was Rumanian or Hungarian, as was sometimes the case, they struck up the forbidden tunes. But if it was a military band, it performed nothing but the classic repertoire.

The dances were directed by the master of ceremony, a colonel with a magnificent, blond beard and a stentorian voice, shouting commands in French: *"Grand Rond, s'il vous plait"* or *"Balancez vos Dames!"* We would all join hands or change partners and this would be the occasion for a quick nod, the pressure of a white-gloved hand, the only chaste signs of love we could exchange. The colonel was slightly drunk and this added zest and vigor to his performance. Nothing escaped his eagle eye; if a wallflower pined alone, a partner would quickly be sent to rescue her.

Though I submitted obediently to all the rites and customs of these grand affairs, I remained an outsider in this closed, clannish Petersburg. I had little in common with it, having tasted the sophistication of Paris and known its intellectual ferment. The men I danced with were absorbed with their own affairs, mostly pertaining to the military, or to horses and the hunt. They seemed unaware of all that was going on outside this narrow world. Politics, at that time hotly discussed by the Russian intelligentsia, were ignored by them. They felt secure in their "status" or "way of life," and the idea that it could ever be upset never entered their minds. As to their cultural interests, they were no less limited and conventional.

However, I am wrong to generalize. Some of my dancing partners were highly educated and brilliant young men. My most interesting friend was Prince Dimitri Sviatopolk-Mirsky, an erudite scholar. He was a close friend of my brother, Grisha, and therefore we met on familiar terms. He was a black-bearded man with strange, Mongol features and a sardonic smile. A revolutionary at heart, he scarcely tried to hide his convictions. Soon after my debut, he was demoted from his rank as officer for refusing to drink to the Tsar's health at a regimental dinner.

Dimitri Sviatopolk-Mirsky's name may be familiar to my readers. After the Revolution, he lived in France and England and became one of the finest literary critics of his time. His *History of Russian Literature* is still a "must" in American and English schools. He was a professor of London University and much of my own literary and academic work was connected with him in the 1930s.

There were many other pleasant and colorful characters at those balls; one was a young man who never danced nor talked with me, nor with any other debutante for that matter. He was a Hussar whose remarkable good looks and proud bearing impressed us all. His slightly flushed, regular features and shining dark eyes made him the picture of self-assured, insolent youth. He reminded me of Tolstoy's hero Vronsky, in *Anna Karenina*. He only appeared for a few moments at our balls, drank a glass of champagne and departed. It was whispered that he spent the rest of the time in nightclubs with the fast young women who also left our balls early, and supped and listened to Gypsy songs in the "islands' " famous restaurants.

Could we have foreseen the future, a very different and somber picture would have met our eyes. Only a few months later, World War I broke out. A number of my dancing partners fell in the very first engagements, for the guards regiments were immediately sent to the front. The "blue" cuirassier, the "yellow" lancer, Count M., the handsome Hussar, the colonel who took care of the wallflowers, all were killed in the tragic battle of Tannenberg.

A few years later the Revolution brought further destruction. As I think of all these people, young and old, gay or sad, dancing, talking, falling in love, gossiping or planning a happy future, I can only say in retrospect: *"Morituri te salutamus."* It was the phrase of the gladiators of Roman days, being sent into the ring of the Coliseum to fight each other to the death: "We who are about to die, salute you."

To go back to the time of my debut, I learned to know quite a different set of people at Kamenny Ostrov. The princess invited my mother and myself to the little dinner parties she gave, off and on, to her most intimate friends. These reunions were always interesting, for the guests, though few, were all men of distinction. I remember Senator Knoi, a little old man, leaning on his cane, so quiet and unpretentious that he passed almost unnoticed. And yet he was a famous jurist and scholar, a great humanist and a leader in Petersburg's most progressive, legal and political circles. No less famous was the pediatrician Dr. Rauchfuss, a defender of the highest scientific and ethical standards in medicine.

Another guest was Prince Serge Wolkonsky the former Director of the Imperial Theaters. He had been demoted after his protégé, Nijinsky (who was to become the world's greatest dancer), appeared on stage in an immodest costume. Ever after, Wolkonsky was at odds with court circles. He was a fine connoisseur of the theatre and the ballet, a brilliant conversationalist and gifted writer. Tall, handsome, dark-eyed, wearing a black, pointed beard, he looked like a Mephisto or an Italian nobleman of the Renaissance. A few of the military were also represented at these dinners; the Princess' brother, Grand Duke Michael, commanding an artillery unit, and General Polivanov, on the Tsar's military staff. I name these guests at random, for I cannot recall them all. I can only say that they all had one thing in common: they represented what I could call "His Majesty's loyal opposition."

I have already mentioned the sadness and concern which hung over the Princess. This feeling was shared by the persons who came to dine with her. They were all deeply aware of the tense atmosphere which reigned at court. Rasputin's fatal hold on the Tsarina was no longer a secret. Everyone knew about this shrewd, debauched Siberian peasant who pretended to be a monk, and who had gained the confidence of the Tsar, and particularly that of his wife, Alexandra; they believed that Rasputin could heal the little Tsarevich Alexis, heir to the throne, who suffered from hemophilia. Nobody could explain how this uncouth "miracle worker" could stop the young boy's hemorrhages and relieve his terrible pain. Some said it was hypnosis, others that he was endowed with a medicine man's uncanny power. Still others thought he had a secret assistant within the palace. The Mongolian doctor Badnaev was one of the court physicians and practiced Chinese medicine; he could, supposedly, provoke or stop hemorrhage which Rasputin pretended to treat.

Whatever the explanation may have been, the pseudomonk's apparent cures made him indispensable in the eyes of Alexandra. Nicholas either shared her belief or obeyed her wishes to allay her growing hysteria. Rasputin's own orgies of which the Tsarina was unaware and the irresponsible behavior of his "clique" were the talk of the town. The imperial family were now cloistered in their palace of Tsarskoe Selo, some thirty miles from Petersburg. Only a few persons including Mrs. Vyrubova, the Tsarina's intimate friend and devotee of Rasputin, were admitted into this *inner sanctum.* Meanwhile, the quack Siberian monk was ruling not only the court, but Russian political circles as well. The story of Rasputin has often been told and I can add little to it, except to stress the fact, often ignored or minimized, that all Russian society was fully aware of the situation and only the ultraconservatives tried to hide it, or subscribed to the slogan: "Our Tsar, right or wrong."

During my stay in Petersburg in January, 1914, rumors had already grown to enormous proportions and could no longer be controlled. Gossip was passed around, discussed in every home, at the Yacht Club, favorite haunt of the male aristocracy, in grand dukes' residences, to say nothing of the Duma, the Russian parliament, from its radical members to its most moderate wing. Meanwhile Mr. Paléologue, the French ambassador, was busily taking notes in high society circles. (He wrote a revealing book, later, about the period.)

There were many who wanted to stop Rasputin by depriving the Tsar of his crown. Others wished to oblige him to moderate his behavior, and particularly that of the Tsarina, in some way, and yet remain loyal to the dynasty. The persons who came to the Kamenny Ostrov belonged to this category. The Princess was not inclined to broach this subject openly with her friends; it was often referred to at her dinners at which everyone spoke in French, so as not to be understood by the servants. There were probably a few spies in the Princess' household, as there were undoubtedly a few members of revolutionary cells. They all kept a "poker face" and went on with their chores, to run the impeccable machinery of the Palace.

At the end of the season I had the opportunity of seeing the Tsar and two members of his family. This was a very rare occasion for, as I have said, the sovereigns had practically abandoned St. Petersburg and saw almost no one of the capital's political and social world. The Tsarina, especially, had become suspicious of everyone who did not belong to her immediate entourage and who did not idolize "our friend," as she called Rasputin. But in the winter of 1914, Nicholas' two older daughters, Tatiana and Olga, had reached the ages of eighteen and nineteen and were to be, like myself, debutantes of that season. Their mother still refused to come to Petersburg, so the Tsar decided to chaperone his daughters. He was eager to let the young girls see something of Petersburg's gay and elegant life, of which they knew nothing.

The first ball at which the Grand Duchesses appeared with their father was at the Anichkov Palace, the residence of the dowager Empress, Maria Fedorovna (whom we had known in Copenhagen). A few days before the ball, the dowager received my mother and myself in private audience. I have already mentioned her friendly attitude toward our family and during our interview she was warm, cordial and informal, a living contrast to her daughter-in-law, the poor Tsarina.

On the night of the grand ball, we all crowded into the immense hall where we were met by masters of ceremony in gold-embroidered court dress, black silk breeches and stockings, and buckled, patent-leather shoes. They held thin ivory canes decorated with blue bows which made them look like rococo shepherds. They herded us along the walls facing the main doors at the end of the hall, which were hermetically closed. The doors, elaborately carved and gilded, were guarded by two tall black Ethiopian footmen in Oriental costume and high turbans; they seemed to have stepped out of *Schéhérazade* with their bright sashes and long earrings. The dowager alone had Ethiopians in her service.

After a long period of waiting motionless against the wall, I saw the great doors open and two stately figures in dazzling uniform appear on the threshold. These also held ivory staffs with blue bows, and their chests were covered with docorations. One was Count Benkendorf, a Grand Court Marshal and brother of our London Ambassador. The other was Count Fredericks, the Minister of the Court, who knew more about the Rasputin affair than any of us, and was the least inclined to talk about it.

Tapping his cane on the parquet floor which shone like a mirror, the Grand Marshal announced in a loud, basso voice:

"His Majesty, the Emperor."

After such an announcement, almost liturgical in solemnity, one could have expected the *Roi Soleil* (the Sun-God, which used to be the title of Louis XIV) to appear. Instead, the short, timid man who now came forward was a complete anticlimax. He was wearing as usual his uniform of a colonel in the infantry, and stroking his beard with a mechanical gesture, Nicholas II surveyed his subjects almost with awe. As he advanced toward us, we curtsied low. (I had practiced all day for that moment.) The men bowed even lower. Now the Tsar was passing between the rows, smiling feebly, nodding right and left with a strange, almost youthful awkwardness. This was the monarch convinced that he was called by Almightly God to absolute power.

The two grand duchesses, Tatiana and Olga, followed in their father's wake. They were tall, slim, lovely young creatures and they looked at us with a sort of amused curiosity. They wore very simple, classic white gowns, for it would have been considered bad taste to dress them up. Other members of the Romanov family walked in procession: the dowager Empress and her two daughters, Xenia and Olga, laughing gaily, bowing to friends they recognized among the guests. The Tsar's sisters were known for their charming, simple manners and were very popular among us.

There were many grand dukes, too, in the cortege. I had seen them at other *fêtes* but now they appeared in a new light, full of authority and prestige. The gods had met and were descending from Olympus.

The Tsar opened the ball with his eldest daughter in the ceremonial polonaise march. All the others followed in pairs and the grand ball was launched into orbit.

But as soon as the orchestra struck up the first quadrille, there was embarrassment. Not a single young man made a move to ask the two grand duchesses to dance. Were they all too shy to make the plunge? Or was it the sudden realization that the two girls were strangers? There was disaffection for the Imperial family, so long absent; there was hostility and wounded pride. But the masters of ceremonies hastily remedied the situation. A few officers were jockied into position. They were the Tsarskoe Selo (Special Guards of Honor) who knew the young ladies and had often danced with them at small family entertainments. These young partners did not belong to the smart set; they were completely unknown, rather uncouth, common looking, for it was the Tsarina's policy to recruit her guards among the ordinary, unglamorous regiments who had not "made the grade." She suspected all the others.

Silence fell upon the guests while the Grand Duchesses and their obscure partners seemed to enjoy themselves immensely. This was too much — jealousy was awakened in the hearts of the reluctant cavaliers. When the next dance was announced, the most brilliant young officers stepped forward and asked Tatiana and Olga for this and all the other dances. To everyone's relief, the ice was broken.

But a cloud of suspicion and coldness still hovered over Anichkov Palace. During supper, a strange thing happened, which my mother described to me later. As the Tsar, according to protocol, made the rounds of the tables, he saw my mother and stopped before her. He recognized the young girl he had danced with several years ago in Copenhagen when visiting his mother, the dowager Empress. His face lit up, then his eyes grew sad again. He whispered in French: *"Je ne connais personne ici"* (I know no one here!) Thus spoke the Tsar of all Russia, in his mother's house, among the flowers of his own most loyal subjects, the aristocracy. By now, he was completely isolated.

The Anichkov ball was an exhausting affair for everyone. It lasted until daybreak, but the main cause of our fatigue was that we had to stand nearly all the time we were not dancing. We were not allowed to sit down as long as a grand duke was standing. After the Tsar departed with his daughters and the other Romanovs were gone, we were ushered out of the ballroom by our "shepherds." All the ladies sat down on the grand staircase, took off their ballroom slippers and rubbed their swollen feet. I can still almost feel the pain in my toes!

On two other occasions I saw Nicholas and the two grand duchesses at close quarters, although in the eyes of protocol, I was too young to be presented to them. Grand Duchess Maria Pavlovna, widow of Grand Duke Vladimir, gave a *folle journée* at her residence, known as the Marble Palace. Its beautiful halls of marble had given it this name. Maria Pavlovna was in the camp openly hostile to Rasputin. She gave her *fête* almost in defiance of the cloistered Tsarina and made a great display of luxury and decoration.

The other occasion was a performance of Wagner's *Parsifal* in the little Court Theater of the *Hermitage,* the museum adjacent to the Winter Palace, which has now become a picture gallery. This miniature theater, to which only the select were admitted, was a jewel of baroque architecture. This was the first performance of *Parsifal* outside of Bayreuth, for Wagner had stipulated in his will, that it should not be shown elsewhere before 1914. The cast was excellent and the Court orchestra was directed by its conductor, Count Sheremetev. The Tsar presided in the Imperial box with his two daughters and his suite. The audience sat on rather hard and uncomfortable benches. Being a junior, I was given a place in one of the last rows, next to a plump, young lady-in-waiting who took up considerable space. In spite of my love for Wagner, the performance seemed endless as I sat, barely able to balance on the edge of my hard bench.

At the end of the season, I attended the wedding of Prince Felix Yusupov, one of Russia's wealthiest young men, who, three years later, was to shoot the mad monk, Rasputin. I remember his extraordinary, large, gray-blue eyes with long lashes, the delicate nose, the thin, red lips which had a slightly sardonic twist, all seeming to hide a mysterious secret. His bride, Princess Irina, was the daughter of Grand Duke Alexander Mikhailovich, the Tsar's cousin. (This was the first morganatic marriage permitted officially) and the wedding took place in the chapel of the Winter Palace. Felix Yusupov served neither in the army nor in the civil government. So he had no uniform, an unheard of breach of protocol for such a grand occasion. A special suit of clothes was designed for him of fine, blue cloth with gold buttons and epaulettes which was called the "uniform of the nobility." Princess Irina's modest attire enhanced her severe, almost icon-like beauty. Both bride and bridegroom seemed to step out of some ancient legend as they knelt before the gold-envested priest who joined their hands in matrimony. This marriage, marked by so many dramatic events, was to last for fifty years, until "death did them part."

By now the season was almost over and we had still had no word from the Tsarina, as to the audience she was expected to give us. We began to wonder whether it would ever come. Mother was nervous, especially since we could make absolutely no move to hasten the event, and the approaching Lenten season would put an end to all court activities.

At last the long expected sign arrived, and we were commanded to take the special train which transported debutantes and their mothers to Tsarskoe Selo, to be presented to the Tsarina. Besides myself, only one other girl had an appointment for that day. She was Mademoiselle Artsymovich, who, like myself, was a diplomat's daughter; her mother was an American. We had again practiced our curtsies and were briefed on how to deport ourselves during the audience. Among other things, we were told not to speak first, to await the Tsarina's questions and to answer them briefly.

At a contrast to the pomp and luxury of the other Romanov mansions I had seen, the imperial family's home was of extreme simplicity. Nicholas and his wife never cared for the main building of the Tsarskoe Selo Palace, erected by the Empress Catherine; they preferred the small annex known as the Alexander Palace, into which we were ushered upon our arrival with a minimum of ceremony. We were served a light lunch in the small diningroom, supervised by a timid lady-in-waiting. After the meal, each girl, with her mother, was led in turn to the Tsarina's private sitting-room.

And now I was curtsying low and kissing the hand of Alexandra Fedorovna, Empress of all Russia. My first and lasting impression was how handsome this woman looked. Though no longer young, and indeed rather matronly, she resembled a magnificent, cold statue with features chiselled in pure marble. She did not seem like a living creature; she sat stiffly in a straight-backed armchair, with hands clasped and sealed lips. She wore a flowing "tea gown," a string of pearls and pear-shaped diamond earrings. The straight nose, the pale brow, the golden hair bound in simple, maiden-like braids around her narrow head — everything was utterly calm and majestic. Only the sudden flush that would pass over her face betrayed the passionate storms that raged in the secret depths of her heart.

The Tsarina was seated next to a small table covered with framed photographs. There were also many large pictures and snapshots of every size hanging on the walls. The members of the imperial family were continually taking photographs of each other. The room was furnished in the so-called *art nouveau* style fashionable in those days. The furniture was of light polished wood and bamboo, upholstered in pale, green satin with a peculiar flower-design. The glass lampshades were also decorated with flowers, mostly waterlilies of a sickly hue. This setting would have suited a play by Ibsen or Strindberg. While clinging to all the attributes of Imperial power, with unyielding obstinacy, Alexandra Fedorovna rejected its pomp with equal determination.

Needless to say, the interview was strained. Mother and I were invited to sit on the hard *art nouveau* chairs and the Tsarina seemed to have difficulty in finding the words of greeting for which we were respectfully waiting. A forced smile was all that she could muster up for a few moments, and when she spoke it was with downcast eyes and in a strange, hollow voice.

Alexandra's extreme coldness, usually attributed to shyness, was one of the causes of her unpopularity in Russian society. In spite of her great beauty she did not attract but rather repulsed her subjects harshly. I felt frozen to the bone and when at last she spoke, I heard myself giving her the most absurd answers. Thus, for instance, when she mentioned her son, the Grand Duke Alexis, I recalled that on the day that he was born, we were happy because our professors canceled our lessons. The Tsarina gave me a severe look.

I was not *persona grata* because of my father's liberal ideas and his frequent interventions on behalf of the Duma. Neither was my mother liked, because the dowager Empress, the Tsarina's mother-in-law, had befriended us, and she was also hostile to Rasputin.

We could clearly realize — and the fact was later confirmed — that this statuesque woman was on the brink of hysteria. The flushed face, the red patches on her open neck and arms were the signs of a growing disorder. Yes, that much we could guess — but who could have foretold the tragic death that awaited the unfortunate Tsarina?

The audience did not last long; it was like a visit to the shrine of a goddess who could not be propitiated. I did, however, receive a gold plaque with the Tsarina's initial *A* on it in diamonds. This meant that I was appointed *Freylina Eë Velichestva* — Maid of Honor of Her Majesty. I had been inducted into the Russian court, which I was never to see again.

Souvenirs from the Growing Up Period

Coronation of Tsar Nicholas II, 1895. In foreground, Helene's great uncle, Count Constantine Pahlen, between the candle bearers

On the way to Japan, Helene and Grisha with their parents, governess and staff on their Trans-Siberian journey

Daban, their Cossack bodyguard

Helene and Grisha with their governess, Miss Mukhanova, aboard the Ryurik

Alexander Iswolsky with staff at Russian Embassy in Japan

*Helene's mother in her Embassy in Paris (1912)
with Japanese dog Bu-Chi (a gift of the Mikado
on the earlier post in Japan)*

Alexander Iswolsky (right) with Prince Alexander (later King) of Yugoslavia (center) and Mr. Vesnich, the Serbian Minister

1894. Helene's father with Grand Duke Vladimir (left)

and with King Edward VII (left) at Marienbad

Alexander Iswolsky, then Foreign Minister, with Premier Stolypin May 4, 1909, on board the imperial yacht, Polyarnaya Zvezda, *awaiting Tsar Nicholas II's arrival for his meeting with Kaiser William II (off the Finnish coast)*

Alexander Iswolsky with Raymond Poincaré, President of France (in the foreground), and General Gouraud, reviewing the troops in Champagne, France, World War I

Fedor Chaliapin, who performed at the Russian Embassy in Paris in 1911

CHAPTER VII

End of a Golden Age

THE PARIS SEASON which opened soon after our return from Russia was a complete contrast to my Petersburg debut. Though brilliant and sophisticated, it was still ruled by etiquette, but there was none of that "clannishness" and old-fashioned rigidity I had found in Petersburg. We were not corralled with people of our own age, but could meet older men and women and make friends with them, regardless of the age barrier. Neither did people all belong to a single group. They represented many elements of society.

There were aristocrats of ancient lineage, the *gratin* (top society) such as the Luynes, the La Rochefoucaulds, the Castellanes. There were representatives of the *haute bourgeoisie,* financiers, industrialists: the Schneiders of the famous Creuzot plants, the Wendels of the Lorraine foundries, the banking family of d'Haussonville, magnates of the sugar industry and owners of the bathhouses on the Seine which have existed for 200 years and which can be seen on eighteenth century prints.

Diplomacy was represented by the Rouviers, the Cambons, the Montebellos. And there were the great Jewish families: the Rothschilds, the Goldschmidts, the Blumenthals.

It was an open society; industrialists married titled young girls, Jewish girls married French dukes. Though they were received into the Catholic Church, they retained their connections with their former *milieu.* Related as many Frenchmen were to influential families in England and America, they often crossed the Channel or the Atlantic. Long resistant to foreign languages and mores, many were now speaking English and playing golf.

Many wealthy Russians also came to Paris for the season. The men sat at the boulevard cafés; the ladies shopped for hats at Reboux, for shoes at Perugia, for gowns at Worth, Paquin, the rising star of Coco Chanel was only known to a fastidious few.

Cartier, of course, had a display of tempting jewelry which made our Fabergé settings look hopelessly *passé.* Only court circles patronized him. Who would have guessed that some thirty years later, the least of Fabergé's trinkets would have become collectors' items? Father never cared much for them, but still had a few left after the Revolution. We could sell them at a good price when our finances ran low. Such are life's little ironies.

Released from the pressures of official Petersburg, our Russian friends were rejuvenated in Paris. They could do as they pleased, felt relaxed and, at times, a little reckless; the ladies showed off their new clothes at the races of Auteuil and Longchamp, where their husbands gambled on the horses and you did not have to bow to the President of the French Republic in his box.

I, too, felt stimulated and renewed in Paris. At French balls, quadrilles were banned and one-steps and tangos *de rigueur* (requirements.)

I even had to take a few dancing lessons and progressed rapidly. I found that French dancing partners were gay and charming, and amusing conversationalists. We tangoed to langorous Argentine rhythms, we waltzed to the strains of *The Dollar Princess,* and one-stepped to a tune called *Très Moutarde.* I wonder if any record of this syncopated tune, as "sharp as mustard," still exists. If so, I would hesitate to play it. This gay tune would remind me too vividly of the approaching tragedy of the war which put an end to our golden age.

The 1914 Paris season was particularly brilliant. There were more dances, more musical and theatrical events than ever. Once more, Serge Diaghilev, the great impresario, brought the Ballets Russes to the French capital. This time he was accepted without reserve. He influenced not only art but also fashions. The Russian painter Leon Bakst, who had designed the sets and costumes for *Schéhérazade,* was all the rage. Paris became infatuated with the Orient. The Countess de Chabrillan gave her famous *Bal Persan* (Persian Ball) in which the loveliest young women, and even the plainest ones, became mysterious and glamorous; turbans, shimmering gowns and flowing scarves became popular. The dressmaker Poiret made exotic dresses, and the Italian artist Fortuny created the material: gold brocade and arabesque designs. The ballet *Petrushka* also influenced the scene, with its bright Russian costumes.

Russia was popular and so was her ambassador, with his wife and daughter. I no longer had to fear a lack of young men with whom to dance. It was quite an experience for them to waltz with a descendant of the boyars, although they had only the vaguest notion of what the word meant. My mother won the prize for popularity, and she was well-fitted for her role. Even she appeared more glamorous because of this reflected glory of *la Sainte Russie* (Holy Russia). During the World War, this halo continued to shine brightly, then suddenly paled and faded when our acquaintances turned from us, to greet the newly installed ambassador of the Revolution. Only a few of our Paris friends kept their interest in us after 1917.

When Father was transferred from Petersburg to Paris, he found a carefully selected circle which was "ready made" to welcome diplomats.

They were assigned to cater, not only to my parents, but to other ambassadors as well. Reading the diaries of the British envoy, Lord Bertie of Thames, I found that he entertained and was entertained by the same little circle as we. This "inner circle" was in full sympathy with Russia and England, friendly to Italy, tolerant to Austria, but they did not frequent the German Embassy; the defeat of 1870 and the loss of Alsace and Lorraine was still a smarting wound even though the amenable ambassador, Baron von Schoen, did all he could to improve relations and his son appeared at our dances.

Included in our "circle" were the Duke and Duchesse de La Tremoille, descendants of a French feudal family, the Princess Murat, descendant of Napoleon's Marshal who had risen from the ranks, the dowager Duchess de Rohan (of historic lineage). Other names from our circle were: the Countess de Chevigné, the Marquise de Ganay, her sister, the Countess of Behague, and the Countess de Ludres — all highly cultivated women. There was also Count Joseph de Gontaut who was a friend of the Russian Grand Duchess Maria Pavlovna, who opposed Rasputin and lived in the Marble Palace. Gontaut often visited Petersburg and his brother Paul, married to Princess Golitsyn, had many Russian connections.

When the Grand Duchess Maria Pavlovna came to Paris, the "inner circle" was there to welcome her. One of her closest friends was the Countess de Chevigné, whom I would like to describe, not only because she was a delightful and brilliant woman, but also because she is believed to have been the prototype for Marcel Proust's Duchesse de Guermantes in his great novel *Remembrance of Things Past*.

There were, of course, living at the time of Proust, others who also inspired Madame de Guermantes' portrayal, as for instance the handsome Comtesse de Greffühle, who was also a member of our circle. But I can say nothing about her that has not already been said by Proust's biographers. Whereas I very often heard Madame de Chevigné speak about "little Marcel" as he eagerly observed her, promenading on the rue St. Honoré and fell deeply in love with her image. She still possessed the hat "with the cornflowers," described in his novel. She said she had never read his book; she was piqued because he did not present her with a first edition of *Le Côté de Guermantes*.

Laure de Chevigné was everything that Proust admired in French aristocracy. The widow of Comte Adheaune de Chevigné (who may have been the *Basin* of the novel), she was the epitome of distinction, shrewdness and self-control. To read Proust is to see Laure; the birdlike profile, bright, blue eyes, the color of the sky of France, the long neck, complete with choker, the severe coiffure with only a few frizzy curls to soften the effect, the low, slightly hoarse voice which could sometimes sound almost gruff and reminded one of the French peasants' accents—all the attributes which Proust so passionately admired. Speaking of his work, he wrote to Laure: "This book, in which there is so much of you."

But even outside of Proust's interest, Madame de Chevigné was a most attractive and unusual woman. In the Gay Nineties she was the first woman who appeared at the races in a tailor-made suit and soon after, suits were considered the height of fashion. When I knew her she was well beyond middle age and her attire was quite conservative, but she used to say: "To be old-fashioned, you have to start by being fashionable."

When the Countess died, all of Paris came to her funeral, including the famous *couturiers,* and Mademoiselle Chanel, whose style she had promoted. Even the seamstresses who had fitted and sewn her gowns placed roses on her casket.

Madame de Chevigné had always remained our friend, and was one of the treasured members of our "inner circle." Another, was the Rumanian writer Princess Marthe Bibesco, a Brancovan, whose ancestors had ruled her country in feudal times. Literary talent ran in her family and her cousin the Comtesse de Noailles was a French poet.

Marthe Bibesco is considered a gifted writer whose books are masterpieces of French style and human pathos; all are true and vivid chronicles of the first decade of our century. She also had a rare beauty combined with her literary and intellectual talents. Indeed, she seemed to have everything except peace of mind.

Perhaps her very beauty caused her more sorrows than joys and involved her in complex, emotional dilemmas. Her scholarly, almost masculine mind was at war with her femininity. Her religious problems and the tragic circumstances of her life were not easily solved, until she met Abbé Mugnier, the Catholic priest who was her spiritual director for some forty years, and whose correspondence she published in two volumes, entitled *Life of a Friendship.*

Abbé Mugnier was also a member of our inner circle, and a good friend of ours. He was actually the only Catholic priest whom my parents could invite to the embassy. An official envoy could not have any part in French religious affairs because of the strict separation of Church and State and also because of the link between the Catholics and the fanatical *Action Française,* the Royalist movement. But the Abbé did not represent these anti-republican factions. He was invited everywhere, even by Protestants and Jews and the staunchest defenders of secularism and even of atheism. I remember only two ecclesiastics who were *persona grata* in the eyes of the anticlerical milieu; one was Monsignor Baudrillard, Bishop *in partibus,* a learned scholar and member of the French Academy, and the other was Abbé Arthur Mugnier, obscure chaplain of a small community of nuns of St. Joseph of Cluny.

What was the secret of the Abbé's extraordinary prestige? He was also a scholar of erudition, like Baudrillard, but without the Bishop's pedantry. He was passionately fond of the humanities, especially of French romantic literature. In fact, Princess Bibesco had started her friendship with him by quoting his favorite author, Chateaubriand. Moreover, he had an excellent sense of humor and his *reparties* were passed on from one salon to another. But his greatest gift was his inexhaustible charity.

Nothing could have been less impressive than this elderly little man coming to dine with the "select" in his threadbare cape and *soutane*, with a shabby felt hat perched on his head. He wore thick laced boots, carried a large umbrella and came on foot or by bus, while the other guests stepped out of their limousines. His features were quite plain, his candid blue eyes were watery and a somewhat clownish wisp of hair adorned his otherwise bald head.

How clearly I remember him, with that silvery tuft of hair which looked like a tiny, pale flame, and was his distinctive hallmark. In the sophisticated hard and often cruel *beau monde*, he was the merciful and gentle being to whom each instinctively turned for comfort. Some would try to hide their secret sorrow, or fear, or perhaps some dreadful doubt, by hurling a *boutade* (witticism or sarcastic remark) at the defenseless little man. He did not mind such provocations and always had an answer ready.

My father grew very fond of him and would engage him in lively conversation. Impressed by the priest's worldly wisdom, he would draw him aside and whisper: "But Monsieur l'Abbé, you are not at all Catholic . . ."

The small man would raise his arms to heaven in a mild gesture of protest. He could count the souls he had directed and pulled out of the mire, saved from despair, brought back to the Church. He could recall the French novelist Jaris-Karl Huysmans, whom he had led all the way from satanism to a Trappist monastery, and who had portrayed him in his book *En Route*.

The sayings of the Abbé were collected by his friends, repeated and some of them written down, mostly by his devoted friend Marthe Bibesco. These sayings were often humorous, often profoundly philosophical. He could use sarcasm, too, but with a gentle prudence. The famous actress Cécile Sorel, who was already middle-aged, asked him whether she was commiting a sin by looking at herself in a mirror and finding herself beautiful. "No Madame," he replied, "this is not a sin, but merely an error." Remarking that he often dined out, an acquaintance said: "Monsieur l'Abbé, you will be buried in a tablecloth." Immediately came the quiet answer: "No, in linen from the Communion table." He had given out so many communions, absolved so many sinners: "I have heard a great number of confessions," he said to Princess Bibesco, "I have heard them in confessionals, of course, but also in railroad stations, on park benches, in the streets and in public gardens."

Love, in the Abbé's mind, was the surest key to faith. He summed up his conviction by saying: "To believe in the presence of another in one's heart is to prepare it to receive God."

The Abbé lived to the age of ninety-seven. He had witnessed three wars waged by his country, and minor ones by other nations. World War II broke his heart. "God lets Himself be moved" he said to Marthe, "Will mankind not be moved by anyone?" And he added, quoting Jeremiah: "With desolation is the land made desolate, because there is none who is considereth in his heart." (Jer. 12:11)

I met him often that Paris season and later had many opportunities of seeing him and consulting him. He was one of the last to visit my father on the eve of his death. He blessed my brother's marriage. He always seemed to be participating in events that directly concerned us, or which conveyed to us a sense of drama. It was thus that we learned that in 1922, the dying Proust asked for his prayers.

I visited the Abbé in his small, modest apartment, 7 rue Méchain, not far from Notre Dame Cathedral. If I have dwelt at length on the Abbé Mugnier, it is because this remarkable priest and scholar is well-nigh forgotten. True that his devoted friend, Marthe Bibesco not only published his correspondence but wrote his biography. But there are few who actually remember him as clearly as I do, and after I pass on, there will be still fewer. I can still see his small, but radiant figure, his face lit with a gentle smile, his shabby soutane, the thick boots, the old umbrella, and that silver tuft of hair crowning his head. It might have been a halo.

It is difficult to follow the fortunes of political men whose lives belong to history rather than to the saga I am relating. My father and mother went out to dinner parties or formal affairs almost every night, and though debutantes were not invited, I heard from them about these grand occasions. Political overtones were not lacking. Most of the ambassadors and minor envoys entertained each other during the Paris season. The senior of the Diplomatic Corps was Lord Bertie of Thames, the plump and pink British ambassador. His wife had been the daughter of a diplomat and she was born in Russia. All her life she had preserved a love of things Russian. Lord Bertie shared her sympathies, but they did not extend to my father, judging from his memoirs. On the other hand Robert Baker, the American ambassador, was on excellent terms with my father, as was his successor, Myron Herrick. But everyone in Paris liked Mr. Herrick; he was one of the most popular diplomats I have ever observed.

It was hard for my mother to understand all the political currents and intrigues going on in that period. Distrust grew as rumors of pogroms, parliamentary unrest and the misdeeds of Rasputin reached our ears. God only knew what was going on in "our great and beloved Russia" — *notre grande et chère Russie,* as we called it. Mother remained unabashed, and smiled her reassuring smile. The "inner circle" and even sophisticated politicians enjoyed her company.

It was as a hostess that she excelled, always tactful and gracious. She wrote all her invitations by hand, except for a few that were officially printed or engraved. I have preserved some of these notes in her large beautiful hand, as well as some of the answers she received.

Mother grew very close to the Protestant circles of Paris. They formed a special group, known as the *Bonne Société Protestante* or (BSP) and they were mostly descendants of the Huguenots. Though mingling with Catholic society and with anticlerical circles, they rarely married out of their own group. They were more or less a closed society. They welcomed my mother because of her own Protestant background. The veteran Countess Mélanie de Pourtalès, who had been a friend of Empress Eugenie and a famous beauty of the Second Empire, was the matriarch of the BSP. Mélanie de Pourtalès came from Alsace, the province torn away from France by the Germans after the war of 1870. The Countess still retained a vast estate near Strasbourg and resided there. But when Emperor Wilhelm expressed the wish to visit the great lady, she closed her door to him and came to live in France. The annexation of Alsace-Lorraine cut many families in two. Friedrich Count Pourtalès was German Ambassador to Russia when World War I broke out. He wept after presenting Germany's declaration of war to Foreign Minister Sazonav (who had taken my father's place.) Mélanie's son-in-law, General Bercekheim, was French military attaché in Petersburg while his cousin was a German landowner. Countess de Pourtalès' granddaughter married a high Austrian officer on the eve of the war, which was to cause no end of trouble. This marriage showed the complexity of French society. I must say that at the time I describe, the hopes of a "revenge" and return of Alsace-Lorraine were very strong, but more emotional than realistic. Nobody dared think of armed conflict.

To take a last look at our "inner circle," it was our small dinner parties at the embassy that gave me the opportunity to learn much about that golden age of society that was so soon to change.

Without being too formal, the "little dinner parties," comprising twelve to twenty guests, were governed by considerable etiquette requiring low-necked evening gowns for the women, with pearls and jewels; white tie and tails for the men, who usually carried fine, gold cigarette cases. The menu was elaborately composed and served by our French chef, but carefully supervised by mother who was a gourmet. The wines were chosen by father and the *maître d'hôtel* announced them by name. Food was served on silver platters; there were tall silver candlesticks on the table and the centerpiece was a group of Sèvres figurines in white biscuit porcelain, a gift from the French President. They were the property of the Embassy, as were the crystal glasses and the silver. But Father and Mother took pains to enhance these settings with fresh flowers and modern arrangements, and even went to considerable expense to do so.

The guests for whom these settings were created were worthy of the effort; each was a personality—attractive, brilliant and experienced in discussing all topics from politics to art and literature. They went from discreet gossip to biting satire; witty remarks launched at the Embassy would later make the rounds of every salon in Paris. The three brothers de Castellane were truly striking figures. The second brother, Jean, was the shortest, but carried himself with military elegance. His wife, Dolly, was tall and matronly; she always seemed to have the leading role and was determined to retain it. Count Stanislas was tall and slim, well-matched to his charming Cuban wife. He was a member of the *Chambre des Deputés*, the French Parliament, an energetic, intelligent man who took political life very seriously.

Family pride was boldly displayed by the Marquis Boni de Castellane, who came to our home but whom Father never considered a friend. In fact, he disliked us intensely because his sympathies lay with Austria, a country which Father had resolutely opposed. Boni favored Austria for reasons too complicated for me to explain, especially now that time has effaced many things that then seemed important. But at the time, Boni de Castellane did not spare criticisms of the Russian Ambassador. He even complained of the food served at our table. It should be recalled that the Marquis had married the American heiress, Miss Gould. He was enormously rich and his pink marble house was a copy of the *Trianon* of Versailles. He entertained lavishly, and he boasted that when a member of the royalty came around, he had only to order an extra cover to be put on the table. (The story of Boni's subsequent divorce has often been told in the gossip columns and does not belong here.) He looked like a typical nobleman of the time of Louis XV. His blond fluffy hair could have been a *perruque* (wig), his slightly prominent eyes of porcelain blue, his rosy cheeks and strutting air reminded one of a portrait by Fragonard.

Another decorative guest was the Count de Gabriac, a famous wit and dandy who wore a frilled shirt and frilled cuffs which were as delightfully strange and outmoded as Dali's *moustachios*.

Before the end of the season, the "inner circle" was widened to include many scholars, writers and journalists. I met members of the French Academy René Doumic and Gabriel Hanotaux; journalists Gauvain and Joseph Reinach; historians such as Fréderic Masson; lawyers like the noted Maître Henri Robert, the most famous defense attorney of that time. I met sociologists like Gustave Le Bon, pioneer of mass psychology; novelists like Paul Bourget and Marcel Proust; and the formidable literary critics Henri Bidou and Paul Souday.

Father's connections with Paris intellectual circles were growing closer and I feel very much indebted to him for my cultural formation, even though he did not encourage me to study at the university for a degree. Very few girls of my "set" followed academic careers so I do not blame my parents for not helping me toward this goal. I was obliged to "do it the hard way" later on when the necessity of making a living overtook me. In the meanwhile, the lack of academic training was largely compensated for by all that I learned simply by listening and absorbing the "tabletalks" in our own home.

Father often told me about his contacts with learned men and women whom he met in private gatherings and at the luncheons held each month at the Café de la Paix for a distinguished group of which he was a member. They were attended by Fréderic Masson, Gustave Le Bon, Princess Bibesco, Princess George of Greece, *née* Bonaparte, who was a follower of Freud and pioneer in France of psychoanalysis. General Maxime Weygand also came to these luncheons. He was later a member of the French Academy.

Grand Duke Nicholas Mikhailovich, uncle of the Tsar whom I had seen at the gala receptions in Petersburg, came to Paris and attended the luncheons at the Café de la Paix in his capacity of historian. He was the author of an important book devoted to Tsar Alexander I and held long discussions with Fréderic Masson on the subject of the Napoleonic Wars. He was a true scholar and liberal; he was openly opposed to Rasputin and his clique and was not afraid of criticizing the Tsar and the Tsarina. He was a great friend of my father and often came to see us at the Embassy, where he knew he could be quite frank and outspoken. I remember very clearly this broad-shouldered man with a black beard and dark eyes full of kindliness and intelligence. He had a Jewish strain as a descendant on the maternal side of a Shaphirov (Shapiro), a famous Russian diplomat of whom the Grand Duke, as historian, was very proud.

He would often talk, in a veiled and noncommittal way of the research he was making concerning Alexander I. He had been allowed to study the secret Imperial archives and headed the committee especially appointed to investigate one of Russia's historical enigmas: the identity of the Siberian hermit and mystery man Fedor Kuzmich. It was believed by many in Russia and abroad that Alexander I had not died in 1825, but had staged a mock funeral and a mock burial (of a corpse unknown) while he himself took refuge in the Siberian wilderness. The committee had come to the conclusion that the legend of Fedor Kuzmich had no foundation. But it had no right to elaborate on its findings and the Grand Duke was bound to silence. However, in his talks with us he would sometimes hint that there was more to the legend than he could reveal. He used to have long conversations with Father in the privacy of his study. With Mother, he would chat and play solitaire. His favorite game was called "the Pyramid" and we played it for many years. Nicholas Mikhailovich was executed in 1919, with several other grand dukes and Grand Duchess Elizabeth Fedorovna, the sister of the Tsarina. If he knew the Siberian hermit's secret he took it to his grave. The Soviet historians are now investigating the mystery of Fedor Kuzmich and may have solved it as I am writing these lines.

During that last Paris season before the war I had many friends among the young girls already described, and I would like to mention the two charming daughters of the organizer of the Persian ball, Anne-Marie and Isabelle de Chabrillan; Méraude de Chaponay, who shared my intellectual interests; and several other girls who remained my faithful friends and companions after the Revolution. But I had few young men friends among the French golden youth. However eager they might be to dance with the Ambassador's daughter, they remained quite aloof and diffident. They feared to get involved with a foreign girl, especially if she was a non-Catholic and could offer no dowry. Parisian marriages were not made in heaven but in the offices of lawyers and stockbrokers. (I learned my lesson a few years later, when my prospective engagement to a young Frenchman was called off under the pressure of his family, as I shall relate.)

Later, in the twenties and thirties, I established many close ties with young Frenchmen, students, teachers and leaders of the avant-garde. But the society I met in my early youth was a closed circuit which reflected only a small section of French life.

Meanwhile, the staff of our Embassy offered many resources. Not only the young attachés but also older, more mature secretaries would drop in for a cup of tea in my little sitting room. Among these almost daily visitors was Prince Argutinsky-Dolgoruky, whom I have already mentioned and will surely refer to again, as he was the man who did more for my artistic and intellectual development than anyone else, before or after. During my Petersburg debut, I had the surprise of being invited to his apartment there, for he had come to the capital on a short leave of absence. I joined a few of his friends in his wonderful rooms on Millyonnaya Street, opposite the Hermitage where I had attended the performance of *Parsifal*.

It was just the right place for the Prince, for he worked daily in the Hermitage doing research and studying eighteenth-century paintings in which he was particularly interested. His apartment itself was like a museum. It was crowded with antiques and the walls were hung with priceless pictures and engravings. I was quite proud to have been invited to this inner sanctum. This tea party sealed our friendship and when we returned to Paris I often visited the Prince.

His apartment on the rue Jean Goujon was a replica of his Petersburg lodgings and even more crowded with precious objects. Argutinsky was a recognized art collector and was often consulted by art dealers and picture galleries. We often wondered how he could find room for himself to live amongst all this fantastic array of treasures. Among them were some masterpieces, such as Brueghel's "Massacre of the Innocents," the Bethlehem story transposed into a Flemish winter scene.

Argutinsky's hobby was, as it had been when I first met him, the Ballets Russes. He was a friend and consultant of Diaghilev, who highly valued his opinion. A word from the Prince might determine some change in the final production.

Leon Bakst of *Schéhérazade* fame and Alexander Benois, who created the costumes and sets for *Petrushka*, often came to the rue Jean Goujon when the Ballets Russes were in Paris. I met both of these artists at Argutinsky's, as well as the prima ballerinas and Stravinsky himself. His *Rites of Spring* had been rejected in 1913 by the Paris public but now he had risen to fame. The Prince was "at home" on Friday evenings and these little reunions in his small, cluttered but hospitable apartment were unforgettable. When I met Stravinsky much later in New York, he did not remember me, but when I mentioned Argutinsky's name his face brightened. It was sufficient to mention the rue Jean Goujon to gain the great master's attention.

The enjoyable Paris season was coming to a close when I was offered an even more exciting prospect. Our friends, the Kochubeys, invited me to visit their estate, Dikanka. It was to be my last visit to Russia before the Revolution.

Tania and Sonia Kochubey were my best friends and co-debutantes. Their father, Prince Victor Kochubey, held an important official position. He was the director of the *Udely*, the special agency administering the immense and numerous estates of the Tsar and of the entire Romanov family.

Not only was Prince Victor an able manager of imperial domains, but he was also one of the most experienced and progressive landowners of his time. I do not remember how many acres Dikanka represented, but I can say without exaggeration that it was one of the largest in Russia, as far as cultivated acreage was concerned. It was located in the Ukraine, which was imperial Russia's breadbasket. The great Russian poet, Pushkin, wrote in his narrative *Poltava:*

> Wealthy and noble is Kochubey,
> His fields are immeasurable.

The Dikanka estate could be traced back to the eighteenth century when a Prince Kochubey was fighting Mazepa, and Peter the Great defeated the Swedes in the battle of Poltava, located a few miles from the historic estate. A small chapel on the Dikanka grounds still contained the blood-soaked shirts of two of Kochubey's lieutenants executed by Mazepa. This was a family shrine which Prince Victor and his family cherished but which I found rather terrifying.

Many battles have been fought, lost and won around Dikanka, from the times of Peter up to those of Hitler, who invaded the Ukraine and seized Poltava and Kiev. He was finally driven out again by Soviet armies, after killing 30,000 Jews at Babi Yar, a ravine at Kiev.

But all was quiet and serene in the Ukraine when I arrived in Dikanka, June 1914, with my faithful companion, Miss Mac.

The Kochubeys lived in an enormous house which looked like a palace, with its own art gallery. There was a beautiful, shady park with century-old oaks, flower beds and neatly swept gravel paths. Beyond the park was a large area reserved for stables, paddocks and an enclosed riding ring or *manège*. Princess Ella Kochubey was a great horsewoman who bred Russian pacemakers. Her stud was famous in the entire country. During the first months of the Revolution, the peasants burned the palace and the stables and butchered all the horses. But today, the pacemaker breed has been restored by the Soviet government.

In spite of the impressive setting, life at Dikanka was actually very simple. Like that of all the country estates, big and small, it consisted of horseback riding and excursions into the steppes or forests for picnics.

At night, there was crayfish catching by torchlight. Compared to the entertainments of young millionaires in France or America, they were extremely limited. A great event was the arrival of my brother, Grisha, with Tatara, the Prince's son, in an automobile. They had covered a distance of over a thousand miles, from Moscow to Poltava, a tremendous feat considering the cars available in those days and the Russian dirt roads. The car had chains on its tires to keep it from skidding in the thick dust which covered these roads in dry summers and was as hazardous as snow.

There were many houseguests gathered at Dikanka; the Prince and Princess' friends, and Tatara and Grisha's fellow students. Though simple in most of their ways, the Kochubeys entertained lavishly at table. We had truly gargantuan meals; the meat, the dairy products, fruits and vegetables, all came from the estate and were deliciously prepared. We had Ukrainian and Russian and French dishes and caviar in large jars, and pots of fresh crayfish soup, which is a delicacy in the Ukraine. Wines and vodka were served, as well as peach, apricot and cherry homemade brandies. The Prince, always a busy man on his estate, did not overindulge and saw that the young people remained sober. Only once, I recall, he gave Miss Mac some extra vodka to see "how she would take it." Dear Mac obediently emptied her glass, winced, stood up on her feet — not without difficulty — and turning angrily on her host, forbade him ever to play such a trick on her again!

But the best food and drink I remember at Dikanka, was not what we had during those sumptuous meals, but the ones we had in the fields when we rode out to watch the old Prince supervising his harvest.

He had introduced McCormick harvesting machines when most Russian landowners still resorted to outdated methods and back-breaking peasant labor. Prince Victor was an experienced, thrifty and far-sighted man and his estate was a model of good farming. He would spend most of his day in the growing and harvesting of his immeasurable fields of wheat, rye and barley. When we joined him at noon, we shared with him and the harvesters the millet porridge, cooked in earthen jars, and drank the icy water brought from a nearby brook. The blue, cloudless sky of the vast fertile Ukraine was like a glorious dome over our heads. Somewhere, high above us, a skylark sang.

The two weeks spent at Dikanka were exciting and gay, or at least they could have been so, had it not been for a strange growing feeling of depression that crept into my heart. Was it the immensity of the steppes stretching as far as the eye could see, and as mysterious as the ocean? Or was it a foreboding of some approaching terrible event, the doom of a people which I sensed in spite of the dazzling Ukrainian sun? I can not say exactly what caused this anxiety, but I very clearly remember it, as the end of that month grew near.

Then came the news that the Archduke Ferdinand and his wife had been assassinated in Sarajevo on June 28. It was the first step in a series of events that started World War I. The golden age was coming to an end.

CHAPTER VIII

War – The "Hôpital Russe"

THE FIRST TREMORS of the approaching earthquake were scarcely felt during those high summer days at Dikanka. News traveled slowly and no warnings came from my own family. I even received permission to prolong my stay in Russia and visit my cousins at the Golun estate. So I left Dikanka accompanied by my faithful Mac while Grisha left to hunt in the Bavarian Alps and to join Mother at *La Chère Villa*.

Looking back upon those days, I still wonder how it was that my father let my brother go to Germany, where trouble was brewing, and did not recall me from Russia, where tensions were rising. The European chancelleries seemed as yet unaware of the dangers arising from the Sarajevo assassination. If France, Russia and England had wanted a war, as some historians have suggested, they would not have timed it at this period of complete unpreparedness.

Meanwhile, Father had left for Petersburg, where he was to escort President Poincaré of France, with his Premier, René Viviani, to pay an official visit to the Tsar. On July 20, he joined Foreign Minister Sazonav, and the French Ambassador to Russia, Maurice Paléologue, on an Admiralty yacht which transported them to the Peterhof harbor. Tsar Nicholas, wearing an Admiral's uniform, arrived on his own yacht, the *Alexandria*, and had luncheon on board, with Sazonav, Father and Paléologue. Poincaré's ship came into view just as coffee was served. The guns of both yachts and shore batteries fired a salute; the French and Russian anthems resounded in the harbor. There were cheers from thousands of spectators as the French President stepped on board the *Alexandria*. There, seated at the stern of the Imperial Yacht, Poincaré immediately entered upon a conference with the Tsar.

In the evening there was a gala dinner at the Peterhof Palace at which the Empress was present. She had a tense smile on her lips, her face was flushed, betraying some secret agitation, as was often the case when she appeared in public.

On that very night, there was a brawl between the French sailors who went ashore, and the crew of the *Alexandria* who were on leave. Petersburg society made jokes about the incident, and also about Mr.

Viviani, who belonged to the extreme left of French government circles, and was scarcely "in tune" with the Russian autocrat he was visiting.

But Poincaré seemed to enjoy the pomp and circumstance with which he was being received. He offered presents to the Tsar and his family, including an automobile with gold fittings, and diamond watch-bracelets for the four grand duchesses.

During a reception at the Winter Palace, the diplomatic corps was presented to the French chief of staff whose cheerfulness was dampened when he was told that the Serbian minister had informed the British ambassador that a note from Austria was about to be sent to Serbia. Nor did he feel reassured when the Austrian ambassador told him point-blank that Austria held Serbia responsible for the Sarajevo assassination. Poincaré answered with a few prudent words. He did not know that the Austrian ultimatum had already been drafted. The text had been received by Germany's Foreign Minister, Herr von Jagow, and by Germany's Ambassador to Russia, Count Pourtalès.

On July 23rd, all unaware of the ultimatum soon to be made official, the Tsar and his French guests attended a military parade where Russia's elite troops marched by, saluting the grandstand, while Sikorsky's huge warplane, the *Ilya Murometz,* designed for a twelve-man crew, flew overhead. It was named after the hero of an ancient Russian epic song and everyone was impressed. Poincaré made a speech about "Peace in honor, strength and self-respect."

That very night, the French party boarded their ship, the warship *France,* and steamed out of the harbor. It was bound for Sweden, the next country to be visited by the President. While at sea, late at night, the news of the ultimatum delivered by Austria to Serbia came over the radio. Poincaré, unperturbed, continued his voyage to Stockholm.

As soon as the news of the ultimatum reached Father he took the first train to Paris. Before leaving, he sent a telegram to Golun telling me to leave immediately for Tegernsee.

I received the telegram on July 24th, which was my birthday and also the feast of Saint Olga, the name of my aunt and a cousin, also at Golun. We were in the middle of a festive meal when the telegram arrived. Surely, this meant bad news. I asked Aunt Masha to let me have a carriage and horses to get to the station. But my aunt declared that no horses were available, as they had just brought guests from the station. I spent a sleepless night, and the next morning asked again for horses. Again she refused. "Why, you have just arrived," she objected. In the afternoon, our mail arrived by horseback. The newspaper from Petersburg carried headlines about the ultimatum. But only the next day Aunt Masha, still reproachful at our leaving, allowed us to get the horses harnessed to catch the only daily train for Moscow.

After an hour at a fast pace, one of the horses stumbled. Our coachman examined his foreleg and said we could continue, but at a slower pace. We felt sure we would miss the train, but when we got to the station we were surprised to see the engine and coaches standing there, with many people crowding around them. We were told that a woman had committed suicide by throwing herself under the wheels as the train entered the station. Tolstoy had witnessed just such a scene at a small station near Tula and this tragedy had inspired him to write *Anna Karenina*. Horrified as we were, we realized that this tragic episode enabled us to reach Moscow and from there, to take a night train to Germany before it was too late.

Russia was already mobilizing. After a long wait at the frontier we got into a small compartment and continued to Berlin. Only later, we realized that ours was the last train to leave the country. After more delays, we were able to travel through Germany to Munich, on the very day that the *Kriegsgefahr* — the state of war — was declared throughout Germany and Bavaria. It was July 31, 1914.

Mother and Grisha met us in Munich having come by car from Tegernsee. No train reservations could be had to Paris; Mother decided that we must drive, but first we must return to pack what belongings we could take with us from our *La Chère Villa*. All night we packed. Our German staff was paid and dismissed. We had a French chauffeur and footman, and Grisha, all of military age. We heard that anti-Russian feelings were running high. Grisha was suspected of being a Russian spy, while pretending to be out hunting in the Alps.

In the morning, we all rose early and started to load our car. There were a few moments left before our departure. I ran over to say goodbye to one of my German girlfriends, Mousie Berckheim, who lived across the lane. Mousie and her brothers had been my playmates during many past summers. She came down to meet me in her dressing gown. I will always remember her, a small, forlorn figure, motionless, dramatic. I seized her hand: "O, Mousie," I exclaimed, "this is too dreadful, are we going to be enemies?" But we both knew that this could never be, and we parted with words of friendship, as Armageddon was rolling up our little lane. Mousie's brother, a submarine commander, went down with his ship in a sea battle, and I never saw any of the Berckheims again. But they always remained in my heart, the best of friends.

If ever there was a guardian angel at our side, it was surely on that day, August 1st, as we rolled along the dusty highway. More and more uniformed men began to appear at frequent checkpoints and military convoys moved slowly northward. In the evening we reached Constanza, the frontier town on the lake, with Switzerland in sight. Here our chauffeur reported that we were out of gas and could not get permission for refueling except from the local *Kommandatur*. Our hearts sank, for the town seemed in turmoil and people surrounding our French car (one of the early Renaults) began to grumble. This was when Mother suddenly revealed her spirit of decision and courage. She asked to be directed to the *Kommandatur,* all of us following in silence. There she said she wanted to speak to the general in charge. Hearing that there was a lady waiting, he gallantly stepped out of his office, into the square, where we stood in awe. With her most charming smile, she said that she must leave Germany immediately to join her husband in Paris, where he was Russian Ambassador. She mentioned her cousin Durckheim, well-known in Bavaria. While she was negotiating, an officer on a motorcycle thundered into the square. Dismounting and saluting he said he had a most urgent message for the *Herr Kommandant.* He started to report, but the general interrupted him, telling him to stand by, as he once more turned his attention to my mother, who renewed her plea: "I must get to Paris, please give me gas."

The general argued that even if we got gas, we were not allowed to travel at night under the *Kriegsgefahr* rules, nor, as potential aliens, could we stay at the hotel. Our arrest seemed imminent. Other Russians traveling in Germany at that time, including the dowager Empress, our friend Maria Fedorovna, had been molested and even stoned. We were more fortunate. To the General's objections, Mother imposed her simple logic: "Since we cannot travel by night, you must give us rooms." And the general did so, saluting politely. Then he turned to hear the messenger's report. In a loud voice, he declared, "Germany has declared war on Russia." Then he jumped on his motorcycle and thundered away. At the sound of that departure, it seemed to me that the very heavens were coming down over my head. I heard the crash of a world that would never again be the same.

I am sure that the general knew what that report contained, but as long as he had not heard it officially, he could still issue us the necessary permits. Early the next morning we were able to leave Germany without further ado. But strangely enough, new complications arose in Switzerland. This neutral country was mobilizing its small but efficient army for its own protection and there were more checkpoints and inspections. We spent two more days and nights on the road and, on entering France, were slowed by military convoys and troops jamming the highways. We arrived in Paris on August 3rd — the day that Germany declared war on France.

Driving into our Embassy courtyard, we found a dense crowd milling around the doors of the consulate. These were the Russian residents of Paris who had come with various claims—hundreds of them, wealthy tourists, businessmen stranded in the French capital without money. A moratorium had been set on money transactions and all the banks closed until further orders. But the people gathered in the courtyard were mostly the *émigrés* of the clothing district, of Russian-Jewish descent, or political, middle-class exiles who had to verify their status in a country at war.

When we entered the Embassy hall, Father rushed to meet us. He was in a state of extreme agitation and anger, blaming me for our delay and not even listening to my explanation as to how Aunt Masha had refused to give us transportation for two days.

But Father had many reasons for being upset; the whole world was in a turmoil and one dramatic event followed another. The day after our arrival, Belgium was invaded; England declared war on Germany and prepared to send an expeditionary force to France. I must repeat that not once during those days which I so clearly remember, did I hear my father rejoice over the military developments taking place, nor show the militant attitude of which he has been unjustly accused.[1]

In the meantime, the crowd in our courtyard kept growing day by day. Most of these people were destitute; they needed money, food and clothing. We organized a relief center in one of our basements and I went down to join the volunteer workers. I suddenly realized that, at last, I was doing something that "made sense," bringing me closer to my fellowmen. It was as if I had previously seen them through a windowpane. Now I was one of them.

The stranded aristocrats and financiers were received in a special room, by the Embassy staff. They took out loans to pay their hotel bills and obtain transportation to Russia. But all communications were cut off; the only route possible was by ship to the port of Murmansk, but even that itinerary was uncertain and there was a long waiting list for passengers. There were complaints, tears, supplications. Among the applicants was Mr. Kh., one of Russia's richest men. All he could obtain from the embassy funds was a modest sum for his most urgent expenses.

We were not the only ones to offer relief to forlorn travelers. Some four thousand Americans were also stranded in Paris and the United States Ambassador, Myron Herrick, distributed relief funds and did what he could to arrange their return home. He, himself, was actually caught in the storm. After Woodrow Wilson's election to the presidency, he was to be replaced by Ambassador Sharpe, after considerable delay. Herrick had to await a ship to take him home, so it was decided that he should continue to exercise his functions until Sharpe arrived. This he did with his usual tact and generosity. He was extremely popular among the Americans in Paris as well as with all the members of the diplomatic corps.

A relief worker who helped out in our basement canteen was Alexander Trubnikov, a curator of the Petersburg Museum of the Hermitage. He specialized in the study of the great masters of the Dutch school of painting. He, too, was awaiting passage on that elusive ship to Mur-

---
1. See the *Memoirs of Alexander Iswolsky: Formerly Russian Minister of Foreign Affairs and Ambassador to France.* Edited and translated by Charles Louis Seeger. See also, *The Politics and Diplomacy of A.P. Iswolsky* by William L. Mathes, Academic International Press, Box 555, Gulf Breeze, FL 32561, 1974.

mansk, but instead of lamenting he spent long hours in the midst of the crowd, serving soup and coffee. I enjoyed his company for he was a very charming, highly cultivated man with a great sense of humor. He finally left for Russia and I saw little of him for the next twenty-two years, but strangely enough we came together in Paris, just before the fall of France in 1939. Once more, he was intent on getting out of the city and since I had good connections in the south of France, he asked me to help him get to a safer place, where I, myself, was going. I last saw him in 1960 when he was in his eightieth year and I was far from resembling the young girl in the Embassy basement. We started to reminisce, but could only exclaim with one voice: "Two World Wars, two dramatic departures from Paris—that is too much!"

Many political exiles came to the consulate; they were socialists who had been opposed to serving in the Tsarist army or taking any part in Tsarist politics or diplomacy. But they had been caught up in the wave of emotion which had swept over their comrades in Russia. Many of them hoped for an amnesty which would permit them to return home and enlist. But communications were still cut off, and so they were enlisted in the French Foreign Legion. Many displayed great courage at the front and a number were killed in action.

There were also elderly political exiles who could not be in active service but who also hoped for amnesty, in order to make themselves useful at home and regain some kind of social status. I remember one of them who, surprisingly enough, bore a famous historic title. He was a descendant of Count Nesselrode, who represented the Tsar at the Congress of Vienna in 1814 and 1815. He is also remembered by a gourmet dessert named after him (Nesselrode pudding)!

The descendant of this statesman was a convinced socialist and had lived many years in Paris, as a "dangerous" political foe of the Tsarist regime. He was a tall, extremely handsome old gentleman with noble features and silver hair, and resembled my Uncle Constantine. All the political exiles were not as distinguished and romantic-looking as Count Nesselrode, but they certainly had a conspiratorial air about them. Among them were men and women who had led a migrant existence for years. As they turned to me for help they produced identity papers and many among them had several passports, each with a different name. I was thrilled to discover this mysterious population and did my best to win their confidence.

Since Grisha was also of age to be drafted but could not get to Russia, he was enrolled as a private in the Foreign Legion, like all the other Russian nationals in France. He went off cheerfully to the recruiting station, and was soon sent to the front. We heard very little from him during the next two or three months and had no idea where he was since the movements of troops were kept strictly secret. Later, we learned that his regiment had been sent to join General Lanrezac's Fifth Army, which was engaged in combat by von Gluck, and defeated before the month of August was over.

It has been noted by all historians of that period that the people of France and the people of Russia displayed the same spirit of exalted patriotism in their common effort to resist the enemy. Perhaps this is difficult to believe in the light of subsequent events, and for those who did not observe it personally. But it remains a fact that all parties in Russia (except the Bolsheviks under Lenin) were united in August 1914. As for the French, their pacifism had retreated after the assassination of Jaurès (Socialist leader) and the soldiers marched off to the war with flowers stuck in the barrels of their rifles and their women waving frantically. Enthusiasm also accompanied the departure of the Russian soldiers who had enlisted in the French army, immediately at the outbreak of war. Most of them were left-wing socialists who had left Russia to avoid service in the tsarist army. But now, like their brothers in their native land, they had been swept into the patriotic wave. Lenin and his followers remained in their antiwar positions. But the majority of the political exiles in France believed, as their joint declaration stated, that the "defeat of the rulers of Germany and Austria will inevitably mark the victory of democracy." [2]

With this conviction in their minds, the Russian volunteers were enrolled in the only French army unit that accepted them, the Foreign Legion, the famous military force brought over from its African base and composed of men belonging to all nations and backgrounds, including adventurers, jail-birds, and riff-raff from everywhere. The *Légionnaires*, shown on the movie screen in their romantic glory, were in reality a tough and ruthless breed. Their commanders, at least many of them, were known for their brutal and inhuman treatment of their subordinates. Some of these commanders were former German criminals which made service even harder for the volunteers. A few of them rebelled and were shot or condemned to hard labor. Others tried to be transferred to other units, but were refused, and accepted the hardships imposed on them. They fought courageously and many of them died heroically. Their story has remained almost unrecorded and mostly forgotten. I want to speak of it here, because their idealism and sacrifice has never been sung by historians of World War I, which is rapidly receding into the past of another era.

But in those days, we were entering into the most disastrous period of the early months of the war. The rapidity of events was overwhelming. It was something like being on board a ship, supposedly safe on the high seas, and then being torpedoed and about to sink. Before we

---

2. I found a small brochure by Lydia Krestovskaya entitled: *History of the Russian Volunteer Movement* published by Éditions J. Povolotsky, Paris (no date). I knew the author personally and remember her collecting the material for her booklet with great devotion.

were fully aware of what was happening, Liège and Namur had fallen; the German army had swept through Belgium. Brussels was occupied and the Belgian government took refuge in France, making its headquarters at Le Havre. Uncle Vania Kudashev, who was then Ambassador to King Albert, was also moved to Le Havre. Tales of horror and devastation came in from the occupied territories and refugees crowded the roads. The tragic situation inspired Debussy's "Song of the Children of Belgium": *"Nous n'avons plus de maisons."* ("We no longer have any homes.") A theme which, alas, has had to be repeated many times in many countries, but Debussy's sad little song seems to have been forgotten.

Sometimes the strains of the *Marseillaise* and *Sambre-et-Meuse* drowned out the bad news pouring in. The French armies, including General Lanrezac's forces which had engulfed Grisha and his fellow *Legionnaires*, were retreating. And on the Eastern front, the Russian army had suffered a crushing defeat at Tannenberg (mentioned earlier). The toll was staggering — 30,000 men killed or missing; over 90,000 taken prisoner; two generals committed suicide and several others surrendered to the Germans — the debacle being due to the fatal blunder of the high command.

Among the victims were the soldiers and officers of the Tsar's elite regiments — many of my partners of the debutante balls of less than a year ago, and my first love, Dimitri. Nobody has described the tragedy more vividly than the great Russian writer Alexander Solzhenitsyn, comparing the scene to a blood-soaked threshing of human bodies, a precious harvest sacrificed in vain — but not entirely — the commander in chief and his staff could no longer boast that the Russian armies would be in Berlin in a few weeks. But neither could the German high command be sure that it would be feasting in Paris that fall, as it had previously declared. In order to check the Russian advance in East Prussia, and confirm the Tannenberg victory, the Germans had to withdraw two army corps from the Western front, a maneuver which permitted the French to make a stand, and achieve what was called "the Miracle of the Marne."

The chain of events has been described by historians of World War I. Of course we could not see the whole picture so clearly, but we could feel the terrible sword of doom hanging over our heads. When the first German airplanes appeared over Paris, they were called ironically enough *tauben*, the German word for "doves" and pronounced by the French as *"les tobes"* with a sinister intonation. The tiny planes, high in the clouds, appeared several times but did little damage to the city, though they killed several civilians, and brought the war much closer. However, nobody panicked. Paris remained calm even when it was rumored that the spearhead of German cavalry, *Les Uhlans*, had been seen at Compiègne, 25 miles from the capital. The French government and the military command then realized the danger. It was clear that Paris could not be defended, nor declared an "open city." After rapid consultations it was decided to evacuate the President, members of the Cabinet, the personnel of the Ministries and diplomatic corps, except those of the American and Spanish Embassies who would take over the affairs of the absent diplomats.

We were notified of this at noon of September 2nd and told that we must be ready to leave on a train for Bordeaux at 10:30 that night. We started to pack, while the Embassy staff began burning or destroying all documents which could not be taken along.

When we boarded our train, we found that eight compartments had been assigned to the Russian Embassy staff, while the British had only three at their disposal. (Sir Francis Bertie, the British Ambassador, noted this in his *Memoirs* with some irritation.)

As we started to move, the tall figure of Myron Herrick, the American Ambassador, appeared in front of our window. He was wearing his official frock coat and top hat. He solemnly removed his headgear, to wave us goodbye. I will always remember his graying, curly hair and friendly smile as he stood bareheaded on the platform, his dark, Spanish colleague by his side. It was as if they were part of a funeral procession.

While the government and the diplomats were on their way to Bordeaux, under strict orders, other panic-stricken individuals had arranged a private exodus. As no trains were available, they were crowded into cars, and one of them hired a taxicab. It must have been the last one available, for soon all Paris taxis were requisitioned to transport troops to the front, a bold maneuver which reinforced the army, faltering under German pressure, and made the stand on the Marne possible.

Only a minority, the rich and the influential, participated in this flight to Bordeaux. The main population of Paris remained at home, showing remarkable calm and resignation. They looked down upon the fugitives and with the usual Parisian wit, found a name for us. We were called *"tournedos,"* a famous Bordeaux dish consisting of specially prepared "turned-over steak" which could also signify people who had turned their backs, to run away. There was a feeling that the government had also done this.

Our *tournedos* train made good time and we were not intercepted by the *Uhlans,* as had been feared. While we were traveling by rail, the caravan of official and unofficial cars proceeded as well. A number of people managed to get transportation, without permit, including some ladies of questionable reputation and there was much criticism of their indiscretions. There were humorous incidents as well, such as the story of a chauffeur who was asked to carry a pet monkey and a parrot; the monkey opened the parrot's cage and let it fly away, causing havoc all around!

The municipality of Bordeaux received us with great courtesy. Each Embassy and Legation was assigned to a private house. We were offered one of the most beautiful homes in this ancient and wealthy city. It had a staircase designed by a famous, 18th century architect. It was classified as an historic monument. However, the house did not have enough space for our large staff and the family, so my father was invited to move our personal living quarters to a country estate a few miles outside of the city. This was a chateau belonging to the Cruse family, well-known wine-makers. Their bottled wine bore the name of our residence, *Château Giscours,* and its owner's name is still important in the international wine market.

A few miles from Giscours lay the estate of the Pillet-Will family, Château Margaux, which produced the greatest of Bordeaux wines. The Duchess la Trémoille's brother was owner of the estate, so she and her husband came to stay with him. She resumed her role of playing hostess and Paris *tournedos* society gathered around her.

It was the time of the *vendange*, the grape harvest, followed by the making of the great wines. Every day, cart loads of grapes were brought in and crushed in the huge sheds of Giscours, Margaux, Mouton-Rothschild and all the other wineries of the Bordeaux region. The rich juices began to ferment in the giant vats and the air was filled with pungent, almost inebriating odors. There was something Rabelaisian in this atmosphere of superabundance and it also pervaded the city of Bordeaux which was enjoying a boom. The *Chapon Fin,* most famous of its restaurants, was crowded at lunch and dinner, serving authentic *tournedos* and mushrooms *à la Bordelaise,* to cabinet ministers, diplomats and all the gourmets of the exodus crowd.

But in spite of all these gastronomic revelries, there was a grim feeling of expectation as the news from the front brought little reassurance. True, Paris had not been occupied by the Germans, but it lay bare and undefended as the enemy advance continued. Father, who commuted to Paris, would return with no words of comfort. It was as if a heavy curtain had suddenly been drawn, separating us from the familiar world we had known; our home, Paris, and the French countryside which we had grown to love, had now become the "theater of war" where a crushing defeat was imminent and where Grisha had become a ghost.

During those anxious days, Mother was kept busy by a project which took our minds away from the feeling of helplessness in the face of disaster. Here was something we could do to help.

The Russian Embassy had been entrusted with a large donation from the dowager Empress, to establish a military hospital for the French soldiers. The wealthy Louit family, owner of a chocolate firm in Bordeaux, offered a building for the hospital; it was the Louit's summer residence, the Château Dulamon, located on a vast estate. It had many rooms and halls and was equipped for many guests and personnel. Mother had quickly assembled a medical, surgical and nursing staff. There were both military and civilian doctors and a number of registered nurses. I was allowed to volunteer as an auxiliary nurse, having proudly produced my Red Cross diploma. The first wounded were arriving in Bordeaux and we immediately got ready to receive them.

Mother held a meeting to organize the purchase of equipment and the various activities on which the work of the hospital depended. It was to be called the *Hôpital Russe,* and our aim was to produce services of the highest quality. At this meeting, a beautiful, strikingly dressed woman suddenly appeared. She was so tall that we all felt like pygmies around her, and her slim figure was extraordinarily graceful. She wore a complete Red Cross nurse's uniform, (which none of our personnel had yet donned) but instead of twill, it was made of the finest white silk, and the veil was lightly poised on top of an elaborate *coiffure*. She wore a large red cross on her bosom and another one on her veil, and introduced herself as Madame Ida Rubinstein. Then we realized that our mysterious visitor was none other than the famous actress, mime and ballerina who had made a sensational debut a few years before, as Salomé, in the play by Oscar Wilde. Madame Rubinstein presented mother with a large check as a contribution to the hospital and promised more gifts to come. She then retired, with a queenly bow, as we watched her in mute admiration. We later learned that her uniform had been designed and executed for this one occasion by the great couturier Worth. When the hospital began to function, she did not return to visit the wounded. But she did keep her promise and was lavish in her gifts, in one instance, sending colorful pajamas for the officers' ward.

After the war, I saw Madame Rubinstein often, in plays and at her private home in Paris. Her generosity was then extended to artists, musicians and writers. (She played an important part in the development of modern art, and in Paris had a fabulous collection of her own. — Ed.)

At the end of her life, Ida Rubinstein, whose great wealth and theatrical career had brought her but little happiness, turned to religion. Of Russian-Jewish descent, she had become a convert to Catholicism and lived in retirement in Vence, not far from the chapel decorated by Matisse. I shall always remember her with gratitude; for all her eccentricities, she was a noble and compassionate soul.

I can remember the day when Father came back from his Bordeaux office and said that the German advance had been stalled. But there was not much cause for celebration when the facts of war grew more apparent as the first convoy of wounded arrived at the *Hôpital Russe*.

It was a shocking sight. The men were borne on stretchers or hobbled on crutches, with blood-stained bandages and mud-caked uniforms and boots. It may seem unbelievable but the French infantry soldiers wore bright red pants, an easy target for the enemy. The light blue, so-called horizon blue uniforms had not yet been introduced; the first convoys were horribly mutilated. Field hospitals and transportation had not been adequate to cope with the casualties; most of them arrived unattended or with improper dressings and various degrees of infections. The worst ones were *tetanos* or gaseous gangrene leading to death, or in some cases, to immediate amputations. There was no sulfa, no penicillin in those days, so the broken, mutilated bodies just had to take their chances, which were slim.

If soldiers at the front receive their baptism of fire, in those first dreadful hours, I received my baptism of pain and horror; whatever was left of the "debutante" I had been fell apart with the tattered uniforms and purulent bandages of these convoys from the Marne.

There was a man on that battlefield who was not brought to the *Hôpital Russe,* because he was struck and killed by a bullet where he was standing; this was the great Catholic poet and writer Charles Péguy. I had not heard about him in those days, and could not suspect that he would deeply influence me and some of my dearest friends, in the future.

Although Paris was no longer threatened after the Marne victory, the government was advised not to return as yet to the capital. So it remained in Bordeaux for three more months, and so did, of course, its satellite diplomatic corps. The prolonged absence of the *tournedos* was frowned upon by the Parisians.

We came back to our Paris Embassy in January, 1915. Though it was good to be home, the setback suffered by the Germans had brought only temporary relief. Almost overnight, the Marne had changed the trend of military activities. It brought the trench war—both sides frozen into positions facing each other.

Paris, too, had changed. It had acquired a severe, unsmiling atmosphere. Many families had already lost their kin. The men who came for a few days to the city on leave were now wearing "horizon blue" uniforms, but looked harassed or exhausted. There was little relaxation for them, for nightclubs and shows were closed down, the streets were darkened at night, cafés and bars were shuttered, and blackouts ordered at the least threat of air raids.

Grisha came back for a short stay with us. He had been in the midst of troop movements around the Marne. He, too, looked harassed and confused in the unfamiliar background of the Foreign Legion. Luckily he was detached from his unit and sent as interpreter and secretary to Count Ignatiev, the military attaché whose headquarters were near the front, in liaison with the French Army Command.

Ignatiev, who was not in sympathy with my father, for reasons I am not able to explain, liked Grisha well enough. He speaks of him in his memoirs as a "young man filled with humor" and adds: "I took him into the office because he had *not* shown himself to be a coward during the retreat of the Sixth Army." (Evidently, some of Grisha's comrades had done so.) My brother displayed his sense of humor by giving imitations of his superior officers, including Ignatiev himself, and to his face. He was never unkind in his mimicry, but irresistibly funny. When on leave, he would drop in to see us and tell us amusing tales, not exactly for the general's ears. Ignatiev had a most unflattering opinion of Général Joffre, commander in chief of the French armed forces, stating that a man of low birth could not make a military leader. He referred to the commander as "that son of a cooper" (maker of barrels and casks) ignorant of the fact that Joffre had precisely the qualities of a French artisan, solid, wise and practical, which had made him the winner on the Marne.

Count Ignatiev, a tall, handsome, broad-shouldered man with a proud, military bearing, had a certain cheerfulness and charm which attracted the ladies. Estranged from his wife, the lovely Mimi, *née* Okhotnikova, a great favorite among Parisian socialites, the Count was romantically involved elsewhere and corresponded with this lady through the field telegraph. Grisha had great fun receiving their love messages. After the war, Ignatiev married the dancer Trukhanova, who had appeared in a ballet suite at one of our embassy garden parties. A practical and ambitious woman, she persuaded her husband to return to Russia, under Soviet rule. He became inspector of military schools training cadets for the Red Army. He rubbed shoulders with many a military commander whose ancestry was more like General Joffre's than his own. His family disowned him, but I felt and still do, that he returned to his homeland, not because of any Communist affiliation, but because of his deep love of Russia.

Although not a great strategist, Count Ignatiev was a professional soldier, and as military attaché he had proved his mettle. This could not be said of his assistant, Colonel Osnobishin, who in peacetime was aide-de-camp to a member of the Imperial family. He had been in charge of the Prince's festivities, specialized in Gypsy songs and knew little about military affairs. When the Germans started their bombardments of allied positions with a new type of artillery, my father asked the colonel about the calibre of the guns. The colonel could not make any precise answer, but made the classic gesture of a fisherman who boasted of a big catch. Father was adamant, but could get no better answer. From that time on, if not before, he began to have great doubts about the efficiency of the Russian military *cadres*. Alas, as the war dragged on and on, the Russian army's failures became more and more apparent. Colonel Osnobishin's gesture became symbolic of approaching disaster.

On the French front the war took an ever heavier toll. The *Hôpital Russe* was transferred from the Bordeaux region to Paris. It was allocated the Hotel Carlton on the Champs Elysées. It was a splendid setup and the greatest brain surgeon of France, Dr. Thierry de Martel, was appointed chief of our medical staff. So casualties with the most severe head wounds were brought to us, as well as other critical cases for Dr. de Martel was also a master of general surgery. This great and profoundly humane physician lost a son in the war. He served selflessly, in the operating theatre and in the wards, saving many lives. But when World War II broke out, and Paris was occupied by Hitler's armies, he committed suicide.

As soon as our hospital was transferred to Paris, I resumed my duties as nurse. I was assigned to the small rooms and suites formerly occupied by the wealthiest residents of the hotel and now reserved for the heaviest casualties. Many were brought to us for major operations, and recovered. Others died before having been treated, and then there were the paraplegics, who lived, and went on living, as half-men. There were the great battles: Ypres, Artois, Champagne, Aisne, Verdun. Each of them meant more convoys of wounded, more torn and maimed bodies. As I read the names of those historic battles, they recall to me such and such a man, such and such an operation and the long days of suffering in between.

One day, one seemingly quite hopeless case was brought to my attention and placed in a separate room we kept for the dying. It was quite a young man who had been blinded by a burst of shrapnel, and had other injuries as well. To my surprise, he could not speak French, but only German. He came from Lorraine which was under German rule, but had deserted to join the French army. Thanks to my knowledge of German, I could communicate with him and help rekindle the tiny flame of life which was still flickering in his skeletal frame. It was almost a miracle that he did not die that night, nor the next day, and we gradually brought him back to life.

His name was Joseph Meyer; he became not only my patient, but my pupil, for he had to learn everything anew because of his total blindness. When he was strong enough to sit up in bed, I taught him the gestures of feeding himself, and when he could get out of bed, helped him with his first steps. I studied Braille in order to show him the signs and he soon learned to read and write. We also practiced French conversation in which he became quite fluent.

When Joseph had recovered sufficiently to leave the hospital, he was accepted as a resident of the Paris section of the American Lighthouse. He learned to make brushes and could earn a living. He presented me with a clothes brush, with my initials spun into it. Years later, when I came to live in America, during the Second World War, I spoke on the radio, a broadcast in French, and beamed to occupied Paris. Joseph was still plying his trade at the Lighthouse. He heard my name announced and recognized my voice immediately. He wrote me a letter full of warmth and gratitude. Of all my First World War soldier friends, it is Joseph, who knew me only by my voice, whom I remember most vividly.

But there are many others, too, whom I recall, not as much as individuals, but as a group of unique and wonderful people: the French peasants and workers. I came close to them when I was transferred to the larger wards, the former ballrooms and restaurants of the Carlton. These spacious halls were occupied by hundreds of soldiers who had been slightly wounded and were making a quick recovery. They were a cheerful lot, whose good humor, wit and confidence persisted, even though, immediately upon release, they might be sent back to the front. They rarely complained, rarely swore and treated their nurses with extreme respect and gratitude for the least care received. These men had a refinement such as I had seldom met in "high society."

In those days the French army had no chaplains. Young priests were drafted like any other citizen and were not allowed to minister in public. I had wounded priests in my ward but only knew their calling because of breviaries among their belongings. But there were always elderly clergymen who visited our men. They administered the last rites to the dying, and also held religious services. Most of the soldiers were Catholics and practiced their religion quite devoutly, especially the Bretons and the Basques. Sunday mass was celebrated in the lounge. I believe that it was the first time that I, as a Russian Orthodox, attended a Catholic service. I liked the simplicity and feeling of familiarity with which these men on their crutches or swathed in bandages, followed the Mass. More than once, I was working at the bedside of some patient, when the priest administered Extreme Unction or gave Communion to a dying man. I was discovering day by day the meaning of life and death, of suffering and the noble acceptance of it. Thus together with the realization of the infinite suffering and injustice caused by war, there came to me something like a faint awakening of faith, which I had long taken for granted but had remained dormant. Something that could illumine this darkness—but as yet it was only the spark of a flame that would later come to life.

Another very distinct and poignant memory of my experience at the *Hôpital Russe* was the friendship of Lieutenant M., a paraplegic condemned to his bed and later, to his wheelchair, with no hope of recovery. His large, blue eyes reflected the angelic beauty of his soul. He was the first to speak to me of Charles Péguy, and to make me read his poetry. M. lived only a short time after his release from the hospital. But his deep faith had, long before his death, opened the doors of that other world for him, which he entered as Péguy had, following the poet who had been his model and his inspiration. It was through M. that I, myself, was irresistibly drawn to Péguy, who was to have a decisive influence on my spiritual life, as he had on the lives of many young people of my generation.

The end of April, 1915, was marked for us by a family event. My brother Grisha, having wearied of clerical work in Ignatiev's headquarters, volunteered once more for active service at the front. He was attached as a liaison interpreter to the French Expeditionary Force which was to support the British landing on the shores of the Bosphorus, in order to seize the straits of the Dardanelles.

The French landed on the Asiatic shore at Kum Kale in an operation ending in disaster. The heavy casualties suffered by the expeditionary forces during the battle of Gallipoli and the final defeat of both British and French forces made one of the gloomiest pages of World War I. Providentially, Grisha was saved from the inferno. While carrying a message to British headquarters he was hit in the foot and evacuated to the rear. The wound was not severe, but incapacitated Grisha for several months. He was brought back to France, and thanks to the French military government, directed to the *Hôpital Russe*.

What a joy it was to see Grisha in one of our own wards. He was a sergeant and placed with other soldiers of his rank, among whom he immediately became popular, due to his jokes and friendliness. But he spoke of his latest war experience with horror. He showed us a letter from his unit's commander who had also been wounded, but much more grievously, than Grisha. I still have his letter:

> . . . I am still on my back and I suffer very much from my wound in the mouth and neck. At times, it drives me crazy. . . . Goodbye, little Grisha. In memory of the Baptism of Fire, where he was your godfather, your old general embraces you.
>
> Vandenberg.

While still laid up in his hospital bed, Grisha was informed that the regimental canteen owed him 130 francs, that he had been cited for a promotion to second lieutenant and awarded the *Croix de Guerre* and the *Médaille Militaire*. He took very little pride in his military achievements and could not forget the cries and moans of the wounded in the hold of the ship which transported the Kum Kale casualties to safety. His story, I believe, put an end forever to any enthusiasm for war still lingering in my heart. But the fighting went on and convoys continued to be brought to us.

During Grisha's stay at the *Hôpital Russe* President Poincaré visited our ward and started, so to speak, a chain reaction. Cold, stiff, devoid of the least trace of "charisma," the little, bearded man went from bed to bed with a frozen smile on his tight lips. The chain reaction was one of disappointment and an expression of irony on many faces. But the worst was yet to come.

Having learned that the Russian Ambassador's son was among the wounded, and in spite of his ill-concealed dislike of my father, Poincaré hastened to the ward where Grisha lay. The bed next to his was occupied by an Arab from a native Moroccan regiment. He had a severe skull injury and his head was heavily bandaged. He and Grisha had become great friends and they both watched with round eyes as the President's cortege marched through the hall. Stopping between the two beds, the President hesitated, then reached out for a bouquet carried by an attendant, and in his ringing voice, bent over the Arab's head: "Congratulations, Mr. Iswolsky." He then placed the bouquet in the Arab's arms, adding, "You must have had quite a suntan on the Bosphorus."

Someone whispered a few words in the President's ear, and he snatched the bouquet away from the Arab, giving it to Grisha and then hastily withdrew. The story was told to me by my brother exactly as I tell it here.

But it was not the only faux-pas committed by the President. He marched on down the hall to visit the blind Joseph Meyer. Once more, in that ringing voice, he made a speech about how "losing both eyes was a great and glorious sacrifice for *La Patrie*" (his country). Joseph had not yet been told that he had lost both eyes. He was still too weak to receive this blow and hoped that one eye might be saved. Once again, Poincaré walked on without seeing the terrible sight: Joseph's tears were flowing from empty sockets.

We all felt that it might be some solace to Joseph Meyer to receive the *Médaille Militaire*, but his papers were not in order; he had enlisted under another name, in case he was captured by the Germans, and there was no one to speak for his cause. Finally, all was arranged by a politician whose son had been wounded and who was in our officers' ward. He was Lazare Weiler, a member of the *Chambre des Députés*, a wealthy industrialist, with both practical and intellectual vision. He was also an art collector and the owner of a beautiful estate. He often came to visit his son and then came to our ward to see the blind Joseph. We struck up a friendship which lasted long after the war. He was a man of great charm, of old Alsatian-Jewish stock and I was captivated by his understanding and kindness. He was actually the first promoter of my literary career. Reading one of my translations from Russian into French, he complimented me on my style and choice of vocabulary and said, "You must write, Mademoiselle!" I was soon to follow his advice.

I must add a few more words about our most unusual staff which was mostly Russian. Many of my compatriots living in France who could not be drafted into the army, were serving in Red Cross units and were usually assigned to our wards in the Carlton. Some were former cooks of the grand dukes who had residences in Paris. They cooked excellent food for our wounded and Russian recipes became quite popular among the men.

Many Russian intellectuals who were working or studying in France when the war broke out became members of our staff. The section for disinfections was run by Jacob Povolotsky, publisher and owner of a bookstore, where in later years I came to browse. He was a Russian Jew, as was our pharmacist, whose wife worked in our wards.

The Stermans, Anatole and Fanya, brother and sister, were the most unforgettable characters among all my colleagues at the *Hôpital Russe*. They had come to Paris and enrolled in the School of Medicine without knowing any French, except a few colloquialisms. They studied the French language as they took courses at the School, and conquered the difficulties they encountered with superhuman courage and persistence. As soon as they mastered the language, they were absorbed not only in their studies but in French literature. They read voraciously and bought books with their meager savings. Their most-treasured acquisition was a complete set of Balzac's works.

Anatole's devotion to his profession was proverbial at the hospital. He gave up his own room, when the wards were overcrowded and slept on the table of the X-ray room. He would spend days and nights watching over critical cases, forgetting to eat. When I asked him why he insisted on fasting, he smiled and shrugged his shoulders, saying, "I do not usually abstain from food; I eat a lot, when I have time!"

The Stermans were both socialists, political exiles and fervent champions of revolution in the name of the oppressed, and for a just society for the people. I would listen spellbound to my new friend who would look at me with his dark owlish eyes through thick bifocals. He would say, "If you ever turn against us, I will not forgive you." How often, in later years, I remembered Anatole's words, and his dark eyes, full of compassion, yet ready to condemn me. My ideas may have changed in some ways, and developed since those days of youthful enthusiasm, but I can still say, "No, Anatole, I have not turned against you."

Other members of our staff who were politically inclined were not as idealistic as the Stermans, but were also quite convincing. In our spare hours, we used to assemble in the pharmacy and engage in lively discussions. We were quite unaware that one of our group was an informer. After the Revolution, when the secret files of the former Paris agent of the *Okhrana* were examined by a committee of the Provisional Government the reports of our pharmacy meetings were discovered. My words, scrupulously recorded read something like this: "When the war is over I want to be independent and do honest work like other people." In Chekov's play, *The Three Sisters*, the young girls also dream of work as a token of liberation. The *Okhrana* saw this as a danger.

Another unusual character on our hospital staff was a young male nurse, recommended by my friend Argutinsky. He was a gifted artist, very shy and withdrawn. He had great difficulty in adjusting himself to military life. His name was Ossip Zadkine, who was to become one of the best sculptors of modern times. He soon relaxed in our friendly atmosphere. When working in my ward at night, he would draw fantastic doodles, which I collected. After a few months of training with us, he was sent to a field hospital and brought back a series of drawings. They were no longer doodles but ghastly scenes of suffering and death which he saw at the front. Being a mere private and as yet unknown in artistic circles, Zadkine was given the hardest jobs. The caricaturist Albert Forain, famous for his political cartoons, adored by the public at large, and feared by the establishment, was also in uniform but he had a pleasant job, assigned to "Camouflage."

A strange incident in our ward opened my eyes to certain undercurrents of opinion of which I had been completely ignorant. It was my twentieth birthday and some wounded natives of Tunis, of Jewish origin, offered me a bouquet of flowers. We were photographed together and the picture fell into the hands of a journalist of an extreme right, anti-Semitic paper who published it with a column accusing the *Hôpital Russe*, and the daughter of the Russian Ambassador, of showing favoritism to Jews at the expense of their French comrades. This attack was so ridiculous that we paid no attention to it. Yet it troubled me. It was my first taste of anti-Semitism — a dark spot in the *Hôpital Russe* experience. As an old Russian proverb says, "a spoonful of tar can spoil a barrel of honey."

As months dragged into years, all dreams of glory faded and the harsh reality of a deadlock stared us in the face. On the Western Front, almost at our doors, began the mud of the trenches, the ratholes, the desolate no man's land, torn by bombardments, moon craters left by bursting shells, the ghost-like woods with crippled trees and charred stumps. A little farther away were the forts and barbed-wired defenses of Verdun, with desperate offensives, to "break through" mostly in vain, and in the air the dogfights between the French ace Guynemer, and the German Red Baron (now remembered by a Lufthansa advertisement).

We, too, had our share of air war, which did not demand heroic deeds on our part, but were dramatic and eerie to behold, as Zeppelins appeared in the sky at night over Paris. They hung, like monstrous cigars, the beams of searchlights sweeping over them, and antiaircraft guns chasing them, while explosions shook the air. A Zeppelin bomb fell a few streets from us, hitting the Ministry of War and pock-marking the building. Little damage was done by these attacks on Paris, compared to those aimed at London. Far more tragic was the shelling of the French capital by the "Big Bertha," the giant, long-range artillery gun which hit toward the end of the war. Such an attack appeared incredible, and the shelling was first attributed to an air raid. Father himself did not believe in the existence of Big Bertha at first. But it made itself manifest with all its might on Good Friday, 1918, when one of its shells hit the Church of St. Gervais, killing a number of people assembled there for the solemn service.

Father would sometimes gather us all in the first floor parlor, for safety's sake and read to us from a book which he thought would improve our minds. It was a history of Byzantium. I must admit that I was not interested in this historic book, when the action was right outside our windows, heavily curtained for the blackouts. Outside, the *badauds*, as the Parisian "gapers" were called, stared into the sky over the darkened streets and boulevards, making ironic remarks and straining their eyes until the phantom cigar ended its performance, sometimes fleeing the flack or being destroyed by it. Grisha preferred to mix with the *badauds*, and did not join the family readings. He had not lost his sense of humor and told us that during one of the air raids he was out with his "date" who lost one of her earrings, a costly jewel. "Every one around us was looking upward," he said, "but we were bent double, searching the gutter . . . people thought we were crazy."

No one has described these eerie Paris blackouts better than Proust. No one seemed very afraid and the *badauds* kept us smiling. However, the German pressure on the front began to be felt more and more. It was wearing out the people's patience. There were too many bereaved families, too many war widows. Since full mourning attire was *de rigueur* in France, black crepe veils for the women and black armbands for men, it was impossible to hide the cruel facts from the public. Dissatisfaction was growing; there were bitter attacks in the leftist press against the *Marchands de Canons*, profiteers, who grew rich while men were being killed or maimed for life. The rightest, patriotic papers demanded more supplies and more men, and so the war industries intensified their efforts.

The news from Russia was even more ominous. We were involved not only in the tragedy of France, but in the oncoming revolution in our homeland, Russia.

CHAPTER IX

Endings and Beginnings

BY THE FALL of 1916, casualties in the Russian armies had reached more than one million killed, four million wounded and two million taken prisoner. There had been large territorial losses, with Poland and the Ukraine occupied by German forces. Even when military operations had been successful, the lack of guns, ammunition and war supplies was disastrous. During the great offensives, soldiers went into battle without rifles, waiting for a fellow combatant to be killed and then picking up his arms. The firing power of the German guns could scarcely be matched by their Russian counterparts, poor in quality and insufficient in numbers. The story is well-known and has often been recorded, as well as the incredible courage and endurance of the Russian soldiers. Alexander Solzhenitsyn has masterfully revived these tragic scenes and there is little that can be added to his picture.

Russian public opinion reacted strongly to the blunders of the government's highest authorities and to the palace intrigues which were impeding every plan to direct and intensify the war effort. Meanwhile, certain of his prestige and trusting to the almost mystic adoration of the Russian soldier for the God-appointed Orthodox ruler, the Tsar had assumed the high command of his army. He had actually taken the place of the Grand Duke Nicholas Nicholaevich, the military figure still enjoying true popularity among the army's rank and file. His demotion and banishment to a faraway post in the Caucasus had caused a disappointment which the Tsar's "mystical image" could not dispel.

Not only those in political circles, but religious figures such as the Very Reverend George Shavelsky, head chaplain of the armed forces, had known all along that the change of High Command was due mainly to the bitter opposition of Grand Duke Nicholas to Rasputin. The latter's unrestricted entries into the Imperial Palace and their disastrous effects created a growing anxiety among well-informed officials and military men. There were rumors of a lack of security, of German agents approaching Rasputin. Did this *éminence griese* in the garb of a *muzhik*, have access to military secrets?

By this time Rasputin's occult power, his influence at court, his uncanny, hypnotic hold over the Empress (while masquerading as a "holy man"), his unashamed behavior in nightclubs and in private homes had ceased to be a secret. He was deeply resented by Russian society and this resentment had become almost unanimous, except for a few groups belonging to court circles who still tried to refute the Rasputin story.

During the summer of 1916, diplomatic couriers and Russian military missions frequently came to Paris. A hopeful picture was brought to us by a parliamentary delegation, including members of the Duma and of the Council of State who arrived in Paris. A banquet was offered to the delegates by the League of Human Rights, presided over by the famous French writer Anatole France, but after their departure Russia's political sky grew darker and darker. Casualties at the front were increasing, catastrophe seemed inevitable; the question was, would it take place immediately or after the war? There was among us a freer discussion of things happening or yet to come.

After the dismissal of Foreign Minister Sazonav in July, and his replacement by Sturmer, noted representative of reaction, many aspects of our war diplomacy had become all too obvious. Sazonov had been dismissed because of his desire for Poland's independence. The recognition of this independence was a part of the program linked with the victorious outcome of the war. During his visit to headquarters in July, 1916, Mr. Sazonav had reminded the Tsar, now commander in chief, of a manifesto to be prepared regarding Polish home rule. He had received the assurance that the manifesto would soon be proclaimed, and very much relieved, he had gone on a short trip to Finland. Soon after his departure, another visitor, Sturmer, had arrived at Mogilev. The manifesto was laid aside and Sturmer was appointed to take Sazonav's place. My father, Sazonav's lifelong friend, saw eye to eye with him on the Polish question. The Polish democratic leader, Mr. Dmovsky, and his assistants often visited our home in Paris. We all shared their bitter disappointment. But the changes due to the most reactionary party in Russia were not restricted to foreign affairs. With growing pessimism we watched the game of ministerial "leapfrog" as the constant reshuffling of the Russian cabinet had been ironically called.

I still recall the mood of irritation, puzzlement and anxiety reflected in my father's conversations in the family circle and when he did not speak, in his taciturn look. And then the curtain rose on the great drama.

In November, 1916, Paul Milioukov, leader of the Progressive Block, the democratic wing of the Duma, made a public speech denouncing Rasputin and his entourage in thinly veiled terms: "Is this stupidity or treason?" demanded Milukov in thundering tones. The press reproduced his speech and the nation was stunned by these ominous words.

Rasputin's murder in December, 1916, was a prologue to the approaching tragedy.[1]

The assassination was brought about by Purishkevich, a leading reactionary of the Duma, and the young Prince Felix Yusupov, who volunteered to help him. The gruesome story is well-known; Yusupov lured Rasputin to his own apartments, offering him poisoned cakes and tea. When these had no effect, he fired a shot from his pistol. Rasputin rallied with uncanny strength and staggered toward a courtyard. Purishkevich, who had been waiting in the background, then fired two more shots. The "mad monk" fell dead.

The reaction in court circles and in general, was one of relief. Yusupov was merely banished to one of his estates. But, it was too late to stop the fatal drift of events. Conditions in Petersburg grew steadily worse. Demonstrations mounted and could not be contained. After a few bloody encounters, the garrison went over to the Revolution. Nicholas and Alexandra had remained in seclusion; he had lost all control over events and seemed on the verge of a mental collapse. He, himself, realized that he must abdicate. In a long, unrealistic Manifesto, he handed his throne over to his brother, Grand Duke Mikhail Alexandrovich, urging him to "lead the Russian State to victory, prosperity, and glory."

The news of the Tsar's abdication appeared in the Paris press on March 17, two days after it had taken place. There were few details. The Tsar's decision was supposedly to leave the throne to his son, Alexis, with Grand Duke Mikhail as regent. The news had been relayed from London where Mr. Bonar Law had made the announcement to the House of Commons. Answering Asquith's request for further explanations, Bonar Law could only add: "There have been some mutinies."

The Paris press brought a more specific account of events in Petrograd (as Petersburg had been now renamed): strikes, demonstrations, the soldiers refusing to shoot at insurgents, street fighting and the passing of a number of regiments of the guard over to the revolutionary camp. The members of the Duma were acclaimed by the people with shouts of "Long live freedom! Long live victory!" There were enthusiastic ovations at the gates of embassies. The French envoy, M. Paléologue, had to make his way through shouting demonstrators.

The Russian Embassy in Paris had been advised, but the news of abdication was still patchy. It had been received by the Russian naval attaché Captain Dimitriev, who brought it to my father. But the final decisions of Emperor Nicholas as to his successor were not yet known.

To the French public, the Russian upheaval came as a shock. The man of the street knew very little about the situation, which was protected by strict military censorship. He believed in the heroic army and

---

1. Here the original manuscript skips to the Tsar's abdication in March, 1917. The description of the murder of Rasputin is taken from *The Romanovs* by Bruce Lincoln, The Dial Press, New York, 1981. (Ed.)

in general had a love for the Russian people, since the alliance had been concluded with them. But the average Frenchman was scarcely aware of the situation on the Eastern front, or of the political tensions that had reached their climax at Petrograd.

Of course, in government circles there had long been grave apprehension. As early as January 17, President Poincaré had noted in his diary that a "palace revolution" was possible in Russia. Even so, the prospects of a continued war against Germany were improving. Supplies and munitions were being brought in for the Allied offensive, including the Russian front, which was planned for the spring. Early in March, the Allied Conference held in Petrograd had reached important decisions. The French delegate, Gaston Doumergue, had returned to Paris almost on the eve of the Revolution, with a personal letter from Emperor Nicholas reaffirming his own and Russia's full cooperation.

In spite of these encouragements, the mood at the Russian Embassy, "rue de Grenelle," continued to be one of extreme anxiety. Though far away from their country, the Russian diplomats had a clear view of what was happening, perhaps a clearer and more somber vision than many a Petrograd official surrounded by discreet silences.

When the abdication of the Tsar became for us an accomplished fact, we were stunned indeed, but what else could have been expected? From my father to the youngest secretary, decoding messages day and night as they kept pouring in, there was a unanimity of feeling; all had to carry on and avoid further catastrophes, not only because of the war but also for the peace that Russia would win through all her sacrifices. All accepted the inevitable calmly, and went back to their desks with renewed resolution. What a dying, petrified regime could not do, might yet be achieved — except for some new, unexpected development.

The question of allegiance to the departing monarch was not even discussed, since he himself had relinquished his power. But who was to take over? A minor incident reflected the uncertainty and confusion of the moment.

Father J. Smirnov, rector of the Russian Orthodox cathedral in Paris, held a conference with my father. He wanted to know who was the chief of state to be mentioned during the litanies of Saturday vespers and Sunday Mass? Was it to be young Tsarevich Alexis, or the Regent, or the Provisional Government? No one could give an answer. Father Smirnov, the gentlest of men, retired without a directive.

Meanwhile, French public opinion and especially Paris newspapers were no less confused; editorials were sent to the printers as fast as they were written, but they were still full of question marks. However, there seemed to be a unanimous decision to greet the Russian Revolution as a new and hopeful beginning.

The rightist daily *Le Gaulois* wrote: "The political leaders who have taken power [meaning the Provisional Government] are indisputably enlightened minds and men of action." The aggressive journalist Gustave Hervé wrote in *La Victoire,* a radical-socialist paper, that "the war had brought liberation to the Russian people." The conservative *Figaro* proclaimed that the revolutionary movement in Petrograd was "national and patriotic. The new Russian state appears to be an organizing power, ready to function normally if it maintains its close link with the Duma." As for *L'Humanité,* the extreme leftist organ, it saluted the Russian socialists for taking a decisive part in the Revolution.

As a general conclusion, the French press and after it public opinion, acquired the firm conviction that the Russian Revolution was a step toward victory. Germany's wish to obtain a separate peace through the leaders of reaction had been defeated. A sincere faith was placed in the Russian people, saved from betrayal and ready to march once more side by side with the Allied forces.

This was a moving and inspiring picture indeed — but what of the Russian people themselves? Alas, they were considered to be trustworthy and excellent war material, but the new sacrifices demanded of them were simply taken for granted. The social, economic and human problems raised by this sudden change of Russia's political structure were not even recognized as such. Nobody seemed to realize that many years of peace and reform would be needed to solve only half of these problems. And yet a war-weary people in a war-torn country were asked and expected to march on *jusqu'au bout* (to the bitter end).

Miles away from Russia, we could not realize nor even imagine, the cost that renewed effort demanded from our country. However, I did have an opportunity to grasp some of the tragedy it represented when we learned the plight of the "Russian Brigades." These were contingents sent to France in August, 1916, as a "token force" and stranded on the plains of Champagne where the Revolution overtook them.

There were some 14,000 men stationed at the Camp de Mailly, awaiting almost immediate action. These Russian soldiers (mostly Siberians) had been hastily trained and were unprepared for warfare in a foreign land. The food supplied by the French army was unfamiliar; the discipline they were supposed to follow, fighting side by side with the French soldiers was different from that which they had been taught at home. The total ignorance of their Orthodox faith and of their native customs created a feeling of depression, gloom and later rebellion.

President Poincaré, accompanied by my father, reviewed the Brigades from a grandstand and complimented their commander, General Lokhvitsky on the troops' good order, fine marching and spirited air as they paraded before him. They were all tall, erect, broad-shouldered and robust, typical Siberian giants.

When the Revolution broke out, the Russian Brigades took their oaths to the Provisional Government, but far from home and lacking political briefing, they did not grasp the situation nor what was expected of them. In April, however, they went into battle heroically. After a period of trench warfare, they took part in an attack where, according to a military expert, they overcame the most difficult moment, the fear which forms a psychological block at the moment when they must leave the trenches and climb into the open. On many occasions the Russians were ahead of their French comrades during the attack.

After the attack which took place in the Rheims-Chalons sectors, I visited the Camp de Mailly with a Red Cross unit. This dismal, flat region was quite near the front and our cars were shelled by the Germans. Although I was a nurse of the *Hôpital Russe*, I had not yet seen the face of a wounded Russian. It was an austere, infinitely sad ikon-like face. How unlike the French soldier who, even in suffering, preserved something of Gallic humor. As we entered the ward where the wounded lay or sat in their beds, they intoned a Russian folksong. It was as sad and beautiful as their faces. It reminded me of the songs I had heard long ago in a Russian village. In the distance, the German guns kept pounding away like a continual, dull thunder accompanying the voices.

A famous Russian opera singer had come with us on this visit. She was Felia Litvin, a very kind and generous woman who made her home in France. She had brought cigarettes and chocolates for the wounded and did her best to cheer them. "Tell them," she whispered to me, "that I am a soloist of the Imperial Opera." I repeated the words to the men, but they did not smile. They had never been to the opera, where Felia Litvin sang her grand arias. Let me add that Madame Litvin showed great kindness to the Russian émigrés who came to Paris after the Bolshevik Revolution. She gave free singing lessons to many young people, who later found their way in musical careers; she gave generously to the poor and died almost penniless.

A few months after the operations in Champagne, the men of the Russian Brigades lost courage. They felt abandoned, misunderstood, forgotten. Even their chaplain, Father Sokolov — who had lost an arm in combat, though he carried no weapon, but only a cross — made bitter complaints. There was a rebellion in the camp which was kept secret, but severely punished. *"Qu'ils partent,"* wrote Raymond Poincaré in his diary ("Let them go away"). And the British Ambassador, Lord Bertie, commenting on the same rebellion noted: "They [the Russian soldiers] have been disposed of."

After the Bolshevik Revolution took hold, the Russian Brigades were disbanded. Some of the soldiers did get home, some were scattered among the émigrés; others did not make it on either side of the frontiers. Their memorial, a Russian Orthodox chapel, still stands at Mourmelon-le Grand, in the plains of Champagne where they fell. Pilgrimages are still made to these graves of almost unknown soldiers.

Only a month or two after the Tsar's abdication, the first euphoria of the Revolution was over. Grave doubts arose as to how Russia could sustain her war effort under the new government. The entire country was in a turmoil. The former administrative machinery had collapsed. New rules permitting removal of officers and their replacement by commanders elected by the soldiers did not appease the general discontent, but revealed the deep, long-suppressed hatred of the men for their superiors. There were calls for immediate peace here and there, fraternization started on the front lines.

It soon became obvious that Russia was ruled by a dual power: the Provisional Government representing the liberal but moderate bourgeoisie, with only one socialist member, Kerensky, and on the other side of the picture, the Soviet of Workers' and Soldiers' Delegates, taken over by Lenin immediately upon his arrival. Their demands were drastic: immediate peace and land reform, granting the peasants millions of expropriated acres. Lenin harangued enthusiastic crowds in the rear, while Kerensky visited the troops at the front. His passionate orations were intended to stimulate the soldiers in view of the summer offensive. He, too, stirred enthusiasm but it was short-lived, while Lenin's laconic speeches and hammered-out slogans acted as a powerful catalyst both at the front and behind the lines.

The tension grew and to ease it, there was another shuffling of the cabinet: the Minister of Foreign Affairs, Paul Miliukov, was replaced by a more radical politician, Tereshchenko, and a number of socialists received the other portfolios. The rule of the Soviet was making itself strongly felt and there was continuous insistence on peacemaking "without annexations and contributions."

Father took the political and military developments quietly in his stride. But late in May, he took a few days off and went down on a solitary trip to Biarritz, a resort near the Spanish border.

Father had often told us about his favorite brother, Gregory, after whom my brother Grisha was named. He had lived in Biarritz when incurably sick with tuberculosis and died there. Father found the small villa where he had lived, and finding it was for rent, he signed a lease for it, "in case anything unexpected happened."

The "unexpected" happened soon after his return. My father went to the Quai d'Orsay as usual to make his report to the Foreign Minister, Jules Cambon. Hardly had he entered, when a messenger from our embassy caught up with him and handed him a cable from the Russian Ministry of Foreign Affairs. It had just been decoded and said: "You are requested to suspend your functions and to put Counselor Sevastopulo in charge of the embassy." Father read the cable, then turning to Monsieur Cambon, with perfect calm, he said: "I entered here as an Ambassador; I am making my exit as a private individual."

The reasons for this abrupt dismissal were never made clear to me. There must have been severe disagreement between the new Foreign Minister, Mr. Tereshchenko and my father, for he had always been on good terms with Mr. Miliukov, the former Minister. The Ambassador sent to replace him was Basil Maklakov, a famous lawyer, for whom my father had the greatest respect. But in November of that same year, Maklakov himself was suspended by Lenin.

We now had to face a situation which was far from reassuring. We had no assets except some savings and what we might get from the sale of our furniture, Mother's jewelry and other objects representing some value. Father made arrangements for the publication of his memoirs, and looked around for a position. But there were no openings in France for a man whose country was near collapse. We made ready to go to Biarritz, where a refuge had wisely been prepared for us.

Before we left Paris, Mother and I were invited to a farewell luncheon, an intimate affair arranged as a tribute to my mother by President Poincaré. The popularity of the ex-ambassadress had survived, but Father was not invited. Protocol must keep this honor for the new envoy. It was the last time I entered the Elysée Palace.

Poincaré noted in his diary: "Friday, June 19, farewell luncheon offered to Mme. Iswolsky and her daughter, very saddened, and seeing poverty ahead. Iswolsky has an 1800 ruble pension. Mrs. Iswolsky like her husband, seems very preoccupied." Incidentally, no such pension had been mentioned by the Russian government.

In fact, Poincaré must have been very preoccupied himself if not deeply disturbed, because he notes two days later in his diary that France had lost her nerve and that a spirit of defeatism and rebellion was rampant on the front. There had been mutinies in the army, soldiers refusing to go to the trenches; while in Paris, three thousand women walked down the Champs Elysées demanding immediate peace.

These were indeed dark days for Russia as well as for France, and none of us were in an optimistic mood. And yet I do not recall that my parents were "preoccupied" or gloomy nor were we saddened by the prospect of poverty. I was fully aware of the drastic changes in our life, but I considered them rather as a liberation from an artificial security which we had long ceased to rely upon. If I was saddened, it was because we had to leave Paris where I had many friends, including those of the *Hôpital Russe*, where my work and interest were centered. This was another parting, another farewell to people and scenes which had become familiar.

We settled down in the little villa at Biarritz only a few blocks away from the beach where the stormy waves of the Atlantic were continually breaking against jagged rocks. This thundering noise, accompanying our new life, will always be part of my memories of Biarritz.

These memories are not too happy. Most picturesque and famous for its bracing climate, Biarritz was a resort for the wealthy and idle. There was little for me to do, no intellectual interests to pursue. Father loved the villa because it reminded him of his late brother, and because it was very old, built in classic Basque style with the date 1600 engraved over the front door. He found an architect who remodeled its tiny patio according to Basque tradition, so our abode was all whitewashed with bright red shutters and tiles. Just as he had admired Japanese gardens and had had the embassy garden on the rue de Grenelle remodeled into classic French style, Father enjoyed these artistic restorations.

But outside of the Basque villa, there was a void to be filled. I found a part-time service in a military hospital, and spent the rest of the day at the country club where visiting Spaniards, Latin Americans and other young people from neutral countries played golf. Most of them were the offspring of millionaires, and I had little in common with them in my new situation, but no other "set" was available. So I learned to play golf. It was the only sport I ever practiced, and far from brilliantly! There was also a sprinkling of Frenchmen at the country club, who had been wounded at the front and had come to Biarritz on convalescent leave. Among them was Lieutenant B.—handsome, clean-cut and chivalrous. And so it started as a romance, with smiling asides at the country club, and then long walks along the beach and the pine-clad bluffs above the sea. There at the foot of the lighthouse, Lieutenant B. proposed to me, and I accepted without the slightest hesitation. For the young man, who came from a good family of southern France, seemed to have all the qualities I most admired. He was a war-hero, he was well-educated, sensitive and kind.

The lieutenant was to return to the front in a few days and I was eager to tell my parents about our engagement and to introduce my young hero to them. I thought that he would wish to inform his own family, but B. said his sister was coming to visit him and he would wait until she came. This rather surprised me, and my heart was suddenly filled with a vague anxiety.

The sister duly arrived and held a long consultation with her brother. I was not invited to join them but was only rapidly introduced to the young woman. She was severe and tight-lipped and might have been a character from a Mauriac novel. After two days of "secret" talks with his sister, the lieutenant came to see me. He had a sheepish look on his face, and bowed his head as he told me that he must break our engagement. He realized, as did his sister, that there were serious obstacles to our marriage. First, I was a foreigner, and the B. family never married foreigners. Second, I was a Russian Orthodox, and a mixed marriage was out of the question. Third, he played the violin and I did not. The last reason seemed quite absurd; the others were valid in the eyes of the sister, who was older than the lieutenant and seemed to have complete control over him. I had never imagined that my hero had so little independence. He left soon after for the front.

After B.'s return to civilian life, he married a girl of his own milieu, French, Catholic, and probably playing the violin. By an irony of fate, an acquaintance who knew nothing of my brief romance, asked me to deliver a wedding present to the place in Paris where he was staying. I did so; by then, I did not care too much, the wound had healed. But it has left a scar, even though it was such a brief encounter.

My brother was also contemplating matrimony at that time, but he was luckier than I. In Paris he had met Princess Natividad de Faucigny-Lucinge. She was a native of Cuba and a widow. Natty, as we called her, was one of the most charming, brilliant and wealthy women of Paris society and many a suitor would have envied the Russian boy, ten years younger than herself, whom she decided to marry. She fell so deeply in love with Grisha and he was so irresistibly attracted to her that the difference in age did not matter to either of them. We all went up to Paris for the wedding. The marriage was performed by our friend, Abbé Mugnier, beloved by my family and the only priest of the Paris diocese who dared to bless a mixed marriage at the altar, and not in the sacristy, according to the strict regulations of that time. Neither did he object to a second marriage conducted in the Russian Orthodox cathedral which was in principle forbidden, since Natty was a Catholic. Grisha was not practicing his religion very fervently, but to be married outside of his Church was out of the question.

Natty had three children by her first marriage, a boy, Jean Louis, and two girls, Aymone and Charlotte. Mother and myself were happy to have young children as part of our family. They, too, became attached to their stepgrandmother, whom they called *"Bonne Maman,"* and I was considered an older sister. Alas, Grisha's marriage went on the rocks and ended in divorce, but our relationship with Natty and the children remained close. Natty died in 1960 and I last saw her in Paris a year before her death. Her children are all married, and Aymone's daughter later became the wife of Valéry Giscard d'Estaing.

Soon after my unfortunate romance in Biarritz, I had a pleasant surprise. I tried my hand at writing, and sent an article to the *Revue de Paris*, a leading literary and political journal. I had been recommended to the editor by our friend, Joseph Reinach, a columnist in *Figaro*, a most dynamic man, who wrote under the name of *Polybe* (from Polybius, Greek historian of antiquity). Reinach was of Jewish descent, and a political figure of some caliber. He had a great, almost sentimental love for Russia. He had become my father's enthusiastic friend although his French rationalism could not always cope with the "Russian Enigma." He gave luncheon parties over which his wife and daughter presided and many political and literary people came to these meals; merely sitting next to them was like taking a course in the humanities or in political science. I was just a greenhorn, hoping to have my first paper published. I am grateful to Joseph Reinach for giving me the occasion of meeting the French intellectual elite; grateful to him for having started me on a literary career, and especially grateful for his great love of Russia. He remained our friend after we had lost our "ambassadorial glamour," and now I felt he had become my friend in a professional way. The article I had written was about the "Decembrists," the officers who had rebelled against Tsar Nicholas I, and were sentenced to hard labor in the Siberian mines. They belonged to our family saga, as after they were released, they were obliged to live in Irkutsk and were often hosted by my father's parents when my grandfather was governor of Irkutsk, as I have already related.

I showed my article to my father, who was very pleased with it. It was already in galley-proof, and he asked me if I knew how to make the required corrections. "Why, of course," I answered, "I can correct a manuscript." He smiled at my ignorance of printers' symbols and explained to me the mysteries of proofreading.

Now I was set on becoming an author, a dream I had cherished ever since Monsieur Weiler had suggested that I should write. But first, I felt that I should complete my education which had been interrupted by the war work at the hospital. I decided to prepare for a bachelor's degree. According to French education laws, you could study for a bachelor of arts at home, by correspondence, and then register for the required examinations at a university of your choice. I subscribed to correspondence courses and with a few savings I had managed to get together, engaged two teachers for my home studies. One was an aged priest from a neighboring parish, with whom I studied Latin; the other, a Jewish boy of sixteen, a mathematics prodigy, who gave me algebra and geometry lessons. The rest I did on my own in accordance with the official program of the Sorbonne examinations for undergraduates.

Meanwhile, in Russia, the democratic Provisional Government had fallen and Lenin's armed sailors had stormed the Winter Palace. The Communist regime was established in the "Ten Days that Shook the World." Strangely enough, Lenin's coup d'état — like Hitler's *Putsch,* in the thirties — was not taken seriously at first. Certain optimists thought that such extremists had little chance of lasting. Inside Russia, there still lingered a certain mood of expectation. The White forces were mobilizing men and resources against the Reds, who represented, as many believed, merely an anarchistic minority; I can remember how my father disagreed with many of his colleagues who predicted Lenin's inevitable downfall. He felt sure that the Bolshevik regime had come to stay.

Down in Biarritz, I had completed my preparations for the exams. I took off for Paris without telling my parents the reason for my trip.

My sister-in-law, who was on her honeymoon with Grisha, had said I could stay at her apartment which was to be their home. It was in one of those picturesque old houses of the Faubourg Saint Germain. The living room was furnished in grand style, with heavy curtains and Louis XVI furniture, which had somewhat abashed my Bohemian-leaning brother. The children were away and I had the whole place to myself. It seemed rather eerie and lonely, but I hastened to unpack my books and was soon deep in reviewing my material for the examinations.

The next day, I went to the Sorbonne in fear and trembling. The written tests were given in a large hall, filled with a great number of young men and women, seated at their desks in mute expectation. I was assigned to a place and the doors were closed. Then the theme of the Russian composition was distributed to us in sealed envelopes. I opened mine, and was thunderstruck—as far as I can recall the wording was as follows: "Describe Russia's defection and betrayal of her Allies."

To be sure, the exam was held only a few months after the treaty of Brest-Litovsk was signed by Soviet Russia and Germany; France was smarting with the blow dealt to the principle of the *guerre jusqu'au bout* (war to the bitter end) which the Allies had espoused. I do not think that there were any other Russian students taking the written test, but for me, such a theme was insulting and cruel. I had to make an immediate choice, either to leave the hall as a demonstration of protest, or to sit down and write a defense of my own country. I chose the second alternative and wrote a flaming eulogy of Russia's heroic stand against the Germans and the strong support she had offered the Allies, making possible the victory of the Marne and the defense of Verdun.

My writing must have been read with sympathetic eyes and a belated feeling of remorse; not only did I receive an excellent mark for my paper, but during the oral exam, Professor Haumant, a noted scholar and expert on Russian affairs, called me aside and whispered an apology for the faux pas committed by the faculty members who had made up the test. Thus I passed my exams successfully.

Once more, I hastened to report to my father, and once more he looked surprised at his daughter's spirit of enterprise. But we had little time to discuss my Sorbonne adventure. We were both stricken with the flu, that epidemic which played havoc with millions of lives in Europe and America at the end of the war.

My case was relatively benign, and I was convalescing when on November 11, 1918, the Armistice was signed outside of Paris. The French, English and Americans celebrated wildly.

Father's condition was far more serious than mine, in fact it was critical for several weeks. Worse still, he seemed to be morally at the end of his tether. Grisha and I sat at his bedside filled with anxiety, and saddened by his haggard features. But his mind was clear and one day, sitting up in his bed, he said, in a firm, resolute voice: "If I die, I do not wish to be buried in the Russian Orthodox Church. Let your mother's Protestant pastor say the funeral prayers."

He made no further comments, but we felt that this decision was final. It laid bare the long-repressed bitterness he had felt, at seeing the abject subserviance of the Orthodox hierarchy to the Tsar, and the corrupting influence of Rasputin. True, Father had never been attracted to the institutional forms of religion, but this did not mean that he was an agnostic. On the contrary, during the last years of his life he had acquired a new, wider conception of the mystery of life, mainly through reading Bergson. Probably if he had known that at that very time, a religious renaissance was taking place in Russia, and that many profound and eminent men felt much as he did about their church's failings, he probably would not have adopted such a drastic attitude. But he had been cut off from his own country's intellectual and spiritual life by the war and revolution. He was not drawn to Protestantism, either, though he respected its integrity and most of all, he admired Mother's simple, candid faith to which she had never sought to convert him.

Whatever the reasons for Father's sudden announcement, it stunned us because Russian Orthodoxy was so much a part of our education and cultural tradition, that to reject it seemed to us like an amputation or the cutting down of an age-old tree. At the same time, we were impressed by the passionate sincerity of his statement, so unlike the usual reserved tone of this man who had ceased to be an official personage, and now spoke as an emotional individual.

After a prolonged illness, Father did recover from the flu, but his health had been badly impaired. He tried to resume an active life but soon had to give up every effort except that of writing his memoirs.

He had written a few chapters when, in the fall of 1919, he was once more taken seriously ill. His lungs had been affected as an aftermath of the flu and he had to undergo surgery in a Paris clinic. After the operation, he suffered a complete loss of voice and never spoke again. Neither did he seem to wish to communicate with any of us. He seemed entirely detached, immersed in his own world. He read some books that he had asked for and corrected galley-proofs of the chapters of his memoirs, soon to be published in a Paris review. We visited him daily, and his two great friends, Abbé Mugnier and Princess Bibesco dropped in to see him, but he did not react to their presence. What struck me most was that the anxiety for himself, and especially for his family, which had always been his chief concern, now seemed to have vanished entirely. A person who knew Father well during the last years of his life, remarked to us, later: "I have never known a man who wanted so much to die."

This discovery altered my own way of looking at people and at life. I had always thought of my father as a dynamic and ambitious man in whom there was a certain vanity and self-assertion. But hidden below the surface, there was perhaps a different person, for whom the transient meaning of life's achievements had become clear, even though he still remained in the limited dimension of human experience.

Father died on November 16th, 1919. He was sixty-three years old. Recalling his last wishes, his funeral service was conducted by Mother's Protestant pastor; Grisha and I had a requiem sung for him in the Russian Orthodox cathedral, and our good Abbé Mugnier said a Mass for his friend at the convent for which he was then chaplain. Thus Father's death was one of my first ecumenical experiences. In spite of sadness, I now stood on the threshold of new beginnings, unaware of what life might bring me.

In France

Helene Iswolsky, journalist and translator

Helene Iswolsky's mother with the Hospital staff at the Russian Hospital in Paris; Miss MacCulloch, the Iswolsky children's governess (2nd row, 3rd from right)

Helene Iswolsky's mother on steps in St. Raphaël, France (1923) with her dogs

Count A. Ignatiev, Military Attaché, with Grisha Iswolsky, a private on his staff

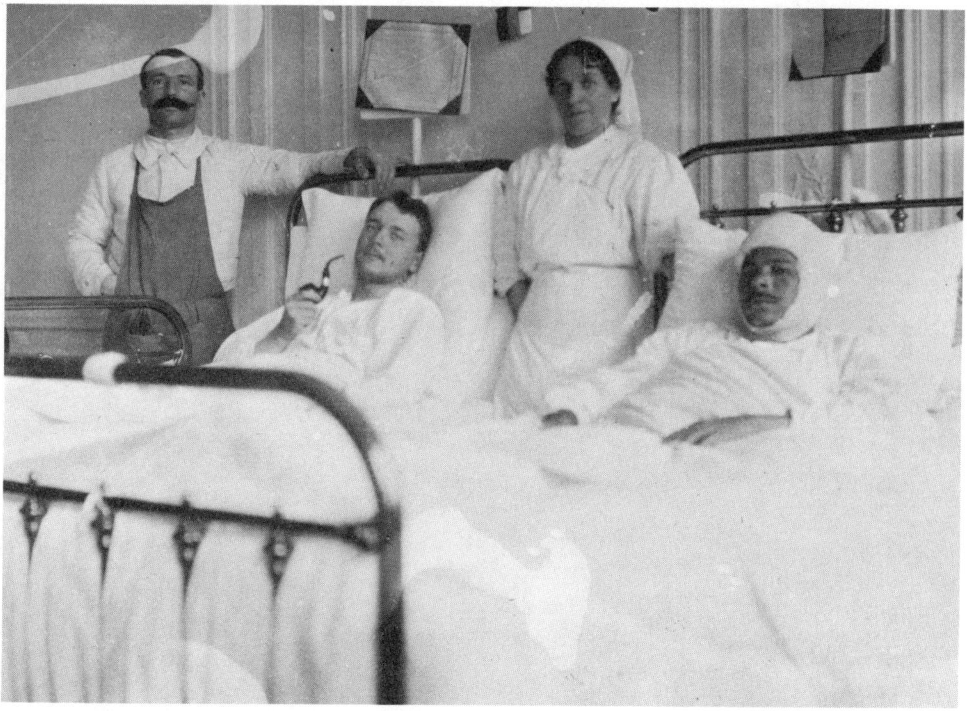

Grisha Iswolsky while hospitalized following being wounded in action, at the Russian Hospital in Paris

Helene Iswolsky vacationing in the Alps

The Biarritz House

Father P. Teilhard de Chardin with Helene Iswolsky and M. Quersaint

Helene Iswolsky with the poet Marina Tsvetaeva, in Savoie, France, 1930

Helene Iswolsky with Kerensky

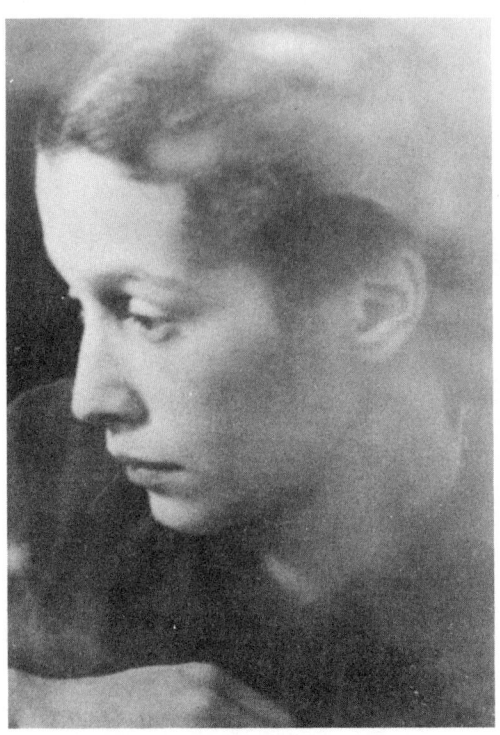

Raïssa Maritain

Mother Mary Skobtsova

Lady Abbess Marie Cronier (1857-1937) founder of the Abbey Sainte Scholastique de Dourgne, France, and her sister, Mother Cécile Cronier, prioress (1869-1944) (picture taken in 1936)

*Mother Paule Komarov, née Varvara Turgenev (1865-1934) and her daughter, Mother Eustochie Komarov (1881-1939). These Russian Benedictine nuns were influential on the conversion of Helene Iswolsky to Catholicism.
(picture taken around 1930)*

Nicholas Berdiaev

CHAPTER X

New Horizons

FATHER'S DEATH following so closely upon the breaking up of our lives was a severe ordeal for all of us. Mother was deeply affected, but preserved her courage and confidence. She felt, however, quite lost, used as she had been throughout so many years to relying entirely upon her husband. Soon after the funeral, Grisha left for America with his wife. He planned to enter a New York banking firm and was convinced that the future was full of promise and that then, of course, he would come to our rescue. For better, or for worse, he loved America, became a U.S. citizen and paid only occasional visits to Europe.

Grisha made many excellent connections in America. Thanks to his charm and good looks, he became popular in the best of New York and Washington society. Natty was a member of the smart set wherever she went, so their prospects seemed most heartening. Unfortunately, they did not materialize.

Grisha's marriage ended on the rocks and so did his career as a businessman. He was divorced and left very much on his own, while far too weak to face life's realities. Like many young men in New York, he was involved during prohibition in "bootlegging" and "speakeasy parties." He got into trouble with most of his friends, attempted another marriage which also broke up, and held various jobs which he almost immediately lost.

His life was getting more and more stormy and desolate until he met Mashenka. This charming Russian, *née* Princess Lieven, had suffered the fate of many women of the emigration. She had driven a truck in Paris, had started her life in America on a shoestring, and ended up as a saleswoman in the millinery department of a Fifth Avenue store.

Grisha married Mashenka in the thirties and she became his guardian angel, never tiring of extending to him a helping hand, understanding his weakness. They deeply loved each other.

Unfortunately this beautiful and apparently vigorous woman was stricken with an incurable form of tuberculosis and was to live only a few years after their marriage.

Grisha's misfortunes caused considerable grief to Mother, but she never ceased to love him just as much as when he was a lively, happy little boy. She always welcomed him when he came home and never rebuked him. The only sign of her secret sorrow was a picture of the Prodigal Son which always hung in her room.

I did my best to understand my "prodigal brother." I did not have Mother's forbearance, but I too never ceased to love him. To be sure, however, his prolonged absences left me to cope with many difficulties.

We were informed by Father's creditors that he had died leaving a considerable number of debts. He was apparently living very much above his means, for his salary did not suffice to maintain the Embassy on the level he considered necessary for the prestige of the country he represented. He had borrowed almost continuously, and the Revolution had cut off all possibilities of paying his debts.

Turning to a lawyer, an excellent advisor and friend, I found out about the legal procedure we were to follow. We were stripped of the little money Father could have left us; all that remained was Mother's small capital and a few of her personal belongings which she could sell. This was at least sufficient for us to weather the first storm, but we soon had to share these remains of our fortune with our relatives who had fled the Bolshevik Revolution and had arrived in Paris.

Aunt Olga had made her escape from Russia and joined her brother, Peter, and his wife somewhere on the way, so they all turned up together, thankful to be alive, but penniless. Though they all finally made a new start, this could not happen overnight, and Mother and I were, so to say, the only stable members of the family to whom they could turn; we did our best to help them.

My cousins were scattered in various other refugee camps and many years passed before I found all of them again. Our own difficulties were nothing compared to the ordeals some of them had been through. Aunt Olga had lived through quite a suspense story. She had been arrested in Kiev, where she was living at the time. She was jailed and condemned to death after having been made to sign a paper admitting that she was "the sister of two Tsarist ministers."

Night after night the executioners came to fetch the prisoners with whom she shared a common cell. She would hear shots in the courtyard below where the executions took place. Finally, she remained alone and was quite sure that her turn was next. During the night, the guards came to fetch her, but the lock of her cell snapped and she heard voices behind the door saying that they would have to wait until next day for a locksmith. The next day Kiev was captured by the White Army and Aunt Olga was liberated.

In spite of this nerve-racking experience, she lost none of her cheerfulness. She would often say how much more she appreciated life after having almost lost it. She had managed to bring her typewriter with her, and immediately set about looking for work. She soon had some translations assigned to her and, after a few months, needed our help no longer.

As to my Uncle Peter, he could at last realize his lifelong wish: to become a priest.

My Aunt Kudashev had died during the war and her husband, Uncle Vania, had been appointed Ambassador to Madrid shortly before the Revolution. Though he lost his post in 1917, he was more fortunate than most of us. He had no debts and had managed to make a few savings. He bought a farm in the Pyrénées and settled down in a small homestead. The transformation of the conventional diplomat, holding the rank of equerry of the Tsar's court, into a farmer was quite remarkable. His skill in managing his estate, working in the fields and vegetable garden with his own hands, gave excellent results. He grew corn, asparagus and melons with such dexterity that he gained the respect of his peasant neighbors. Mother stayed at his farm for a few months, recuperating from her sad ordeal, while I attended to our affairs and prepared for a future which seemed far from bright.

I was intent on getting a job as soon as possible, but Countess Jean de Castellane, a friend of Mother's, who took a great interest in us, insisted that I continue my studies. She offered to pay my tuition and, thanks to her, I enrolled at the Ecole de Droit, the law school of Paris University, in graduate studies. Great kindness was also shown to us by another of our friends, Countess Pastré, who paid the exorbitant hospital bill for Father's operation. Madame Pastré was a refined intellectual and art collector. She was of Jewish descent and had a warm and humane understanding of people in distress. I want to mention these two women's sympathy and love, for they were about the only friends who cared. The rest of the "inner circle" soon forgot the former *"Ambassadrice"* whom they had called "the smile of Paris." One of them showed quite unexpected callousness.

He was the Marquis de L., who belonged to that "inner circle" of the Embassy. Though he lived in Paris, he happened to be the owner of the house Father had rented in Biarritz, and where we still had all our belongings.

We had not, as yet, had the time to move from there when the Marquis sent us a notice advising us to leave the little house immediately, since our lease had expired and he would not renew it. If we did not comply, he would throw our furniture out into the street.

Dismayed and shocked, I called our lawyer who told me that the Marquis had already been to see him and had been so rude, that he would have nothing further to do with this man. But with a little legal advice, I could perhaps manage to tackle him.

I asked our landlord to come and see me at a time when I knew Mother would be out. Meanwhile, I made a few preparations. I had just completed my first semester at school and knew the main points of French civil law which pertained to our case. I took out my voluminous law textbooks and piled them on a table well in view. I still remember the angry Marquis as he entered my "sanctuary of learning." He was a middle-aged man, with close-cropped hair and hard, unpleasant features. He had often lunched and dined at the Embassy and was reputed as a dilettante and a wit. I had never liked him, especially when he used to look at me with the sugary smile he reserved for young ladies.

Now he stood frowning somberly, hat in hand, without removing his overcoat, in a hurry to finish the business he had come for. He scanned the books on the table, and I explained *en passant* that I was now immersed in law studies. This seemed to disturb him.

I plunged into the heart of the matter as our lawyer had instructed me. I explained that Father's estate was not yet settled and that we were forbidden to break the seals and enter the Biarritz house under severe penalties.

The gentleman promptly retreated. When the estate was settled, everything we had left there was sold to satisfy the creditors. We could only save a few personal pieces of furniture, so there was little moving to do. Soon after these events, we managed to find a small apartment which we made as pleasant as possible. I continued to attend law school and entered my second semester with considerable confidence, since I had defeated the Marquis in the first round.

Besides the basic curriculum, I attended seminars and student discussions, wrote papers, and learned to think with greater clarity. We had fine professors, many of whom later became well known in the French political and social arenas. They were extremely cordial to us as students, and we could consult them as often as we liked outside the lecture period. As to the student body, it represented many classes of French society, from the affluent and titled to the poor and obscure boys who were either typical Parisians, or young men and women from small provincial towns. They lived in dingy rooming houses, ate in cheap restaurants where rabbit was served instead of chicken, and horsemeat instead of steak. I would often share their scanty meals, which seemed to me delicious, because of the table talk that went with them, and the camaraderie which reigned amongst us.

In the spring I passed all my tests successfully, and registered for the second year of law school which was to open in the fall. Meanwhile, I returned to my literary work and tried my hand at translations. I had discovered some of the poems of Sergei Esenin, young Russian peasant. He had joined the Communists, but was later disillusioned and plunged into drunkenness and debauchery. Esenin came to America and married the famous dancer Isadora Duncan. They were divorced and Esenin returned to Russia; he committed suicide in 1925 at the age of thirty.

Esenin was a rebel. His poems denied the God of his childhood and he believed that a real paradise would be created here on earth. But there was a mystical, almost prophetic tone, in his writings; a messianism which was born not from the Marxist dogmas, but from the Russian legends of mother earth.

I translated several of Esenin's poems into French and they were later published in an anthology of modern poetry; this book was edited by Yvan Goll.[1]

After this first experiment, I continued to watch for Soviet publications. My source was Povolotsky, the owner of a Russian bookshop who had been one of our male nurses at the hospital where I worked during the war. He was quite a scholar and often helped me in my research.

I discovered several Soviet prose writers belonging to a group called the Serapion Brothers. The "Brothers" had gone along with the Revolution without accepting its dogmatism and regimentation, and were later known as the "fellow travelers." They remained free of Party directives and defended freedom of expression.

A Paris periodical published one of my translations. This periodical, the *Revue de France*, was directed by Marcel Prévost, a French novelist and member of the French Academy. I met the assistant editor of the *Revue*, Horace de Carbuccia, at a luncheon given by Countess Jean de Castellane who had taken my literary career, as well as my university studies, to heart.

I had also done some creative writing and had published an article on the great Russian nineteenth-century poet Alexander Pushkin. A recent biographical work had appeared in Soviet Russia concerning Pushkin's death, and the author of this book had used some until then unknown research material. The poet had been killed in a duel by a young Frenchman, George Dantes, who had aroused his jealousy by courting his beautiful wife. The circumstances surrounding the Pushkin-Dantes affair were highly dramatic, and I described them in this vein, defending the memory of the Russian poet. With youthful passion I laid all the blame on the killer, Dantes. The article was published in the important French periodical *La Revue des Deux Mondes*. This juvenile endeavor would have brought me considerable satisfaction had it not been marred by an embarrassing incident. I had signed my article, "H. Iswolsky," so that the reader was unaware that the author was a woman.

One of my Russian friends was approached by a Baron Dantes, who was a direct descendant of Pushkin's assassin and of whose existence I was totally unaware. Neither could I suspect that he was dedicated to the defense of his ancestor.

---

1. Yvan Goll and his wife, Claire, were poets belonging to the postsurrealist movement. They have been described by the French literary historian Clouet as "the high priests of hermetic ministry."

In angry tones the Baron demanded to know who was this "Mr. Iswolsky" who had spoken ill of Baron George Dantes in his article? Such an insult was to be avenged without delay by a duel.

Learning about my identity, the Baron changed his mind. He invited me to dinner at his home where I met his charming wife and Count Felix de Voguë, son of the literary critic Melchior de Voguë, who had been the first to reveal the Russian novel and Russian poetry to the French public. Count Melchior had married a Russian and his son, Felix, was no less devoted to my country than his father.

I believe it was Monsieur de Voguë who helped the angry Baron to make peace with me, and we spent a very pleasant evening. It was hinted, however, that in the future I should avoid such a delicate subject in my writings.

I was twenty-three and launched on my literary career. I was able to support myself with my translations, and while sharing my mother's apartment, enjoyed the freedom and independence of a Paris student. Soon we had to make a place in our modest home for a youthful boarder, my brother's stepson, Jean-Louis. He was the eldest child of my sister-in-law, Natty, by her first husband, Prince Guy de Faucigny-Lucinge, and had been placed in a boarding school when Grisha and his wife went to America.

Jean-Louis, or "Johnny", as we called him, was a sensitive young boy in his early teens who was unhappy in school and needed a home. It was decided that he should live with us and study with tutors.

Mother and I grew very fond of the young boy, who became part of our family and brought us a spirit of youth, mutual affection and confidence. He enjoyed complete independence, yet spent a great deal of time with us and shared many of my interests. He collected rare books, was fond of modern art and literature, and I often went with him to the avant-garde movies at the Rue des Ursulines, a small theater.

Through him I met his charming uncle, Emilio Terry, who, like my sister-in-law, was a Cuban of English descent. He was a brilliant architect and everything he built was marked with great originality and taste.[2]

Emilio's apartment was beautifully decorated and he gave small dinner parties, at which superb food was served and conversation was brilliant. The Abbé Mugnier often came to dinner at Emilio's. Other guests were the Latin American essayist Ramon Fernandez and Jacques Rivière, editor in chief of the periodical *Nouvelle Revue Française*, which became at that time the leading revue of modern French literature. Rivière had been a soldier during World War I and was captured by the Germans. He related the religious crisis he had gone through as a prisoner-of-war, in a book entitled *A la trace de Dieu*. His religious quest,

---

2. Emilio Terry died in the nineteen seventies. The French novelist Julien Green (his friend and of whom I speak of in Chapter XV) devoted articles to Terry's architectural work which was a modern version of the classic Palladian style.

which was dramatic but led to no solution, revealed an exceptionally delicate and sensitive soul. I was fascinated by him.

These dinner parties were carefully supervised and presided over by Emilio's lady housekeeper. This middle-aged and dignified Englishwoman had been at one time governess of Mademoiselle Haas, the daughter of a Jewish banker known to be the prototype of Proust's hero, Swann. Thus, the lady had actually brought up the famous Gilberte Swann! This little episode will give the reader a flavor of the 1920s when the Proustian world was all around us.

Marcel Proust was still living at that time, and though already seriously ill, made a few last appearances in the Paris salons which he had so often described. I saw him at a party given by Princess Winnie de Polignac, *née* Singer. The wealthy sewing machine heiress was a patroness of the arts, especially of music. I was brought to her home by her niece, Daisy Singer, one of my dearest friends of early debutante days.

The Princess's party presented a program of chamber music during which strict silence was observed, and I had little opportunity of meeting the guests. I remember sitting next to a good-looking, racy, elegantly dressed and bejewelled woman in her late forties. I recognized her immediately, having seen many portraits of her, as the poetess Anne de Noailles. This great lady of the French Parnassus was known as the most talkative woman of Paris society. It was said that if someone interrupted the flow of her brilliant, but irrepressible conversation, she would place a hand over the person's mouth.

I can say that, because of the string quartet in full swing, I never heard Anne de Noailles' voice. As the concert proceeded, I looked at the audience; some of the later arrivals stood at the door. Among them was a man of medium height with dark, shiny, carefully parted hair and a dark moustache, of sallow complexion, and enormous, dark, penetrating eyes. They dimly glowed under the half-closed eyelids and were lined by heavy pouches. He looked exhausted, scarcely able to stand up, until an armchair was hurriedly brought for him. The aspect of this man was so unusual, so tragic, that during the intermission I asked who he was and was told that it was Marcel Proust. I most clearly remember his eyes and will never forget them; they were like two dark mirrors or projectors deeply sunk into their orbits, scrutinizing the world with terrifying accuracy. Such was the man I saw at the eve of his death when his physical frame had become almost spectral.

Proust left before the concert was over. He died a year later, in 1921. I regret not having been able to get closer to him at the Polignac party, not having spoken to him nor heard his voice. My brother was luckier. He had several occasions to meet Marcel Proust and had, before he went to America, often told me about these encounters.

He made Proust's acquaintance at some mutual friends and amused him with his jokes and comic imitations which always made people laugh. The novelist invited my brother to come and see him. He was already in poor health, though not as yet cloistered in his insulated, sound-proof apartment. He was always seeking a place to live where he could breathe in spite of his asthma, which was growing more and more acute.

At the time Grisha met him, he had found that the Ritz was the most appropriate habitat. He invited my brother to dinner in the hotel's restaurant and they sat at a little table which had been specially reserved for them by Olivier, the most famous maître d'hôtel in the Ritz's history. Proust sat throughout the meal wrapped in a heavy overcoat. Grisha wondered why the table reserved for them was near a door, half-closed, in the most drafty corner of the restaurant. Why should Proust wear an overcoat, instead of moving to a less drafty area? "This is my special draft," his host explained, "it makes me breathe better."

Proust asked his young guest to tell him more of his stories and anecdotes, and was again highly amused. Grisha enjoyed his dinner and Proust's reaction to his wit, but was not impressed by the fact of meeting so great a writer. He would joke with anyone who was a good audience and never boasted about it. He saw Proust on a few other occasions and each time their conversation was full of wit and humor. My brother's amusing and vivacious talk appealed to another distinguished writer, the novelist and playwright Jean Giraudoux. He, too, made my brother tell his stories and make his comic imitations.

I must confess that I was envious of Grisha's success with these men of letters whom I approached with fear and trembling. Though more or less indifferent to literature, my brother had a fine sense of all that these two masters really represented. He could respond to them by mere intuition. But he had had no ambition.

There was no need for me to be envious. I was myself able to participate, perhaps in a smaller way, in an interesting social and intellectual life, thanks to an American young woman, Marie-Louise de Sinçay, *née* Logan. She was married to a Belgian, but was separated from him and lived in Paris. Her little private house on the Left Bank was most charming and hospitable. Many distinguished people were her friends.

Marie-Louise was a very intelligent, bright young woman. She spoke French fluently and was remarkably well-read. In fact, she was continuously immersed in books. Typically American by birth (she was the descendant of General Logan of the Civil War), she had become an international figure, living now in Paris, now on the Riviera, now in England or Italy. She was most generous and devoted to her friends, but at times slightly eccentric. One of her peculiarities was to be continually late.

When invited to a dinner party, she would appear when everyone was already at table, starting the second course. At home, her guests would wait as long as an hour before she finally appeared to greet them. But we all got used to Marie-Louise's unusual behavior and laughed it off, though we did get, at times, quite impatient.

At Madame de Sinçay's dinners (though always late), she entertained frequently and most pleasantly; thus I met Lord Beaverbrook, Bernard Berenson, the art critic and painter whom we called "B.B.," and Walter Berry, the American lawyer and literary connoisseur. The latter had been a friend of Proust and is best known as Edith Wharton's unhappy suitor and, later, her devoted companion.

Life could have been once more secure and pleasant had not my health suddenly broken down. Maybe the strain following my father's death, and the excessive load of work I had assumed, had been too much for me. There was also another, deeper psychological reason for my physical condition. In spite of my many satisfying achievements, I felt a void, or rather a jumble, in my life. No real pattern was emerging from it. I was doing too many things at the same time, getting involved with too many different people. Somehow, I had lost the sense of the spiritual values which formerly had guided me. In fact, I belonged to the "lost generation."

I consulted several doctors. They all advised rest, a change of environment and various treatments, none of which worked. I finally decided to visit Uncle Vania at his farm in the Pyrenees mountains. I interrupted my studies at law school and my writing projects and got on a train to the little town in the Pyrenees near which my uncle's estate was located. I was not aware that this would lead me to new and wider horizons. I was much too sick to stay more than a month at my uncle's place without medical care. So it was decided for me to go to Pau, the main city of that region, the Béarn, where there was an excellent medical staff.

The night before leaving for Pau, I dreamed of a wide, light-blue mountain stream, peacefully winding between wooded banks. When I arrived in Pau by train, I saw the very landscape of my dream; the stream was the *Gave de Pau* which has its source high in the mountains, and after flowing past the city I had reached, goes on to Lourdes, skirting Our Lady's grotto. Mother came to join me, and we settled in a hotel. The doctor came and prescribed a new treatment. I needed someone to take care of me, so an old nun came to nurse me. She was a naive, simple woman, but very compassionate and patient. I was attracted by her and by the faith which shone in her homely face.

And now I began to have a good look at myself, and the picture was not a very pleasant one. I saw myself as I really was: no longer the successful author, the diligent student, Mother's strong support. I was now a poor weakling, dependent on others, needing attention and protection. And in the moral and religious sense, I had also been slipping. I had not exactly lost my faith, but I had ceased practicing it. Father's final revolt against the established Orthodox Church had shaken my own beliefs. And the sophisticated, secular milieu of Paris intellectuals had imbued me with their own cynicism. There were some dark spots on my conscience and they had spread, leaving no rest for my troubled soul. I was just one of those "lost" young men and women.

During an anxious, sleepless night, as the old nun was bending over me, I suddenly sat up in my bed and made a promise: if I recover, I will search for a way to get back to the God of my childhood.

Things did not go much better after I had made that promise. My doctor came to see me and said that he had done all he could; he was through with me. I should consult a specialist and would probably have to be hospitalized. On that day of gloom, Mother made the acquaintance of a neighbor, an American woman whose name was Miss Natalie Harris. This charming and intelligent woman inspired her with such confidence that she told her all about my woes.

Natalie came to see me immediately. She recognized my symptoms, having suffered from a similar sickness a few years earlier. A famous doctor in Switzerland had cured her and she suggested I follow his treatment. It was a very simple one, consisting mostly of plenty of rest, light food and fresh air. No hospital rules. No medicines.

Natalie visited me daily, bringing books, magazines, and some American desserts and goodies, which she had taught her Bearnese cook to prepare. I found my visitor always cheerful and entertaining. She was a very refined and cultured woman from a distinguished American family, related to the Barrymores. She understood that my condition needed an atmosphere of calm and mutual confidence.

Maybe the Swiss doctor's treatment really worked. Maybe it was the quiet kindness and reassurance that Natalie Harris brought me, but in about three weeks I had regained the strength to stand once more on my feet. I took my first walk on Pau's beautiful *promenade* with a view of the Pyrenees and the winding vistas of the *Gave*.

Now that I was well, my search for God had to begin. But I did not know exactly where to start. Natalie Harris was a Catholic convert, but her church seemed to me too different from mine; it had too strict a theology and liturgy alien to me. Later I discovered other, more appealing aspects of Catholicism. These aspects were brought to me by some young people with whom I had contact. They were students, like myself, yet they did not resemble those I had known at law school, who were mostly rationalists and atheists.

My new friends were interested in a religious movement which sought to counteract the *Weltschmerz* of the lost generation with a constructive ideology. It was founded on Catholic theological premises but was, at the same time, oriented toward the problems of our times. Their masters were Leon Bloy, Jacques Maritain (the neo-Thomist philosopher) and the poet Péguy, who had been killed at the battle of the Marne. I had already heard about Péguy's great poetry from a wounded officer, dying in our hospital. But I now learned the names of Bloy and Maritain for the first time.

This meant discovering the religious revival which was inspiring French Catholic youth with a new dimension. I was attracted by the ideal of Christian social justice and of a purified, positive way of life which the students I met in Pau exemplified. Somehow I had the feeling of having been freed from a burden of confusion; freed from the selfish, bourgeois, hedonistic society which I had known until then, both in the "Embassy days," and in the years that followed.

I began reading about Western saints. Saint Francis had always attracted me, but I now seemed to see him in a new light. I also found the works of Charles Péguy, his essays on social ideals and his poem about the Chartres Cathedral and about Joan of Arc. And there was a book about the desert hermit Charles de Foucauld. I think de Foucauld's life story was one of the decisive influences in what I would like to call, but dare not, my spiritual rebirth. I had still a long way to go. One thing became clear to me: my own Eastern Christian faith and that of the west were not basically opposed to each other, as people were told on both sides of the barrier. But how could the barrier be lifted?

Soon after my discovery, we decided to give up our Paris apartment and to transfer our home to Pau; we had grown very fond of the Pyrenees, where life was so much calmer and cheaper, as well as more pleasant for Mother. As to myself, I would have to look for a job, and the one that was already offered to me would mean some traveling. Uncle Vania gave up his farm to take care of Mother. They rented a large apartment which cost half the price we should have had to pay in Paris. There was a room for me, so I could always come back on vacation. My only regret was that my studies at law school could not be resumed. My long sickness had drained our meager savings, and I had to start all over again.

Shortly after my recovery, I was offered a job as private secretary to a certain Count Jean Bertier de Sauvigny, the youngest member of the French Senate. His wife had known me in Paris and thought I could fill that post because of my diplomatic background and my own writings.

Count Jean was considered a radical, though he was actually a mild liberal: dynamic, ambitious and like most politicians, concerned with re-election. His wife, of old Breton stock, was pleasant, vivacious and charming. They had two lovely children. I worked both in Paris and in the Thionville region, in Lorraine, which was the Senator's electoral precinct and where the de Bertiers had an estate. My work in Lorraine taught me something about the difficulties for any administration functioning in a zone between two countries, speaking different languages, and bitter over the recent annexation of Lorraine by the Germans. I was also aware of the immense working population of the industrial region, the monstrous blast furnaces, the poor, primitive housing conditions of the workers. Many refugees from Russia were hired at these plants, ruled by dynasties of steel magnates who lived in opulence. Politicians visited these works on their campaign tours, but very little progress in bettering conditions was made, in spite of many promises.

Monsieur de Bertier's office work was not complicated, it was mainly correspondence with members of his electorate. Some asked for small favors, such as a license for a tobacco shop, a government monopoly. One of the letters was highly dramatic; it was written by the wife of an inmate of a prison, condemned to death. The wife implored the Count to obtain a pardon for her husband. He did all he could, but the case dragged on and on, until it began to haunt me. I do not know the end of this drama, for de Bertier died suddenly, of a heart attack during a political speech for his reelection.

A few months before the Count's death, I had resigned my position. I had not been unhappy at the de Bertier's chateau, nor at their Paris apartment. They both showed me great kindness and I had become part of their family. But I had realized the vanity of political life, and the artificial character of its *soi-disant* humane ideals. I longed to go back to my literary work, and there was the *Gave*, the blue mountain stream, calling. I was happy to find my room waiting for me with a brand-new writing desk and Mother's and Uncle Vania's loving welcome.

I picked up my writings where I had left them: translations, book reviews and articles. The view from my window was magnificent. The high peaks of the Pyrenees and foothills covered with vineyards, glistening in the southern sun. It was all so peaceful, and yet, my heart was troubled. I felt that I had not kept my promise; that I had again been driven by my literary and worldly ambitions. I really had to put my house in order.

I looked up the Russian Orthodox priest who was the rector of a small chapel where the small Russian colony of Pau came to worship. But the pastor was a man who was excellent for the old, traditional members of his flock, but I could not possibly lay before him the troubles of the "lost generation."

A Catholic priest learned that I was interested in religious problems and came to visit us, under the pretext of bringing me books. But his intentions to "convert me," as he believed was his duty, were all too obvious. In the year 1923, there was no dialogue between the churches, only missionary endeavors; the very word *ecumenism* had, as yet, not come into existence.

And then, as it seems often happened in my life, things began to move quite unexpectedly. We had befriended a young Russian musician, stranded in Pau due to ill health and extreme poverty. This young man, whom we called Sasha, was a remarkably gifted pianist, besides being a brilliant causeur and raconteur. He had studied under Rimsky-Korsakov and could play the main scenes of his operas transcribed for the piano. Thanks to the connections we had made in Pau, we introduced Sasha to a number of people interested in music. He was invited to play in their homes and started giving music lessons. One of his new admirers was a doctor who treated him without any fees, only asking him to play for him. Sasha regained his health and independence in no time. He was pleasant as a companion and we became great friends. He told me that he and his family were originally Orthodox, but his sister, Katia, had become a Catholic and had entered Saint Scholastica, a Benedictine abbey of strictly cloistered nuns in the Toulouse region. His mother had joined the Catholic Church and, in spite of her advanced age, was also admitted into the community. Sasha had often visited his sister and mother at the monastery, and had later made a retreat at the men's Benedictine Abbey of En-Calcat, located not far from Saint Scholastica. He had been so deeply impressed by these two great monastic centers that he, too, had recently joined the Catholic Church. He was thinking of becoming a monk of En-Calcat.

This seemed surprising for a young man so full of life and of such a strong artistic temperament. But I believe Sasha was quite sincere, and though he never became a monk, he had a deep and unwavering faith to the end of his life. He told me about the Benedictine monastic tradition, which he described with his usual enthusiasm. He had written to his sister Katia, whose name in religion was Mother Eustochie, and told her of all the help we had given him, and the nun wrote us a letter of thanks; it was half in French, half in Russian. Mother Eustochie had not forgotten her native tongue even though she had lived in the cloistered community for twenty-five years.

I answered her letter in Russian, and so began a correspondence which brought new light into my troubled soul; how was I to reconcile East and West, the Orthodox faith and the Catholic? How to find the peace of mind that eluded me?

Mother Eustochie invited me to Saint Scholastica, which was not far away. And what joy for her, she wrote, will it be to be able to speak with me in Russian! But there was still some hesitation on my part. I sensed that for me this was to be no easy adventure.

On a sultry September afternoon, I took a local train to Castres, the ancient *Castrum Romanum*, lying at the foot of the Cévennes mountains. I had placed in my bag a pack of cigarettes, a volume of Proust, and a manuscript I was working on. Would the nuns object to my smoking? Would I have the time to read and write as I wished? The prospect of life in a monastic community was suddenly confusing and awesome to me. Though nominally an Orthodox, I had lived long enough in France to be familiar with the Catholic Church; it inspired me with respect and admiration, but it did not definitely attract me. On the other hand, Orthodoxy did not seem to give any answer to the religious problems which had begun to loom before me, as for many young people of the war generation. I had always been a believer, but there was a veil drawn between me and the God I worshipped.

Sometimes this veil was lifted — I remember that once, during the war, while nursing in the *Hôpital Russe*, I had once had a revelation of the supernatural world when one of my patients died. He was a soldier from Brittany, a humble peasant who had asked for a priest to assist him. There were three of us in that room, the priest, the dying man and myself. That day I believe that my soul was suddenly awakened to spiritual life as a reality. Later, I began to read the works of Péguy and they made a deep impression on me. This was, as I have said, the first deep Catholic influence in my life.

And now I was on my way to Saint Scholastica. I will always remember that hot September day, the scorching south wind blowing over the sunbaked villages. As sometimes happens on the eve of a great new experience, I felt weary and listless.

A monk in a black habit, with a typical Benedictine hood, left the train with me and we boarded a bus, drawn by horses. When he learned that I was going to the Abbey, he smiled and said: "Welcome to the peace of Saint Benedict." He was from the men's monastery of En-Calcat, which we were approaching; a plain building of rough-hewn stone and a square church tower. We had reached a little stream and the air was cooler. The landscape had become a little bleaker and the *Montagne Noire*, the black foothills of the Cévennes, rose to view. Beyond En-Calcat, I saw tall white walls and another pinnacled church tower glistening in the evening sun. "That is Saint Scholastica," the monk explained as he alighted at the gates of his monastery.

At the gates of Saint Scholastica I was met by lay sisters and escorted to the *parloir*. The tall, iron bars and wooden grille of the reception room filled me with vague dismay. Dark figures loomed behind the bars. It was the Abbess and my Russian friend, Mother Eustochie. I could dimly see their faces which stood out, pale and eerie from their white starched wimples, their black merging into the shadows of the room. They looked to me like weird apparitions.

Then I was aware that the Abbess was speaking to me in a kind, motherly voice, asking whether I was not tired and hungry? Mother Eustochie addressed me in Russian — it was surprising that after twenty years in a French cloister, her Russian was pure and perfect. Then she drifted into French. "It is a great joy for us to receive you here, but this is just a preliminary visit. We shall see more of you when you join us in the enclosure. . . ." "The enclosure?" I murmured in astonishment, for I knew that entrance into the cloister is strictly forbidden to visitors.

"Yes, we have a surprise for you," Mother Eustochie explained, "the Bishop has granted you special permission to spend ten days inside our cloister. This is a rare exception."

The opening of the inner cloister door was an impressive moment; two lay sisters took me to the white-washed entrance hall. Slowly they unlocked the great, oaken doors, which swung noiselessly open. As I passed through them I could not help thinking of those who had preceeded me, never to return. And also—may the comparison not seem too profane—I had something like an "Alice through the Looking-Glass" feeling, as I stepped into this unknown world.

The Abbess and Mother Eustochie were waiting for me. Now I could see the superior in the light of the cloister. I saw, not an apparition, but a tall, robust woman of sixty-five, with a kindly face and intelligent, hazel eyes that peered at me benevolently through large spectacles. She extended both hands to greet me with the Benedictine welcome: *Benedicamus Domino!*

"*Deo Gratias*," responded Mother Eustochie, grasping my hand. The Russian nun was of medium height with bright, blue eyes, full of gentleness. And yet an indomitable spirit shone in them. As I later found out, she was the life and soul of the community, an accomplished artist and one of the most devout and fervent nuns of Saint Scholastica.

She led me through a long passage to an oaken stairway. Everything was immaculately clean, the woodwork elaborately polished. The whitewashed walls and stone-flagged floors reminded me of a modern sanatorium. Saint Scholastica was designed to admit plenty of sun and air; it was equipped with running water, baths and modern sanitation. Mother Cronier believed in keeping her children physically fit. "Nowadays," she explained, "girls cannot stand the extreme hardships that former generations of nuns bore easily. Yet even in the present, the Rule of Saint Benedict is stern enough. During the winter, the cells are not heated, and in summer there is the scorching heat. We get up at dawn and work hard. . . ." The cell I was to occupy was a small, white cubicle, with a straw mattress, a table, a chair and a *prie-Dieu*. A washstand held an earthenware basin and bowl. A black crucifix hung on the wall.

Left alone, I looked out of the window; the black crests of the Cévennes rose before me, shutting out the horizon. Complete silence reigned. I could hardly believe that over a hundred nuns lived in this great, silent building, yet I felt their invisible presence. A feeling of apprehension stole over me. What was the reason for all this? How could it be explained? For years and years, these voluntary prisoners had nothing to gaze upon but this bleak mountain range. For a time, I was one of them.

"And now," said Mother Eustochie, who had brought me my supper on a tray, "there is something I want to show you." She drew out of her deep pocket a small volume, bound in black cloth. I opened it and saw that it was printed in Slavonic characters.

"This," she explained, "is an old Russian prayer book. It belonged to my uncle who was an Orthodox priest. Our Abbess has permitted me to keep it and I often read in chapel. Only here, after years of monastic life, have I understood the prayers of the Eastern Church. They are so beautiful."

"But not quite in the Benedictine spirit?" I observed, smiling.

"On the contrary, Saint Benedict was the direct spiritual descendant of Saint Basil the Great, whose Rule is followed by all the Eastern monasteries, including the Russian ones."

"So, we stem from the same root?"

"Yes, from the same root," she echoed. "You will see for yourself that our Benedictine liturgy is more primitive than the common Latin liturgy. It bears the mark, as does yours, of the Byzantine tradition. Even our Gregorian chant is of Greek origin. And so is your early Russian Church music."

"Indeed!" I exclaimed with interest, "and this means that after all these years in the Abbey, you have preserved a link with Russia. Now you know what all our countrymen say, that a Russian who is converted to the Catholic faith is denationalized and becomes a Latin."

"But that is absurd," Mother Eustochie objected, "the Catholic Church is universal and respects all rites and religious customs. There is a special Papal encyclical dealing with the Eastern Rite. If a Russian is converted to the Catholic faith, unless he deliberately chooses to be a Latin, he becomes a Catholic of the Eastern Rite. In Paris, there is a Russian Catholic priest who says Mass according to the genuine Slavonic liturgy, the very one contained in my uncle's prayer book. . . ."

As I pondered this new vista, Mother Eustochie drew up a chair and continued, "I pray every day for our beloved country. When I took the veil, I wrote to my family and asked them to tell the peasants on our land that I had retired to a monastery. They did not ask where, nor how, but simply thanked God for this great favor. Yes, the Russian people are profoundly Christian; they have a knowledge of the ascetic and mystical life far deeper than the peoples of the West. And now you have come to help me. We shall work for unity; it is the wish of our Abbess, and that of the Benedictines in general. *Ut unum sint in Christo.*"

The church bell struck seven and Mother Eustochie rose, "It is recreation time, we must go down to Our Lady's garden, where the community is waiting to meet you." I expected to see a solemn assemblage of prim, quiet figures; instead, I saw an animated group of young women, talking and laughing as they walked around carefully tended flowerbeds. They wore broad brimmed peasant hats over their veils and wooden *sabots*. They came up to me, nodding and smiling. I felt somewhat confused, but noticed that they had beautiful faces, not all handsome, in the usual accepted sense of that word, but they all seemed to reflect the same joyful, mellow light. It shone on every brow, transfiguring even the plainest features. They seemed full of an intense life, dynamic, as though swept by some mysterious wind—the breath of the Spirit.

Mother Cronier, the Abbess, did not seem like a formidable matriarch. She, too, wore a straw hat and *sabots*. She chatted informally with the novices who gathered around her. I was encircled with greetings, questions and friendly laughter; they took a lively interest in their young visitor from "the world." Soon, I found myself also laughing and talking as if we were old friends.

The monastery bell struck eight, and suddenly there was a complete hush. Conversations ended in the middle of a phrase. Mother Eustochie had just time to whisper to me, "This is the Great Silence which lasts until after tomorrow's early Mass."

My first experience of the Great Silence, that night at Saint Scholastica, has remained an unforgettable memory. It wrought its message deeper in my soul than all the sermons and books of piety could have done. Being admitted to the cloister had exhilarated me. It was like the feeling one experiences after a stiff climb, when one has reached the summit of a mountain. I had been breathing the clean, brisk air of high altitudes.

But now I felt suddenly cold, abandoned. This silence which had come so unexpectedly, was oppressive; it seemed to paralyze the soul. I was alone and face to face with a great mystery which seemed to fill the Abbey. How small and helpless I felt in this unknown world!

It was with a sense of relief that I followed the community to chapel where Compline, the evening office was to be sung. My sinking heart found comfort in the gentle *Salve Regina* chanted in pure Gregorian modes. For the first time, I experienced the beauty and harmony of a Benedictine service, but I still felt anxious and unnerved.

The night seemed full of threatening shadows and hushed, evil voices. It was here in the vast Abbey, which drifted like a ship through the terrors of the night, that one understood the dark forces of temptation and doubt which assail man at the hours of darkness. Then only did one realize the protective powers of prayer.

After Compline was over, I stole up to my cell, and lay down on my straw mattress. A thousand images whirled through my mind. A thousand questions arose in my mind and I could find no answers. At last I fell asleep at dawn, after I had heard the shuffling feet of the nuns going to Matins.

When I awoke, the sunshine was flooding my cell and there was Mother Eustochie on the threshold, a rough kitchen apron tied over her habit; she was carrying a steaming cup of coffee and a loaf of brown bread. *"Deo Gratias,"* she called out cheerfully as I sat up in my bed. A great feeling of joy and security came over me. It was as if, after those dark hours of the night, I had been reborn, with a new, vigorous spirit. The peace of Saint Benedict had come to me.

During this first visit, two great personalities dominated the life of Saint Scholastica. One was the Abbess, Mother Marie Cronier, who had founded the Abbey, and the other was Dom Romain Benquet, the retired Abbott and founder of En-Calcat. He was the son of a country gentleman who owned the farm of En-Calcat. He entered monastic life at the age of 17, at the famous Benedictine monastery of *La-Pierre-qui-Vire*. After his profession he obtained permission to turn his home, which he had inherited, into a monastery of En-Calcat. He had known Mother Cronier when she was a wealthy young Parisian, and was amazed by her ardor and purpose. When she said that she intended to abandon her fortune, and to enter a Benedictine Community, he encouraged her. But she, too, felt led to found her own small community after some years in the convent. This was the origin of Saint Scholastica. The two communities flourished side by side, training their own architects and artists to follow the Benedictine style of simplicity and beauty in every detail of decorations, vestments and liturgical music. Through the years, both communities received a great number of visitors. Besides friends and relatives, many distinguished Catholic writers, artists and scholars came to seek advice or guidance, or to relax in the peace of Saint Benedict.

When I met Dom Romain Benquet he was a frail old man of eighty, thin and worn from long years of prayer and fasting, and the great activity that he had expended while building up his monastery. But his eyes were still bright, with a keen, youthful spirit. He was confessor and spiritual director of the nuns, the beloved father of both communities who venerated him like a saint. I had many talks with the nuns, and also with Dom Romain.

In my talks with Mother Eustochie, she continually stressed the importance of our common spiritual and cultural heritage, the Russian religious tradition. She was the first to tell me that, due to circumstances, I was being received into a Latin community but that I was to remain in the Byzantine, or Slavonic rite, in which I had been baptized and brought up. Such was the wish of the Pope, Pius XI, as expressed in his encyclical *Orientalis Dignitas*. This was essential for my future work, as it later turned out, and I was now more than ever aware that East and West are not opposed to each other.

These fundamental ideas about the perspective of reunion of both Churches, or branches of the Church universal, were expressed in the

1890s by the Russian philosopher Vladimir Soloviev. I had read his remarkable works before meeting Mother Eustochie, who had also been inspired by him. Soloviev's position was generally adopted by the Catholic Church at Vatican Council II, and by Pope John XXIII in particular. The dogmatic differences are being studied by the Secretariat for Christian Unity in Rome. Later, in my work for ecumenical understanding, I made a study of Soloviev and other philosophers such as Nicholas Berdiaev, but at that time, I felt simply impelled to make a gesture of complete acceptance of a closer bond to the universal Church.

My talks with Dom Romain were also preparing me for this step, on an even deeper, spiritual level. I found myself confiding in him, able to talk to him as I had never been able to do with anyone before.

It was astonishing that having left the world at seventeen, he should have had such a deep knowledge and intuition about our hectic, modern life and all its problems. The monks or laymen who consulted him were rarely disappointed; his advice was always enlightening, practical and to the point. He had the gift of penetrating the most hidden secrets of the human heart. Those who came to him for confession, and who did not know how to "explain their case," were soon relieved. They found that Dom Romain knew all about them before they opened their mouths.

I cannot relate what depths of soul I explored with Dom Romain. I went through a last, hard struggle familiar, I believe, to all those who are near the final goal; the unconditional surrender to the unknown God. It was a revolt that lasted through one terrible night. It ended quite suddenly as it had begun, never to return. At least, I trust and hope that it will not, though none of us is protected against such buffetings.

When morning came, my decision was made. By evening, I had made a general confession and was received into the Universal Church. I had laid bare my entire life to Dom Romain whom, I felt, knew human nature better than any psychologist I had known. There was something of the Curé d'Ars about him, or of Dostoevsky's *starets*, Father Zosima.

The next day, September 14th, 1923, on the Feast of the Exaltation of the Cross, I received Holy Communion at the Conventual Mass. I had been away from the Sacraments for at least ten years. When asked why I became a Catholic, I answered, "I wanted to get back to the Sacraments." The Catholic Church helped me to do so at the time of a complete spiritual blackout. It was as simple as that.

During my stay in the cloister, I had also met Mother Eustochie's mother, whose name in religion was Mother Paule. This distinguished Russian woman was born a Turgenev, and was a relative of the famous author of *Fathers and Sons*, Ivan Turgenev. She, too, had a perfect command of her native tongue, as well as of French. The strange story of what happened after she entered the convent was something that might have been imagined by Dostoevsky, but it was told to me by the Abbess just as she had witnessed it herself.

Barbara Turgenev had been the wife of a Russian diplomat, who had a post as consul, in Constantinople. A highly educated man, refined and brilliant, he was at the same time, completely immoral, a typical *viveur* and unfaithful husband. When his daughter, Katia (Mother Eustochie), was eighteen years old, he took her to Petersburg, to make her debut, just as I had made mine. Then she returned to France and found her true vocation; she became a Catholic and afterwards, a nun. She entered Saint Scholastica, and her mother joined her daughter, under rather unusual circumstances. She was extremely unhappy with her husband and was actually made to feel unwelcome in her own home, for Mr. Komarov had fallen in love with a young girl whom he wished to marry as soon as he could obtain a divorce. When Mrs. Komarov wished to retire to her daughter's convent, the kind Abbess, seeing her piety and devotion, admitted her to the cloister, but only conditionally.

When Mr. Komarov was advised of the date of the profession, he arrived for the ceremony in formal dress: frock coat, top hat with a number of decorations pinned to his chest. He pretended to be deeply moved by the event; in reality, he was delighted. The divorce he had requested from the Orthodox Church was slow in coming. In his confused mind, he recalled that Russian Tsars of old could repudiate a wife and remarry, provided the former spouse entered a monastery. This practice was now obsolete, a fact he preferred to ignore. He could see his wife and daughter through the grill, and though he shed a few tears to show his emotion, his face was extremely cheerful. After the two women had made their solemn vows, the Abbott, Dom Romain, mounted the pulpit and gave a short oration. He welcomed the newly professed, young nun. And then came the surprise: turning to Mrs. Komarov, now wearing the black veil and the great cowl of a choir nun, he reminded her that she was, and ever would remain Mr. Komarov's wife. Whenever he needed her, she would have to fulfill her marital duties and go back to him. Mr. Komarov's hopes were shattered. As the ceremony ended, he rushed to the grill and shouted in French, at the top of his voice: "Adieu, Barbara Turgenev!" He then rushed to the parlor, and demanded an interview with the Abbott and the Abbess, stormed and cursed and finally drove away, shaking his fist at the monastery and its inhabitants.

Years went by, Barbara Turgenev, now Mother Paule, lived in peace. One day, a telegram came. Mr. Komarov was seriously ill, in the south of France alone, abandoned, afraid of death. He implored his wife to come back. Mother Paule was not easily persuaded. She resented this man who had made her suffer. She declared that she would never leave Saint Scholastica. But the Abbess insisted that it was her duty to go back to her husband.

There were difficulties. The clothes which Mother Paule had worn had long since been disposed off. Her head was shorn. But the nuns consulted some fashion pictures; clothes were provided as well as a wig, and Mrs. Komarov set out tearfully on the dreaded journey.

Not only did Mr. Komarov make peace with his wife, but was deeply repentant and made a full confession of his sins and received communion on the eve of his death. Now Mother Paule could return to Saint Scholastica to pursue her life in peace.

As I packed my suitcase to leave Saint Scholastica, I found my volume of Proust unopened, the unfinished manuscript and the package of cigarettes untouched. I had never even thought of them. As I was to catch the early morning bus, the bells rang out for Mass. Once more, I saw the community pass in procession to the chapel. The nuns smiled a goodbye, and Mother Eustochie took my hand. We did not speak, for this was still the "Great Silence" — and it was better so. What words could have conveyed my gratitude!

I came back to Saint Scholastica more than once but I was never again allowed to enter the cloister. But I had learned the importance of the contemplative life, the meaning of prayer, which gave the community its thrust, its dynamism; it was like a power-house from which even those who did not belong to it could draw a new flow of spiritual energy.

I was not the only one of the "lost generation" to make this discovery. Many young intellectuals who were my contemporaries went through a similar experience. Some of them entered contemplative religious orders such as Saint Scholastica or En-Calcat. Others became oblates, settling down near Frances ancient monasteries: Jouarre, Solesmes, Saint Benôit, Vezelay, Le Saulchoirs, *La Pierre-qui-Vire*, etc.

However, the monastic or half-monastic way of life was not for me, as the wise old Abbess Cronier was quite aware. She did not try to keep me in the monastery, but she gave me a definite goal to carry away: the ecumenical dialogue, which in those days, had just begun to take form. Mother Eustochie would have wished me to stay on. She even planned that I should make a Byzantine rite Foundation of the Benedictines, such as that at Chevetogne in Belgium. This plan never materialized, but I left Saint Scholastica and returned to the world a different person. It was as though I had visited another planet and had come back to earth with memories of another dimension.

Mother Eustochie gave me the little cross which she had worn on her leather belt during the twenty years of cloistered life. It still hangs on my wall, one of the few objects I could save when I fled France in World War II. I made a promise never to hang anything else on that wall except Mother Eustochie's cross.

CHAPTER XI

Writer's Progress

RETURNING into the world after the days spent at Saint Scholastica was like leaving the flowers of the holy mountains to descend into a barren plain. This is, I believe, a common experience of those whose religious euphoria is not shared by others.

My difficulties were in part due to the fact that my Russian Orthodox relatives and friends blamed me for joining the Catholic Church and considered this as a betrayal. Most of these émigrés, who had suffered the loss of their country and former status, clung to their Faith as all they had saved from the disaster. A strong conservative nationalist trend reigned in this milieu, which was anti-Catholic even more deeply than it had been previously in Russia. I do not pass judgment on them. Following a century-old tradition, they were aggravated by everything "Roman." Neither was the Catholic Church prepared to dispel this hostility, which I felt deeply.

Mother Eustochie's dream, and my own wish to build a bridge between Rome and Moscow, was unfulfilled. Following the suggestions made by the Russian nuns of Saint Scholastica, I sought out a Catholic priest of Byzantine rite who had a small chapel in Paris with an iconostasis, vestments and other religious objects, and even a choir in strictly Slavonic style. But this chapel was only a beginning, something like an experimental center, and there were only a few Russian Catholics besides me who attended the liturgy. The priest was Monsignor Alexander Evreinov, later consecrated a bishop.

Many mistakes were made in the set-up of this experimental center. It took more than a decade to build up a Russian Catholic community in Paris. In other cities of Europe, America, and the Far East, similar attempts encountered as many difficulties as ours did.

Nor had I greater success in trying to rediscover in Pau, and later in Paris, the signs of the Catholic renaissance that had so deeply impressed me. Actually, this great spiritual reawakening was not made manifest, except among some contemplatives or in small circles of Catholic lay intellectuals. The religious houses I approached, unlike Saint Scholastica, received no guests and offered no spiritual direction.

My quest was disappointing, but I was not discouraged. I felt that if God wanted me to wait, if He seemed silent until things had matured, I would be patient and content with that which I had received already. Perhaps it saved me from excessive enthusiasm and that proselytizing zeal which makes converts commit so many blunders.

Meanwhile, I tried to practice my faith as well as I could, without further direction. The clergy of Pau was conservative and provincial.

Strangely enough, it was my Protestant mother who took the greatest interest in my newly adopted Catholic devotions. She said, "Now you will go to church every Sunday"—something I had not been doing for a number of years.

My mother was very particular about serving fish on Fridays and during Lent. She would have been surprised at the changes that Catholics have now made.

Alas, the Sunday Masses at our parish church of Pau were routine and cold compared to the beautiful services of the Benedictines. I preferred the early weekday Masses which gave more time for silent recollection. A tall elderly priest said the nine o'clock Mass in our parish. There was something unusual about him, and I learned that he was the Abbé Henri Brémond, a Jesuit and a scholar, who lived at Pau in semi-exile. He had been banished for having given absolution to Lord Tyrrell, who had been excommunicated by Rome for having opposed the dogma of papal infallibility. Brémond, called to Tyrrell's deathbed, ignored the ban. He was not expelled from his order, but dismissed from his community. He lived alone in a modest apartment near the parish church.

This distinguished Jesuit was in disfavor, not only because of the Tyrrell affair, but also because of his masterful work *The Literary History of Religious Feeling in France*, which was considered dangerously original. At the time I went to his early masses, he had just published another work, *Prayer and Poetry*. This book offered a comparison between mystical and poetic experience. It led to an exchange of letters between Brémond and Paul Valéry, the leader of modern French poetry.

I had read both Brémond's book and his correspondence with Valéry and was excited by both of them. Since he was our neighbor, I invited him to our home. He came most graciously, but he and my mother fell into a discussion about Luther, whom he attacked and she defended valiantly. Her charm finally disarmed him, and they parted good friends though neither one had given up one inch of their convictions. Brémond was later elected a member of the French Academy, and went to live in Paris. I clearly remember his visit because this unusual and brilliant old priest had reawakened my interest in literature. I felt that the time had come for me to go back to my writing.

In Paris once more, I found many openings; I was asked to help in the writing of a book by the young Frenchman Joseph Kessel. He was the son of a Jewish doctor, and though he wrote in excellent French, he also spoke and took a great interest in all things Russian. The book we were to write was a novel set in the time of the Tsarist regime, on the eve of its downfall. I was to provide the historic and political background to Kessel's daring plot, built around Rasputin's influence at Court and his murder.

My own recollections provided some colorful material to which I added considerable research. I collected and summarized all the books, magazine and newspaper articles pouring in from Russia, or from émigré circles, throwing new light on the last days of the Romanovs. The most striking document was the collection of the Tsarina's letters to Nicholas when he was at the front as commander in chief of the Russian army. The letters, published by the Soviets, were more exciting than anything that could be written by others about this dramatic era.

I interviewed a number of persons whom I knew or could get in touch with who were witnesses or indirect participants in this tragedy; politicians, journalists, ladies of the court or soldiers who had fought at the Russian front—a most exciting journey into the not-so-distant past.

My most interesting interview was that with Prince Felix Yusupov, the chief conspirator in Rasputin's assassination. He had himself written an account of what happened on that fateful night. I had been told that the Prince sued any person who had distorted his story, so I decided to get the facts personally from him.

Prince Yusupov, his wife, Irina Alexandrovna, and his daughter, as well as Irina's mother, the Grand Duchess Xenia, all lived in a large house in the Bois de Boulogne, the most elegant residential district of Paris. He was still quite wealthy, due to the jewels he had brought out of Russia, some of them priceless, as was a famous necklace of pink pearls. His house was always full of guests, many of them living on his bounty, for he was not only hospitable, but also most generous.

On the day of my visit, however, the house was very quiet. The Prince was recovering from an operation and had been ordered to rest. He received me, reclining on a divan, dressed in white silk pajamas. I was struck by the extraordinary beauty of his face. I had not seen him since his wedding day, when he had appeared as a prince charming. Now he was a mature man and one who had been through a frightening ordeal. His features had become even more striking. The large, gray-blue eyes were like two pools of light, mysterious, hypnotic; the dark eyebrows straight as arrows, the long eyelashes, the smile on the thin, slightly twisted lips made him look like an angel of the Renaissance.

His wife, Irina, entered. The radiant young bride I had seen in my debutante days was now austere and melancholy. But she had what Russians call an icon-like beauty. She stayed only a few moments, shy and silent as a ghost. The next person to appear was not ghostly but also shy. She was short, plain and dignified, nodding briefly to both of us. "My mother-in-law," said the Prince, introducing the late Tsar's sister.

When we were left alone, Prince Felix beckoned me to a chair and offered me a cigarette. It seemed strange that this beautiful, mysterious creature should greet me so casually, as if he had known me all his life. And yet, there was something satanic about his twisted smile. He talked for several hours about the assassination, and seemed quite pleased to reminisce, going over all the horrifying details. In conclusion, he showed me a ring he was wearing, with a bullet mounted in silver. He explained that this was the bullet that had killed Rasputin.

After this investigation, I went a step further and visited a young woman who had been one of Rasputin's fervent disciples. She said that she firmly believed that he was a holy man and compared him to Saint Francis. I was getting more and more bewildered and so was Joseph Kessel, who was sorting out all this fantastic material with me. She made us understand, even better than Alexandra's letters, the evil spell that Rasputin had cast, not only over this unfortunate woman, but also over all those around him. But this did not exonerate those who had taken advantage of this spell, and who had let Russia slip from one disaster to another until her military defeats had cost millions of lives.

Our book finally came out, under the title *The Blind Kings* (Les Rois Aveugles) published by Les Editions de France, 1925 and later, reprinted by Plon, Paris, 1970. There was also an English translation. It was well received by the French press and both Kessel and I enjoyed a brief moment of notoriety. At least, for me, it was a brief moment, before disaster struck. The emigration's monarchist circles were outraged. The same people who had condemned me for becoming a Catholic, now denounced me for betraying a sacred cause. Actually, I had never been a monarchist, but this mattered little to those who attacked me. They did so violently, by word of mouth and in the newspapers they published in Paris. They also tried to influence French society and the French press against me. The wave of hatred grew so fast that I found myself cut off and ostracized by people I had known, trusted and even loved. It was a hard awakening. But I had nothing to retract. The historic facts were on my side. Even my enemies recognized the validity of *The Blind Kings*. One of them said: "The book is true, but I hate it."

Characteristically enough, Joseph Kessel was not chosen as a target by these angry people. In their eyes, he was "just another Jew" whereas I belonged to their set and must be punished accordingly. This adverse criticism hurt not only me, but my publisher. However, our editor in chief was Marcel Prévost, a novelist of great repute in those days. He was a member of the French Academy and enjoyed tremendous prestige. He wrote an article in my defense, asserting that historic truth was above partisan opinions. This helped me, but not entirely. People long afterwards would say to me, "Were *you* the woman involved in that book?"

There is no youthful experience, however disastrous, that does not bring some good. I discovered my enemies, but also my real friends. A few French and Russians, even though they belonged to the conservative group, gallantly stood up for me and invited me to their homes. One incident which happened on the Riviera, was at first embarrassing but had a pleasant ending. I was visiting my friend, Anne Golitsyn, whose family was noted for its hospitality and gourmet food. One afternoon, unexpected visitors were announced. They were Grand Duchess Elena Vladimirovna, the wife of Prince Nicholas of Greece, with her two daughters, Elisabeth and Marina, the future Duchess of Kent. It had been noted that royalty on vacation loves to pay such impromptu visits, so the Golitsyn's chef busied himself to prepare a hasty but succulent meal. It was a bouillabaisse, the famous fish soup or stew which is a specialty of that region. It was a truly excellent production, but the Grand Duchess did not seem to like it. I sat opposite her and suddenly realized that the object of her dislike was not so much the soup as it was myself! "Good gracious," I said to myself, "Here we go again — she is mad about *that* book!" I could not help remarking, quite casually, that the Grand Duchess's own brother, still heir presumptive to the Russian throne, had not only accepted the Revolution, but had hailed it, though this had been forgotten as a lamentable incident.

The Grand Duchess cast a stern look at me. Tall, handsome, every inch a Romanov, she was quite intimidating. I bore the ordeal bravely. The rest of the meal was so delicious that the great lady relented or at least forgot about me. After luncheon, we played games and everybody laughed, including my severe judge. Later in the afternoon, the younger people, the two Princesses and I went swimming in the blue waters of the Mediterranean. We all had a good time and the Grand Duchess departed with her daughters in an excellent mood.

If I had lost some of my old friends, I found new ones among the emigré intelligensia: writers, poets, journalists and former left-wing members of the Duma. Although bitterly opposed to Communism, which had defeated them, they had retained their critical attitude toward the Tsarist regime. Many of them were socialists and all were confirmed liberals. Learning about the furor aroused by *The Blind Kings*, they welcomed me in their midst. Thus I entered a milieu that I had not known previously and found it a very stimulating one. I adopted these excellent people and they adopted me. I remember one of them saying: "You have been accepted by our *obshchestvennost*." This was a compliment, but difficult to put into English. It meant something like belonging to a progressive community, political, social and ethical, with high standards of integrity.

Encouraged by my new-found friends, and also not to lose the "feel" of my mother tongue, I started to write in Russian for some of the periodicals published by these liberals, and after that my ties with them were never severed. One of the copy editors of a Russian-Paris daily, who printed my articles in 1935, came to New York, later, as editor of another Russian paper and printed more of my work. He died in 1970, at the age of ninety, pursuing his vocation until his last days. I knew him for all those years as a man who never smiled and seldom talked, but he published everything I submitted without a single cut.

In the mid-nineteen twenties I was almost constantly at work in Paris, leaving my mother in Pau to the good care of Uncle Vania and a Béarnaise cook who had learned to prepare Russian dishes. In Paris I shared an apartment with a Belgian friend, Marguerite Quersaint. She led a bohemian life tempered by Belgian family tradition. The apartment was cheap, old-fashioned and picturesque. It had no electricity but was lit by gas lamps. There was a zinc bathtub where the water was heated by a gas range underneath. We called it "the soup pot." Marguerite wrote poetry, some of which was published, but she later married and dropped literature. She was a most intelligent and sensitive girl, but had no concern for religion. However, a Jesuit priest whom she had met on a ship during one of her travels, stimulated her interest, without ever trying to "convert" her, in the ordinary sense of the word. While I was staying with her, this priest came to luncheon. She introduced him as a paleontologist and geologist, teaching at the Institut Catholique. His name was Teilhard de Chardin.

There was something luminous about this tall, handsome, gracious man in his forties. He already had a high reputation for his scientific discoveries but was practically unknown for his religious and philosophical writings. Although his order had not allowed the publication of these works, Marguerite had some of them in mimeographed form, and showed them to me; but I was quite unaware that our friend Teilhard, as Marguerite called him, would someday revolutionize modern theology.

I was charmed by this dynamic and at the same time, simple and even modest personality. Marguerite had three cats and Teilhard was delighted with these pets. After luncheon, we took them down to our small backyard, and I took a picture of them. Teilhard is holding one of them as shown in my photo, wearing the plain, rather shabby garb of a poor, French cleric, a typical "country priest."

I had another opportunity of lunching with him at Marguerite's a few years later when she was married and had a little girl. She defiantly declared that the child would receive a strictly secular education. Teilhard patiently argued with her, proving that it would be best to let her little daughter know about God. He spoke smilingly, almost lightly, but so convincingly that Marguerite finally conceded. She promised Teilhard to follow his advice and, being a very straight and loyal person, she kept her promise.

I think it was my friend's loyalty and her fine sense of true values which attracted certain unique and delicate souls to her. Such was, of course, Teilhard de Chardin. Another was the poet Rainer Maria Rilke.

Rilke had asked her to check some poems he was composing in French. He would drop in at our little apartment with his faithful companion, Maria Klossovska, and her son, the young surrealist painter Baltus. They would spend hours in our sitting room under gas jets which emitted a gentle, hissing sound when they were lit. Though the poet already suffered from the illness which was soon to carry him away, in those days he still seemed in good spirits and absorbed in his French poems.

I remember him as an extraordinarily gentle person, dreamy, enveloped in a veil of loneliness even when he was with other people. He looked like a Slav more than a German, and this impression was conveyed to me especially because he spoke Russian to me. He had known Tolstoy intimately and had a deep veneration for him, having stayed with him during his visit to Russia. He also knew the painter Leonid Pasternak, the father of the young poet Boris Pasternak, whose work had just appeared. At that time, I was, myself, interested in this poetry and discussed it with our guest. This created an understanding between us which he remembered kindly, as it later appeared.

During those years I had kept up my interest in Soviet literature, which I followed as closely as possible. We received but little material from the U.S.S.R., but some of it was exciting. There were these poems of Boris Pasternak, hailed by expert Russian literary critics. Another poet whose work was of great classic beauty was Ossip Mandelstam. Boris Pasternak became known the world over some thirty years later due to his novel, *Doctor Zhivago*, while Ossip Mandelstam's poems began to be studied in the West in the nineteen sixties, years after his tragic death in a concentration camp.

I tried my hand at translating some of these poems into French. If I succeeded, I consider this as something as a *tour de force* which I could never repeat again. It required all the enthusiasm and also the boldness of youth. It led me to a pleasant surprise.

In the fall of 1926, my contribution in this field was requested by the editors of a new literary review which bore the rather ambiguous name of *Commerce*. This word currently used for trade, has another, old-fashioned, sophisticated French meaning. It can be interpreted as an intellectual intercourse. And such was obviously the aim of this review which published the works of avant-garde French authors, as well as the translations of contemporary works or classics of other countries: Germany, Italy, Spain, Russia, etc.

The editors in chief of *Commerce* were the poets Paul Valery and Saint John Perse (whose real name was Alexis Saint Léger), former Ambassador and a top adviser of the Ministry of Foreign Affairs. In fact, he was considered the *éminence griese* of French diplomacy between the two wars. As Saint John Perse, he was also the *éminence griese* of *Commerce*. His major poem *Anabase* was first published in this review. It was translated into English at the time when the author, who had fled France in World War II, held an important post at the Library of Congress in Washington. He was the last survivor of *Commerce's* brilliant galaxy of writers.

Saint John Perse is a "poet's poet" whose work is difficult to describe. His solemn verses have been compared to incantations. They are like the measured sounds of a brass gong. The literary critic Pierre de Boisdeffre describes his poems as "giving the *feeling* of the sacred without being sacred."[1]

The founder and director of *Commerce* was a wealthy American woman. Born Marguerite Chaplin, she was married to Prince Gofredo de Bassiano of ancient Roman stock, who was an amateur composer. They lived in France most of the time. While her husband was absorbed in his compositions, Marguerite de Bassiano patronized all the arts: music, painting, and modern literature. Her home in Versailles was full of invaluable pictures, including works of Picasso. She helped support needy writers, painters, and composers, among them Eric Satie. Her house was indeed a promised land, into which I wandered by pure chance. At that time, there were few observers of Soviet authors in Europe, and even fewer translations of their work. One man, however, was fully aware of what was happening on the Soviet literary front. He was Professor Dimitri Sviatopolk-Mirsky of the University of London, who had been my former partner at the debutante balls in Petersburg. Even in the old days, he was far more cultured and sophisticated than the other young men with whom I danced. He had been Grisha's friend. Since I had last seen him, he had fought with his regiment and was amongst the few who survived the battle of Tannenberg. He escaped from Russia at the time of the Bolshevik coup d'état and took up residence in England, combining teaching with literary criticism. He often came to Paris and was Marguerite Bassiano's adviser for Russian literature.

Mirsky saw my translations of a poem by Boris Pasternak and of another by Ossip Mandelstam. He approved them, though he was a severe, and often inexorable, critic. Princess Bassiano was looking for Russian material, and Mirsky recommended me. My translation was accepted and published in one of her 1925 issues. The Princess paid for my contribution generously. Best of all, she invited me to be a regular guest at the Sunday luncheons in the Bassiano residence at Versailles.

---

1. Librairie Académique, Perrin, Paris 1964.

These gatherings which lasted all afternoon remain as the most vivid remembrances of my life in Paris in the twenties. It was all done in great style and yet an intimate, almost family atmosphere, was preserved.

A fleet of chauffeured cars was sent to Paris to pick up the guests at their respective homes and bring them back in the evening. Luncheon was served in the large, sun-flooded dining room, and conversation started almost immediately as the guests sat down to a delicious meal. With fear and trembling, I observed the great men, poets, artists, and writers, who represented the epitome of modern *belles-lettres*.

There was Paul Valéry, the high priest of poetry, and the gentle blue-eyed Rainer Maria Rilke, as modest and relaxed as when I met him at Marguerite Quersaint's.

Shortly before his death in Switzerland in March 1926, Rilke wrote to his friend, the painter Leonid Pasternak, father of Boris Pasternak, who lived in Munich at that time: "The very fine Paris revue *Commerce*, edited by the great poet Paul Valéry, has published very impressive poems by Boris in a French translation by Helene Isvolsky, whom I have also seen in Paris." (In his autobiography, *I Remember*, Boris Pasternak tells of his meeting Rilke as a child when the German poet visited Tolstoy in Russia and knew Leonid, who painted Tolstoy's portrait and also made a sketch of him on his deathbed.)

Another guest at these luncheons was Leon-Paul Fargue, the "cosmic" poet. Two other critics of our society were also of this group. They were the French essayist Julien Benda, author of *The Treason of the Clerks*, and the German Bernard Groethaysen, who, a few years later, was to publish his *Origin of the Bourgeois Spirit in France*. Goodnatured, absentminded Groethaysen was a chain smoker, continually sprinkling cigarette ashes on his beard and shirt. Benda was correct, stiff, and biting in his denunciations.

The Russian adviser, Mirsky, came to Versailles as often as he visited Paris. He was still the black-bearded and rather fierce-looking man I had known in uniform. He was now more mature, however, and had acquired prestige which made him resemble a "Byzantine emperor," according to Marguerite Bassiano's enthusiastic opinion.

Saint John Perse never appeared at the Sunday luncheon. I was told that he avoided crowded receptions. Paul Valéry was the literary personality whom I most clearly remember as presiding over us all. To me he was very intimidating, and I hardly dared address him, though when we drove home together in one of the cars of the chauffeured fleet, he was much easier to approach and actually seemed quite relaxed. I gathered that this most outstanding poet was extremely "hard up," his works being known only to a special public. Princess Bassiano offered him much needed financial help. When Valéry was elected to the French Academy, his situation was considerably improved, but the patronage of the angel of *Commerce* should be acknowledged.

There were so many other remarkable people at the Versailles Sundays, that I'm afraid I cannot remember them all. From America came Archibald MacLeish, a young poet; Arthur Wales, an Englishman, brought us the translation of the Japanese 17th-century novel *The Tale of Genji*.

There were the composers: Igor Stravinsky, whom I had already met at my friend Argutinsky's, and Eric Satie; also the tall, fair-haired, and rosy-cheeked Sergei Prokofiev, soon to return to Soviet Russia, where a new period of his music was to start. Modern French composers were represented by François Poulenc and George Auric of the group known as *Les Six* (The Six). On one of the Sundays, Maurice Ravel lunched at the Bassianos. He lived in a villa nearby, and we drove him home. He asked us to come in, and with complete simplicity, played some of his compositions on the piano just for three of us.

The painters I most often saw at Versailles were Raoul Dufy, as sprightly as his pictures, the stocky, square-shouldered Derain, and Dunoyer de Segonzac, handsome as a movie star. As they gradually rose to fame, their pictures began to fetch enormous prices, but in the twenties, life must still have been a struggle for them. Derain gave painting lessons to Marguerite Bassiano's young daughter and was also commissioned to paint her portrait.

There were amusing or exciting incidents at our luncheons as when a young and "promising" pianist, whose name was Vladimir Horowitz, played chopsticks for us, or when we heard that Charles Lindbergh, on his transatlantic flight, was nearing the shores of France.

There was often an empty seat at these luncheon parties. It was reserved, half-jokingly, half-reluctantly, for a guest who was known to arrive hours late. In fact, he usually arrived after the meal was over, but I am sure there was always a snack ready for him. The culprit was Léon-Paul Fargue, whose poetry ranked with that of Valéry and Saint John Perse, but is still little known outside of France.

Fargue was a man who never conformed and preferred poverty and obscurity to the fame of a poet laureate. Since his poems could secure him no income, he ran a ceramic workshop, made his own designs and could operate a kiln. He was an able craftsman but had no interest in business. He spent most of his time in cafés where he could discuss literature with a few devotees or chance acquaintances who had read his poems. He stayed awake till dawn and I was told that during the wartime blackouts he suffered greatly for he could no longer roam the dark streets of Paris and his favorite haunts were closed. He would drop in at the police station of his precinct which was open all night and there he could always find a friendly audience.

Fargue was almost continually in debt. His participation in *Commerce* and Marguerite Bassiano's generosity improved his situation to some degree, but he was still known to make his taxi drivers wait for hours at the doors of friends he visited, until the cabbies grew impatient and demanded to be paid by his unwitting host. He would borrow money from anyone. One day, he attended a reception at the home of a duchess, famed for her literary salon. He conversed so delightfully that when he took his leave, she accompanied him to the hall. There was his hat with a note pinned on it from the butler: "Mr. Fargue owes me 50 francs." The duchess hastily paid the debt, a small compensation for the pleasure the poet had given her.

On the Versailles Sundays, Fargue adopted a "big brother" attitude toward me. While other famous guests kept their distances, he would make the most amusing and slangy remarks, as we strolled in the Princess' beautiful rose garden. Leon-Paul was then in his forties but looked older due to his insomnia and fondness for alcohol. Yet he was solidly built, with clear-cut, handsome features and large, penetrating dark eyes, and carried himself with princely dignity. There was something of the sleepwalker about him, as if the world around him was almost a dream or a nightmare. He was a brilliant talker, though sometimes extremely gross; then he would suddenly mingle Parisian slang with a burst of flashing, elegant epithets. I was attracted to this wonderful poet to the point of being infatuated. But this could only be a fleeting and most evasive relationship.

I do believe that he quite liked me, however. One day, we had a date to meet at the Café des Deux Magots, the haunt of many writers and painters, later, the headquarters of Jean-Paul Sartre. I waited two hours before Leon-Paul finally appeared, quite unconcerned and brilliant as usual. Another time, we arranged to meet at a station café where I was to catch a train. Hours passed, while I watched the clock move relentlessly toward the time of my departure. Fargue did not appear and I had to catch that train. In fact, I almost missed it. When we met again, neither of us apologized—I felt that he rather resented that I had not waited for him.

I saw him for the last time a few years later, just before the fall of France, when I was working on an illustrated magazine. We met in the editor's office, for Fargue was also writing color stories for them, being as usual desperate for money. Seeing me correcting proofs in the shabby, little office, he exclaimed: "Alas, my dear Helene, what have we come to?" *(Ah, ma Pauvre Helene où en sommes-nous?)* and he added: "They have shut off everything in my apartment: gas, electricity and even the camembert!" This was a typical example of Fargue's imagery; he talked as he wrote, in metaphors and fanciful analogies. One day at the Deux Magots he looked at my drink, a rum toddie in a tall glass, with a piece of lemon floating in it. "Why, that's a night-light," he said dreamily—thinking of the tiny wick floating in oil, that was used in those days for vigil lamps or sick rooms. Fargue's poetry was filled with strange, sometimes wild images, as in his poem *Vulturne* picturing the Last Judgment with loudspeakers instead of Angels' trumpets. His doomsday was terrifying in its truly Biblical dimensions and his rising of the dead was a modern version of the prophet Ezekiel.

The writer Colette said of Fargue that he spoke of things that others could not see. She visited him during his last illness when she herself, was in a wheelchair, and in her last book, *Break of Day and the Blue Lantern* (The Noonday Press, 1966), she described his lodgings on rue Montparnasse, a narrow lane opening on the great boulevard of that name. She also recalled his voice so vividly that I seemed to hear him speak: "his fat, rich, infinitely elastic voice, with a shade of suffocation over it, caused by chronic bronchitis." It was also caused by the cigarette which always dangled from his thin ironic lips.

Fargue died in 1947, when I was in New York. Later, returning to Paris, I wandered along the famous boulevard. I stopped at a street corner and read the sign: "Square Leon-Paul Fargue." There was a little sidewalk café on the square, so I sat down and ordered a rum toddy with a slice of lemon in it. If my old friend was not there, it simply meant that he was late, as usual.

For a while, *Commerce* brought out a few more of my contributions, but then the Bassiano's went back to Italy and the magazine was discontinued. Princess Bassiano founded another periodical, however, for Italian consumption, called the *Botega Oscura*, along the same lines.

Thanks to the generosity of a friend, I obtained a grant to write the biography of Michael Bakunin, the father of anarchism, whose escape from Russia I have related in a previous chapter on our early trip through Siberia. New material has been published in the U.S.S.R. about his extraordinary personality, which compares with the personality of a character in Dostoevsky's novel *The Possessed*. According to a Soviet scholar, Leonid Grossman, this romantic rebel may have been the prototype for the hero Stavrogin.

Considerable research has been done in Russia, France and America, since the publication of my slim volume, but it was one of the first to reopen this history of the early Russian revolutionary movement in Paris. It was published by the N.R.F.: *Editions de la Nouvelle Revue Française*, the leading publishing house of that time, connected to the *Revue* of the same name. It was the house of the French literary elite. Under Gallimard, its director, it brought out the works of Proust, Gide, Valéry, Drieu la Rochelle, Jacques de Lacretelle, to name only a few. It was a privilege to be even the smallest star in that great constellation.

But alas, once more I suffered a setback. This time it came from Bakunin's youngest daughter, who was a teacher living in Italy — a fact I had totally disregarded. Her students had somehow gotten hold of my book and began to tease her about some of my remarks. Miss Bakunin took a train to Paris and called on me in a state of great excitement. She would not listen to any apologies, but threatened to sue me and my publisher. We finally succeeded in calming her, by promising to delete the passages that offended her. But after my work on *The Blind Kings* and this on Bakunin, I have always remained somewhat nervous about my published writings.

In spite of these frustrating episodes, I look back at this period of my life as one of the happiest. The Paris literary world was kind to beginners. I found encouragement on every side. It was customary in France for young authors to send their books personally to critics or writers of repute. These gentlemen acknowledged our efforts by writing friendly notes of appreciation, and usually meant it.

A good friend of mine at that time was Suzanne Bertillon, a decorator, who gathered in her studio an interesting group of young painters, writers and musicians. This brilliant young woman was the daughter of Alphonse Bertillon, the inventor of anthropometry or fingerprinting. Her mother, a Russian Jew, was a surgeon and the first woman doctor to practice in Paris.

But Suzanne was interested in neither medicine nor criminology. She was a fine artist and had excellent taste in modern painting, music and drama. We often went together to avant-garde plays or concerts, and usually ended up at the *Dôme* or the *Coupole*, the two main cafés of Montparnasse where artists and intellectuals of all ages and nationalities met every night. Several young men of Suzanne's set usually accompanied us. One of them, whose name was Christian or *Cri-cri*, as we more familiarly called him, was our most constant escort. He did not impress me as particularly imaginative nor creative, but was always a pleasant companion, most courteous and correct. Only a few years later, he rose to fame as Christian Dior.

Though participating in French literary and artistic life, I never lost my interest in things Russian. A growing number of Russian intellectuals had come to Paris. I made the acquaintance of the novelist Ivan Bunin, considered the finest prose writer since Tolstoy. In the thirties he received the Nobel Prize for literature, and in the forties was invited by the Soviet Government to come back to Russia. He refused the invitation but granted permission to have his works reprinted in the Soviet Union. Two other émigré writers, Alexis Tolstoy (not related to the author of *War and Peace*) and Alexander Kuprin, a gifted short-story writer, did go back to the Soviet Union. I had a last glimpse of them as they left for Moscow.

There were many other gifted men and women who made up the Russian Parnassus in exile. Alas, France did not offer the opportunities that Russian émigrés found in America; they were not allowed to teach in schools or universities; their books were not translated (except for a few), their paintings or other works of art, seldom exhibited.

Two daily newspapers and several monthly reviews were founded by Russians who had preserved their wealth, and they did their best to help writers in exile, but royalties were scarce. A free university was founded and a music school, but they were not accredited and professors received minimum fees. However, the intellectuals, artists and musicians carried on with remarkable courage and devotion. It was a great example to meet these brave and talented people who were content with the mere necessities of life, living in small, dingy apartments, educating their children against great odds and seeking to perpetuate in foreign and often unfriendly surroundings, the best traditions of Russian humanism.

I was often asked how I have preserved, through so many years of exile, the correct use of my native tongue. I would say that I did not as much "preserve it," as perfect it, for during the twenties and thirties of my Paris period, I went through a thorough training which I could compare to postgraduate studies; the final polishing which I had missed in Russia. So that thirty years later, when I returned on a trip to Russia, my countrymen could not believe I had been away so long.

On my dutiful trips to Pau, my mother became aware of my urge to live and work in the great city instead of the quiet, provincial town of the Pyrenees. One day, she said to me: "Helene, let us go back to Paris."

So back we went — not to Paris itself, where rents were above our means, but to Meudon, a Parisian suburb halfway to Versailles. The apartment house where we came to live, 1 avenue de la Gare, was almost entirely occupied by Russian tenants, like a Russian enclave within French suburbia. It even had a Russian grocery store which sold everything we needed: including homemade borsch, pickles, vodka and Russian newspapers.

This house was described by our finest poet and prose writer and I would like to quote a passage from her, which is more colorful and vivid than anything I can say. She was our neighbor, the unforgettable Marina Tsvetaeva.

> The famous house of the emigration, avenue de la Gare — all-émigré barracks, which was lighted up at night like a ballroom or a hospital, each window with its own insomnia. The house with music pouring down, like a shower on the passerby from each of its seven stories. Every window with its own music — (Don't you ever sleep?) strings, wind, chorals, piano, soprano, children's music, the Russian nostalgia in many different voices. The house where old people died, every day, and new people were born. Full of christenings and funerals, with priests and mailmen ever present. (Are you writing letters all the time?) The house where you never find anyone at home because everyone is visiting everybody else in the house. Where Ivanov does not find Petrov at home, because he is at Ivanov's. The house which stays alive, aglow with festivities til Carnival, spilling over to Easter, for there is always someone late with celebrating (because of sick-

ness, lack of funds). A continuous New Year's, a continuous Easter. Last Easter, 1931, the entire house took off at the same time to the five Paris churches, the three Meudon churches and one in Clamart (to one God, but separately). And in spite of differences of confessions and distances, everybody stumbled home together with candles and embraces. The house which that night, did not sleep at all because of the midnight Easter Mass, and in the morning was full of sounds: "Christ is risen!" "We were at your place" — The house where all would visit each other so hurriedly, up and down the stairs, that they never met — An inanimate object animated by the Russian soul; a wide-open fortress whose doors remained unlocked until morning.

This picture may be somewhat of a poetic exaggeration, but its spirit is true. It is clear from what Marina said that we found in that house an extraordinary community life—an example of solidarity and brotherhood.

No one was lonely on the avenue de la Gare and nobody was destitute. It was jokingly said of our suburban "stronghold" that we all survived thanks to a certain thousand-franc bill which we lent each other in an emergency. When reimbursed, it was immediately passed on to someone else and so on, *ad finitum*. But it was not only financial aid which was available at avenue de la Gare, but the kindness of everyone which made our life far more secure and pleasant than that in many deluxe apartments. My mother was in her late sixties and in poor health; I would not have been able to leave her alone when I went to work in Paris, had it not been for good neighbors who kept an eye on her, when I was away. If I stayed in the city for a lecture or an evening show, there was always someone ready to "baby-sit" until I came home. One of our neighbors was a doctor, another a typist who helped me with my work. There was also a professor and a journalist among the many intellectuals under our roof.

I remember particularly one family of devoted parents who had a number of children whom they struggled to feed and educate. The eldest daughter painted scarves to make a living, but she also found time to study. Her main interest was French medieval history and she grew up to become an accomplished scholar and writer. She published several historical novels which were best sellers in France and later, reached America in translation. Her name was Zoe Oldenburg, author of *The Cornerstone* and *The Crusaders*.

But most remarkable of all, was Marina Tsvetaeva, now acknowledged to be one of Russia's greatest poets. I first met Marina at a small party arranged by a group of young Russian intellectuals who called themselves "The Eurasians." They were inspired by a new concept of Russia and its culture as being neither European nor Asian, but a combination of both. This idea was reflected in a periodical called *Versty* which, for a time, played an important part in Russian émigré circles. It was not communist, but took a constructive view of the deep, social changes brought by the Revolution. Only a few writers belonged to this group, among them, Dimitri Mirsky and Marina's husband, Sergei Efron. The movement was short-lived but had a considerable influence on the younger émigré circles and even on some Soviet intellectuals.

Marina's party was held in the Paris suburbs, very much like our Meudon. The room was crowded and full of cigarette smoke. As I was introduced, a young woman with short-clipped, graying hair, rose from a divan and hurried toward me, waving a cigarette holder in one hand, and a lorgnette in the other. She was very shortsighted and her face was white and drawn. She was not tall but slender; her thin, pale lips were smiling mysteriously, reminding me of some young woman of the Renaissance, and her movements were quick and precise, as if she were driven by an inner rhythm.

"I am Marina Tsvetaeva," she exclaimed, fixing her pale, blue eyes on me, "and I have a message for you from Boris Pasternak." She grasped my hand firmly and we sat down, side by side on the divan. Lighting another cigarette, she told me in rapid, staccatto phrases that she corresponded with Pasternak — something that an émigré could rarely do. He had written to her that he read my translation of his poem, and liked it.

I was in "seventh heaven" — at last I had a link with a world from which I had been cut off, with which I longed for contact. I also felt suddenly close to the young woman who had brought me this surprising news.

This marked the beginning of a great friendship which lasted until Marina left France during World War II, and met a tragic death. In the following chapter, I shall write about Marina, her creative life and the sad fate that awaited her and her son Mur, as well as her husband, Efron, and our friend Dimitri Mirsky, all of whom returned to Russia during the War. Little could we foresee the doom that would overtake them.

As soon as we were settled in Meudon, I began to look for a regular job. Commuting presented no difficulty since we were linked by an electric train to Montparnasse. I made the rounds of my literary connections, but, alas, there was no work available at the high level I had hoped for. Joseph Kessel finally referred me to his younger brother, George, who had started an illustrated police magazine called *Detective*.

I was reluctant to apply, but Joseph said that his brother was a gifted and already experienced journalist. I went to see the young man who knew of my knowledge of languages and he told me that he wanted foreign news items; he suggested that I try my hand at a color story. I was not too happy about this assignment but I knew that my colleagues, some quite famous, like Léon-Paul Fargue, had to write for small magazines to make a living. There were no "grants," no "writers in residence" in the Paris of those days.

I bought all the French, English-language and German newspapers that I knew; in vain, I searched for a crime that would provide a sensational color-story — until I found the account of the St. Valentine's day shooting in Chicago. I realized that this was a "scoop." But I knew nothing about American "gang warfare." I spent several days making inquiries visiting American newspaper offices and information centers; I called on reporter friends who consented to open their files — their so-called "morgue," to my scrutiny. Finally I attacked the story. The subject did not appeal to me. I had a deep distaste for violence. But this was, on the other hand, an extraordinary human document which stirred my imagination. I wrote the story, with the result that I was hired as a contributing editor of *Detective*.

My friend, Marie-Louise de Sinçay, was shocked when she heard of my new job. "Are you a detective?" she asked, sarcastically. I reassured her that I was merely a crime reporter, and added that most of the crimes I had to write up were "made in America." This puzzled her still more.

But there was also a Russian crime I was asked to cover. It was committed right in Paris, only a few blocks from the home I had shared with Marguerite Quersaint. On January 26, 1930, a Russian émigré and former general of the White Army was kidnapped in full daylight at the corner of a narrow street where he lived, next to a Catholic hospital. He was General P. A. Koutiepov, leader of a secret paramilitary organization which was sending its agents to Russia to promote an illusory counterrevolutionary action. The rightist émigrés who had fought under his command considered him a hero. His conspiracy was doomed, many of his agents perished, but he may have had important plans which the communists wanted to get hold of.

Several neighbors who knew him saw the General go out on foot, to do some shopping. A nurse of the Catholic hospital who happened to be looking out of the window, observed the kidnapping scene: a car drove up, a man in uniform, impersonating a French policeman, got out, arrested Kutepov and drove away with him. No one knows what happened, but speculation had it, that he had been taken to a mystery ship, docked at Le Havre, and spirited away to the Soviet Union.

Since I was Russian, I was assigned to follow various trails which might lead to the fake policeman and his victim. But the kidnapping had been so cleverly carried out that the trails led nowhere. The police were as confounded as I was. I found the "case of the vanishing General" so scary that I turned it over to a reporter with stronger nerves than mine.

Later, I switched to another periodical which was not quite so grim. I wrote travelogues, nature and science stories, and also wrote up some interviews. I learned that a journalist's life is sometimes exciting, but mostly exhausting. It was an experience very different from that of living in the Bassiano's "Ivory Tower."

I would have welcomed a change and felt hopeful when I was summoned to do an emergency job for an important magazine called *Match*, the equivalent of the American *Life*. The material had to go to the printer's early in the morning. I thought this might give me the break I needed, and hurried to the office of Pierre Lazareff, then editor in chief of *Match*. I had heard that he was one of the youngest and shrewdest Paris journalists. I found him to be a small, bespectacled man, seated in his swivel chair in his shirt-sleeves and suspenders, smoking a cigarette; both his feet were stretched out on his desk, which was littered with papers.

Lazareff uttered a few brief commands and I was rushed to the copy editors' room where I spent the night at the job assigned to me. As soon as I had finished it, I issued forth into the deserted and chilly Paris streets; dawn was breaking and life faintly stirring. My hopes had been in vain. I was not hired by *Match*. I did not see Lazareff again for a number of years. But he had not forgotten me. The next time he gave me a job far more interesting than any in *Match*. But that was in New York, 1942.

As I look over the past, I see that many events which marked my life were brought about not through my own will, but through coincidence. Or shall I call it Providence, which brought important changes in my life? Though I am not a fatalist, I have become aware that our wishes are not fulfilled by our power alone, nor at the hour that we have chosen.

During the years which I have just described, I was drifting further and further away from my original intention, of working along spiritual lines, especially for the union of the churches of East and West. I found no support in literary circles, nor in the tense atmosphere of journalism. I did not know anyone to whom I could turn in matters of religion.

Through a chance meeting with a young girl on a train, I found the key to my dilemma. We were travelling by night and shared a sleeping compartment. The girl's name was Madeleine du Bos and since neither of us could sleep, we struck up a conversation. Madeleine's interests were horses, races and fox hunting, not exactly mine. But she was a bright, sympathetic young person. When I told her that I was a writer she exclaimed: "Why, you must meet my brother, Charlie!"

"Charlie" was none other than Charles du Bos, the Catholic writer whose fame as an essayist, literary critic, editor of avant-garde reviews was widely spread, in France and abroad. Seeing my interest, Madeleine gave me an introduction to her brother and he invited me to his home.

I shall always remember the warm welcome and understanding given to me by Charles du Bos and his wife. Thanks to them, I found at last the environment I so much needed, that of the new Catholic "Renaissance" which was sweeping over the rigidity or cool complacency of the Church. Here was a spiritual revolution in its purest expression. But there was nothing revolutionary in the aspect of this quiet, middle-aged, kindly man with his blue eyes and heavy, dark mustache, as he had risen to greet me in his book-lined study. He was a typical French scholar, correct, precise in every word, constantly seeking to clarify his thoughts and that of others.

Du Bos had an international background; his mother was an Anglo-American and he had studied at Oxford and in Germany. He spoke English and German fluently and his literary criticism embraced world literature. With André Gide, the novelist, he had founded the international *Décades de Pontigny,* a yearly symposium of philosophers and writers held in a former Benedictine abbey, later the residence of the humanist leader, Paul Desjardins. Du Bos had later drifted away from Gide because of the latter's amorality and skepticism, retaining, however, his interest in Pontigny and its participants. (His dispute with Gide was published under the title *Dialogue with André Gide*). Intellectuals from many countries came to his Paris home. Among them were German Jews and Catholics who had fled Hitler's persecutions which were then growing more threatening from day to day.

Thanks to du Bos' knowledge and sympathy for many nationalities, he understood me better than certain French intellectuals I had sometimes encountered who regarded me as an exotic "Cossack," while the left-wingers thought of me as a tsarist. The novelist André Malraux (who was later the Minister of Culture under de Gaulle but at that time a Communist), flatly ignored me, as being a "White Russian." Du Bos had a broader outlook on things in general and on Russian émigrés in particular, knowing several philosophers and writers exiled from the Soviet Union for whom he had the highest opinion. Tolerant of the religious convictions of every man, he was himself a devout Catholic. For many years he had been estranged from his Church, but he had recently returned to his faith and practiced it with great fervor. He was a daily communicant, made retreats at Saint Scholastica, where one of his nieces was a novice; so, like myself, he was inspired by the Rule of Saint Benedict and by Gregorian chant.

I learned to appreciate the erudition and literary subtlety of du Bos when he asked me to work with him on the translation of a Russian book which I had recently discovered. It was an exchange of letters, something like the Gide-du Bos dialogue, between two Russian writers, the symbolist poet Viacheslav Ivanov and the literary critic Michael Gershenzon. The letters had been written in Leningrad in 1921, when the authors had both been hospitalized and lay each in his corner of the public ward. So the book was entitled *Correspondence between Two Corners*. They discussed from their sickbeds the meaning of the Revolution which had just taken place; Gershenzon saw it as a *tabula rasa* necessary for the creation of new values, whereas Ivanov defended the idea of the *Thesaurus*, the necessity of preserving the cultural values of the past. This dialogue was in its own time, and remains today, an important document, due especially to Ivanov's extraordinary personality. As a poet and philosopher he had dominated the Russian literary scene on the eve of the Revolution. He was known for his book *Dyonisius, the Suffering God*, in which he showed the Greek divinity as the prefiguration of Christ. He was also the author of a profound work on Dostoevsky. So great was his prestige that he was called "Ivanov the Magnificent."

During the early days of the Revolution, Ivanov escaped with his family and came to live in Rome. He taught at the Pontifical Gregorian Institute; he had been a Russian Orthodox believer, deeply imbued with his country's religious tradition, yet at the same time attracted by ancient Greek culture and mythology. Rome came to represent to him the Catholic *Thesaurus*—he joined the universal Church, preserving the Byzantine rite and thus following the precepts of my master, Vladimir Soloviev. This formed a link between me and Ivanov, although I had never met him at that time. He once wrote: "We have been baptized in Soloviev."

As we set to work on Ivanov's *Correspondence*, I translated from the original Russian text, while du Bos, who knew no Russian but was an expert on religious and philosophical terminology, checked every word of my French translation. It was like the task of a jeweler, examining each gem before setting it. We submitted the result of our joint effort to the "Magnificent," who approved it and added an introduction, clarifying his Catholic position, which the *Correspondence*, written earlier, could not have anticipated. Our translation was published in the Catholic review *Vigile*, and later in book form by Correa, Paris, 1928. Ivanov's letter to me was unfortunately lost when Hitler occupied Paris, in 1940.

My work with du Bos had been a hard but interesting job. I was rewarded when Ivanov wrote me a personal letter of appreciation, saluting me as a Russian Catholic, like himself. Much later, his son, Dimitri Ivanov, became one of my good friends when I visited Rome.

Thanks to Charles du Bos, I made another connection with the movement considered the Catholic Religious Renaissance, indeed, I met its leader, the neo-Thomist philosopher Jacques Maritain. He had found in the *Summa* of Thomas Aquinas the principle of the common good, the very basis of social justice. Charles du Bos was a good friend of Jacques, as he familiarly called him, and suggested that I make his acquaintance. By another "coincidence," he lived not far from our house in Meudon. I would have been shy about approaching Maritain, even with du Bos' letter of introduction in my pocket, had it not been for a certain china plate, with a pussywillow pattern.

This plate had been described by the poet Jean Cocteau in a letter to Jacques Maritain, to whom he owed his return to the Church. The letter, published with an answer from Maritain, had moved me, because I had seen Cocteau at Madame de Chevigné's, the friend of Proust and prototype of his character Madame de Guermantes. He lived in the same apartment house as the old Countess and would often drop in for a chat, while we were visiting her.[2]

Jean Cocteau was the *enfant terrible* of literary Paris; the unruly, fancy-free poet, critic and dramatist, filmmaker, opium addict and homosexual. He was on the brink of moral and physical collapse when a chance visit to the home of Maritain brought him back to life. There he had encountered a missionary of the White Fathers of Africa who had given him a "spiritual shock treatment" that had restored his sanity and his hope.

In his letter, Cocteau speaks, in his vivid style, of the philosopher and his wife, Raissa, who had welcomed him with such kindness and understanding. He also described the surroundings, the house, its atmosphere, its set-up and the blue willow plates. This had been my favorite pattern, remembered since childhood; its mention by Cocteau was like a sign to me that I should go there. So I had written to the Maritains and a few days later sat at their hospitable table with its blue willow plates, just as Cocteau had described them.

Maritain was a small, fragile man with delicate features; his physical frame seemed to have just enough consistance to enclose and hold the spirit that filled it. Gentle in manner, courteous in speech, Maritain immediately captivated me by his charisma, which I can best describe by one word, luminous.

As to his wife, Raissa, Cocteau compared her to "our Lady's thread," a fine web or rather filament, spun by the tiniest spider. She was indeed, a frail and often ailing woman, but spiritually and intellectually as strong as the silvery web to which she was compared. I cannot think of the Maritains as two separate persons. Though different in origin, they were linked by a common destiny. Raissa was Jacques Maritain's faithful convert from their student days, when they had come as agnostics to the study of Henry Bergson and then approached a further spirituality together through the influence of Leon Bloy, the great Catholic reformer. Through his guidance they found the fullness of Christian faith, and became Catholics.

Of Jewish descent and born in Russia, Raissa had retained her native tongue and culture. She was, therefore, most helpful to me later, as I worked to establish contacts with the Russian Orthodox. On the other hand, firmly rooted in her race, Raissa was a pioneer of Judeo-Christian relations. No one had a deeper insight than she into the "mystery of Israel," which was one of Maritain's major concerns.

---

2. I knew of the letter as it was published in *An Answer to Jean Cocteau* by Stock, Paris, 1927. It was later translated by John Coleman into English and called *Art and Faith, Letters between Jacques Maritain and Jean Cocteau*, Philosophical Library, New York, 1948.

The teaching of neo-Thomism, as presented by Jacques Maritain, rejected the humanism of the Renaissance, centered on Man alone, without the transcendant dimension of God, creator of man, and of Christ, man's redeemer and ultimate goal. Putting it in another way, Maritain sought to establish the primacy of spirit over matter; the importance of the human person not centered in itself, but in a Supreme Being or God.

Although I have been attracted to the great masters of Eastern spirituality and by the thought of Teilhard de Chardin, I still consider Maritain's teaching on man and society extremely valuable and unique in those days. Far from offering us an ironclad doctrine, which is usually associated with that of scholasticism, he made a dynamic and creative appeal to the spiritual forces. He gave us the feeling that we stood on the threshold of a new era in which heaven and earth, the City of God and the city of man, would be brought together. His criticism of Marxism and of the totalitarian societies, as well as of the bourgeois, capitalist establishment, have lost none of their impact. His book *True Humanism* (*Humanisme Integrals*, Fernand Aubies, Paris, 1936) was published in English by Scribners and speaks of this new "heroic humanist of a personalist, pluralistic and communal democracy," and this can still be said to provide a basic pattern for Catholic liberal thought or Catholic social doctrines.

Most appealing of all, as I reread his social-political writings, was his concept of a new kind of saintliness, the saintliness of the dedicated layman, involved in the temporal world yet oriented toward the world of the spirit. This new kind of saintliness could lead the layman to the most radical reforms, but required, first of all, a "purification of means," that is, moral restraint and preparation through prayer and contemplation.

Such was the general character of what I shall call "the Maritain experiment," the search for political and spiritual balance or truth, the great search which I was to follow and share with Maritain for a number of years. If, later, we drifted apart, there remained between us a deep friendship and affection.

From the very beginning, Jacques and Raissa were most kind and understanding. They invited me to their Sunday afternoons when their friends came from Paris and other suburbs to see them. How different were these Sundays from the sophisticated luncheons of Versailles, with their atmosphere of intellectual aloofness.

Maritain's circle was made up of writers, poets, critics and philosophers of the "new wave": Claudel, Bernanos, François Mauriac, Gabriel Marcel, leader of Christian existentialism, Henri Gheon, playwright and biographer, Daniel Rops, author of *Jesus and His Times*, Stanislaus Fumet, editor of the avant-garde Catholic review *Temps Présent* and Emmanuel Mounier, editor of *Esprit* and author of the Personalist *Manifesto* of which I shall speak more fully in the next chapter.

Another guest of the Maritains' was Pierre Van der Meer, head of the Catholic publishing house of Desclée de Brouwer, of Belgium and France, whose story was quite unusual.

In the early thirties, Pierre Van der Meer and his wife decided to separate, to go into two cloistered Benedictine communities, but later, discovered that the contemplative life was not their vocation. So they were released from their vows and reunited. After his wife's death, Van der Meer returned to his monastery, and was ordained a priest. Later, he was elected prior. He died in 1970.

Several religious, Jesuits, Dominicans and Carmelites, came on Sundays, as well as we young professors and students of the Institut Catholique, where Maritain held a chair of theology. And of course, Charles du Bos was a frequent guest at Meudon.

These Sundays were not limited to Catholics. The Maritains had friends among Russian Orthodox and Jews. Interested as they were in modern art and music, they had such visitors as Chagall and Stravinsky. It was, for me, the sharing of a great experiment, in which Catholics and non-Catholics were joining, perhaps for the first time.

The Maritains and their circle understood and welcomed with sympathy, my interest in the developments within Russia. Although we rejected the materialistic character of communism, and the ruthless methods of the Stalin regime, we felt that there were dynamic forces at work in the depths of the Russian people. These forces transcended the narrow framework of the atheistic state. I felt convinced that a "new man" was emerging in Russia. What sort of man was he? Not made according to the official pattern yet reflecting inevitably, the profound changes that had been brought about by the very fact of the Revolution. He represented the new world but also carried with him the *Thesaurus*, the spiritual heritage of Holy Russia. In those days, the Soviet Union was a closed circuit; there were no cultural exchanges. As yet, no tourists penetrated the forbidden city. But thanks to certain bits of information I had managed to collect, a portrait of the "new man" could be constructed. He offered a few promising signs. In spite of the impact of Communist internationalism, he had gradually rediscovered the roots of Russia, a national culture and tradition. He had not lost his religious sense and he was linked not to the dehumanizing, totalitarian commune, but to the ancient Russian idea of Christian solidarity.

I attempted to project this portrait in an essay which was published by Pierre Van der Meer in a series of contemporary studies. It was called *Homme Soviétique* (The Soviet Man), Desclée de Brouwer, Paris, 1936.[3]

Little did I suspect that this booklet had reached America, and was read there by a man named Peter Maurin, who gave it to Dorothy Day.

---

3. The essay was later published in German (*Vita Nova Verlag*, Luzern, 1936) and in English by Sheed and Ward (New York, 1937).

They had founded the *Catholic Worker* movement in 1932, of which I was unfamiliar at that time, and which was later to play a decisive role in my life.

In the meantime I had taken another step in what I might call "Writer's Progress," aided by my good friends and teachers of the "New Wave." Modesty should perhaps prevent me from saying that Maritain was kind enough to quote me in his booklet *Humanisme Intégral* (pp. 71, 94), but I give it as a proof of his remarkable generosity and goodwill toward people younger and less experienced than himself.

CHAPTER XII

The 1930s – Time of Decision

IT WAS THROUGH the Maritains, that, in the late twenties, I made the acquaintance of Nicholas Berdiaev, the Russian Orthodox philosopher exiled from his country and living in Clamart, another suburb of Paris, only two miles from Meudon.

Maritain and Berdiaev were linked by many ties of friendship and mutual appreciation. They held many ideas in common in the sphere of Christian humanism and the search for social justice. On other points, however, they remained in complete disagreement and these differences were eventually to draw them apart. However, the genuine cordiality they felt for each other, and which I often had the opportunity of observing, was never lost.

Soon after I met Jacques and Raissa, they suggested that I accompany them to the ecumenical discussions which were held in Berdiaev's home. I gladly accepted the invitation. For some time, I had been reading the works of Berdiaev and knew of his deep concern with the problems of faith and the destiny of man in the modern world. I had also heard his story. He had been the son of a landowner in the Ukraine, and the young Berdiaev had been involved in student rebellions and was imprisoned and then sentenced to several years of forced residence in a small, provincial town. At first, he became a confirmed Marxist; he shared the fate of other followers of Marx and had been in full accord with them. But during the daily studies and discussions which he pursued with his companions in the hotel where they were quartered, Berdiaev gradually became aware that the Marxist theory of dialectic materialism led to the denial of freedom; it led to a closed, collective society. Seen in this perspective, dehumanization was near. The creative power of man which belongs to the realm of the spirit, had no chance of remaining alive and of expanding.

Having reached this conclusion, Berdiaev not only broke with his companions, but renounced materialism in the name of the transcendent faith which he had found in Christianity. Baptized and raised as a Russian Orthodox by his family, he returned to the traditional religion that he had, for a time, abandoned. But now he sought to infuse it with the humanist, social ideas he had acquired. After he was released from his forced residence, he became one of the leaders of a Russian Orthodox revival, in many aspects similar to the Catholic "new wave."

In this sphere, Berdiaev met Jacques Maritain halfway. Both sought the "true Christian humanism" which could reform society. Both criticized the materialistic, bourgeois structure of the modern world around them, as well as the excesses of the totalitarian regimes, communist, nazi, or fascist. However, Berdiaev had deeper insights into the Marxists, having been one himself. He had experienced the pressures of the Communist rule, having lived under it for five years. He was twice arrested and, finally, exiled with his wife, Lydia, and threatened with the death penalty, if he ever tried to return. But in spite of all this, he retained a deep love of his native land and was entirely imbued with its culture. Dostoevsky, Tolstoy, Vladimir Soloviev were the source of his religious inspiration, even more than the Church to which he adhered, without accepting its total authority.

So it is easy to see that Berdiaev differed from Maritain, without contradicting him in any essential way. I believe that Russian religious thought as represented by Berdiaev not only attracted Maritain but also influenced him and his entourage, especially the younger members.

As to the Russian philosopher, due to his French friends he took a broader view of Catholicism as expressed by its new, progressive leaders. He was an admirer of Leon Bloy and brought him to the attention of his own Orthodox followers. His objections to Maritain's dogmatic positions were due to his reliance on St. Thomas, on Aristotle and on the Western mode of speculation, typical of scholasticism, and so deeply opposed to the more mystical spirituality of the Eastern Church.

In spite of these disagreements, Berdiaev had not only sympathy and understanding for Catholic religious culture, but a direct "feel" for it due to his own affiliations. His maternal grandmother was a French woman, born Countess de Choiseul, who had fled her country during the French Revolution. She had married a Russian nobleman, but retained her Catholic faith. She even continued to use the de Choiseul prayerbook. She objected to any allusions to the difference between Catholics and Orthodox and so, in her way, was a precursor of ecumenism. Berdiaev mentions her in his autobiography *Dream and Reality* (Macmillan, 1951). This was the origin of his interest in promoting a rapprochement with Catholics; this interest extended also to Protestants. There was also a family link between Berdiaev's family and our own. His grandmother, whose Russian name was Kudashev, had a son, Prince Ivan Kudashev, who was my Uncle Vania's father. Although a distant connection, I was happy to find it in our respective family *sagas* and was eager to be admitted to the Clamart talks.

My first glimpse of the famous philosopher was not disappointing. He was somehow, just what I expected him to be, a typical, Russian gentleman, both attractive and imposing. I remember him sitting in his living room in the midst of a small circle. From time to time, he would shake his dark, lion-like mane of hair which was streaked with silver; or inhale the smoke of a small cigar which seemed a part of him. His handsome, somewhat ruddy face with straight nose and pointed, graying beard and bright hazel eyes under heavy eyebrows, gave him a grave, concentrated look, but he never lost his amiable expression.

There were only a few Orthodox guests present at this discussion, as they were wary of ecumenical perspectives. There were no Protestants, at Maritain's request, for in those days, his views on the Reformation were strictly negative. He gradually softened his attitude, but he remained unbending on the main issues which concerned Calvin and Luther.

Catholics, on the other hand, were well-represented. There was, of course, Maritain himself, Charles du Bos, Gabriel Marcel, Etienne Gilson, Henri Massignon, (one of the most distinguished authorities on Moslems) and Father Gillet, a Dominican scholar who later became head of his order. There was also, Father La Berthonière, a secular priest with modernist tendencies, who opposed Thomism.

Due to the tensions caused by various arguments during the meetings, they were soon discontinued, never to be resumed at Clamart. During these few encounters, I hardly had the time to get close to Berdiaev; this opportunity came a few years later and, as so many things in my life — quite unexpectedly. My closer contact with Berdiaev came not through these ecumenical attempts, but because of my involvement in certain youth movements of the "new wave." One of these was led by Emmanuel Mounier, a young, French Catholic philosopher who was inspired by Maritain and Berdiaev, with their Christian humanism, and gave it his own original and dynamic form: a call to the "Personalist and Communitarian Revolution." The concept was explained in his book *Revolution Personaliste et Communautaire,* reprinted by Editions du Seuil (Paris, 1961).

Mounier had an acute sense of the crisis in the modern world. He denounced the social and economic evils of capitalist countries as "the established disorder." Personalism as opposed to selfish bourgeois *individualism,* affirmed the dignity of man, "created in the image and semblance of God." It held that each person was unique, informed by the Spirit. But at the same time, he was related to other persons, a part of a community and called to serve all men.

Like Maritain and Berdiaev, Mounier made a careful analysis of Marxism. He recognized, as his masters did, that Marxist criticism of man's alienation within the capitalist framework was justified. So was the Marxist attempt to offer a remedy to economic slavery. However, he also pointed out that Marxist materialism did not take the spiritual value of the human person into account.

Mounier's view of the modern world was not a condemnation, but rather an attempt to rebuild it according to a positive, transcendental philosophy. He stressed the primacy of the spirit above matter, the primacy of the human person and a relation between man and society based not on constraint but on love. He called for a revolution without violence, but based on the transformation of every separate person and of his way of life, liberated from the struggle for money and from the pressures of an impersonal state. A community of men, linked by love and mutual service was to replace the centralized, all-powerful state. Such a transformation could not take place overnight. The immediate goal was for each person to dedicate himself, to have his own change of heart, before changing the world. Such idealism or *personalism* appealed especially to young people. It meant sacrificing material interests and gains, for a spiritual way of life. Such demands could only be made by a leader whose own standards and integrity were on the highest level, and such was the case with Mounier. He was twenty-six years old when I first met him at the Maritain's. Fair-haired and blue-eyed, he had the clean, clear features of youth: a sincerity and strength of conviction, untouched by the chilling breath of skepticism. At the same time, his manner of life, his way of meeting the hardest challenges were like those of a mature man.

Mounier had renounced a successful academic career to devote himself entirely to the personalist movement. He made many sacrifices, accepting poverty for himself and his family. He met with considerable opposition, because his ideas did not fit any conventional mold. He was a Catholic but worked with Protestants, Russian Orthodox, Jews and unbelievers. He was critical of the Church which was allied with the power of money and of bourgeois reaction. He defied the all-powerful press which he considered corrupt and servile to vested interests. His radicalism went against the grain, not only of the capitalist establishment but also of the communist dogma.

Although the personalist movement did not have a large following (it was not supposed to be a mass movement), it attracted a youthful élite, consisting mostly of intellectuals: students, young teachers, journalists, and representatives of other liberal professions. The movement had its own publication, *Esprit*, founded in 1932, and its bill of rights, *Manifesto in the Service of Personalism*, published in 1936. Yearly congresses were held by this group calling itself Friends of *Esprit*, and it rallied active members which came from all over France, as well as from abroad.

At one of these congresses which I attended eagerly, I met an American delegate, Governor Paulding, editor of *Commonweal*. When I came to America in 1941, Paulding was one of the first to welcome me. He actually helped me start my literary career over again, in the land of my adoption. Another man in the United States who was influenced by Mounier and his personalism was Peter Maurin of the *Catholic Worker*, already mentioned with Dorothy Day in the preceding chapter. They greeted me in America with much cordiality because we had found a common denominator in personalism.

Many books have been written about Mounier and his movement. His own complete works are contained in four volumes. I have recently read a doctoral dissertation on the founder of *Esprit*. It has some three hundred pages of text and thirty pages of biography. But this study, though excellent and respectful of his memory, cannot convey the unique atmosphere in which Mounier and his disciples lived and worked and fought their battles. Who could describe the editorial office of *Esprit*, the small, cluttered room in an old building blackened by the smoke of a nearby railroad station? There Mounier and a few volunteers worked all day and night, getting the review ready for the printer. Who could recreate the excitement we all felt when the first issues of *Esprit* came out, calling for the personalist revolution, or with Berdiaev's essay *On the Dignity of Christianity and the Indignity of Christians*.

Sometimes we spent entire days at congresses debating on the choice to be made between pacifism and violence. How often we were confronted with conflicting ideologies and with problems of ominous world events: Hilter's growing power, Mussolini's invasion of Abyssinia, Stalin's purges, the Spanish Civil War. We lived in an atmosphere of drama which increased from year to year, and realized how essential it was for us to close our ranks, to think clearly, to act with integrity. That was Mounier's greatest example to us. (On the occasion of Mounier's premature death, in 1950, at the age of 45, Father Jean Danielou S.J., later a Cardinal, wrote: "The work, the whole life of Mounier was a passionate fight in the name of the Spirit and the claims of the person." Published in the *Third Hour*, V, 1957.)

The personalist movement however, had not drawn me away from my interest in following the religious and social evolution of the Russian people under the Soviet regime. On the contrary, Mounier's ideas helped me to clarify and define my own attitude toward my country and the fate of humanism in the Soviet Union Stalin's ruthless methods of collectivization, the famous Moscow trials and purges, left little hope that ethical and spiritual values could be saved. Still, even in this darkness, there were the positive signs that I had listed in my book *Soviet Man*, mentioned above. But I found little support among my Russian friends. The older ones were too deeply obsessed by an overall criticism of communism and the younger ones were either entirely indifferent to what was going on in Russia, which they had left as children, or attracted by certain fascist tendencies or chauvinistic doctrines. I felt almost isolated in this respect, until I found a small group of young men and women who shared many of my views. They were led by Yuri Shirinsky-Shikhmatov, a highly educated and aristocratic young man in his thirties, who started a postrevolutionary youth movement. It was based on a few principles which offered a general outlook on conditions in the Soviet Union: The Russian Revolution was an accomplished fact that could not be turned back. But it should be open to constructive criticism. The Christian ideal of social justice was deeply rooted in the consciousness of the Russian people. It should be the answer to the problems which beset our modern times. This ideal was the common responsibility of each for all as expressed in the religious concept of *sobornost'* and illustrated by Russian Orthodox writers such as Khomiakov, Dostoevsky, Tolstoy and, in our day, Berdiaev.

Shirinsky-Shikhmatov was a devout Orthodox and came from a well-known family. In fact he was a prince in his own right, but did not use his title, and his faith was not linked to reactionary trends and traditions, as was the case with most of his fellow aristocrats. He was strongly influenced by Berdiaev and belonged to what might be called the small Russian Orthodox left. I remember him as a tall, slender, charming man with an extensive knowledge of the social and political sciences.

His wife had been earlier married to a militant Russian socialist who was tried by the communists and committed suicide. He had left her a son who had the dynamic spirit of his father. He was very fond of his stepfather, Shirinsky, and under him, had become one of the leaders of the postrevolutionary movement. But inspite of various talents, the family was poor and there were no jobs open to them, so Yuri earned his living as a taxidriver.

He managed, somehow, to combine his daily task with work for his movement, and he founded a review entitled *Utverzhdenie* (Affirmation).

He would often write his editorial in his driver's seat, while waiting for customers. He made great sacrifices, living almost in destitution, often leaving debts unpaid. Once, I remember that a wealthy Frenchman, who had made a generous contribution to the review, drove us all home after a meeting of *Affirmation*. As we approached the apartment house where Yuri lived he whispered in my ear: "This is really embarrassing. I forgot that this man is the owner of our building and we owe him three months rent!" But luckily, the Frenchman was a true friend of left-wing Russian youth.

Unfortunately, *Affirmation* did not last long. Support failed and the movement never gained many followers, but it saved many of us from the pessimism which was the prevailing mood among young émigrés of the thirties. It helped us to dedicate ourselves more fully to Christian humanism in spite of the difficulties we encountered from rightist or leftist extremists. This was the third force which had become the goal of the religious youthful elite in France, whether Catholic, Orthodox or Protestant.

Affirmation, though short-lived, had so much in common with *Esprit*, that I arranged a meeting of Yuri Shirinsky and Emmanuel Mounier. Afterwards, the Russian postrevolutionary delegates attended the congresses of *Esprit*, and Mounier gave us a space in his review, to discuss Russian problems. We first signed this column collectively, but later I wrote it in my name. Maritain took personal interest in the Russian postrevolutionary movement and so did Berdiaev. This was, I believe, the first time that our Catholic and Russian Orthodox masters had made a contact with the Russian Christian humanists of the younger generation. Jacques Maritain mentions the movement in *True Humanism*, and Berdiaev in his *Dream and Reality* books already discussed.

I owe a great deal to Yuri Shirinsky-Shikhmatov who did so much to promote a search for truth and the ideal of self-dedication.

He had but a short span of life to devote to this gift of himself. And he did so, totally. I saw him last before leaving Paris in 1940. He remained in the capital under the German occupation and defied the racists, by wearing the yellow arm band imposed on the Jews, because his wife was Jewish. He was arrested, taken to a concentration camp and beaten to death. He is listed among the heroes of the French Resistance.

Although none of us could foresee the tragic events so near at hand, we were all aware of heavy clouds gathering on the horizon and realized how important it was to keep close to each other, regardless of race, religion or nationality.

This common involvement, brought me once more to the door of Nicholas Berdiaev, or rather, he came to my door. After the failure of the Clamart talks, I had lost contact with him. Then came a letter in his characteristic, neat, small handwriting, asking if he could come to see me. He walked the two miles between Clamart and Meudon and arrived cool and composed, like a man who knew how to get along without a car. Seated in our small living room and lighting one of his small cigars, he told me the purpose of his visit. He knew of my connections with *Esprit* and *Affirmation* and had read some of my articles in French and in Russian. He was in full agreement with the points that I made, and considered that the two Christian humanist youth movements to which I belonged were making a worthwhile contribution to the causes that he himself defended, so quite simply, almost modestly, he invited me to come to his Sunday afternoons, where he gathered some of his closest friends for intimate discussion. He made no mention of my Catholic affiliation, which he knew, but he took for granted my ecumenical approach to Russian Orthodoxy and spiritual culture. It was thus that I became a regular visitor at Berdiaev's home.

This did not mean that I gave up the Maritains' Sundays completely; I still felt part of their circle. But I must admit that I was more and more drawn to the Clamart meetings. They were less formal, less subject to the framework of scholasticism. There was something more home-like to me in the whole atmosphere surrounding Berdiaev, a combinaton of learning and intimacy, and there was also much that was unusual and surprising.

While Berdiaev was the leader of left wing Russian Orthodoxy, his wife, Lydia, was a Catholic who also held advanced views, but kept very much to herself and to a small group of Russian Catholics not too popular with the Orthodox. She was particularly interested in Judeo-Christian relations. She shared this interest with her husband, but it may have seemed that for all the rest they had drifted far apart.

I say, "it may have seemed" because Lydia did not attend the Sunday "at homes," she received her own friends in her room, while her unmarried sister, Eugenia, a confirmed Russian Orthodox, played hostess to Berdiaev's circle. Another part of the house was occupied by Berdiaev's mother-in-law, an amiable old lady in a wheelchair, wearing a lace cap and wrapped in a shawl. Ministered to by her two daughters and the philosopher, who took his turn, she was the object of their quiet devotion. One might say that Berdiaev's home life was lived on three levels. I visited them many times and felt the peace and harmony which reigned in each section of this family, so full of contradictions.

There were the minor difficulties, like the difference of the Julian and Gregorian calendars at Christmas and Easter time. Arrangements were made so that the feasts were celebrated by Berdiaev and Eugenia at one time, and by Lydia and the old lady, also a Catholic, at another time. So the spirit of *agape* prevailed.

Lydia was to die four years before her husband, after a long and painful illness. He watched her sufferings in deep distress, at the same time admiring her courage and faith. He spent many hours at her bedside, talking to her and reading the notes she wrote as the only means of communication left to her (she suffered a paralysis of the throat). I was in America when her death occurred and he wrote to me about his grief with the directness and simplicity so characteristic of him: "Death is an absurd thing, it is difficult to be reconciled with it, but there is also something luminous in it, the revelation of love, obscured by everyday life." This excerpt from Berdiaev's letter was dated Clamart, October 12, 1945. The original Russian letter was published by me in the *New Review (Novy Zhurnal)*.

Though she was my fellow Catholic, I did not get to know Lydia very well as she was quite shy and reserved. As to her old mother, she often slept in her wheelchair, and if awake, was satisfied with a few friendly words. It was the level of Berdiaev's own friends assembled around the large dining room table that held the greatest attraction for me. Though the setting was that of the Paris suburb, I felt transported to my native land, to a typical Russian family homestead. Tea was served by Berdiaev's sister-in-law, Eugenia, who used to bake large Russian cakes for the occasion. They were delicious and all enjoyed them with their tea, as a sort of ritual.

When I began to take part in the Clamart Sundays, Berdiaev had become extremely popular in Catholic and Protestant circles, but he was sometimes an object of controversy and even hostility in the Russian Orthodox emigration. Even the priests and laymen who had started a religious revival, the Russian Christian Student Movement, in which Berdiaev participated for a time, turned away from him. Their hostility was mainly due to their traditional thinking—their adherence to a purely liturgical form of the Christian life, with little concern for the problem of social justice. They could not follow Berdiaev in his philosophical explorations, but considered him a modernist, a heretic. Only a few leaders remained in touch with him, and most of the young students refused to accept his radicalism. This hurt him deeply, more deeply than the distrust of people of his own age. The need for youthful sympathy and support was the reason he relied on us, the friends of *Esprit* and *Affirmation*, and so had sought the little cooperation I could offer.

The group at Clamart was relatively small and compact, but each of its members was sincerely committed to his search. Most of the older men and women were connected with the Religious-Philosophical Academy, a free institution at which Berdiaev taught. He was also editor of the review *Put'* (The Way), which published articles devoted to the latest trends in Russian Orthodox theology. It also reflected similar trends in Western religious thought. The contributors of this review, priests and laymen, and a few young people from *Affirmation*, also came to the Clamart Sunday afternoons, which were not so much a symposium as a never-ending tea party.

Among the group that sat around the large table in the friendly, quiet Clamart dining room was Professor George Fedorov, historian of the Russian Church and of its most radical thinkers in the fields of social justice, and Constantine Mochulsky, who lectured on Dostoevsky and Soloviev at the Sorbonne and who became one of my dearest friends. There was the remarkable Mother Mary Skobtsova, a nun who had founded a house of hospitality for the poorest Russian émigrés, relegated to the Paris slums. Mother Mary herself observed the rules of monastic poverty, wearing a threadbare habit, a crude leather belt, torn sandals, and a faded black veil which never seemed to rest quite straight on her shorn head. She scarcely resembled the image of the angelic *igumena* (mother superior) shown on old Russian icons. Yet no other religious of the Paris Russian emigration reflected more of the spirit of Russian Orthodox charisma.

The Jewish philosopher Leo Shestov came to the Clamart tea parties very often. Berdiaev was especially fond of him, and their affection was mutual, although as philosophers they disagreed on many points. Shestov opposed the essence of what is usually called philosophy, the Western way of thought founded on reason and inherited from ancient Greek concepts. For him, the only truth was in the revelation of the Bible, of a God who transcends all rational categories. Shestov was practically unknown in France, but recognized by a few French intellectuals, among them Camus. He can be considered one of the initiators of modern existentialism of the pre-Sartre period. Camus discussed Shestov's ideas in his *Myth of Sisyphus*.[1]

Berdiaev wrote smilingly about Shestov's thought, saying that it sought to liberate man from philosophy, whereas he wanted to liberate man through philosophy. They had one thing in common — the search for man's freedom — and I believe that it was this common concern that brought not only Shestov, but all of us, to the Clamart round table.

It was indeed a "round table," not merely a piece of furniture, but the symbol of a spiritual banquet, which we enjoyed at the Berdiaev's. There are, alas, only a few survivors of those unforgetable Sundays. Here in New York, I still have the opportunity of reminiscing with Dr. Paul Anderson, the retired director of the European branch of the YMCA. It was this American organization which financed the publications of émigré Russian Orthodox theologians, as well as the review *Put'*. Dr. Anderson was a frequent guest at the "round table." He spoke Russian fluently and worked for many years, one of the most active workers in the ecumenic field. After World War II, he paid many visits to Moscow and knew the successive patriarchs who ruled the Russian Orthodox Church. He also had many friends among Catholic ecumenical leaders.

I think that every vital problem, religious, philosophical, moral, and social, was discussed in our little group, presided over, or rather led, with kindliness and patience by our host, Berdiaev. He did not "officiate," but addressed each one of us in his own charming, trustful manner.

It was thus that I learned from Berdiaev himself the main trends of his religious and social teaching. They were often developed by him right there, at our "round table," and later revised, rethought, and put into final shape in his major works. Speaking for myself, I have realized throughout the years how much I owe Berdiaev. When he called me to his "round table," he offered me the rare opportunity of widening and activating my spiritual development without, in any way, interfering with my basic faith. His contribution to my ecumenical formation was essential.

Soon after I started to attend the Clamart discussions, Berdiaev entrusted me with the translation of two of his most recent books into French. One was the biography of the Russian philosopher Constantine

---

1. The English translation of Shestov's *Athens and Jerusalem* was published in 1956 by Simon and Schuster, New York. It is also in paperback, 1968, a Clarion Book.

Leontiev, and the other was a work which also appeared in an English translation, called *The Fate of Man in the Modern World*.

I spent many months working on these two translations and Berdiaev carefully checked them with me. Thus I grew to know him better than at the Sunday teas. He would often launch into an explanation or analyse the meaning of a word which revealed to me, so to speak, the inner workings of his mind. How often, rereading Berdiaev's books, I recognize whole sentences from his conversations with me with the carefully weighed terminology he used. He often said to me that he wrote exactly as he thought, and he also spoke as he thought, or viceversa. That is why, each time I find even a brief quotation from Berdiaev, I seem to hear his voice, and he comes alive again.

If I have called this chapter "Time of Decision," it is because it was precisely at this time of my life that I made certain decisions, certain commitments that shaped the pattern of the years to come. This does not mean, however, that I shut myself up in a closed world where every one agreed, and no longer sought the contradictions of other worlds outside of my own.

During those years, I formed another one of my lifelong friendships, but it was not with one of the *Esprit* nor of the *Affirmation* groups, but with a man who was in many ways a stranger and opposed to them. I must say that this excellent friendship actually started with an unfortunate jolt.

It happened that one day, a friend of mine connected with the older émigré socialists asked me if I would like to meet Alexander Kerensky. I had met several former political leaders ousted by the Bolshevik Revolution but I had never met this man who had been the last head of the Provisional Government and had fled when Lenin seized power in October 1917. Kerensky had been premier at a time when a free democracy was in the making in Russia. Even before his rise to power, he had played an important part in the downfall of the tsarist regime. To me, as author of the epilogue in *The Blind Kings*, he appeared to be a humanist and an idealist who, though unable to succeed, still retained a heroic quality.

Of course, I was interested in meeting him, and asked my friend why she had made this suggestion. To my surprise, she said that the suggestion had come from Kerensky. He had heard that I had written a book about the anarchist Bakunin which intrigued him. He invited me to lunch hinting that I might bring my book and autograph it for him.

It was a "blind date" for I had never set eyes on him, but I had seen photos and movie shots of him and was sure I could recognize him. We met in a quiet, decorous restaurant near the French Parliament where politicians and diplomats often took their meal. I spotted him immediately, sitting at a table in the back of the room, enveloped in mysterious shadows. The chalk-white face, the pale, half-closed eyes, the slightly graying hair, close-cropped, *en brosse* (crew cut). How familiar it all seemed to me and at the same time, uncanny, as if I had seen it before in a dream. I introduced myself, and he rose, courteously bowing. He gave me a brief smile and motioned me to my seat.

He ordered cocktails and an excellent meal, which he chose carefully, in gourmet fashion. When the drinks and food came, I was prepared for a friendly, interesting talk and timidly handed him my book on Bakunin. He took it rather gingerly, looked at it severely and suddenly launched a *blitz* attack on me. Why did I choose Bakunin as a subject for my book? Why was I interested in anarchists? He was against all anarchists, against their role in Russia and elsewhere. He spoke ironically about youth movements of our time. My *Affirmation* friends and similar young men and women were, in his mind, vain, naive, and extreme in their revolt against society.

I was amazed to hear this man who had been a leader of socialism, and still remained a radical in exile, attack me on the grounds where I had thought we could meet. I explained that, not being an anarchist myself, I considered Bakunin to be an interesting and important protagonist in the history of the Russian Revolution. And after all, I said to myself, you, Kerensky, rode on the crest of the revolutionary wave. I tried to defend myself and my *Affirmation* allegiance, but made little impression. We both fell into silence.

When the meal was over, Kerensky rose once more, bowed with frozen politeness and escorted me to the door of the restaurant. As we stood on the street he said: "Goodbye. I must tell you that I am extremely nearsighted. If I see you on the street, I may not recognize you." He gave me a brusque nod and walked away. I noted that he wore no hat, but wielded a cane, as he walked with rapid strides and soon disappeared from my sight. I stood there, helplessly, as one rejected. But my book, with my autograph in it, was in his pocket.

I do not know why Kerensky made this last remark; true, his sight was very low and later deteriorated into progressive blindness. But I felt his warning was just a way of signing off, of closing our dispute or pretending to do so. Actually, it was a challenge, and a never-ending one. Alexander Fedorovich Kerensky — I call him by his full Russian name — often told me in later years that he enjoyed teasing his friends, provoking and contradicting them. He was also extremely sensitive to a certain brand of political "avant-gardism" which seemed to him superficial and immature, compared to his own tragic experience.

He had not meant to snub me, as shown by our next encounter. I had often heard about his great gift of oratory but had never heard him speak. The announcement of a lecture in a large Paris hall aroused my curiosity and with some reluctance, for I was still annoyed by his last remarks, I went to the lecture. Yes, it was true. Kerensky was a brilliant orator, no wonder that during the first months of the Revolution, he had captivated his audiences, made people applaud and cheer and hail him as the ideal leader of a democracy. But, alas, Kerensky's gift for oratory, and his political integrity, which was unquestionable, could not withstand the plain, direct, precise speeches of Lenin which found the slogans people wished to hear: *"Bread, peace, land"* — these were the fruits of revolution as promised by Lenin, while Kerensky offered a long-range program, to be put into effect only after victory was won. The war-weary people did not wish to fight for victory — they followed Lenin.

I felt all of Kerensky's tragedy, and only those who have heard him speak can realize the powerful magic that political eloquence can produce. I was deeply impressed by the perfectly balanced structure of his rich, elegant Russian. But I was still hurt by this great orator's attitude toward me, and went off, without staying behind to greet him. I thought that my brief contact with Kerensky was over. But someone told him that I was in the audience. He looked for me, but hearing I had left, he sent me a message: "Would I come to tea with him, at his apartment?"

There was an aura of mystery about this invitation. I was given Kerensky's address but told it was a secret closely guarded by a few friends. He lived on a small, isolated street near the Seine river, under the assumed name of Alexandrov. He had no telephone. This secrecy was not a romantic whim, but a necessary precaution. Kerensky was a target, not so much for Communists as for the right-wing émigré fanatics. No man, I believe, suffered so much hatred and persecution as the former head of the Provisional Government. Among his enemies, there were people who had cheered and even worshipped him. All the defeats, mistakes, failures of the short-lived Russian democratic regime, were heaped on his shoulders. He could not take a taxi, since most Paris cab drivers were former White Army officers. So he usually went on foot, walking at a high speed, bent over his cane as if to parry an attack. A woman had once struck him in the face during a public lecture, and he had been constantly insulted and booed. He was no coward, but always on the alert and secretive about his daily life.

This ugly, ruthless persecution, the hatred and calumnies to which Kerensky was subjected, awakened my sympathy far more than his eloquence. Indeed, his tragic fate moved me to a compassion that could never be expressed in words. But he had a fine intuition and was aware of my true feeling. I could have said to him, had I dared, what Dostoevsky's monk, Zosima, said to Dimitri Karamazov: "I do not bow to you, but to your suffering."

"Mr. Alexandrov" lived with a strict, almost ascetic simplicity. The two-room lower income apartment was cheerless, almost bare. He was estranged from his wife of many years, and a prim, old-maidish cousin kept house for him. She served us tea, smiled and accepted me as part of the "Kerensky underground." From that day on, I became a frequent guest.

In the late 1930s, there was a considerable change in his life. Kerensky married for a second time. His wife, a beautiful Australian, drew him out of his solitary den into the limelight. He went on several lecture tours to America and finally settled there. He became widely known in colleges and universities around the United States, gave interviews, and appeared on television. I saw a great deal of him when I myself came to live in New York in 1941. Our friendship grew from year to year, and though we still sometimes disagreed, he remained my loyal and affectionate friend. I owe him much, for he assumed, more than once, responsibilities on my behalf as would an older brother. I will always think of Kerensky as a man of destiny, a man of sorrows. I treasure the vivid memories of our friendship when it was born in the poor little apartment on the banks of the Seine, where he laid before me, not only his own suffering, but that of a Russia he had loved and lost. Solitude, rejection were his natural climate.

He died at the age of 89 after a long and painful illness, blind and abandoned by most of his friends. Only a few of us were with him during those last months. His wife had died soon after their marriage. A Russian Orthodox priest often came to assist him, for, through all his years, he had retained a simple, childlike faith. Only his closest friends knew about it, for he rarely mentioned it himself. How many times I had seen him forgive his enemies in the name of Christ. Even at the height of his political career, he had sought to exercise power without having recourse to violence; his policy was often interpreted as weakness.

During the many years that I was in touch with Alexander Fedorovich he often talked to me about the Revolution, his own role in it, his relations with the Tsar and Tsarina after their abdication, and his struggle against mounting opposition from right and from left, which ended in defeat. He has told this story in his books, and I have nothing new to add to what is already well known. He revealed no secrets to me, no unpublished details of what he called the Kerensky experience. All I can do here is to try to give a truthful portrait of the man, a task more difficult than giving additional historic data. Most comprehensive in my mind is Kerensky's last book, *Russia and History's Turning Point* (Duel, Sloan and Pearce, 1965).

Among the friends I made during the 1930s, the greatest and perhaps most unique was Marina Tsvetaeva, the poetess who had brought me the message from Pasternak. She lived only a few blocks away from "the house in Meudon" she had described in lyric tones. Soon after my first meeting with her, she invited me to her home, and I entered her enchanted world in which poetry was her real life.

Marina had only a few friends, as she did not mix easily. To those who were aware of her value, both as a person and as a poet, she gave herself generously and without reserve. She liked to read her poems, some of which were completed and others, in the making, were born under our very eyes. She was a brilliant conversationalist, steeped in Russian literary tradition, and also familiar with the French and German classics. But she did not try to impress us with her knowledge. Writing, reciting poetry, her own and that of others, savoring every word and sound and rhythm, were as natural to her as her own heartbeat. It can truly be said that Marina lived every line of her poetry. This was all the more remarkable because of the dire poverty she endured, and the heavy family burden she had to carry on her slim and delicate shoulders.

She was married to Sergei Efron, a Jewish writer and journalist who suffered from a chronic pulmonary disease and could not support his family. They had two children, a daughter, Alya, in her teens, and a son, George, known as Mur, a five-year-old, curly-headed young giant and his mother's darling. Marina kept her maiden name as a *nom de plume,* but was Efron's faithful companion, as ever the busy housewife and provider of the little income she could collect selling her poems off and on to émigré periodicals. Alya knitted woolen hats to help the family along. After some schooling, she had dropped out and dreamed of going to Soviet Russia. Efron shared his daughter's homesickness; Marina hesitated. In her poems, she spoke of herself as a constant wanderer, for whom home was everywhere and nowhere. And she did look like a Gypsy, roaming through the streets and lanes of Meudon in a threadbare skirt and faded sweater, a satchel and a shopping bag slung over her shoulders. Besides mother and myself, several families of our "historic house" became her friends. She would drop in to see us, each in turn, and we would fill her satchel and bag with food and clothing. She made the rounds of the markets at closing time to get the cheapest unsold remnants of fruit and vegetables. Taking the boy, Mur, with her, she would take long walks in the woods which grew all around our suburb, and plunged into the thickets to gather mushrooms, berries, and firewood for her stove. I often accompanied her on these expeditions which were for me a sheer delight, for Marina was not only a lover of nature, commenting on each sight we came across, on each shrub or blossom, she was also a poet, composing rhymes, picking out words, weighing them as precious stones, discovered in the forests, arranging them like bouquets of wildflowers, giving expression to each of her own moods with the economy and precision typical of her language. For she spoke exactly as she wrote.

It is difficult to explain Marina's art in so many words, and even more difficult to translate her poetry into a foreign tongue. It is intimately linked with a classic Russian style, as well as with Russian folklore, archaic forms of speech, and a surprising set of colloquial expressions. To imitate this fantastic structure with foreign words is like building a house of cards or a castle of sand; it is sure to collapse. Marina herself once attempted to translate one of her poems into French with little success, although it did one day serve its purpose on a very unusual occasion which I shall describe later.

It takes a poet to recognize another poet. Pasternak, who admired Tsvetaeva as a kindred spirit, wrote about her art as no one, I believe, has ever done before or after, so I will quote his lines, and let the reader make out for himself all that they meant to the older poet:

> One had to read oneself into her. When I had done so, I was amazed to discover such an abyss of purity and power. Nothing at all comparable existed anywhere else. . . . I was instantly won over by the great lyrical power of the form of her poetry, which stemmed from personal experience. It was not weak-chested but wonderfully compact and condensed and did not get out of breath at the end of each separate line, but which by the development of its periods without interruption of rhythm, sustained itself for a whole succession of strophes.

This quotation is from Pasternak's *I Remember* (Pantheon, 1959).

Marina combined these extraordinary poetic gifts with a simple down-to-earth attitude in her daily life. She shopped, cooked meals, sewed and mended clothes with the zeal of a true housewife. She was hospitable and shared the little she had with her small group of friends and admirers. Prince Mirsky, the black-bearded literary critic, whom I knew, would drop in for tea or supper and spend hours in Marina's kitchen where we sat around her listening to her talk or to the recitation of a newborn poem. Her kitchen was her sanctuary, and the rough, unpainted table on which she prepared her scanty meals, was also her desk on which she constantly scribbled, experimenting as in a laboratory on the masterpiece which would finally be produced.

In the summer of 1935, an antifascist congress was held in Paris and Boris Pasternak came from Soviet Russia to attend it. He had several meetings with Marina, her husband, Efron, and daughter, Alya. With Pasternak, they discussed the possibility of returning to their homeland. Efron, though he had fought in the civil war on the side of the White Army, had been convinced in the years following that Russia, as it was developing under the Soviet regime, was a great nation, calling him to be one of its own. His daughter, Alya, shared his view and also wanted to go home. Marina, "the wanderer," hesitated and Pasternak offered no helpful advice. "I did not know what to say to her," he wrote later, "I was very much afraid that she and her remarkable family would find things difficult and not very peaceful in Russia."[2]

And so the "remarkable family" went on living at Meudon, Efron haunted by his dream of going home, and Marina, alienated from most

---

2. The quote is also from *I Remember*, Pantheon, 1959.

of her fellow émigrés, collecting small fees for the poems reluctantly published in the literary journals. Their life of poverty seemed doomed to continue forever.

Marina's friends formed a "Tsvetaeva Aid Society" which managed to reach a few contributors and paid the poet's rent. I spoke of her woes to Ida Rubinstein, the famous ballerina and art collector, who had so generously sponsored our *Hôpital Russe*, during the first World War. During the postwar period, Madame Rubinstein had produced two great performances, one of them Gabriel D'Annunzio's *Saint Sebastian* and the other Maurice Ravel's *Bolero* and had danced in both of them. She was extremely wealthy and generous, and when I sought her help for Marina she responded immediately with a practical idea. She was to appear in a new ballet, *Amphion,* based on a poem of Paul Valéry, and her partner was Russian and did not understand what it was all about. She wanted Valéry's scenario translated into Russian and entrusted Marina with this task, offering her a substantial fee. The two women had never met, so the prima donna decided to visit the poet and present her with the check. The inhabitants of the rue Jeanne d'Arc were all agog to see the great lady of the ballet driving past their modest homes in her shining Rolls Royce. The liveried chauffeur helped her alight at Marina's doorstep. She climbed the long, creaking stairs and entered Marina's shabby lodgings. This unusual visit was described to me by Marina in the vaguest terms and I felt I should not question her further. Madame Rubinstein never returned to Meudon and there were no further assignments.

I thought of another plan. Marina had translated one of her long poems into French and I sought to have it published in a literary review. I was advised to introduce Marina to a Miss Natalie Barney who was very influential in the Paris literary world. A word of recommendation from her from the bizarre American poet was an "open Sesame" to the door of every important literary periodical. So I obtained an invitation for myself and Marina to one of Miss Barney's Fridays which, for more than two decades, had been attended by some of the world's most famous writers, among them James Joyce, Marcel Proust, T.S. Eliot, Paul Valéry, Gertrude Stein, who, incidentally, was Miss Barney's next-door neighbor.

An author and poet in her own right, Miss Barney was also famous for having inspired Rémy de Gourmónt's beautiful *"Lettres à une Amazone."* Moreover, she was known to be the main character in Radclyffe Hall's *Well of Loneliness,* disguised as Valerie Seymour. Ladies with stiff collars, ties and monocles often appeared on the Fridays, but not exclusively and Miss Barney affected the feminine graces, although she was a daughter of Sappho. However, the day I appeared with Marina there were no celebrities nor odd characters; it happened to be a rather dull gathering. Perhaps Miss Barney's Fridays were on the decline in the mid-thirties. Marina read her poems in her brilliant, precise French translation, and with perfect diction, but the audience gave her no more than a cool reception.

The setting of this reading was, however, uniquely charming. Miss Barney held her salon in a pavillion that she rented on the Left Bank, rue Jacob, the old-fashioned quiet street near St. Germain des Prés, the oldest church in Paris. She had lived there for many years and I found a photo of the room where Marina had read her poem in the *New York Times Book Review;* published in 1969, it showed the "Amazone" in her ninety-fifth year, about to be evicted by a man who had bought the pavillion which she had rented for more than sixty years. The photo illustrated an excellent article by Herbert Lottman, entitled "In Search of Miss Barney," estimating her values and eccentricities.

In the photo I recognized the charming scene. There was the living-room, just as we had seen it forty years earlier; the tall French windows opening on the small, romantic garden, the heavy silks and brocades, the antique furniture. There was the round, center table where we were served tea, and the divan where Marina and I sat despondently after the unsuccessful poetry reading.

Following the visit to Miss Barney, Marina never sought again to contact French literary circles. She returned to her seclusion and to her kitchen table to which, as she said to me, every disappointment flung her back, to write.

There were changes among those who were nearest to her. First, it was Dimitri Mirsky who came to a fatal decision. He had discovered Karl Marx, and the reading of *Das Kapital* had been like an electric shock. He suddenly felt convinced that communism was the only truth. He applied for membership in the English Communist Party and was readily accepted because of his London connections. He gave up his academic career and obtained a visa from the Soviet government to return to his homeland. There was a period of probation during which he ceased to see any of his émigré friends and when at last he left, he did not say goodbye to any of us.

I was told that he took none of his belongings with him but arrived in Moscow with empty hands, like a postulant entering a religious community. Some of his literary criticism was published in Soviet periodicals, but after this debut, he was never heard from again. Years later we learned that he had been arrested for "Party line deviation" and died in one of Stalin's concentration camps.

In the mid-thirties we knew nothing of Mirsky's fate, but his departure had stimulated Efron's desire to return to Russia. I had friendly relations with Marina's husband and we had many long talks. His nostalgia for his homeland seemed to me, sincere. He was a handsome man in his mid-thirties, tall and dark, with large blue eyes. There was a dreamy air about him. Pasternak described him as "charming, refined and courageous." Marina was devoted to him and saw in him a "young knight in shining armor" whom she had married when he had gone off to the wars against the Bolsheviks. Strangely enough, she never seemed to consider his growing early communist sympathies for the Soviet Union as a contradiction. White or Red, Sergei was to her, almost a saint.

The change that came over him was gradual, and though I could not help noticing it, life at the rue Jeanne d'Arc went on as usual. Except that Sergei was more and more frequently absent from his home. His health had improved, and he now had a job, which explained his long absences. Later, we learned that he was working in an organization which had been formed to help émigrés to become repatriated to the Soviet Union. Efron himself was on the list for repatriation, but could not obtain a visa. One was accorded, however, to his daughter, Alya, who then left for Moscow. There was a rumor that Efron had become a Soviet agent, in the hope that this would finally grant him the right to return to his homeland. Marina was not aware of these rumors. She could not suspect her husband's secret activities, for he did not confide in her nor in any of their mutual friends. In her eyes, Sergei could do no wrong. But I began to feel anxious.

I saw him only once during this period. He was wearing new, well-tailored clothes and seemed better fed than when he depended on his family's meager fare. The organization wanted its employees to be presentable but otherwise, he seemed to be underpaid, for he brought no money home. In conversation with him, I found him different, stiff, dogmatic, lauding the Soviet regime in every sentence. He offered me a free round-trip to the Soviet Union, if I would bring my father's private papers which were in our possession and turn them over to the Soviet archives. It was a temptation to be able to see Leningrad and Moscow again without final repatriation. For one blissful moment, I imagined being home again, even for a very brief visit, but then, sensing a trap in Efron's offer, I politely refused. He was displeased and sulky. Soon after this encounter, Efron and Marina gave up their Meudon apartment, for unexplained reasons and settled in another Paris suburb. After this, I did not see Marina very often. I missed her and was troubled about her, as rumors about her husband's secret occupation continued to circulate. Marina vigorously denied these rumors as soon as they reached her.

The worst was yet to come. One night in September, 1937, when Efron was away, as usual, the police invaded his apartment and not finding him at home, they arrested Marina and took her to the nearest precinct. There she was interrogated for hours by the *Sûreté* (French secret police) as to the whereabouts of and activities of her husband. Terrified and bewildered, Marina could offer no information. When further pressed, she seemed unable to give any coherent answers to the simplest questions; suddenly, she switched to a sort of rythmic incantation. The police listened, amazed, as she recited in full, the translation of her poem, read at Miss Barney's.

The next day we read in the papers that a former Soviet secret agent, Ignace Reis, who lived in Lausanne, had been murdered. The trail of his assassin led to Paris, the center of a conspiracy involving the organization for which Efron worked. He had been warned and had fled to Spain. Again, Marina was arrested, but after hours of grilling, she was released and no charges were held against her. But what little security she had had was lost. The fate of her husband weighed heavily on her mind. She finally learned that he had at last succeeded in getting into the Soviet Union, and now it was clear to her that loyalty to him demanded that she follow. But things moved slowly and she lingered on, a suspect in the eyes of many who did not believe her repeated declarations that she knew nothing of Efron's activities. She was forced by neighbors to leave her apartment and went into semi-hiding, in a small, Paris hotel, then moved to a faraway resort in Normandie. Little Mur, the only member of her family left to her, was her sole consolation.

I saw Marina only twice during those long months, while she was awaiting her permit to leave for Russia, and moving from place to place. She did not contact us personally, but came to one of Berdiaev's Sunday meetings. The second time, I encountered her in Paris; she was mostly silent, on both occasions, proud, and on the defensive.

Like Mirsky, she left without saying goodbye. But the reason for her return to Russia was different. Hers was a strictly family affair. While she was on her way, it was learned by one of her friends in Western Europe that Efron had been arrested as soon as he had reached Moscow, and later executed. Stalin had no use for agents who had failed.

When the news reached us, Marina was on the train and we had no way of reaching her. In Moscow, she inquired about her husband and was told nothing, except that her daughter, Alya, had been placed in a concentration camp. She herself, was not made welcome. So the "wandering poet" had come home, only to face new trials and humiliations.

Marina tried courageously to pick up the broken threads of her life and make a new start. She still believed that her poetry would be recognized by her own people. She sought contacts with Soviet literary circles, but with small results. Only one of her poems appeared in the Soviet press. She was not eligible for membership in the Union of Soviet Writers.

Her situation became hopeless in 1941 when Hitler invaded Soviet Russia and his armies threatened Moscow. The city was to be evacuated but everyone who was a *persona grata* was offered a decent place of refuge. Marina was abandoned to her own devices. Taking Mur with her, she traveled far and somehow got stranded at Elbuga, a remote town in the Volga-Kama region.

She rented a room for herself, while Mur, now a young man in his late teens, took a job in a neighboring town. Marina also looked for work but found nothing to do, except cleaning. Hearing that the poet Aseev, a *persona grata*, was billeted in the neighborhood, living in considerable comfort, she went to see him, asking for help. Again, she met with complete indifference.

Marina Tsvetaeva returned to Elbuga, her forces spent. In her miserable room, she hanged herself. She was buried in the local cemetery with not even a marker on her grave. To complete the tragic epilogue, her son, Mur, fell sick and died soon after his mother, or, according to other reports, he enlisted and was killed at the front.

Alya was the only survivor of this "remarkable family." She was released from the concentration camp and settled in Tarutin, a writers' colony near Moscow. She did a great deal to collect her mother's writings. When Stalin died, and a literary "thaw" brought changes in the scope of Soviet publications, Marina's poems again saw the light. There was a renewed interest and appreciation of her writings and she is posthumously recognized as one of Russia's greatest poets. A volume of her collected works was published in Moscow in 1965 and Alya is still collecting and editing Marina's papers. Her influence on the younger generation of Soviet poets, such as Yevtushenko, Voznesensky and Brodsky is obvious. She lives on in every line of poetry worthy of attention in the Soviet Union and in the Russian emigration, the two literary circles which rejected her when she was in their midst.

Biographical material about Marina Tsvetaeva and analysis of her poetic work has been made by Simon Karlinsky in a book published by the University of California Press in 1966, and other important books in Russian and in French have come out. Two articles by myself were drawn upon by Karlinsky.

Indeed, there may be a great and important vindication for the injustice done to Marina Tsvetaeva in the past. But nothing will heal the wounds in the hearts of those who loved her. Nothing will answer the question which haunts us: did we do everything we could to save her from the tragic fate which Boris Pasternak so wisely foresaw?

In the United States

Helene Iswolsky with student, autographing her publication Light Before Dusk

Helene Iswolsky with the Voice of America staff; standing behind her to the right: Julien Green now of the Académie Française

Helene Iswolsky with staff at Fordham University

Helene Iswolsky in Fordham University's classroom with students

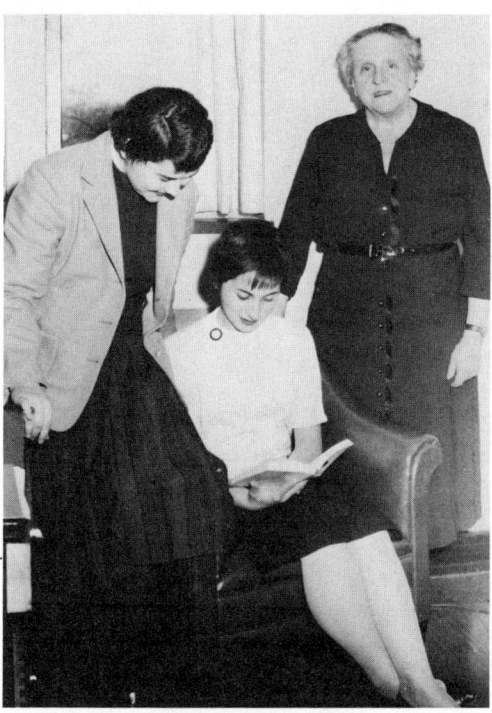

Same at Seton Hall College

Dorothy Day, Helene Iswolsky's favorite picture, photo credit Stanley Vichnevsky

Helene Iswolsky at work

CHAPTER XIII

Farewell to France

THE CASE of Sergei Efron and our tragic parting with Marina brought the deep shadows of Stalin's terror almost to our doorstep. Berdiaev and Maritain, and all of those who were leaders of the religious renaissance, Russian Orthodox, Catholic and Protestant, could not but realize that their philosophy must draw a clear line between Christian personalism and the totalitarian concept of man as the tool of the dictator in the Kremlin.

But there was another dark shadow now being cast by another dictator who was daily growing in power and stature. Hitler's National Socialism, with it *Valhalla*, its pagan "supermen" and anti-Semitic fanatics were obviously just as inhuman as the instigators of the Moscow purges. The remilitarization of the Rhineland and the annexation of Austria left little doubt as to the Führer's warlike intentions.

Besides the small, literary and religiously oriented groups with which I worked, there were, of course, the wide, French intellectual circles and political parties, from liberal to radical, whose thinking was antitotalitarian. But there were also other French groups and movements whose feelings were ambiguous, if not outright anti-Semitic and reactionary, concerning any social change. Some were ready to condone Hitler in their fear of the new "Popular Front," which was taking form, supported by many outstanding intellectuals, artists and churchmen who felt that a reform of working conditions and wages was long overdue. The situation was a very complex one.

Between these extreme positions, there was the limbo of disenchanted youths who roamed despondently without making a choice and having no plan of action. Such was the case of a number of young Russian émigrés. They had no roots, having left their native land as young children, or having been born abroad. They did not have the memories of their elders, for whom tradition, political affiliation, and religion, still meant a great deal. These young people had little communication with French youth. Not only did they suffer poverty, but degradation, receiving no regular education, and lacking the training required for better jobs. They were mostly employed as unskilled workers in factories or coal mines (grossly underpaid) or as Paris taxicab drivers.

Some did manage to enroll in schools of higher education. But this meant further deprivation. A few tried a literary vocation. They did not fare any better financially but at least they had something to live for. They had talent and imagination. The production of some of these youthful writers and poets was quite remarkable, but the note of disenchantment, melancholy, and skepticism prevailed. World events did little to awaken optimism. The religious renaissance was as far from them as the traditional faith of their fathers. They were the beatniks of that time, not by choice but due to the storms that had cast them out on foreign shores. There were the problems of alcohol, drugs, tragic love affairs, which were harder to face for them than for their French contemporaries.

They would assemble at Montparnasse cafés, where they would sit listlessly for hours, spending their last francs on drinks and cigarettes. The waiters knew them and would often let them go without demanding payment, a generosity extended to many writers and artists, both old and young, in that particular bohemian circle. They proudly called themselves "the Russian Montparnasse." They had at least one place where they were not treated as strangers.

The "Russian Montparnasse" showed its grim aspect when the most gifted of the group, Boris Poplavsky, died, allegedly from an overdose of drugs. He had lived in destitution and solitude for so long, that his death was an almost inevitable end to a tragic tale. All those who knew him were deeply moved and wondered what could be done to help the young émigré intelligentsia. The answer was found by a remarkable man, Ilya Bunakov Fondaminsky, a friend of Berdiaev, whom I had often met at the Clamart Sundays.

He was a Jew and had been married to a Jewish girl, who died some time before I had made his acquaintance, but he was still under the impact of this loss. His wife had been deeply attracted to the Christian faith, but hesitated to be baptized, as many Jews did, particularly at the time of the Nazi anti-Semitic persecutions. It seemed to her that to abandon her faith would mean abandoning her people. After her death, she was buried according to the Jewish funeral rites, but Father Sergius Bulgakov, the outstanding Russian Orthodox priest, who was her friend and knew of her desire to receive baptism, celebrated a special memorial service for her. It was an ancient liturgical office which was used for the burial of catechumens.

Ilya Bunakov Fondaminsky (or Ilyusha as we familiarly called him) was attracted to the Christian faith no less than his late wife and remained no less hesitant to take the final step. But he regularly attended the Russian Orthodox liturgy and blessed himself. He was one of the kindest, most generous men I have ever known. In his youth, however, Ilyusha had belonged to the most radical wing of the Russian Socialist Revolutionary Party; this was a terrorist group, and though Fondaminsky never threw a bomb, he was said to have carried dynamite sewn in his vest. He had retained a romantic spirit and a youthful enthusiasm. He had a deep love of Russia and faith in her destiny, but, he had, above all, compassion. Vladimir Nabokov, who cast a skeptical look at most of his fellow émigrés, had this to say about Ilyusha: "Everyone who was caught in the radiance of this most human man was filled with uncommon tenderness and respect for him."

Poplavsky's death was a shock to this "most human man." He realized that the "Russian Montparnasse" was disintegrating, because these youthful poets and writers had been neglected, left to their despair. He invited them to his home where they could discuss their problems in an atmosphere of friendship and understanding, and led them toward a spiritual life.

Berdiaev, Fedorov, Mother Mary, and other religious leaders I had met at Clamart, came to Ilyusha's open house to get acquainted with the younger generation. These were entirely informal meetings, but little by little they acquired a certain shape and substance and became a writers' and poets' club called the "Circle." I often came to the "Circle" meetings, attended by so many of my friends, old and new.

"Wonderful, wonderful!" Ilyusha would exclaim, as the "Russian Montparnasse" settled down to a new way of life, so different from the previous "limbo" existence. Not all of the young people joined the "Circle," some remained skeptical and aloof. But more and more visitors dropped in at the "at homes"; they sat in the large dining room where tea, cake, sandwiches and *vin ordinaire* (table wine) were served in sufficient quantities to satisfy young appetites, while others browsed in the no less spacious library with its shelves lined with hundreds of books.

Ilyusha had been a political exile under the tsars, before having become one again, later, when his party was suppressed by Lenin. He had been a wealthy man and had managed to export some of his assets abroad before the Revolution. He could thus afford these comfortable living quarters which he now shared with his new young friends. He assisted them financially whenever necessary, but his main concern was to help them publish their writings. Thanks to this help, the "Circle" brought out books of poems and prose, written by the youthful group, which now no longer called itself "the Russian Montparnasse," but the "Paris School of Russian Authors."

One of the important features of this group was precisely the feeling of "coming of age" which it gradually acquired. Among the "Paris School" writers, I could name quite a few whose poems could figure in anthologies as fine examples of modern verse.[1] And there were gifted prose writers—Dr. Basil Yanovsky, whose first novel *Love Second* started him on a literary career, later continued and developed to full maturity. Yanovsky, who had just graduated from the Paris Medical School, combined in his writings the experience of a young physician and of a humanist seeking ethical and spiritual values, transcending matter.

The senior members of the "Circle" had also this great search in mind. They gave frequent talks at Ilyusha's, and founded a review to express their views. It was entitled *Novy Grad* (The New City) and its very name was a symbol of hope and of the creative spirit of Christianity.

One of the contributors of *Novy Grad* was Mother Mary Skobtsova, whom I had first met at Berdiaev's. Her insight into the problems which troubled the young generation helped them to clarify their own ideas. Her deep compassion for the poor, the sick, the prisoners and mentally disturbed inspired many various activities, which filled most of her time. But she had also time to give to the search of the "New City," where true Christian values would eliminate the misery of a godless civilization.

Mother Mary was deeply aware of the heavy clouds gathering on our horizon. She felt that the decisions to be made here and now were not merely problematic good resolutions, but something which would have to materialize far sooner than we thought. These feelings we all began to share and were intensified after the Munich pact had revealed to us how close we stood already to the danger zone. I will always recall a conversation we had at Ilyusha's. Someone had mentioned Hitler's ruthless methods and the possibility of each of us having to face persecution, imprisonment, torture. How would we react in such an eventuality? Ilyusha beat his breast, saying, "I am a weak man, I must admit that under torture I might betray my dearest friends." Each of us confessed to a lack of courage, expressing the hope that God would give us strength, or protect us against the worst. When it was Mother Mary's turn to speak, she merely said, looking as it were, to an immediate future: "Whatever we do when the time comes we must prepare ourselves now for great trials."

Indeed, the great trials she spoke of were indeed reserved for Mother Mary and Ilyusha. After the fall of France, they were both arrested, interned in concentration camps, and died heroically. Mother Mary suffered for having sheltered Jews in her Paris House of Hospitality. Ilyusha, far from betraying his friends, shared their fate. After his internment, he was offered the means of escape through the underground, but refused to take advantage of them, saying that he wanted to share to the end the fate of his brothers, the Jews. He died in a prison hospital after an operation and was baptized shortly before passing away.

---

1. In fact such an anthology was published in New York in the 1950s by the poet and literary critic Yuri Ivask (Chekhov Editions).

I do not know what we all did to "prepare ourselves" for the approaching disaster, as Mother Mary had urged us to do, except during those years of the late thirties, we did live in a serious and recollected mood. I remember discussing the international situation with Father Mailleux, a Dominican, who was one of the editors of progressive Catholic reviews and publications. I asked him whether it was still possible to pursue any creative work in our respective spiritual endeavors while already breathing the stifling atmosphere of an inevitable cataclysm. Father Mailleux answered: "Go on doing whatever you have to do, no matter what happens in the future. God will take care of it."

And such was also Ilyusha's firm belief. He went on with his work at the "Circle," exclaiming, "Wonderful, wonderful" — rejoicing at the smallest progress in his various plans and experiments. His motto was, "We must create a secular religious order, the Order of the Intelligentsia."

One of his plans was to promote a rapprochement of young Russian Orthodox men and women with Catholics and Protestants. It was actually one of the first ecumenical endeavors of that kind. I found at the "Circle" the opportunity of realizing some of my own dreams. Our first ecumenical meetings took place in the summer of 1939, on the very eve of the war. We could only start on our project of bringing together young people of various faiths, and it all proved to be quite tentative and sporadic. We did obtain, however, some satisfying results, when a noted Catholic existentialist philosopher spoke at the "Circle." "God took care of the rest," as Father Mailleux had put it, for a few years later, when I made my home in America, I found in New York some of the friends who had also arrived there and whom I had last seen at Ilyusha's interfaith meetings. Together, in memoriam, we founded an ecumenical group called the Third Hour, to which I will return in one of my concluding chapters.

I have mentioned, speaking of Ilya Bunakov Fondaminsky, the testimony of Vladimir Nabokov, today famous as an English (as well as Russian) novelist. He was already known among us as a brilliant young writer in the nineteen thirties. He did not belong however to the "Montparnasse group," for he lived with his wife in Berlin, but he often visited Paris. He wrote exclusively in Russian in those days, and in spite of the high reputation he enjoyed in the émigré literary milieu, his royalties were few, providing him with only a meagre means of subsistence. It was in America that the Nabokovs found the way to prosperity, but not without a struggle. During his visits to Paris, young Nabokov stayed at Fondaminsky's, but did not mingle with the writers of the "Circle." I would see him as he hurriedly traversed the entrance hall, to find a refuge in the only spare room not invaded by our crowd, a slender, sprightly figure, the pale face with an ambiguous smile of a man wiser and sadder than his age.

Our "Circle" activities came to a sudden end in September, 1939, when the storm we had been expecting actually broke. Many members of our group were drafted or enlisted and one of them, the young author Vladimir Varshavsky, became my *filleul de guerre*, (war godson), which meant that I adopted him for the duration of the war, to send him packages with foods and cigarettes. This was quite fortunate for Varshavsky, who volunteered for a dangerous reconnaissance job, was made a prisoner and spent the rest of the war years in a German P.O.W. camp, where he suffered great hardships and where my packages were at least some comfort.

In May 1940 came the breakthrough and Hitler's armies poured into Belgium, the Netherlands and, scarcely six weeks later, were at the gates of Paris. As soon as the blitz started, I took Mother to Pau, where we still had many friends to take care of her. I returned to Paris for a while, where I continued to work, hoping against hope that there would still be a "miracle of the Marne." As things grew worse from day to day, I consulted Alexander Kerensky as to what to do next, but he himself was undecided, now planning to stay in Paris where he lived with his young wife (they had been marrried a few months earlier) or leave for America, where he had a speaking engagement. One day, in early June, I met Maritain's friend the composer Arthur Lourié walking despondently in the Paris streets. He told me that Maritain and Raissa were at least safe, for Jacques was in the United States on a lecture tour and his wife accompanied him. "And what about yourself?" I asked Lourié, "what are you planning to do?" He looked at me with surprise, "What a question," he exclaimed, "I have no plans, I am staying right here in Paris, whatever happens. I cannot part with my grand piano." Only twenty-four hours later, Lourié parted with his beloved instrument, and fled with his wife to the south of France and thence to America.

I went to Clamart to see Berdiaev. He too was undecided, and asked me where, in my opinion, it would be best to go with his wife and sister-in-law in case of an emergency. He did not mind leaving his house and his belongings, but would not part with his adored cat, Nour, which, of course, would go along with them. I advised him to make arrangements for settling in Pau, where we could help him to find a home and friends. He was inclined to follow my advice, but fate decided otherwise. He had to endure four years of German occupation, while I was fortunate enough to escape it.

On June 22nd, my friend Jean de Saint Chamant, who worked at the Ministry of Information, called me to tell me I should leave immediately to join my mother.

He was very hush-hush about the whole thing, because he knew, as I did, that all the telephones were bugged by the secret service. But his message was clear enough, the situation had deteriorated rapidly.

Later I was to learn that Jean de Saint Chamant, to whom I owe my own escape from Paris, left the capital himself only a few hours after his telephone call to me. He was evacuated with the Ministry of Information to some unknown destination, and had to reach safety on foot. For just like in World War I, the entire administration left the great city to its fate, and this time, it was a tragic one.

I began to pack hastily, and got a few of my belongings together in a small suitcase, when my brother Grisha appeared on the scene. He had recently arrived from America with his wife, Mashenka, and it had been arranged that they would stay with us. But my sister-in-law was visiting one of her daughters, so Grisha was alone, expecting her any moment to come back. They had no intention of leaving France, since both were American citizens and the States were not yet at war. Mashenka was already at that time suffering from an advanced tubercular condition, but still quite active and alert. So we all hoped that rest in our little apartment would at least be an opportunity to slow down the progress of the disease. Grisha saw me go without too much anxiety, since panic had not yet spread through the city. We heard loudspeakers in the streets broadcasting Premier Bidault's promise that all would be well. But in an hour or two, just as I was leaving Meudon, another loudspeaker blared. It was Monsieur Renaud's voice telling the people of Paris that everyone should be evacuated. And so, one million people, including myself, left the capital on that tragic day.

History, they say, repeats itself, so do certain events in a person's life. So it was with me, for I actually caught the last train leaving the Paris station for southern France as I had caught the last train leaving Russia in 1917. This time, it was in a dense crowd, milling around the gates, that I pushed my way to the tracks and got on the train bound for Pau. I got to my destination the day that France surrendered; the armistice was signed on June 22; it established two territorial zones. One zone was entirely occupied by the German army, the other remained free, under the new French government, with its seat at Vichy, headed by Marshal Pétain. Providentially for us, Pau was located in the free zone.

I had traveled for three days with innumerable stops, almost without food and drink; we had once been bombed by a German plane flying low over our heads, but the train moved on and everyone remained calm in my compartment. I was exhausted but at least spared the suffering of other refugees, thousands of them, who traveled by car, along jammed roads, short of gas, food and milk for the children, continually harassed and strafed by the German planes. I was deeply shaken by all the misery, and, needless to say, stunned by France's collapse which caused me almost physical pain.

We spent a year in Pau, and though we were secure from German oppression, we knew the hardships of severe rationing; the coupons we were entitled to for meat, sugar, bread and other vital foodstuffs were reduced to a minimum. There were no potatoes, no eggs, no butter, only a few spoonfuls of vegetable oil per person, per week. Foodstuffs disappeared one by one from the market. We were grateful to a woman, who had been our cook when we lived in Pau in the twenties and who had a small farm in the mountains; she provided us with cheese and bacon from time to time, and did not demand the high prices of the black market which did business with the city's more affluent population. Meanwhile, the harvest of the fertile country around Pau was requisitioned by the Germans and transferred to the occupied zone for the military, while Frenchmen were reduced to near starvation.

I looked with anguish at the near future awaiting us, for I could find no job, and the money we somehow managed to get from our Paris bank was rapidly dwindling. In spite of these preoccupations, I drew a great deal of comfort from the fact that several young people of the *Esprit* group had found refuge in Pau, as well as other leaders of the Catholic avant-garde movements. Among them was Stanislaus Fumet and the German philosopher Landsberg, a Jew recently converted to Christianity and a disciple of Husserl. Father Carré, a Dominican, editor of the periodical *Revue des Jeunes*, would say Mass for us and give us retreats. He was a man of deep spirituality and insight who after the liberation of France preached during the Lenten season at Notre Dame Cathedral in Paris, from a pulpit long famous for its great sermons.

It was from these various groups assembled at our meetings that the initiators of the Pau underground resistance movement gradually emerged. They were to show great courage, and some of them died heroically at the hands of their Nazi persecutors. Among them was Landsberg, whose wife survived after terrible hardships and ordeals.

One day, Mother and I had a great surprise. My cousin, Sergei Iswolsky, his wife, Sandra, and his son, Michael, who was in his late teens, suddenly appeared in Pau, as it seemed from nowhere. They had lived in Brussels for many years and Sergei, who was a disabled veteran from World War I, received a pension from the Belgian government. He had been shell-shocked and half paralyzed, but could still hold a small job, and Michael had a free education. When the Germans occupied Brussels, my cousin fled with thousands of other refugees. Sergei, who wore heavy braces, covered many miles on foot with his family, arriving in Pau, which was one of the main refugee centers of the French free zone. They did not know that I was in Pau with Mother and we, of course, had had no news from them since May. We found each other quite by chance, thanks to the love of mystery stories which Sandra and I had in common. There was a small lending library in the city where I had taken out some mystery books and where my cousin had registered. Seeing that two Iswolskys were put down in her files, the librarian asked

Sandra if we were related. With our address in hand, Sergei, Sandra and Michael were soon at our home, where we all embraced, thanking God that we were reunited in a town where crowds of refugees were daily pouring in, and where people scarcely knew about each others' whereabouts.

And it was quite a family reunion, for besides Sergei and his family, we had another cousin, Vera Hall and her boy, Alexander, also staying in Pau. But she had found a permanent home there, whereas the Iswolskys had to be resettled. Many good friends came to their aid, and the Baron A. invited them to stay at his farm not far from the city. They would often come down to have tea with us, and Vera would join us. Thanks to our former cook we always had some tid-bits to be shared at our "tea parties." Vera carefully collected the remaining crusts of bread, to feed her dogs, two beautiful shepherds.

Many other Russian refugees kept arriving in Pau. They were either Jews or socialists, in danger of being arrested in the occupied zone. Among them was Vadim Rudnev, the editor of an important literary review, which was suspended by the Nazis. Rudnev and his wife were planning to go to America with the help of some good friends in New York. But he was stricken with a terminal cancer soon after his flight from Paris. His widow, Vera Rudnev, was disconsolate and quite indifferent to what fate now lay in store for her. But we all urged her to go on with her late husband's plans to emigrate to the United States.

Many Russian Jews and the other leftist refugees had already received emergency visas and the necessary means to leave France as soon as arrangements for their passage had been completed. One of these, Doctor Kovarsky, with his wife and daughter, often visited us. One day, I accompanied the doctor on his way home and walked with him through the park, where the trees were turning to autumn gold. We had lived more than four months under the sway of a powerful conqueror, and I wondered how long his rule over us would last. Suddenly, Doctor Kovarsky stopped and asked me point blank, "How would you like to go to America?"

"Very much indeed," I exclaimed, "but this is quite impossible!"

"Not at all," said the Doctor, "we shall help you."

"We" meant the Jewish and Russian organizations in the United States with whom Kovarsky and his group of political exiles were closely linked. So, once again, Providence opened the doors to safety for me just as they had seemed locked forever. I was advised to write to Kerensky, who was living in New York and who was connected with the organizations providing the emergency visas. The rest, Kovarsky told me, "would be taken care of by friends."

Kerensky immediately answered, telling me he would obtain the affidavits requested for our emigration to America. This was the most difficult step, since affidavits could be granted only by wealthy American citizens who guaranteed that the emigrants would be no burden to the United States. Such a wealthy man was Mr. Bakhmetev, former Russian Ambassador in Washington, who had become a United States citizen after the Revolution and been quite successful in business. He was a friend of the Kerenskys, a very kind and generous man, who helped many of his compatriots and founded the "Humanity Fund" for Russian intellectuals.

These were the preliminaries of our exodus. I had, of course, to consult Mother and obtain her agreement to my plans. But before doing so, I went to see two trustworthy persons. One of them was our family physician, who knew Mother's condition; I asked him whether she was strong enough to undertake the long journey. He said, "She can make it. Go, by all means. Soon we will have no medicines here, no proper medical care will be offered." The other person was Father Carré. I asked him whether I should stay here, in France, with the underground or go on working for ecumenism in a free country. He said, "Go, by all means. We have information that the Germans will occupy the whole of France including the Pau region. You will be in great danger because of your anti-Hitler writings. So, of course would your mother." With these words, he gave me his blessing.

Meanwhile things were rapidly shaping up. The Jewish relief organization "Haias" offered to pay our passage to America. This generosity was due to my late father's stand against anti-Semitism in years gone by and to my own small contribution in defending the persecuted Jews. I owe "Haias" a lifelong debt of gratitude.

Three friends of ours were to accompany us on our journey — Alexander Konovalov (former Minister of Commerce in Kerensky's Government), his wife and the recently widowed Mrs. Vera Rudnev.

The last days at Pau were devoted to our preparations for the voyage and to persuading Mother that we should be leaving soon for America. She was loath to accept our plan and it was only thanks to Mr. Konovalov that we finally obtained her consent.

I had further the problem of transferring some of our money (or what remained of it) to a bank in Lisbon. This involved a great deal of red tape. For a month or so I followed a strict schedule; every day, and hour after hour, I made my rounds to the various agencies which officially and unofficially could take care of our affairs.

The most complicated problem, however, was Grisha. We had been informed through ordinary channels (permitted from one zone to another) of my sister-in-law's death in our apartment. Grisha had nursed her during the last months and weeks with extraordinary devotion and one of her daughters had been with her to the end. Now Grisha was alone, and desperate. Only later did we learn that he had found refuge at our old friend's Prince Argutinsky's home.

I got in touch with Grisha through the underground route. This was through a seafood peddler, who was allowed to bring Arcachon oysters to the free zone. We never saw any of the oysters, probably delivered to the Vichy V.I.P.s; but the peddler smuggled letters hidden under the seafood from us to Paris and brought back the answers for the sum of five francs.

Thus, I let Grisha know that we were leaving for America. He had his passport, and the money I managed to transfer would easily get him out of Paris; he was to join us in Lisbon, and we would then all travel together to America, his home, and soon to be mine and Mother's. The oyster man brought Grisha's answer. He was ready to go along.

The next problem was getting the American visa. The only available United States consulate was in Marseilles. This meant a night's journey. I had to take Mother all the way, find a hotel to stay in and collect enough provisions to last for three days. I had been told that even with our ration coupons, we were unlikely to find any food in Marseilles.

On our way south we passed Lourdes, and the grotto with its blazing candles could be seen for a few seconds, just the time to say a silent prayer for our immediate trip, and for the longer and more perilous one which could bring us to America.

At Marseilles things worked out according to plan, but not without a few unexpected complications. As we presented ourselves at the American consulate, we were told to await our turn with a number of other applicants for the U.S. visa. They were mostly Jews from Germany who had found a temporary asylum in the south of France, but as the threat of extended occupation grew nearer, they were trying to get out of the so-called free zone as soon as possible. While waiting to see the consul, I helped the Germans to explain their case, since they spoke no French nor English. This was a diversion for me and calmed my nerves for the dreaded encounter. When our turn came, the consular employee checked our papers carefully, the affidavit was satisfactory and so were the other documents, but the employee found that a recommendation was lacking for the final approval. What could I do? I knew nobody in Marseilles who could give us a recommendation. As I pleaded and presented our situation the employee suggested I go over to "Haias," across the street. If they gave the needed support, it would suffice. It was another trip, another period of waiting and standing in line, but at last I got to the desk where "Haias" gave out recommendations. I rushed back to the consulate where Mother was patiently waiting. This time we got the visa and were fingerprinted by a polite secretary. I was jubilant, but my mother complained that her fingers were all black from the fingerprinting. She asked for soap and water. There was enough water, but soap was rationed even for the consulate. The kind secretary finally produced a piece of real soap, something we had not seen for months.

Mother washed her hands and with one of her charming smiles, we left the consulate with the precious visas, which were to open the door to a new life.

Back in our hotel we unpacked our food and enjoyed a meal which, however modest, could not have been obtained in Marseilles for love nor money. The city was suffering even greater restrictions than our Bearnese region; meat and dairy products had almost vanished, and the usual immense seafood supplies in this famous fishing area had been completely suspended by order of the German navy, which was guarding the port, and the entire coast was strewn with underwater mine fields. Gone were Marseilles' gourmet dishes, gone its famous bouillabaisse with its lobsters and a variety of fish. Gone the small fry which made every meal in Marseilles such a delightful treat. All that was left were the baby octopus. You could get them in profusion, but their rubbery tentacles were barely nutritious or appetizing.

While I sat with Mother in our hotel room there was a knock at the door, and a young man presented himself as Bertrand d'Astorg. We knew his father, Count d'Astorg, who lived in Pau and who had given us Bertrand's address. The young d'Astorg was affiliated with *Esprit*. He was a friend of Mounier's and one of the leaders of the Uriages Center, a training school for young Christian humanists who hoped against hope to be able to start France's reconstruction according to the personalist ideal. It was heartening to hear our visitor speaking of all that could still be done, in spite of the Germans' presence. There was another, positive presence in France, in fact the entire Christian anti-Nazi movement was called *Présence*; it was a voluntary act of dedication, service and endurance; alas, Uriages and all its affiliates were soon to be closed and Mounier arrested. The Resistance movement, however, gained momentum and went into direct action. But I feel that Uriages and other Catholic Youth centers were a preparation for the great struggle and in this sense a real training ground.

On our way back to Pau we had a pleasant surprise; a French officer in uniform boarded our train at Toulouse and climbed into our compartment. He was Colonel Count de Brantes, the husband of Natty de Lucinge's daughter and Grisha's stepdaughter, Aymone. We had always been very close to Aymone up to her marriage, but we had not seen her since. I knew that she had had five children with François de Brantes, and that he was a devout Catholic. He was a career officer and as such, in spite of his own opinions, had remained loyal to the head of the French government, Marshal Petain.

We were glad to see this member of the family and talked freely with him. He told us that his mother-in-law, Natty, had gone back to America and gave us a tentative address for her. He left the train at Tarbes, with warm words and greetings to the family.

We were never to see François de Brantes again. Much later we learned what had happened to him:

> When all of France was invaded by the Germans, he, like many others, felt released from his bond of allegiance. He joined and played an important part in the O.R.A. (the Secret Army). Denounced, captured by the Gestapo, he was deported to Dachau, and died there.
>
> It was I who brought the news to my sister. It was later confirmed by a priest, a fellow prisoner, who, secretly, had been able to give him absolution.[2]

It was also later that I was told that Jean-Louis (Johnny) likewise had been involved in the Resistance, but fortunately he survived these tragic years. (Both Aymone and Jean-Louis, as well as Lolotte, wife of the author Alfred Fabre-Luce, occasionally visit America, and drop in to see me in my New York apartment. Their children are all married and pursuing various careers; one of Aymone's daughters is the wife of Valéry Giscard d'Estaing, twice Minister of Finance, and later President of France.)

Back in Pau I had to attend to the last items on our agenda. The transit visas through Spain and Portugal were now to be obtained. As I called on the Spanish consul, I was reminded of the fact that I had signed the Guernica Manifesto. I may have been entered on the black list. Trembling, I entered the consul's office, but was reassured when the man who held our destiny in his hands was none other than a former acquaintance. I met him on the Biarritz golf links some years ago and he was still more of a sportsman than a Franco official. It sufficed for me to recall Biarritz for the consul to give me the visas. From his office I rushed to the Portuguese consul, where the problem was how to get the rubber stamps and the ink pads for the transit visas to Lisbon. Pau had no official Portuguese consulate, but a so-called honorary consul, a Frenchman, invested with the necessary powers. His office was located in a room of the gentleman's own apartment; he had received so few customers for many years that his equipment had been reduced to a minimum. His office was stormed by hundreds of men, women and children, who, like ourselves, were eager to leave France before the expected showdown. I got the transit visa via Portugal in a few moments, since there was no time even to check our identifications. From the Portuguese honorary consular authority I went to the Prefecture for our exit permit. It could not be obtained, I was told, before the okay of the local intelligence bureau. This information filled me with fears, for everything now depended on this last step, a most critical one in a fascist-ridden country. The man in the intelligence bureau glanced at our passports and, to my intense surprise, smiled at me benevolently. "Any relation to Monsieur Grégoire Iswolsky?" he asked me, and when I told him Grisha was my brother, he stamped our papers with a courteous

---

2. This was the firsthand story, told by J.L. de Faucigny-Lucinge, brother of Aymone. (Ed.)

gesture. He introduced himself as a man who had been attacked by burglars and saved by my brother when Grisha and Mashenka were living in Pau in 1938. Never has a good deed been rewarded more magnanimously and unexpectedly.

Back at the Prefecture, our passports were duly stamped for the last time, but the employee made a mistake, indicating that we were leaving France through the Eastern border of Perpignan, whereas our exit permit and tickets had been on the line recently opened through the Western divide and linking Pau directly with Madrid. Fortunately, I noticed the mistake in good time, returned breathlessly to the Prefecture and had the mistake corrected. Such mistakes seem to pursue me and my kin, as when my mother's French identification in Paris listed her as seven years old, and the country of my birth on my United States passport was Soviet Union, which did not exist when I came into the world. Besides, my record in the State Department clearly said born in Germany.

Our last days in Pau were hectic and tense. Mother was still deeply antagonistic toward the journey to America, and I began to doubt whether I had undertaken the right step. But my doubts were soon dispelled when I read in the local paper, *Le Patriote*, that all aliens in the Pau area would soon be transferred to "X," a small town in the mountains where they would be subject to forced residence.

On the day when the news broke in *Le Patriote*, our friend, the Countess D.M. visited us. I told her how shocked I was at this measure. "But surely," I added, just to test our visitor, "my mother, a widow of an ambassador and a staunch friend of France, would be spared such a treatment." The Countess raised her tearful eyes to heaven. "My poor child," she murmured, "these are our Marshal Pétain's order. Your dear mother, however honored and loved, will have to accept this ordeal." I must add that the Countess was herself Russian-born, but having married a wealthy Frenchman with a title to boot, was naturally exempt from the Marshal's decree of forced residence. "Yes," the old lady went on to say with a sigh, "you will find, I hope, some comfortable lodgings in X."

At these words, I could contain myself no longer and rising to my feet, I looked into the Countess's eyes dimmed with crocodile's tears and exclaimed in a ringing voice: "I do not think this will be necessary, Madame, for we are leaving for America." The Countess seemed surprised and dubious. She bowed her head and took leave of us without daring to ask any further details of our immediate plans.

Now there was one last problem to be solved. How should we get to the station? There were no cars, no taxicabs available, since fuel was practically drained from our town. After many inquiries, I discovered that the only vehicle which could offer us transportation was an omnibus, which ran on monoxide gas. We got the bus man to promise to fetch us at a certain time on May 2, a hopeless proposition. With the Konovalovs and Mrs. Rudnev, we finally succeeded in hiring this extraordinary contraption and could rest assured that, provided an enormous fee, it would fetch us at our various addresses.

The day before we left we had our last "tea party" with my cousins, the Sergei Iswolskys and Vera Hall. Sergei and Sandra were depressed and anxious for their future; the Baron d'A. was making things very difficult for them at his chateau; the Marshal's warning against alien refugees was a threat to the A's security; the more so because the Baron's brother-in-law, a famous sportsman, was recently appointed Minister of Physical Education. Sergei's son, Michael, was working in local youth organizations but rumor had it that all young Frenchmen would be drafted to work in Germany. Sandra was desperate about her son. I felt that I was abandoning my family, and yet, in our "forced residence" in the mountains I could have scarcely helped my relatives. All I could do was to give Sandra the name and address of Father Z., the priest of a small parish in a nearby town who was, as I knew, an active member of the underground and could smuggle Michael over the border. My cousin Vera was no less preoccupied and sad. She told us that since our bread supply would cease, she would have to put to sleep one of her beautiful sheep dogs. But her grief for the dog was not the only reason for her extremely tense, almost angry, look. I was to discover the reason next day at the station.

When the "tea party" was over and our last evening meal served at the hotel, I still had time to walk over to a nearby parish. It could still hold, more or less clandestinely, the meetings of *Esprit, Temps Présent* and *Jocists;* I took leave with deep emotion of my friends of the underground.

Then came the day of our departure. It took place late in May, a little over a year after my "flight from Paris." Early in the morning the bizarre vehicle with an autobus chassis and a locomotive funnel arrived just in time to pick us up and fetch our three other companions at their respective homes. Our luggage was piled up high on the top of our bus, which crawled along the deserted streets and finally reached the railroad station where our friends and relatives had assembled to see us off.

It was a sad parting. We, who were going to America, were abandoning the little group with which we had shared so many anxieties, but also the trust and solidarity which had drawn us so close together in a hostile, cruel world.

Cousin Vera Hall was there, her face pale and drawn. She took me aside and began rebuking me for leaving France. She had the opportunity of going abroad with her young son, Alexander, but had refused the offer, considering that it was her duty, as well as the young boy's to see it through. It was a heroic decision, but whether it was a wise one is another question. Alexander Hall was in his teens when we left for America. He was already then an ardent Gaullist and had attempted to run away to Algiers to join the Army of Liberation. After the Allied landing, he enlisted in de Gaulle's army. He fought in the unit commanded by Général de Lattre de Tassigny and was killed a few days before the collapse of the Germans. He was awarded a posthumous medal for his courage, accompanied by de Lattre's personal letter to his mother. But Vera never recovered from the loss of her only child whom she loved passionately. I do not think, however, knowing her as I did, that she ever regretted her refusal to take her son away from the country to which she was devoted.

I was upset by Vera's rebuke, but I told her that I felt it would be safer for Mother to be in America and that I could not leave her. I was also convinced that under the pressure to which even the "free zone" was subjected, it would be impossible to continue the work I had in mind and which I considered my vocation. She listened silently to my words and embraced me without her usual warmth and affection. Alas, I never saw her again. But we exchanged many letters after the liberation and the last time I heard of her she was to join a religious community.

There was a tense silence during those last minutes of parting. Then the train came slowly into view. It was to take us to the Spanish border, and as we heard the conductor call out *"En voiture s'il vous plait!"* (All aboard!), we hurriedly climbed into our coach with the sudden realization that we were now "on our way." It was a heartbreak.

We were soon speeding along the line which had been constructed and in part excavated in the very heart of the great divide between Spain and France. It was a desolate country; lonely shepherds were watching their flocks in an almost biblical country. Though strictly guarded on both sides of the frontier, there remained the secret trails of the mountain smugglers. I knew, thanks to my underground friends, that these men, moving like shadows through those trails, hiding in the caves or in ancient monasteries, were not operatic characters like in *Carmen*, but part of a network which got fugitives over to Spain and thence to England or Africa.

At the border we were checked severely by Franco's police and custom officials. The gendarmes, who did recall *dramatis personae* from *Carmen*, took Mr. Konovalov to one room, while we ladies were led to another room by a policewoman. We were all made to undress and thoroughly searched, or so at least it appeared at the moment.

Spain was still under the impact of the recent civil war and starving children gathered around our train begging for food. They were ragged, sickly, the very symbol of the storm which had swept their country; it seemed as if Goya's tragic pictures had come to life again. We gave the children what food still remained from the package our friends had brought us at our departure from Pau as a *bon voyage* gift. Once again the "all aboard" sounded and we hastily climbed back into our compartment and felt relieved when the train began to move. In Madrid where we stopped for a whole day, we had our first square meal. It seemed incredible that butter, milk, coffee, sugar, meat and potatoes could be served by the restaurant in sufficient quantity and without ration cards, but we could not forget the starving children we had seen at the border. I spent most of the day at the Prado museum; the great collections of this famous picture gallery had been hidden for safety during the civil war and had just been returned to their respective halls.

Standing in admiration, almost in awe before the El Grecos, the Velasquez', the Goyas, I could forget for a while our past tribulations and not think of the uncertain fate awaiting us. Nor did the tragic political strife and the stifling air of Franco's regime penetrate these sacred walls. No tranquilizer could have set my nerves at rest more surely than the sight of these immortal paintings which reflected Spain's true genius. While Goya's scenes were like a preview of the recent reign of terror, El Greco expressed the soul of Spain's great mystics and saints. I stopped for a last look at Velasquez' portait of Philip IV, whom my father was said to resemble when he was a young man. He wore the king's costume for a fancy dress; there was also some resemblance to Philip in my own face, or so I used to be told. I gave him a farewell nod as I tore myself away from the wonderful museum and hastened to rejoin Mother and our fellow travelers who were anxiously awaiting me for the last stretch of our journey on land. We arrived at Lisbon early in the morning, and the city was all sunshine, flowers and beautiful dark-eyed people. I shall always retain this first impression of Portugal; it seemed to me like a promise, a ray of hope, a smile of welcome after our long journey through the night. But alas, only a few hours after our arrival, all joy faded from the picture.

The money which was to be transferred for us to a Lisbon bank had not arrived and was not due for a week or more. This meant that we would arrive in America with a minimum sum, amounting to fifty dollars. Moreover, there would be no money available to pay Grisha's passage. The second blow was that Grisha's own exit from France had been delayed. The Franco-Spanish frontier in the occupied zone had been unexpectedly closed for an indefinite period of time. Our "rendez-vous" in Lisbon, as we had so carefully planned, was now an impossiblity; we were booked for the *Ciudad de Sevilla*, a Spanish liner which was sailing in a week, and no other passage was available. The third blow was that "Haias," which had so generously paid for our passage, could not guarantee a cabin for Mother, since the ship was going to be filled to capacity by hundreds of refugees. We might have to be placed in the hold or, if Mother was given a berth, I could not take care of her nor even get near her. She was by now almost entirely incapacitated and could not be left alone. I spent the days following this alarming news in innumerable trips to the bank (the last hope of getting our check on time had faded), to "Haias," where there was still no space available, and to the American consulate, where I tried to make arrangements for Grisha to obtain a loan for his passage. As an American citizen, there may have been some arrangement possible in normal times, but Lisbon was jammed with refugees in similar predicaments, and nobody knew what could be done about it. Back to "Haias" and thence to the Spanish embassy with a letter for the chargé d'affaires which had been given me by a friend in Pau and which would perhaps help us to get that berth on the Spanish ship. But the embassy offices were closed and the chargé d'affaires out of town.

Exhausted, speechless with anxiety and by then, thoroughly discouraged, I took the streetcar back to our hotel. On the terrace of a café overlooking the square, the Konovalovs and Mrs. Rudnev were peacefully having some cool drinks. They, too, had been looking for berths and money for the continuation of their journey. The Konovalovs looked hopeful. As to Mrs. Rudnev, she was content with the prospect of a deck chair which had been promised her somewhere on the lower deck. Hearing my tale of woe, my friends tried to reassure me. "Haias," after all, had not said its last word, and the Spanish Embassy would help. "Maybe," I exclaimed, "but what about my brother? I cannot get in touch with him and when he arrives, he will find us gone and no money for his passage. What will become of him? He is sick, broken-hearted, and after his wife's death, completely incapable of looking after himself."

"How much money would you want to leave him when he arrives?" Mrs. Rudnev asked. I named the sum approximately, and suddenly I heard Mrs. Rudnev's quiet voice saying, "I can lend you this sum, I have it with me." I was speechless for a moment. How could my fellow-traveler have all that money in her possession here in Lisbon when we had been allowed just enough cash for our transit expenses? Mrs. Rudnev smiled mysteriously. Bending closer to me, she whispered, "I have it here, sewn into my slip. The policewoman at the Spanish frontier never found it." And she fished the banknotes out of a secret pocket and handed them over to me.

I do not remember whether I prayed for that miracle, but I certainly prayed after it happened and thanked God for His last minute help.

The rest was easy. I left the money for Grisha with all instructions with Prince Makinsky, a Russian émigré, curator of the Lisbon branch of Carnegie Foundation (the only person I knew in Lisbon and to whom I could explain the situation). Prince Makinsky was an executive of the European branch of the Coca-Cola Company. He was most helpful during our stay in Lisbon and promised to send Grisha a telegram with all instructions, to meet him at the station upon his arrival, to get him to a hotel and contact "Haias"; the latter agreed to arrange Grisha's passage and also, suddenly produced two berths for us.

And so our anxious days in Lisbon ended in a sort of happy glow. My mother never knew about the agonies I had suffered and was unusually cheerful and cooperative. Makinsky invited us over to the health bureau of Carnegie Foundation where we were vaccinated. Next day, Mr. Konovalov ran a temperature and my mother's arm began to swell, but now nothing could stop us from boarding the *Ciudad de Sevilla*.

The day before we sailed, a tall, handsome middle-aged lady stopped me in the hall of our hotel; smiling, nodding, she exclaimed, "Don't you recognize me? I am Irma de Manziarly, we met at Berdiaev's." It all came back to me; the lady's interest in ecumenism and her many travels around the globe. Mrs. de Manziarly was the daughter of a wealthy Moscow businessman of Baltic origin. A convinced Lutheran (she was writing a book about Luther), she had many friends among Catholics and Russian Orthodox. During her visit to India a few years earlier, she had studied Hinduism and had an interview with Gandhi, who made her a present of a spinning wheel. Her lively, dynamic and fascinating conversation helped to while away those last hours on land and to put aside, for a time at least, the many preoccupations which still haunted me. Mrs. de Manziarly, however, was not sailing on the *Ciudad*. She had a reservation on a deluxe liner and a room prepared for her in one of New York's best "little hotels." She had managed to secure a considerable income abroad in spite of wars and revolutions. Though our meeting was a brief one in Lisbon, it was truly providential, like everything which had taken place in this exodus. We were soon to meet again in New York where Mrs. de Manziarly gathered a few friends interested in ecumenism. With her help, we formed a little group which was to continue in America the work started by Maritain, Berdiaev and Mounier.

On the eve of our departure from Lisbon, another voyager came to join us with a reservation on the *Ciudad*. She was Mrs. Helen Fedorov, the wife of Professor George Fedorov, the Russian Orthodox historian and religious writer who had been so often at Berdiaev's Sunday tea parties. Mrs. Fedorov was deeply distressed, as her husband had been stranded in the occupied zone, while she had been able to escape by another route. The professor was on the blacklist because of his violent anti-Nazi writings. He had finally evaded the Gestapo and had been smuggled by the underground out of France. He was believed to have found a passage to Africa with a group of other refugees who, with the help of de Gaulle's associates, were also bound for America along a different route. But nothing was certain, and Mrs. Fedorov could only hope against hope to be reunited with her husband.

On a bright, sunny morning, our little party boarded the *Ciudad de Sevilla*. Our journey was uneventful, except that it took us three weeks to get to New York as our ship followed the southern route, via the Canaries, San Domingo and Havana, to avoid the submarines patrolling the northern waters. Once a British destroyer stopped us and searched our ship for arms and forbidden cargo. The Spanish officers were coldly polite and poker-faced; the refugees assembled on deck, cheered the British. Our cabin was small and became exceedingly hot, with the fan humming day and night under the low ceiling. But we were lucky to get the berths, as the *Ciudad* was crowded from upper deck to hold. Poor Mrs. Rudnev resignedly slept in her deck chair, but had all her meals with us. We did all we could to ease her discomfort. Mother was calm and smiling; maybe she recalled the long journeys she had made years ago, as a diplomat's wife. Once only did she lose her patience, quite unexpectedly. It was the morning we made a stop at the Canaries. Mother was in her berth and as I opened the porthole, she looked out and saw the docks, crowded and very noisy. The various sounds of a port of call were covered with a loud twitter, as peddlers were offering hundreds of canaries for sale, each in a tiny cage. Mother sat up and looked at the scene:"Goodness gracious," she exclaimed, "why so many canaries, where are we?" Shaking with laughter, I explained that we were docked at the Canaries, where canaries originate. I must admit, I had never thought that the birds really belonged to a tiny island, now an important United States military and air base. Many passengers bought canaries and enjoyed their company on board. Mother was not amused and was irritable throughout the day.

As to myself, I did not laugh after the canary incident. I was feeling more and more depressed as the days passed ever so slowly and the hot stifling nights made sleep impossible. I am not a good sailor, even when the sea is calm. My thoughts turned to the great responsibilities I had assumed. How would I be able to make a living in America? Where would we find a home in a city, where apartments were exorbitant and hotels well above our means? I knew I could write in English and had some articles ready, as well as some publisher's addresses. All this would be sufficient were I alone, but with Mother nearing her eighties and Grisha knocked out by his wife's death I had to face innumerable difficulties. I began to question myself as to the wisdom of my project, but every time I thought of the Countess D. M.'s admonition to "obey the Marshal," I felt that this would have been worse than all the uncertainties we had to face. And sure enough, only a few weeks after we left, the "demarcation zone" was abolished, the Germans occupied the whole of France, and all aliens, especially the Russians in Pau, were arrested and crowded into barracks for several days.

The Baron d'A. let my cousins know that they were no longer welcome, and they found refuge thanks only to my underground friends. Michael was to be deported to Germany and was saved by the village priest whose address I had given him. The young boy escaped along the "smugglers" route over the Spanish border, was arrested in Madrid and jailed. I managed to get him freed thanks to the kind intervention of United States Ambassador to Spain, Carlton Hayes. But I am anticipating, since these events belong to a later period.

Michael finally obtained a passage to England where he enlisted in the Army and received his commission. After the war, he immigrated to Canada, was a major in the Canadian army and is now an employee of the Ministry of Foreign Affairs, married to a Scottish wife and has two children. He helped his father and mother to come over and provided for them until Sergei's death. Sandra worked as a saleswoman in a department store for several years and is now teaching Russian in a language school sponsored by the Canadian government. My cousin Peter, his wife, Sonya, and son, Peter junior, who lived in Belgrade, escaped just in time to avoid the German occupation, and after many wanderings, arrived in New York with a visa and an affidavit I managed to procure for them and with the status of displaced persons. It was a long pull before they, too, finally got settled.

Thus it was that nine of the Iswolskys became citizens of the New World. None of them went back to Russia except myself and Michael, who accompanied Canadian Minister Paul Martin on an official visit to the Soviet Union. He told me how surprised he was when the head of the Leningrad Soviet (equivalent to a mayor) told him that Grandfather and Grandmother Iswolsky's mausoleum in Alexander Nevsky cemetery was well preserved and dutifully kept by the municipality with many other monuments, some of them famous, like Dostoevsky's and Tchaikovsky's tombs.

But if the dead were honored, the living were to be wanderers for many years, and were it not for our strong family ties, I would have probably never been able to pull together the threads of my saga. But as the *Ciudad de Sevilla* slowly plowed its way through the Atlantic, skirting Santo Domingo and the beautiful elegant skyline of Havana, I knew nothing of what was happening to my kith and kin, and could only pray that Grisha could follow on our trail. There was a small chapel aboard and I attended Mass on one of the few rough days we had on our otherwise smooth sailing. It is a great experience to hear a Mass at sea, especially in a storm. It corresponded to my own mood: "Lord, Lord, I am sinking," such was the cry, and then I thought of Mrs. Rudnev's quiet grey eyes as she placed her smuggled treasure into my hands.

The night before we landed, the Konovalovs, Vera Rudnev, Mrs. Fedorov and myself got together on the upper deck and leaning over the rails, watched the *Ciudad's* silvery wake and the porpoises frolicking around it. How gay and unconcerned they seemed, as each of us, absorbed in silent thought, tried to look into the future, as impenetrable as a night at sea when land is already near, yet still shrouded in deep mystery.

Mr. Konovalov, who had been quite cheerful during our long journey, now appeared preoccupied and gloomy. As to Mrs. Fedorov, she was quite dramatic, saying that if she and her husband were not reunited, she would commit suicide. Fortunately, Professor Fedorov soon joined his wife in New York where he became a successful author and lecturer. I had many opportunities of working with him and we became great friends until his death in the late fifties. Strangely enough, his wife's "death wish" on the *Ciudad* still haunted her for many years. It was fulfilled twenty years later when after editing her late husband's posthumous papers, she returned to Paris where she suffered a long period of depression and committed suicide.

Of all of us assembled that night on the deck of the *Ciudad*, the only unperturbed person was Mrs. Rudnev. She had nothing more to lose after her husband's death, and nothing she wanted in particular to gain without him. She was content with the humble work some friends had promised to secure for her in New York; a job in a factory producing stuffed animals, elephants and donkeys, the famous emblems of the two American parties.

None of us slept on that night before our landing in America except, perhaps, my mother, who after the "canary incident" had regained her sweet smile and cheerful temper. We all rose early to make ready for health and immigration inspections which were coming immediately after breakfast.

We did not make the spectacular entrance into the harbor past the Statue of Liberty and did not assemble on deck to admire the skyline in the glow of the cloudless June morning. Because of security reasons, no transatlantic ship could dock at the piers of Manhattan. We landed in Brooklyn, quite an anticlimax, not only for us who missed the thrill promised to every immigrant, but also for our friends, who though long-time New Yorkers, had never been in Brooklyn and lost their way in the maze of unfamiliar streets, arrived just in time, hot and out of breath, to greet us at the pier.

It was a joy indeed to see Alexander Kerensky and his wife waving to us, and next to them was a little old lady in old-fashioned attire and a young woman, tall and slim, elegantly dressed whom I did not know at first sight, but who was also waving and smiling. We went through immigration and customs very rapidly; our arrival had been announced by our New York friends to the authorities in charge, and we were spared the red tape. I recall rapidly filling-out the usual questionnaires for Mother and myself, and Mrs. Fedorov doing hers, without any trouble, but the question "Are you an anarchist?" made her hestitate. "I *am* an anarchist," she muttered to me, "I cannot tell a lie." "Never mind," I whispered back. "You are an anarchist at heart, but a sort of romantic and imaginary one, so you can answer the question by 'No' without perjuring yourself." Elena Nikolaevna did so, but she kept on worrying long after we had landed. Had she answered "Yes," she could not have entered the United States.

Alexander Kerensky, his wife, and the two ladies rushed to greet us at the gate. Now I recognized the older woman and her companion. She was Mrs. Alexandra Greaves, my mother's cousin and the widow of a well-known Russian lawyer who had long practiced in America. The younger woman was her daughter, Marguerite Langkyaer, the wife of a Danish diplomat. We had not been in touch with either of them for many years, but they learned of our arrival and were ready to offer their help to us in the strange city. I realized once more how uncertain our future was. Our funds were rapidly dwindling and I dared not tell our friends and relatives about it. There was a surprise for us; Alexander Kerensky told us that his friend Mrs. Kenneth Simpson had invited us to stay at her home until our plans were settled. They drove us in their car to uptown Manhattan and escorted us to East 91st Street, where our hostess was awaiting us in the vast library of her lovely private home.

It seemed to me indeed like a fairy tale when we were taken up to the guest room on the fifth floor by the Japanese butler. We found all the comfort which we could wish for and which I had not even dreamed could still exist. Mrs. Kenneth Simpson has remained my friend since that first encounter. I had the opportunity of appreciating all her remarkable qualities: kindness, generosity, intelligence, good taste; her library was full of the most recent books, among them many French and Russian ones. She spoke both these languages and has been many times in Europe. The walls were hung with the finest modern paintings and drawings. Throughout the years, I was to visit often this most hospitable of houses, and each time I recalled the emotion which filled me on that memorable morning of June 3, 1941, when Helen Simpson held out her hand to my mother and me, as if we were her old and always welcome friends.

CHAPTER XIV

America – The Grand Tour

WE HAD safely crossed the ocean and found refuge in New York. It might seem that our troubles were over; however, our prospects were not very promising. My mother's health was failing and she needed my constant care. There was no chance of my taking a job. A week after we arrived, Grisha landed. He had been met as arranged, by Prince Makinsky in Lisbon, and "Haias" got him a passage, which would have been impossible without the help of this organization. But the only reservation available was a hammock in the overcrowded hold. Grisha spent the entire voyage on deck. He was in poor shape, nervous and exhausted, so I had two invalids on my hands. Though the money delayed in Lisbon had arrived, there was little left after I had paid my debt to Mrs. Rudnev. But, as usual, Providence came to our rescue.

I was advised to consult Alexandra Tolstoy, the daughter of the famous novelist, who directed a relief organization she had set up, especially to aid the Russian émigrés. This Tolstoy Foundation had an office in New York, and in addition, Miss Tolstoy had obtained a rural center in the Hudson Valley, near Nyack. The estate was called Reed Farm and had been given to the Foundation by Mrs. Harkness, a well-known philanthropist. There were many acres of land and several buildings equipped to receive a considerable number of people.

I first saw Alexandra Tolstoy in her New York office. She had been Tolstoy's favorite daughter, the youngest, who had been with him when he left his home in 1910, and died in the local railroad station at Astapovo. As I spoke to her, using the patronymic Alexandra Lvovna, I recalled Lev Tolstoy's tragic death. Her resemblance to her father was striking.

She was heavily built, broad-shouldered with strong features and powerful hands. Her voice was pleasant, and she spoke the most beautiful Russian I had ever heard. Yes, this was the pure Russian in which Tolstoy wrote *War and Peace*, so full of color and music.

After consultation with Miss Tolstoy and her assistant, Tatiana Shaufuss, it was decided that Mother, Grisha and myself, would move to Reed Farm. We were given rooms in a small cottage near the main building and found our new quarters comfortable and cheerful. Several other émigrés moved into the main building and there was a separate cottage where a summer camp for children was opened. Grisha and I could work on the farm for our room and board. All the inhabitants, if they were strong and healthy, were assigned various tasks; working in the house, the gardens, the farm. Others were in charge of the children's camp, teaching them Russian and Russian culture. The head of the summer camp was Martha Knudson, who had been a teacher in one of the "free schools" which Tolstoy had started on his estate, similar to the "Montessori method."

There was a Russian Orthodox chapel at the farm and Bishop Sava, a refugee from Eastern Europe, was in charge of the religious services. He was a kindhearted, friendly man and made his headquarters in a small cabin, something like a hermit's cell. There was a Catholic church within walking distance, where I could go to Mass. I also often attended the Orthodox services and soon became great friends with the good Bishop Sava. He helped Grisha to regain his courage and energy.

I was assigned to a job in the refectory, serving meals to the inhabitants of the farm, whose number kept steadily growing. We also had weekend guests who enjoyed our Russian food, prepared by an expert cook. Grisha was put in charge of the chickens, for Alexandra Tolstoy planned to raise poultry in order to provide income for the farm. But this plan was still in its initial stages. There were few chickens when we moved in and Grisha enjoyed taking care of them. But one evening, calamity almost struck; I was sitting on our porch after supper. It was growing dark, and I savoured the peace and quiet of the country scene. Then suddenly, I saw white forms hovering on the lawn. I thought at first that the wind had blown pieces of laundry from the clothesline, but, no, the ghostly forms were moving—they were Grisha's chickens! He had forgotten to lock them up for the night and he was now fast asleep. I rushed to the rescue and drove the chickens back to their coop, just as Alexandra came striding across the lawn.

She always took great strides and had a commanding look when inspecting her domain. She was a hard worker herself, sharing her father's ideas that manual labor was important and had a deep spiritual significance. It was a philosophy of true Christian living. She would drive out daily to her New York office; then returning, after many strenuous hours, she would hurry down to her vegetable garden or into the fields, to join the farmhands. She spent her weekends helping to plow, hoe, weed, or collect the harvest. She carried bushels of corn or potatoes on her powerful shoulders. Sometimes I helped her, and so learned to plant potatoes. I was thrilled to hear her talk about her father and what he said to her about the meaning of life. It was well worth digging or pulling out weeds, to hear these wise sayings.

Most of the time, however, I was busy in the refectory, serving three meals a day to some twenty or thirty people. I remember getting very tired; my feet ached and I longed to sit down. Ever since, I have had sympathy for waitresses in large, crowded restaurants for I know how they feel. One Sunday, a famous Russian ballet company came to dinner at the farm. The beautiful, graceful ballerinas and their elegant partners were enchanting and as a devotee of the ballet, I did my best to cater to them, but they must have noticed that I looked tired. Several of the young girls rose to their feet and offered to help me serve. They flitted from table to table, laughing merrily and showing their wonderful precision and skill—it was quite a performance!

Soon after we moved to the farm, I took a day off to visit the Kerenskys. At dinner, I noticed that he seemed preoccupied. There was good reason for it. The news had come over the radio that Hitler's armies were mustering at the Russian border.

For us of the emigration, the official news of the German invasion of Russia was shattering. However opposed we may have been to the Stalin regime, we deeply felt the tragedy which now threatened our homeland. The date was June 21st. Some experts predicted that Hitler would enter Moscow within three months. Tens of thousands of Red Army soldiers were killed or surrendered; Smolensk and Kiev fell. Disaster seemed inevitable.

In the hot summer nights, I slept out on the screened porch watching the fireflies dance their ballet, with the frogs croaking not far away. The country reminded me of Russia and my heart sank as I thought of my far away land, torn by war, bombed and plundered.

Novgorod was captured in August and in the south, Kharkov fell. The Germans had penetrated deep into the Ukraine. But then resistance stiffened. The fall of Leningrad and of Moscow, which Hitler expected momentarily, never happened.

On a late, fall weekend, Professor Timashev, a well-known sociologist who taught at Fordham University, came to visit the farm. I asked him what he thought of the war situation, and he answered by another question: "What is the date, today?" When I answered, "October 15th," he replied: "Well, it is now raining in Russia. I was born in the region where the army is concentrated. I know that the roads are turning into a sea of mud. The *panzers* will be bogged down. Then, it will soon be winter, and the snow will pile up. The Germans are late in their schedule." The professor was right. Hitler never made it, irrespective of his initial success.

In spite of many duties on the farm, I was still intent on returning to literary work. I had written a few articles about my experiences in occupied France. They were intended for the American press, so I switched from French to English. I looked up my old friend Governor

Paulding, editor of *Commonweal,* and he accepted my articles. Later, *Commonweal* published other articles of mine on Russian culture and religion.

I was delighted to learn from Paulding that many of my former Paris friends were now in New York. Jacques Maritain and Raissa, who had left Paris just before the war, writing and lecturing, had stayed on in New York and had an apartment on lower Fifth Avenue. The composer Arthur Lourié and his wife, who had fled Hitler, lived in the same building. Father Couturier, my spiritual director, had also arrived in New York. I visited them every time I could get away from the farm. Soon after our reunion, we got up a declaration affirming our position as Catholics, opposing Hitler's tyranny and racism. It was published in French, entitled *Devant La Crise Mondiale* (Facing the World Crisis).

Maritain encouraged me to write about my life in France during the years when we had shared so many friends and interests. He gave me an introduction to Julie Kernan of Longmans-Green. She had lived many years in France and shared our distress at the fall of France. Her brother had been arrested by the Germans in the French zone. She welcomed me warmly and approved my project. I signed a contract with Longmans-Green and set to work immediately.

The book came out early in 1942, under the title *Light before Dusk.* I still feel there is much useful source material in it concerning the French spiritual revival of the thirties. The book was well received by the Catholic press. I have since met a number of priests and religious intellectuals who had read it and felt inspired by the remarkable people such as Mounier and Fondaminsky (now largely forgotten) and the dynamic social, religious and ecumenical movements I described. Julie Kernan arranged an exhibition of my work in the window of a Catholic bookstore with photographs of Maritain, Berdiaev, Mounier, etc. and I met a number of progressive Catholics who invited me to dinners, luncheons and various meetings. For a while, it seemed that I had reached a peak of success, although the book was not a bestseller.

Among others, I met Mr. and Mrs. Robert Hoguet, who were friends of the Maritains and many Catholic intellectuals from Europe. Their home was a center for a true, spiritual elite. I was deeply grateful for their kindness and hospitality, and our friendship subsequently lasted many years.

Back at the farm, my mother had gradually adjusted herself to her new environment and had regained her cheerful smile. She wanted to contribute something to the community life, and gave French lessons to the children of the summer camp.

With the advance I had received on *Light before Dusk* plus royalties and odd sums I was able to make from various translations, I was slowly getting back on my feet, but I was still a long way from independence.

As for Grisha, he had applied reluctantly for several jobs. He would much rather remain at the farm with his chickens. He was very depressed and the urge to drink would suddenly overpower him. Mother tried to persuade him to "pull himself together." But the "prodigal son," as usual, had his way. According to Tolstoy's precepts, drinking was strictly prohibited at the farm. But, as I had learned, alcoholism is a disease which has its own laws and cannot be prohibited from outside. Grisha had to make his own decision, which he finally did.

My book had quite a circulation among Catholic schools in America and Canada, where it had been simultaneously published by Longmans and later translated into French by the Editions de L'Arbre in Montreal, under the title *Au Temps de la Lumière*. Soon after the Montreal publication, I received an invitation to lecture at the Assumption College in Windsor, Ontario. This invitation rather scared me, for I had had an unfortunate experience a few weeks earlier, when Alexandra Tolstoy, who was tied up at the farm, asked me to replace her as speaker at Wellesley College in Massachusetts. I had prepared a text on Russian religious life, but I was very shy about speaking in public and decided to read my lecture, from beginning to end. The lecture was held in a very small auditorium, and though I did find the audience rather cool, I was not worried about it.

Then a letter came from one of my sponsors, giving me a warning. I was not clearly heard, and I did not once look at my audience. Alas, the gentleman was right. I had given a very poor performance. I had never heard anyone lecture in America up to that time and was unaware what is expected of a speaker. To read a whole paper without looking up, without a single ad lib, was a terrible mistake. I was grateful for the criticism, though it upset me so much that I was afraid to accept the Windsor invitation. But finally decided that I could do better on the podium, and accepted the offer.

This was to be a big affair. It was the program of the Christian Culture series; Jacques Maritain, Frank Sheed and his wife, Maisie Ward, Bishop Fulton Sheen and other illustrous guests had been summoned by the dynamic and liberal Dean of Assumption College, Monsignor MacMahon.

My topic was Russia's heroic resistance to the German invasion. This theme deeply inspired me, especially after a poem by Constantine Simonov had reached me from the Soviet Union. Simonov, a war correspondent of the Red Army fighting Hitler, did not reflect the ideology which usually was the stamp of Soviet writing. He expressed the love of the Russian people for their country, their courage and self-sacrifice, and their religious sentiments, which particularly moved me. For was this not the mood I had tried to capture in my little book *The Soviet Man* —published five years before the war? I had predicted that the Russian people were devoted to their Russian land, more deeply than to communism and that religion was alive in Russia, in spite of Soviet persecution.

I wrote out my lecture carefully, with quotations from the Simonov poem and trained intensively in my room, going over the lecture again and again, so that the people who shared the cottage with me thought I was talking to myself. This time everything went well. The audience was warm and responsive. I felt that you can really communicate with people through the lecture medium. Many Americans came over from Detroit to hear me speak, so this was really my American debut.

Soon after my return from Canada, I had lunch with Julie Kernan, who said, "I want you to meet Dorothy Day and see her House of Hospitality." I had heard of the *Catholic Worker* and was eager to meet the woman who had founded it, with the French peasant Peter Maurin. So we set off for Mott Street, near Chinatown, where the House was then located. As we entered the main hall, I immediately sensed that it was an unusual, strange and rather frightening world. However, it seemed aglow with its own brightness. I saw for the first time, the scene that became familiar to me, yet always deeply stirred me. Along the stretching, refectory tables, the poor were crowded, seated on the long, wooden benches, some leaning on the tables, others crouched as if half asleep. Large coffee bowls and chunks of bread were placed before them. In their midst, sat a little gray-haired man. He might have come from an old French woodcut. He was speaking English with a heavy, French accent.

"This is Peter Maurin," said Julie, leading me to him and giving my name. "So you are Helene Iswolsky," cried Peter, grasping my hand. "I have read your book, *Soviet Man* now . . ." I was amazed that the little book published in France had reached Peter here in the slums of New York and had found an echo in this extraordinary old man. He told me he read the book in French, then found an English translation. (I was unaware that it had been translated.) He had given it to Dorothy Day — "We both liked it" he concluded with one of his rapid, eloquent gestures.

Soviet Man had actually been my introduction to the *Catholic Worker*. I was immediately accepted into the family, or rather, I had been accepted before I ever came to Mott Street.

"Now let us go upstairs and meet Dorothy," said Julie, leading me up a creaky stairway to the third floor. We went through a small hallway with several doors and knocked at one.

"Come in," said a low, quiet voice. We entered what at first seemed to be a nursery. There were several cribs in the room, with a baby in each one; in the midst of them stood a tall woman with clear-cut features, blue eyes and with thick braids of blond hair wound around her head. There was something full of repose about this figure, in spite of the fact that the babies were quite noisy and loud voices were heard in an adjacent room. For the time, her room was shared by a few of the Bowery's motherless offspring, and the people next door had just arrived from a bout in the neighboring saloon. During the twenty-five years that I have known Dorothy, I have always found her sharing her room or giving it up, and usually exposed to the most varied sounds. And yet that extraordinary repose which I felt on our first meeting never ceased to emanate from her.

During my first visit to the *Catholic Worker*, Dorothy talked about Dostoevsky. I discovered that she knew the great Russian classics and could quote them (in English, of course) as frequently as myself, and even more profusely than I did. But what impressed me most was not her culture, which was extensive, but her way of life, sharing the lot of the poorest, and not as an outsider, patronizing them, helping them at a distance, but as *one* of them, a member of that vast family living under the sign of destitution and misery.

Delighted with the warm welcome which Dorothy and Peter gave me on that first day of our acquaintance, I hoped to see more of them, but circumstances prevented me from doing so for some time. On December 8th, 1941, we celebrated Mother's eightieth birthday. She was in fine spirits and it would have been a joyful occasion, had it not been for the news of Pearl Harbor which came to us over the radio. So America was at war and Churchill could write to Franklin Roosevelt, "Now we are all in one boat!" We were completely cut off from Europe now, but at the same time, we were hopeful that with Russia, the United States and Great Britain allied against the common enemy, the liberation of all the occupied countries would be accomplished.

In the spring of 1942, Mother had a stroke and became bedridden. There were two registered nurses working as volunteers at the farm and they took care of our invalid a few hours each day, while I served in the refectory. Grisha also helped us. For two or three months, we continued in this way, but the situation grew more difficult. Alexandra Tolstoy suggested that we find a nursing home, but I feared these institutions, and insisted that we keep Mother in the cottage. Then Grisha, tiring of his chickens and the almost cloistered life of the farm, suddenly made up his mind to look for a job in New York. He found work as a packer in a match factory. Hard as it was to be left alone with Mother, I realized that this was an important step for my brother. He was determined to make good, and in spite of very small wages, kept his job for a longer time than ever before. Indeed, he worked at the factory until his death in 1951.

My mother, whose mind was mostly wandering, noticed Grisha's absence one day and asked where he was. When told he had taken a job in the city, she murmured, "Thank God," with a smile. Now that her "prodigal son" had picked himself up, she could die in peace. The end came peacefully, but it would have been a painful ordeal had it not been for the help of Alexandra who, during those agonizing hours, helped me face the mystery of death, just as her father had described it in his great writings.

When it was all over, I did not linger long at Reed Farm. I realized that much as I suffered over my mother's death, it was time for me to look for a job in the city. I decided to look for a room in the neighborhood I knew best, the upper East Side. When we had first stayed with Mrs. Simpson, I often went to the Church of St. Jean Baptiste at Lexington Avenue and 76th Street. There was an atmosphere of constant prayer and recollection here and the Fathers of the Blessed Sacrament who were in charge were French Canadians, friendly and compassionate. I had always felt inspired by Saint Jean Baptiste, and so I looked for a room in the vicinity.

I found the first For Rent sign a few blocks away. The door was answered by an elderly lady who led me up three floors where a bedroom–sitting-room was available. The dark blue velvet curtains and studio couch cover, the upholstered furniture, the old-fashioned, folding writing desk and the neat, tiled bathroom were all quite attractive. The rent of ten dollars a week did not exceed my means. There was only one drawback; it had no kitchenette and I would have to eat outside. I did not hesitate, however, and rented the room immediately.

The elderly lady seemed pleased when I told her I was Russian. The last tenant had also been Russian, she said, and a very nice gentleman. He had left the picture which hung on the wall. It was an enlarged photograph of the Kremlin, a good omen, I said to myself, as I unpacked my belongings. The landlady's name was Miss Seary and she allowed me to keep the Kremlin picture.

As soon as I was settled in my new lodgings, I started looking for some means of subsistence. I sent a few articles to magazines to whom I had been recommended, but none of them accepted my writings. Julie Kernan had given me the address of an agent who organized lecture tours. She was Mrs. Josephine Ryan Murphy, who lived in Chicago, a most cooperative and experienced woman. She took me "in tow" and worked out a program of lectures for Catholic colleges. But this was a long-range project, since a tour could not be arranged until 1943.

One of the colleges interested was Saint Mary's in Indiana. The President, Sister Madeleva, a poet and scholar, wrote to me personally and put me down on her schedule. It would have to be late, she said, because of the football season. I was puzzled by this allusion to the sport —what had this nun and highly intellectual woman to do with football? The riddle was solved when it was explained to me that Saint Mary's was the neighbor of Notre Dame University, the venerable institution that had become famous for its prowess in that sport; the whole area was absorbed in it. Nobody would attend my lectures in the football season!

I did have an assignment for a lecture, however, at Fordham University in New York. It had been arranged by Father Andrew Rogosh who came of a Russian family and had graduated from the Russicum, an institution in Rome devoted to the study of the Eastern Catholic tradition. He was then rector of Saint Michael's Church of the Catholic Byzantine rite, a kindly and courteous man who took great interest in my work.

Again I worked hard on my lecture, which was to deal with the prospects for a rapprochement between Catholics and Russian Orthodox. This was a topic which did not concern American Catholics as much as it had my friends in Paris. I was eager to present the subject to Fordham, but had no appropriate dress for such a formal occasion, for the lecture was to be in Keating Hall, the main auditorium of the university. It so happened that a friend had presented me with a long, evening dress; it was of dark red chiffon and gold, very handsome and dignified. I decided to wear it, and made, I believe, a satisfying impression. The talk was well accepted and Father Rogosh was particularly pleased.

Besides the encouragement of this good priest, I had the support of a Russian woman who, like myself, was a Catholic, and deeply attached to the Eastern Catholic heritage. She was Catherine de Hueck, known to the American lay apostolate as the "Baroness," later Mrs. Eddie Doherty.

I had first met Catherine in Paris where she was a reporter for *Sign* magazine, but her main interest was centered in New York. She had just founded "Friendship House" in Harlem, to promote a true Christian relationship between the white and black people of America. She was a pioneer in a field which in those days, with only few exceptions, was a subject taboo in American society. She displayed great courage in defending her position. No greater tribute can be paid to her than the words of Thomas Merton in his diary: "She was one of the most energetic and generous people I have ever met—and one of the most simple. Everything she says and does . . . goes right to the heart of the issue. The Russian Revolution had made her poor, but far from resenting this, she embraced it as a marvelous grace from God. She resolved to make poverty her vocation with a vigor and directness that was thoroughly Franciscan!" *(Secular Journal of Thomas Merton,* Farrar, Strauss and Cudahy, New York, 1959)

I visited Friendship House and it was a new experience for me to walk through the streets of Harlem. When I asked black people for the "Baroness" they smiled approvingly. There had been riots and breaking of windows in the area, but Friendship House remained untouched. I gave some talks in their library, where Catherine had collected translations of Russian classics and spiritual writings. She took a lively interest in my work and recommended me to Frank Sheed, whose publishing house, Sheed and Ward, had brought out some excellent books on Russia and religion.

I submitted a project to Mr. Sheed which I had started in Paris before the invasion of France. It was to present a panorama of Russia's cultural and spiritual trends from an early period of history until the present time. The project was approved and Mr. Sheed gave me a contract to write the book as soon as possible. Since I had already collected a considerable amount of material, and written the first two chapters in French, I knew how to begin again even though my papers had been lost. I spent long hours in the Public Library's Slavonic department, and managed to reconstruct my work, this time in English.

I was comfortable in my new lodgings; it was a good place to work. Miss Seary permitted me to have a hotplate and even an icebox. A few old and new friends dropped in to see me. Grisha came quite regularly on weekends. He was doing very well at the match factory but he still needed care and attention. We kept close to each other. He had become his former, charming self.

Kerensky, with his wife, Theresa, often visited me but she seemed to be ailing, and discovered later that she had an incurable illness. She longed to go home to her native Australia and they both left for Sidney where she died after a few months. When Kerensky returned to America, he traveled almost continuously, giving many lectures. Finally, he took a permanent position at the Hoover Library at Stanford University, San Francisco. I saw little of him the next ten years but our ties of friendship were never broken and we had a long and affectionate correspondence.

Even though things had turned out well in New York, I still suffered from spells of intense loneliness. I had taken care of my mother for so many years and shared so much of my life with her that her death left a void which nothing could fill. I felt this void particularly at Christmas time when the streets and stores were gaily decorated. Hundreds of Santa Clauses rang their bells on the sidewalks and delighted small children everywhere. Even the countryside near the city was sparkling with lights and Christmas trees. People were excited, buying presents, planning parties, but there was nothing for me in all this gaiety.

On Christmas Day I took a bus to Rockland Lake and dropped into Reed Farm. But Alexandra Tolstoy was not there and our little cottage looked abandoned. Everything reminded me of the last days we spent there.

I returned to New York and my small apartment, in a melancholy mood. As I climbed the stairs, I met Miss Seary, who welcomed me with a smile and a hearty "Merry Christmas." There was so much warmth in her greeting that I answered with equal good wishes. "Won't you come to my sitting room," said the old lady and led me downstairs.

Miss Seary lived in the basement and I had only seen her while paying my rent. Now the apartment had a wonderfully festive atmosphere. Several people were sitting around a large table covered by a fancy tablecloth, with coffee, fruitcake, many goodies and snacks. Miss Seary offered me a drink; it was a martini, dexterously mixed. We spent the evening talking, and we sang "Jingle Bells"—that tune heard everywhere at Christmas. I never get tired of it, because it brings back that evening in Miss Seary's parlor when she saved me from a wave of depression.

The people around the table were mostly tenants of our rooming house. Some of them, I learned later, owed Miss Seary several months rent. She was a most generous person and I grew very fond of her. However, there was something mysterious about this old Irish Catholic who had seen better days. She had had a much larger roominghouse and even a few movie stars amongst her roomers, one of them being Bette Davis. Miss Seary enjoyed a good drink and company, but she was no bohemian. Her courteous manner and quiet way of talking were those of a *grande dame*. Some said she came from old stock and called her "Lady Seary." I remember my first landlady with deep gratitude for she gave me my first home in New York City.

Soon after Christmas I finished my book, *The Soul of Russia*, and began to get ready for the lecture tour which had been arranged for me, thanks to Julie Kernan. Mrs. Josephine Ryan Murphy had planned my tour mostly in the Midwest area, but it began with Catholic University in Washington. I had no money for my trip and was ashamed to tell my agent of my financial troubles. A friend lent me a hundred dollars for my ticket and a few dresses. I still had the red-and-gold gown I had worn at Fordham, but needed other items. An old fur-lined coat which I had brought from France looked rather shabby, but I tried to pretend it was the latest thing from Paris. The girls often asked me to speak to them about fashions, and all I could tell them was that French women in occupied Paris could hardly get new clothes when materials were lacking. Stockings were not available and shoes were often replaced by wooden sandals. They looked at me with unbelieving eyes; I came from Paris, I *must* know what's new.

My Washington experience was most delightful, in spite of misgivings; indeed it seemed to me that a minor miracle had happened. As I mounted the rostrum and placed the text of my talk on the lectern, I suddenly realized that I did not need these sheets of paper; I could speak without looking at them. It was as if I had received the "gift of tongues." From that day on, I never used a written text. Of course I made a careful preparation and took a few notes with me, mostly quotations.

Father James Magner, then procurator of Catholic University and founder of the Charles Caroll Forum, where I had spoken, was a charming host. He entertained me and a few faculty members in his own house on the campus. He was an accomplished pianist and played Russian music for us. Next day, as he drove me to the station, I felt I could confide in him. I told him that I was hesitating between two vocations. Should I engage in the apostolate of reconciliation between Catholics and Orthodox which had started in France, or should I do more studying to attain academic status? Father Magner discussed my problem with warm interest. He offered me a teaching job at the Catholic College which would permit me, at the same time, to take some graduate courses. I hesitated to accept this offer, still wanting to stay in New York where all my friends were centered and where I hoped to be able to do some more writing.

Meanwhile, I continued my tour which took me to Toledo, Ohio, and to Chicago, where I spent several weeks lecturing at Catholic colleges in the area. This was the most active and interesting period of my tour, in which I met some outstanding personalities and made new friends.

Josephine Ryan Murphy, my agent, became my daily mentor in Chicago. I would have been lost without her in this great city where people lived enormous distances from each other—so it seemed to me. Mrs. Murphy not only arranged this excellent program for me—my first "Grand Tour"— but she remained my agent for years to come, and organized several very satisfactory big lectures and tours.

My most memorable meeting in Chicago was at the Dominican Sisters' Rosary College. The President, Sister Thomas Aquinas, was one of the most remarkable women I have ever encountered, certainly the most magnanimous to offer me her friendship. She was at that time already in frail health and lame, but her intellectual and spiritual energies never failed her. She was continually limping around in her white habit and black veil, attending all college activities and welcoming each guest personally. She was highly sympathetic to my devotion to the Russian people, for she, too, had faith in their spiritual survival. She was an avant-garde champion of social action or reform, and of racial equality.

I found Chicago's Catholic schools and organizations far more aware of social problems than the New York Catholics. This was due in part to Bishop Sheil, coadjutor of the archbishop of Chicago, whose school of social studies became an important and active center. At nearby Notre Dame University, a young priest, Father Putz, was promoting a Jocist movement. He came to see me during my stay in Chicago and we had a long talk about the youth movements I had known or worked with in

France. I gave one of my lectures at Bishop Sheil's school where I found a very friendly and enlightened audience.

In Chicago, I also met Father Chrysostom Tarasevich, a Benedictine monk of the Byzantine rite. He came from Belorussia, one of the Soviet republics whose language and culture are very similar to those of Russia and the Ukraine. This meeting was the beginning of a friendship of many years with this outstanding priest so deeply imbued with Eastern spirituality and the love of the Russian people, in war and in peace.

Father Chrysostom was impetuous, outspoken, radical and to an extent even considered "suspect" by the F.B.I. But nothing could dampen his zeal and enthusiasm. He published a magazine called *One Church*, the only ecumenical publication in Russian at that time. He was encouraged by his abbot, but after he died his successor suspended the publication. Father Chrysostom also started a radio program in Russian and English which was broadcast for some time, by a small Chicago station. He asked me to speak on it, one evening, followed by Russian folk music. Later, I met him in New York, where he often came to preach at retreats for the *Catholic Worker*. He did much to promote my own ecumenical work. For many years he was a sick man and I wondered how long he would be able to carry on his work, but each time he had a crisis, he seemed to recover almost miraculously. In 1967, he was able to return to his native Belorussia and spent six months in a small village, where he said Mass for the people — a remarkable feat, since Catholics were not allowed to perform services (But his Byzantine rite protected him. — Ed.)

I found that my old friend Catherine de Huek also had a House of Hospitality in Chicago. We discussed the possibility of organizing a Russian-Catholic center in New York or Chicago, but there were many obstacles involved. One day a member of a Catholic women's club came to see me at my hotel. She asked me if the "Baroness" could be trusted, and was she not a dangerous subversive character? I replied that I had known her for many years, and that she was recommended to me by Bishop Sheil. I advised the lady to go and ask the Bishop about her. She left, only half reassured.

A few days later, speaking at Notre Dame University, Catherine was challenged at a discussion which I attended, and I was delighted by her enthusiasm, her deep convictions and her brilliant *reparties* — her most violent opponents were soon disarmed.

Both Catherine and I were scheduled to speak at Saint Mary's College and drove there together from Notre Dame University. There we met the president, Sister Madeleva, who had written to me about the "football games." It did not take me long to discover that she was a poet, a scholar and a remarkable educator. Spread under the glass on her desk was a map of the world. It was characteristic of this American nun who had traveled far and wide, had a doctor's degree from Oxford, and whose friends and visitors came from many countries. During a stay in Paris, she had met Charles du Bos, and in the thirties he was appointed a visiting professor at Notre Dame University. They became close friends and neighbors. In her memoirs,[1] she tells how he came to Mass at Saint Mary's and had breakfast with her every day. The memory of Charles du Bos was a link between me and Sister Madeleva and she kindly invited me to come to Saint Mary's as often as I wished.

I returned to the college in 1945 on my last "grand tour" and it happened that Catherine de Huek was also there. We shared the guest room and spent most of the night talking. She was wavering between two alternatives: to go on with her work in the lay apostolate, as a widow, or to get married. She left Saint Mary's as yet undecided. A few days later, I learned that she was married in Chicago, to a famous newsman of the time, Eddie Doherty. He was a Catholic by birth and after their marriage joined Catherine in her work. Later, in 1970, he was ordained a Melchite priest—the clergy of this Eastern Catholic rite being allowed to marry (as are the Russian Orthodox). Together, they founded Madonna House, a lay-apostolate training center in Combemere, Canada.

My tour was almost over. I had been impressed by the colleges I had visited, the buildings, the comfort, the eagerness of the students, the friendliness of the nuns. Little could I foresee the days when students would rebel and nuns would leave their schools and novitiates. These were the happy days of Catholic education. It was not yet involved in intense competition with secular colleges, nor in large building projects for new laboratories and technological equipment which, later, absorbed the funds of the wealthiest institutions. Enrollments were relatively small and the relations between students and administration were closer than in subsequent years.

After the American tour, I was scheduled to speak in Montreal. I gave several lectures in both French and English, and was most graciously received by the mayor of Montreal. Canadian papers presented me as a courageous speaker, "reasonably optimistic."

I returned to New York immensely heartened. The *Soul of Russia* had come out and was well-reviewed. I was planning more literary work, but I soon discovered that my recent "successes" would not provide for my daily bread. The fees for lectures would soon be exhausted. I decided that I must cut down my expenses. Miss Seary had a smaller room which she could rent to me for half the price of my attractive studio.

While contemplating these sad prospects, the telephone rang in the hall, and my landlady called out my name. I ran downstairs in a somber mood. An unknown voice, apparently someone's secretary, asked me

---

1. This memoir, *The First Seventy Years* (Macmillan, 1959), mentions my visit as one of the European intellectuals to come to her college during the War.

to come and see Mr. Pierre Lazareff, at 250 East 57th Street. He would await me in his office. Pierre Lazareff? I immediately recalled the little man I had met some years before in Paris, on the nightshift of his illustrated magazine *Match*. I remembered the excitement, the feverish work I had done on the captions, the fatigue, the bewilderment of finding myself at dawn, alone on the Paris streets, as the magazine went to press. What was Pierre Lazareff doing in New York and how did he find out my address?

Still completely puzzled, I promised that I would be there at the appointed time. I knew that if it was Lazareff, it must be something important and as I arrived at the address, I recognized the building as the location of the Voice of America. I had applied there for a job several months earlier, to no avail. I did not think they had even written down my name. Now I was being called by one of France's greatest journalists. How many times, throughout my life, I had been taken by surprise, found Providence at my side when my fortunes were at their lowest ebb!

I was escorted to one of the top floors, occupied by the French desk, which broadcast twenty-four hours, around the clock — programs of news, and information to the underground in France. There, in a large office, was Mr. Lazareff in his shirt-sleeves and suspenders, with his feet on the desk — just as I had seen him last, in Paris. He was now director of the French desk and just as dynamic as when he had been editor of *Paris-Soir* and *Match*. Both these publications folded after the fall of France, while Lazareff and his wife, Helen Gordon, escaped to America. She was now editor of a woman's magazine.

Mr. Lazareff told me that he had called me at the suggestion of another well-known journalist with whom I had worked many years ago, in Paris. He was now also working for the Voice of America. They were looking for an editor of religious news and my articles in *Commonweal* and my book *Light before Dusk* had come to their attention.

So it was that I was hired by the Voice of America. I had to fill out a long questionnaire as to my former occupations, life, education and mores. One of the questions was "Do you indulge in alcoholic drinks?" I wanted to set down *NO*, but I was not a total abstainer and hesitated. An official, who was helping me with the questionnaire, smiled and said: "Why not write 'occasionally' " — I did so.

I became a civil servant under the State Department and was submitted to a security check, but with a minimum of red tape, for Mr. Lazareff was in a hurry to put me to work. I was given a badge with my photograph on it and was told to report on July 10th, at nine o'clock. As I sat down at the place assigned to me in the long row of desks, the teletypes were humming, bringing the morning news: the invasion of Sicily had begun.

CHAPTER XV

Wartime and Peacetime

MY ENROLLMENT in the Voice of America introduced me to an entirely new world. I had never served a government agency and American bureaucracy was completely unfamiliar to me. In times of war, such an agency was subject to both civilian and military restrictions. Yet within this rigid framework there was a motley crowd of journalists, novelists, scientists and artists, from France and Germany, speaking to their compatriots of the underground.

Not only the leading scriptwriters and the announcers in charge of broadcasts, but also the typists and technicians belonged to the intellectual elite of the countries which they had fled to escape Hitler's domination and terror.

I had some difficulty in adapting myself to the techniques of scriptwriting and the first days were very tense indeed, until finally I learned the elements of timing on radio; every minute, every second is counted to make up a broadcast and the least mistake may lead to the need for disastrous cuts or disruption of a whole program.

These were technical problems which I soon learned to master. The real difficulties arose when I came into close contact with my colleagues. In Paris, my last years had been entirely devoted to the work of *Esprit*, and the Russian youth movements; I had been almost cut off from other intellectual circles. The people of the Office of War Information (or O.W.I.), belonged to a world which was not mine. They were for the most part, rationalists, atheists or inspired by surrealism which, in those days, influenced nearly all French painting and literature, and was opposed to the Church. Since I was entrusted with religious themes, I found no sympathizers. Two or three of my colleagues observed me with polite curiosity, but most of them were hostile or indifferent.

My two archenemies were the famous poet André Breton and the young typist, Miss G., who was assigned to me. When I dictated my script to her, she would laugh or shrug; once, she cut a halo out of a newspaper and put it on her head! I remember Breton as an imperious figure. He always held his head very high, and with his thick crown of blond hair he looked like a lion. The great man was not a scriptwriter;

he refused to write anything on assignment. But since he wanted to serve the French resistance, he accepted the humbler roles of announcer and narrator. It was ironic that he was assigned to read my scripts, which he despised, especially because they dealt with religion. He was a magnificent speaker and when I listened to him on the playbacks I could not help admiring his beautiful, clear classic French. But there was something strange and disturbing about his antagonism to Christianity. It was almost satanic and frightened me. During the two years he worked at the O.W.I. he never spoke to me, never nodded, and would sometimes sit on my desk, turning his back to me, while chatting with other writers and typists who would assemble around their idol for the coffee break, while I drank my coffee alone.

I felt that I was in a strange world where all the values I had trustfully taken for granted, were turned upside down. My bewilderment would have been complete, had it not been for an unexpected and most fortunate turn of events. It was decided that my religious program should be followed immediately by a daily feature written and narrated by the novelist Julien Green and dealing with life in America at war: "*L'Amérique en Guerre.*" I had read Green's first two books, *Mont Cinère* and *Adrienne Mesurat,* and had been greatly impressed by them. Seeing my name on his program, I was both delighted and intimidated. How would this deep and brilliant author tolerate my clumsy, inexperienced style? In order for us to work together, Julien Green came to consult with me. I was surprised to see that he looked so youthful and shy. His handsome features, dark eyes and gentle voice not only reassured, but charmed me. He had heard about me through our mutual friends, Jacques Maritain and Father Couturier. I had also heard his story. Julien had been a Catholic in his youth, but had lost his faith. He recovered it after a deep, spiritual crisis. He was an essentially religious writer. Green, who is today a member of the French Academy and one of France's most famous novelists and playwrights, is actually American-born, of an old Virginia family. He speaks English fluently. But since early childhood he lived and studied in France. He has made Paris his permanent home. During World War II, he came to New York, enlisted in the American army, and was later transferred to the Office of War Information. After the liberation, he returned immediately to France and still lives there.

At the Voice of America, Green felt as isolated as I did in the tense, noisy atmosphere of the crowded rooms. He often stopped at my desk to chat with me, sensing a kindred spirit. One day, he pulled out of his pocket *The Imitation of Christ,* which he always carried with him. Another time, he brought me a picture of Bernadette of Lourdes in her Bearnaise peasant dress. She reminded me of the young girls I had often seen on the farms of the Pyrenees. Seeing my delight, Julien returned the next day with a small picture frame and said solemnly: "Bernadette needs a house." I still have the picture in its frame and it reminds me of Julien and his gentle voice, amid the clatter of typewriters and teletypes carrying the war news.

Later, other dynamic and spiritual people came to work with us. Among them was Denis de Rougement, the Protestant moralist whom I had met at the conferences of *Esprit* in Paris. Father Couturier gave a few broadcasts for the Resistance and Jacques Maritain was on the air periodically. He learned, through the undergrounds, that his mother had heard one of his broadcasts shortly before her death. Leon Blum, the ex-Prime-Minister, interned in Germany, also listened to Maritain, thanks to the complicity of one of his wardens. As for myself, I could continue my ecumenical work started in France by asking Protestant and Jewish speakers to bring their scripts for my program.

In spite of the initial difficulties, I made many interesting and fruitful contacts at the Voice of America. I established cordial relations with most of my colleagues and some became lifelong friends. One scriptwriter, Dolores Vanetti, who had acquired citizenship papers, was my witness when I became an American citizen. She assisted me on many other occasions and I owe her a great debt of gratitude.

It was exciting to be so closely related to military and political events overseas, and to the great drama in which so many nations, figures and ideologies were involved. Each day, Pierre Lazareff assembled all the scriptwriters in his office, briefing us on the situation as it developed, and giving us his instructions. We transmitted war news on the hour, every hour. Pierre's great experience as a journalist guided us, and I was in charge of some of those transmissions that caused considerable nervous tension; the slightest mistake might have serious consequences and the men of the underground who were listening to us, were risking their lives.

In the spring of 1944, we all lived in expectation of the invasion of France and eagerly listened to every item which could herald the long-awaited day of liberation. But the secret was so well guarded that no sign appeared on our horizon. We were forbidden to make any guesses or bets on the invasion date. On June 5th, there was a false alarm which sent us rushing to the teletypes, only to be told to go back to our desks. Then D-Day arrived, June 6th; the excitement in our office, and on the streets of New York was indescribable.

Back at our desks, we continued to follow the story of liberation at the cost of more suffering and death. Tragedy was only eased by the news of Europe's gradual liberation and the entrance of the Allies into Paris. Then came the time when Hitler's armies were rolled back from the Russian front.

Most of us, in those days, and certainly my colleagues at their desks and broadcast studios, took the continuing bombings and bloodshed for granted as the inevitable premise to our victory in the name of a just war. But then, on August 6th, 1945, an event took place which changed the picture of war forever.

Our teletypes gave us the news, to be immediately transmitted to the whole world. The American air force had used a new weapon against Japan, a lethal weapon of unprecedented power. It had wiped out an entire town called Hiroshima and had spread deadly radiation over a wide area, killing thousands of people, civilians.

No one could grasp immediately the meaning of Hiroshima because this first appearance of the atom bomb was announced in the usual terms of a war communique. A second assault that followed at Nagasaki, was reported in similar tones. There was, however, something sinister in these communiques, something different, overwhelming. They marked the beginning of a new era, the end of wars that could be considered just.

Spectacular as were the dramas of Hiroshima and Nagasaki, they were not the only horrors that had begun to change my attitude toward war. The news we had been broadcasting to the underground up until Germany's surrender, told of the firebombings of Berlin, Hamburg, Dresden, speaking only of attacks on military targets, but said nothing of the loss of civilian lives. These facts began to reach us after the war was over and revealed the terrifying pictures that had been concealed. My thoughts turned to Dorothy Day. I had not been able to share her total opposition to war, but many things that she had said or written, now seemed to be prophetic. I felt nearer to her and from that time on, our friendship deepened. However, I must say that I was not entirely won over to her positions on peace and nonviolence. I cannot forget the French resistance during the war, nor the defense of the Russian people against German aggression. I also admire the liberation movements which have been started by oppressed nations and victims of colonialism. I consider them a manifestation of the noblest human spirit. Yet the idea of nonviolence is higher than all human levels; it is the very essence of the Gospels. As Soloviev wrote: "The teaching of the Gospels are difficult to follow, but not impossible. Otherwise, they would not have been given to us."

After the conclusion of World War II, the Voice of America continued to broadcast information, news and colorful stories to Europe. I remained at my desk but many of my French colleagues returned to France. Pierre Lazareff left to resume the publication of his paper; instead of *Paris Soir* it was renamed *France-Soir*. Our French section had lost its *raison d'être* and gradually folded up.

The axe had fallen somewhat abruptly and I was again left with little more than a few savings. I determined to resume my writing and lecturing. Quite unexpectedly, Frank Sheed looked me up, suggesting that I help him prepare an anthology of Russian religious writings. We asked Professor George Fedotov, a Russian Orthodox theologian and friend of Berdiaev, to edit this collection of spiritual writing. I was entrusted with the translation of a number of texts to be included in it. Thus, the *Treasury of Russian Spirituality* was born. (It is still used as source material by students of Russian ascetic and mystical tradition.)

After Hiroshima and my deeper relationship with Dorothy Day, I often visited the *Catholic Worker's* House of Hospitality on Mott Street and, later, on Christie Street, and spoke from time to time, at the Friday night forums held there. I did not see much of Peter Maurin, who was often away on speaking tours to distant cities. Then suddenly, he had a stroke which incapacitated him almost entirely. The last time I saw him was at Maryfarm, the *Catholic Worker's* rural community. He was unable to walk or speak. He simply sat on the threshold of the little cabin which was his last home on earth.

Maryfarm was my first experience of the *Worker's* role in promoting Christian living in a rural setting. Many of the men and women there were Dorothy's friends and faithful companions; others were men from the road, poor and ragged. I remember sharing their evening meal. A priest who was a member of the community, said grace and recited the Angelus. The men and women gave the responses. When the priest said "and the Word was made flesh," they all genuflected. I was deeply moved and suddenly thought that I would like to belong to this place. To live with these people. But the idea faded as quickly as it had come; I was not worthy to belong to such a family. Yet later, I tried it, for a period.

I was now able to resume my ecumenical work with a few of the original group who had started this activity in Paris, and whom I was fortunate to find living in New York. There was the composer Arthur Lourié, whom I had met on the Avenue Mozart on the day before the fall of Paris, and who had assured me that he had "no intention of leaving France and his beloved grand piano." He was now composing on a similar instrument in his New York apartment. There was Denis de Rougemont, my recent colleague at the "Voice of America" and a leader of Protestant humanism. Basil Yanovsky, the Russian Orthodox novelist who had belonged to the Fondaminsky circle in Paris, was now working as an anesthetist in a New York hospital. Mrs. Irma de Manziarly, who had greeted me so kindly in Lisbon, had made contact with me soon after we reached America. Other ecumenical friends joined us and we met regularly in Mrs. de Manziarly's hotel room, which was small but comfortable and quiet. Our little group wanted to start anew something like Mounier's workshops and Berdiaev's seminars. At each meeting we chose a topic to discuss or read a paper appropriate to our spirit of religious understanding. Each of us was devoted to his own faith, but reached out to accommodate the convictions of others.

In remembrance of our Paris days, we had some red wine to enliven our dialogue, and this custom prevailed as our little circle enlarged over the years. Governor Paulding from *Commonweal*, who had been so close to Mounier and married a girl from the *Esprit* group, would often drop in. A young Russian Orthodox monk, Father John Shakhovsky came to give us a talk. He was a dedicated priest, a poet and writer, who remained with our group for some years. Later he became archbishop of San Francisco.

For awhile, we met in my room which was somewhat larger and had the inviting atmosphere created by the kind old Miss Seary. During these meetings, Paulding brought the English Catholic author and literary critic Anne Fremantle, who in turn brought the poet W. H. Auden, already famous for his poems and brilliant prose. We had so little space that I remember Auden sitting on the floor, propped against the icebox. Another day, Anne brought one of her close friends, Mrs. Porter Chandler (Bebo), a devout Catholic. She was a highly educated woman, related to the writer Marion Crawford, and had often lived in Rome and Paris. She spoke French fluently and brought to our work a truly dynamic spirit. Seeing how crowded we were, she suggested holding our meetings in her large apartment on East 72nd Street. We were delighted with her offer and enjoyed her hospitality for many years.

Some of the papers read at our meetings were so interesting that I began thinking of starting a publication that would reflect our work. I also hoped to obtain material from our Paris friends. We were overjoyed to hear from Berdiaev and Mochulsky soon after France was liberated and were able to send them parcels with coffee, canned goods, and even candles. I wrote to Berdiaev concerning our publication plans. As yet there was no regular mail to Europe, so I looked for someone who was going to sail for France. I found Jean-Paul Sartre, the initiator of existentialism, who had come to the United States on a lecture tour and attended one of his talks.

I had heard so much about the tremendous influence of Sartre on French youth, that I was surprised to see a rather timid and quiet little man, smoking his pipe and looking suspiciously from left to right. This suspicious expression was due to a certain malformation of his features which had become part of his famous image. He was actually riding on the crest of his fame. Sartre was going back to France in a few days, and with a certain hesitation, I asked him if he would take my letter to the Russian philosopher, who had actually spoken of existentialism long before Sartre published his *Nausea*. To my surprise, he very graciously agreed to do this. I must add that in spite of his categorical denial of religious values, Jean-Paul Sartre was far more courteous with me than André Breton had been. Thanks to him, I had the joy of receiving an answer from Berdiaev as soon as mail communication was restored.

The first letters we received from France brought us the sad news of the death of Mother Mary Skobtsova and that of Fondaminsky. When more details reached us, we decided to publish a memorial to them in our new journal, together with articles by Berdiaev and Mochulsky.

We had now assembled enough material and collected sufficient funds to print our first issue, which was to be in Russian, followed by two other issues offering French and English translations of the text. Our aim was to present an international record of our work; a bold project indeed, which did not materialize. We brought out the next issues in English only, since most of our readers were Americans. But we did preserve the original format, something like Péguy's *Cahiers*.

What would be the name of our publication? Even when offered in one language, it would still have an international character, so we decided to use the name *The Third Hour*, which was the time, according to the Scriptures, when the Holy Spirit descended upon the Apostles and they began to speak in different "tongues." Our conception was inspired by Eastern Orthodoxy, which has a special devotion to the Holy Spirit. It has developed the Greek idea of the *pneuma* as the Giver of Life.

Essentially oriented toward religion and ecumenical endeavors, *The Third Hour* had also a deep concern for the problems of social justice, peace and racial equality. Although our group and our publication underwent many changes in the twenty-five years of its existence, it never abandoned these fundamental principles.

Officially we were called The Third Hour Foundation. Our activities were deliberately limited, for we were only "pathfinders." Some people even described us as "an ecumenical underground." But though we acted privately, we did nothing secretly. Our Third Hour meetings were always open and attended by many priests and followers of various religions. The Catholic clergy only made one condition for their cooperation — that we were to avoid all publicity. We were only too glad to comply, for we had always sought to do our work quietly and in a mood of recollection. Our center was New York City, one of the few places where theologians and scholars could meet in an atmosphere of cordiality and mutual respect. We were a center of dialogue before Vatican Council II made this term official.

When Dr. Oscar Kulmann, the Protestant theologian and ecumenist, came to the United States in 1959, he sought our help to make contact with Catholic theologians whom he could not reach otherwise. Contact was duly established, thanks to Dr. John Bennet, who was in those days rector, later president, of Union Theological Seminary. He offered his apartment for a meeting at which many distinguished Catholics were present, and got in touch with Dr. Kulmann for the first time.

To return to my own career, interrupted by the folding of our section of the Voice of America, I had to start once more on a new profession, thanks to the help of a good friend, Mrs. Catherine Wolkonsky. She had just been asked to head the Russian department at Vassar College. Her assignment was a complex and difficult one, so she asked me to take over a course on Dostoevsky, which had been scheduled for that spring semester. I was rather awed at the prospect of giving a course at such a sophisticated institution, but the topic attracted me. The course involved only two hours a week on two consecutive days. I would have to commute to Poughkeepsie, and Mrs. Wolkonsky was kind enough to arrange not only a convenient schedule, but also invited me to stay at her home overnight.

I was surprised to see the strange attire of the Vassar girls, wearing blue jeans and men's shirts on campus and in classrooms, and then in the evening dressing up in the most elaborate manner to meet their dates. Though I soon got used to these fashions, the moods and reactions of my students to my course was not easy to face. To be sure, many of them had read some of Dostoevsky's major works, and others did their share of assigned reading quite willingly, but until I came along, the religious aspects of these works had hardly been discussed by them. Mrs. Wolkonsky, a devout Russian Orthodox, brought her own spirit to the department, but she entrusted this particular course to me, knowing my connections with Berdiaev and other men of the Russian religious revival.

During the first lectures, I felt that there was a stonewall between myself and my youthful audience, and discussion period aroused little response. But as we delved deeper into our subject, the girls' interest was gradually awakened and our dialogue became more lively. I introduced the students to Mochulsky's work on Dostoevsky which had just appeared in Paris. Other sources of Russian literary criticism were also available, and these works made a deep appeal to the girls in my class. I believe they had a direct influence on their approach to religious problems in general, and to Dostoevsky's spirituality in particular. The exams at the end of the term showed that my efforts under Catherine Wolkonsky's leadership had not been in vain. We were delighted with the term papers as they presented a wide range of thoughtful analysis of the great Russian writer. I even asked the students' permission to publish some of them in an issue of *The Third Hour*. As I glance through its pages, I still recall the enthusiasm both teacher and students shared at the end of that term which started me on my teaching career.

The satisfaction and pleasure that I experienced at Vassar was marred by two deaths which occurred almost simultaneously. I had received a letter from Berdiaev dated March 18 answering one of mine. He informed me that he had refused an offer to come on a lecture tour to America. He considered this too great an effort because of his not speaking English well enough. He also spoke of fatigue and illness. This letter reached me on the very day that we learned of his sudden death on the morning of March 19th. In my letter, which must have been written on the very eve of his passing away, he sent a last message to his friends: "The world atmosphere is now very unfavorable. But I still think that there will be no more war. One must struggle against the psychosis of war."

More than two decades have passed since Berdiaev's last letter to me, and "war psychosis" is still poisoning the atmosphere of our world. If anything, as I am writing these lines, I understand more fully what this posthumous message really meant.

We learned that our dear friend Constantin Mochulsky had passed away only a few days after Berdiaev. He died from tuberculosis contracted during the years of cold and hunger, in occupied Paris.

Berdiaev's influence on my work and destiny lingered on. A memorial meeting was arranged by his friends and I was asked to be the last speaker. As I listened to those who preceded me, I was amazed to hear comments that were critical and even hostile toward the great philosopher. This was due to certain rumors that had reached Russian émigré-writers that Berdiaev had shown tolerance and even sympathy for the Soviet regime. He had received Soviet visitors at his Sundays in Clamart and expressed himself favorably on their behalf.

The truth was more complex than presented, or misrepresented, by Berdiaev's enemies. Recent events in the Soviet Union, the Russian people's heroic struggle against Germany and the revelation of a deep, national consciousness, appealed to Berdiaev's generosity and faith in his country. I was informed about the Clamart atmosphere, and knew that a representative of the Soviet Ambassador to France had urged Berdiaev to return to Russia. He refused on the grounds that he might not be able to write as he wished, nor publish his works freely in the Soviet Union. His article "The Evolution of Marxism" (published posthumously, in *The Third Hour*) spoke clearly of the negative traits of Russian Communism: "linked to the compulsory acceptance of dialectic materialism, the desire to achieve brotherhood by means of violence, while denying spiritual freedom." It was on this knowledge of Berdiaev's true position and of his teachings that I based my defense of this man. I had prepared a paper before hearing the negative criticism that seemed to me unfair and unjust. Now I put my paper aside, and defended him passionately.

My words were received in almost complete silence. I went home feeling that I had failed miserably in my attempt to bring out Berdiaev's true image. Only later, I learned that all my words had not fallen on arid soil. The next day while a friend was visiting me, there was a knock on my door. Once again, fate was knocking. I went to open, and saw a dark, good-looking young man, who smiled and introduced himself as Richard Burgi from Fordham University. I often received visits from students who wanted to interview me about Russia, so I asked the young man to come back the next day. He presented himself at the appointed hour, and as I invited him to sit down, he told me he was teaching Russian at Fordham University. He was an American but could speak Russian and had been the first to offer such a course at the Catholic university. He told me he had read my book *Soul of Russia* and that my work had awakened his interest in that country. He had learned the language first by linguaphone and later studied at Columbia University's Russian department. He had attended the meeting in honor of Berdiaev and liked my speech. He had now come, not only to get acquainted with me, but to make a request — would I like to teach Russian at Fordham?

As I expressed my surprise, Burgi explained that I could be a substitute for him as he was writing a thesis for his doctorate and needed a year of seclusion and intensive work. When I accepted my young visitor's offer, he asked me to report to the two Fordham centers: the College of Arts and Sciences at Rosehill in the Bronx and the Business School in downtown Manhattan. This unexpected turn of events marked not only the extension of my work as a teacher, but the beginning of a deep and lasting friendship. From that day on, there was hardly an occasion in my life, joyful, sad, important, or exciting, at which Richard Burgi was not present: first as a brilliant Ph.D. and later as chairman of the Fordham Russian Institute and of the Russian departments of Yale and Princeton. He always remained the same generous, devoted and dynamic man who had knocked at my door.

In the fall semester of 1948 and during the two years that followed, I taught Russian on the two campuses, which meant long rides on the subway from my home to the Bronx or down to City Hall, sometimes traveling both ways on the same day. My new job did not have the attraction of the Vassar course, but I gained the experience I had lacked in language teaching, as well as in the paperwork and academic red tape which became part of my duties. The young students, who took my courses in elementary and advanced Russian, were not as sophisticated as the Vassar girls, but they were attentive and friendly; the work on Rosehill was pleasant enough, but the Business School, where space was limited, did not even have a regular room for my class and I sometimes had to teach in the lounge or in the cafeteria. However, I remained quite satisfied and even optimistic knowing that my friend Richard, who by then had successfully presented his thesis, was working on a plan which he had long cherished: the founding of a Russian Institute at Fordham with a staff of native teachers and American scholars qualified in this field. Father Thurston Davies, the dean of Fordham College, was in full agreement with Burgi's plan. However, it still needed the president's approval, and sufficient financial support to launch the institute.

During this period, I was in constant touch with Richard, sharing his views which were close to my own and encouraged by the trust he put in me. I had the opportunity of meeting his parents who lived on their farm at Chatham, New York, and who heartily welcomed me as they did all of their son's friends. In fact, the Chatham farm was a meeting place where young and old would gather during vacation time to enjoy the Burgi's boundless hospitality.

Mr. Burgi was of Swiss-Bavarian origin and had emigrated to America in his youth. His wife was Irish and she, too, came from the "old country." When on his father's farm, Richard would help him with the harvesting of corn and with hay-making, while his sister Betty, who was getting a doctor's degree in biology, took care of the flowers and vegetables. At mealtimes family and guests would assemble in the spacious diningroom to share Mrs. Burgi's delicious cooking. This was American country life at its best, and it also reminded me of my childhood in Bavaria, especially when Mr. Burgi would talk German with me and reminisce about his own youth in the Alps. In the evenings, Richard would play Russian records or we would browse in his library stocked with Russian literature, and other books and picture albums representing every aspect of Russian culture.

During one of my visits, we motored into the Catskills to see the famous philologist Dr. Roman Jakobson at the summer resort where he was recuperating from an automobile accident which had crippled him for months. Now he could walk again, with the help of a cane. I always enjoyed the company of this wise and amiable scholar, one of the greatest Slavonic linguists of our time, whom I had formerly met in Paris.

Richard Burgi was studying for his doctorate under Dr. Jakobson when his accident occurred. He often visited him in the hospital, and when he could get into a wheelchair, Richard and some other students would take him out for a walk. But one day they pushed the wheelchair with such vigor that it got out of their hands and started down a hill. They caught it just in time, with Dr. Jakobson waving his arms in dismay. This little incident was typical of Richard's impetuous and sometimes reckless nature. With the same enthusiasm and zeal, he pursued his dream of creating a Russian Institute at Fordham.

Immediately after his graduation, Richard began working on his ambitious project. He left no stone unturned, appealed to the highest authorities, fought opposition and inertia. In the late summer of 1950, a telegram from Richard informed me that his dream had finally come true.

His program was ready and he had recruited a teaching staff of American and Russian native scholars. They were to offer language studies, as well as history, literature, religion, arts and journalism. Richard was to be temporary director (for he was later to teach at Yale). I was assigned courses on Dostoevsky and Tolstoy, and another, on Russian culture. I was also to teach elementary and advanced Russian language.

The Fordham FM radio station was to offer a weekly broadcast on Russian cultural topics, and I was to prepare the scripts for the programs and arrange the general set up.

The general purpose of the Institute, open to undergraduate and graduate students, was to bring them to a better understanding of Russian culture and of the Russian people. We all felt strongly that it was not enough to oppose communism. We must seek through Russia's historic and spiritual heritage, the positive values which would lead someday to a renaissance within Russia herself and bring her greater freedom.

The Institute of Contemporary Russian Studies was solemnly opened on October 19, 1950. The ceremony started with the Benediction, offered by Father Laurence McGinley, Rector of Fordham, Father Thurston Davies, Dean of the College, and Father Gerald Walsh, University Provost. The service, in the University church, was followed by an address by Eugene Cardinal Tisserant who was, at that time, Prefect of the Congregation of Oriental Rites. The French-born Cardinal had come from Rome on a visit to the United States, and was an ideal person to give our Institute its headstart. He had a deep knowledge of Russia and of the religious spirit of its people. He firmly believed that this spirit was still alive, in spite of the atheistic regime which tried to surpress it. "I am very happy," the Cardinal said, "to have a part in this opening, as I am always seeking what can be done to promote a better understanding between East and West."

Before leaving, the Cardinal bestowed the Papal blessing on our new Institute, and our faculty was presented to him. Later, I had several other occasions to meet the Cardinal and had long talks with him about the survival of religion in Russia, a subject about which people are very misinformed, especially today. Cardinal Tisserant's enlightened interest and encouraging attitude was a good omen in those early days. We strove faithfully to bring Russia nearer to our students.

On our staff we had two gifted Russian writers: Sergei Maximov and Michail Koriakov, both of them trained in Soviet schools. Though they had become political exiles, opposed to the Soviet regime, they brought to our classes a knowledge of modern Russia, both in language and literature, which we could not have offered. Among the American professors, we had such distinguished teachers as Dr. Robert Pollack, who lectured on Marxism, and Father J. Franklin Ewing, the anthropologist who had made a special study of tribes in the Russian far north. Besides his classes, Father Ewing took great interest in our radio broadcasts and was a regular announcer for some of our programs.

Russian friends, who had been stranded in Paris by the war, still turned up in New York. Some had suffered greatly and there were few jobs to be had in France. Among this late immigration was the young

Alexander Obolensky, his wife and son, as well as his uncle, the brilliant actor and musician George Flevitsky. The Obolenskys and George Flevitsky were able to rent rooms from Miss Seary and she welcomed them with her usual cordiality. So we became a little Russian colony. There was no more loneliness for me but, instead, a constant coming and going, with Russian songs and music which even our neighbors began to enjoy. The young couple and "Uncle George" shared the icebox which I had recently acquired. Our atmosphere was far from gloomy.

Later, the Obolenskys were quite successful in business. Their uncle found parts in a play or two. Alexander took time off to take graduate courses and obtained a Ph.D at the University of Pennsylvania. He became a professor of Russian language and literature at New York University, and held various academic jobs thereafter. When we met in later years, we never failed to recall the happy days when we had shared the icebox!

In the meanwhile, I had found time to devote to *The Third Hour*, which continued to grow. We had frequent meetings at the Chandlers and found a series of speakers who shared our ecumenical aims. From France came Father George Tavard, who was interested in a rapprochement with Protestants. Father Tavard, who was an Assumptionist, later became one of the leading theologians in America. He was a special envoy *(periti)* at Vatican Council II. But at the time that he came to us, there was very little encouragement for his ecumenical work. The understanding and hospitality he found at the Chandlers' home did a great deal to relieve the tensions he had to suffer.

We also had visits from Father Voillaume, founder of the "Little Brothers and Sisters of Charles de Foucauld" and from Abbé Pierre, who started a great drive to house the poor in France. Father Carré, the Dominican whom I had consulted in Pau about my coming to America, was now welcomed at our meetings. The Jesuit scholar and writer Jean Danielou, spoke at our forum as did another Jesuit, Father Jerôme de Suza, Indian delegate to the United Nations.

We had the active cooperation of Claire Huchet Bishop, a French author and journalist. She was especially dedicated to improving Judeo-Christian relations, as was also Monsignor John Oesterreicher, who often joined us. He was director of Judeo-Christian studies at Seton College, and a scholar of note.

Dorothy Day spoke at many of our meetings. She had actually been involved in ecumenical work for years, without thinking of it as such, since the poor of all creeds and nationalities came to her breadline and to her Houses of Hospitality. She had a direct, spontaneous and intuitive understanding of our problems which were becoming more complex. We had a number of Protestant speakers, Episcopalians and Russian Orthodox. Some of them, like the Lutheran Pastor von Schenk and

Father Alexander Schmemann, rector of Saint Vladimir's Russian Orthodox Seminary, were to play an important role when the ecumenical movement officially "surfaced." They were active at Vatican Council II and in the great assemblies of the World Council of Churches.

Many of the guests who came to the Chandlers contributed papers for *The Third Hour* issues, which now had a fair number of subscribers. But with no publicity, no advertising and only a few financial friends, it was difficult to distribute our publication. Hundreds of copies remained unsold. They kept piling up in my lodging. This reminded me of Péguy's *Cahiers,* which accumulated in his office, until he had to make armchairs and sofas out of them (to be able to sit down) — these books which are now collectors' items.

Occasionally, I was asked to speak to various Catholic organizations such as the Council of Catholic Women in Hartford, Connecticut. I remember this lecture because of two incidents, one comic and one leading to new spiritual contacts. Arriving at the hotel where my talk was to be given, I found the elevator full of strange-looking people. They wore bizzare costumes and had the air of vivacious, carefree stage performers. I followed some of them into a suite where a man stood near a table in evening dress, gesticulating with a wand in one hand, a top hat on his head. I inquired what this was all about, and they told me that this was a magicians' convention! I left, reluctantly — I would rather have stayed to watch these showmen than to give my own performance.

In the ballroom, my real audience had gathered around small tables with snowwhite linen and glistening silverware. I was led to a larger speakers' table, presided over by Reverend O'Bryan, bishop of Hartford and I was seated next to him. During the luncheon, the Bishop told me that two Benedictine nuns had arrived in his diocese and hoped to found a monastery there. "In fact," said the Bishop, "the French nuns have been asking after you." "But who are they," I questioned with surprise? He could not give me any answer, but seemed puzzled himself. He gave me an address in New York, however, where I could get further information.

The next day, I went to the address the Bishop had given me, and the mystery of the French nuns was solved. They were Benedictines from the Abbey of Jouarre. Mother Benedict Düss and her companion, Mother Marie-Aline, who had arrived in America with the intention of founding a Community of the Strict Observance, on the pattern of their motherhouse. They had read my book *Light before Dusk* and thought that my own experience in a Benedictine Abbey would help them to explain to American Catholics what a cloistered monastery of their order was like. There are many Benedictine Sisters in the United States but most are engaged in teaching or parish work and are not contemplative nuns. It was difficult to bring the old monastic tradition to America.

I was extremely happy to hear about this project which was to bring me the atmosphere of recollected prayer and the beauty of the Benedictine liturgy of which I had long been deprived. I hastened to make arrangements to meet Mother Benedict and her companion.

They were staying at the home of Lauren Ford, a painter and devout Catholic convert, who had a large farm near Bethlehem, Connecticut. She had named it "the Sheepfold" and actually had quite a large flock of sheep that enhanced the country scene. It was a joy to visit this charming artist and to make the acquaintance of her Benedictine guests.

How vividly I recalled the memorable retreat at Saint Scholastica now more than twenty years ago. It seemed as if it had all happened yesterday!

The Benedictine Mothers delighted me with their beautiful, distinguished and precise French. Curiously enough, Mother Benedict was American, but she had lived in France since early childhood, and was educated there. She had graduated from the Medical School in Paris. She impressed me as a very remarkable, dedicated woman of exceptional intelligence and at the same time, having a deep understanding of the basic, contemplative life of the Benedictines.

Thanks to Miss Ford's hospitality and the kind interest that the two Mothers took in me, I often visited the Sheepfold; step by step, I witnessed the foundation of the new community, today, known all over America as Regina Laudis. The story of this foundation has often been told and even been shown in a film called *Come to the Stable*. Finally, six more nuns arrived from Jouarre and the community opened its first monastery, a converted barn, with an adjacent guesthouse.

During Christmas time, I made my first retreat at Regina Laudis. The beautiful Connecticut countryside was blanketed with snow. On Christmas Eve, Matins and Lauds were sung by the nuns, conducted by Mother Benedict, an expert in Gregorian chant. Midnight Mass was celebrated by the Chaplain of the Community, Father Damasus Winzen, a monk from Maria Lach in Germany. He had left his native land when Hitler came to power.

Father Damasus was a great scholar and liturgist, and was to help me through many years, toward a deeper understanding of the Rule of Saint Benedict and of the liturgical wealth of the diurnal Office. He brought together a number of men and women, including myself, who became oblates and formed a spiritual family under the guidance of this kindly, wise and scholarly man who was later to found his own community of the strict observance known as Mount Savior Priory at Elmira, New York.

Thus I had the privilege of being connected with the contemplative Benedictine life once again, and in the years to come, I drew much strength and spiritual renewal from it.

Later, another Benedictine monastery, Our Lady of the Resurrection, played an important part in the last chapter of my life. It was led by Brother Victor d'Avila, whom I met at the Catholic Worker Farm and who became one of my most faithful friends.

Brother Victor had lived in many countries and spoke English, Spanish, French and Italian but he remained strongly attached to the French monasteries of Saint Benedict which had had a formative influence on his monastic life. His project of starting a small community aroused my interest and sympathy. He wished to follow a life of prayer and contemplation by living in great simplicity and poverty according to the Gospel. Dorothy Day and I, as well as the *Catholic Worker* community, gave him our moral support. Finally, a small, deserted cottage was found to serve as the incipient monastery. It followed the rule of Saint Benedict and also the Eastern Orthodox monastic tradition, where early monasticism originated. Emphasis was put on the celebration of the daily Offices, repetition of the Jesus Prayer, silence, dedication to the land, manual work, study and hospitality. Whenever possible, the Divine Liturgy was celebrated in the chapel. The tiny chapel in Barrytown, and also the subsequent chapel at Cold Spring, impressed me by its simplicity and good taste. From the beginning, the monastery started to attract many visitors who came for prayer and recollection, for solitude and silence. There were laymen and religious, Catholic and Orthodox, Protestants and Jews, students and intellectuals of all sorts.

Later, when the monastery was transferred from Barrytown to Cold Spring, New York, I was staying at the Catholic Worker Farm and was able to have a small part in the move, by carrying the wooden statue of Our Lady in my arms, to her new home. As I entered the larger, freshly painted farmhouse, I remembered Brother Victor's words: "God never closes a door without opening another." The new monastery was blessed by Bishop Pernicone, Vicar of the Poughkeepsie area, who concelebrated Mass with three religious. Monastic life was then resumed, with scarcely an interruption.

Here was the same beauty and simplicity that Brother Victor had created in the smaller monastery. The many icons, handpainted in the true traditional style, were both prayerful and decorative. Brother Victor was an excellent artist and everything he did was in the finest taste. He was also a trained musician and retained in the singing of the Offices, both the Gregorian and the Byzantine chants. Since study is part of a monk's life, there was a large library of classical and spiritual books. While the guests enjoy the quiet and comfortable artistic ambiance, there is nothing superfluous in this little monastery. I always enjoyed its simple and recollected atmosphere of prayer. It answers an urgent need of our times. It helps us to become free of worldly matters and to rediscover the richness of spiritual values.

It was a long time since my conversion experience at Saint Scholastica in France, and now these Benedictine monasteries had brought me back again to the spirit of Saint Benedict. They helped me to renew my own spiritual commitment after the tumult of the war years and their aftermath. This was a most necessary renewal for there were still difficult and trying years ahead.

CHAPTER XVI

From Noon Till Twilight

As I entered my fiftieth year and time seemed to be rushing on, I suddenly became aware that I had lived half a century. This realization came as a shock to me, but I could not linger over it; I was too busy with my teaching schedule, as well as writing and enjoying the friendship of my many friends.

But scarcely six months after joining the Fordham Russian Institute, I suffered the worst loss of my mature life — the death of my brother, Grisha. Although we had lived separately for several years, we were still very close to each other and there was no more tension between us since he had gained control over his drinking. He was working hard as a packer in a match factory, when he was struck with an incurable disease. After a time at the hospital, he was sent home with the diagnosis: terminal cancer. Nothing could be done but to make him as comfortable as possible in his small apartment, and to ease his pain which had become acute. I could not give up my job at Fordham, but I found a good woman to take care of my brother in the daytime, and I set up a cot in a back room, where I could spend the night. Had I been completely alone to face the situation, it would have been an almost impossible task, but during those last months, as throughout his entire life, Grisha had been so popular with his many friends, that now they really came to the rescue, visiting him constantly and assisting him financially, so that the dingy match-packer's apartment became a salon of high class Petersburg society. Grisha delighted in these visits and talked gaily to all those who sat around him. Even when his condition grew worse, he could still laugh and joke.

As the end approached, we had to take Grisha to the hospital again. A Russian Orthodox priest came to visit him, discreetly advising him to consider the state of his soul. But Grisha would have nothing to do with this well-intentioned clergyman, and we had to usher him out as tactfully as possible. Yet, only a few days later, a great change came over my brother. After a long spell of unconsciousness, he suddenly came to himself, and saw the large crucifix which was hanging on the wall opposite his bed (for it was a Catholic hospital). He seemed deeply moved by this silent symbol of love — it was as if Christ Himself had come to the rescue of the prodigal son. Then we felt that this time, he would not refuse to let a priest bring him Communion. This time nothing interfered with God's grace. My brother received the last rites with childlike simplicity.

How different this final acceptance of his Church was compared to our father's dramatic revolt against it. But they had this in common: great honesty and dignity in the face of death, sensed as a mystery beyond our human understanding.

Grisha's funeral was held in the Russian Orthodox cathedral of Our Lady of Protection. The Mass was sung by the Afonsky quartet, highly trained singers from the cathedral choir. The beauty of the Byzantine funeral service, so deeply consoling, and the presence of so many loving friends helped me to live through those painful hours. But all the courage I could summon would not have been enough had it not been for the tall, white-haired quiet woman at my side. For Dorothy Day appeared as I was ready to break down, bringing me that strength and peace which she has always given me in times of stress and suffering.

Just a month after Grisha's death, I had an accident which could have been fatal. I fell down the stairs of our roominghouse and hit my head against a sharp angle of the balustrade. It happened late at night, and George Flevitsky, coming home in the small hours, found me unconscious. He alerted the other tenants and I was rushed to a neighboring hospital. So I owe my life to the members of our little "commune."

I woke up in my hospital bed, swathed in bandages. Yuri was holding one hand, while Father Lynch, a friend from Fordham, was holding the other, trying to restrain me. Several others sat around me. When they saw me open my eyes, they all sighed with relief. Indeed, I had returned from a long journey which had taken me almost to death's door. For three days I had been unconscious, and in that state was operated on by one of New York's most expert neurosurgeons, who had removed blood clots from my brain. I was lying in a public ward, as no private room was available, and had been given Extreme Unction. Luckily, my friends had been around me when I recovered consciousness, for my first wish was to tear away my bandages, but they calmed me, reassured me. I think of the old Russian proverb: "No need to have a hundred rubles; better to have a hundred friends."

I felt happy and grateful, until I discovered that I could not move my left arm and leg. Would I be a cripple the rest of my life? But when the surgeon who had performed the almost miraculous operation, appeared at my bedside, his kindly smile, attentive, serious eyes won my confidence immediately. "But what about my arm and leg," I asked anxiously. He went on smiling and told me that I would very soon regain the use of my limbs. He was right, of course.

Dr. Eichlin, quiet, dignified, good-looking, was one of the finest brain specialists in New York. When he came to take out the stitches, we talked for a while, and he was interested to learn that I had been a nurse on the staff of Charles de Martel and had seen the famous French brain specialist operate. Dr. Eichlin himself had studied neurosurgery in France, under Claude Vincent, de Martel's brilliant pupil.

As I began to recover, my experience at the hospital was altogether delightful. Many friends came to visit me and so it was an interlude that took the edge off the great sorrow caused by Grisha's death. I was released from the hospital after three weeks, but still felt rather shaky and uncertain, so I had to use a cane. The Louriés invited me to stay with them throughout the summer, and gradually my strength returned in time for the fall semester at Fordham.

I was to have a final checkup at Dr. Eichlin's office, and this somehow, frightened me. Supposing I was not allowed to work? Two of my dearest friends agreed to accompany me. They were Jane O'Donnel, one of the devoted staff members of the *Catholic Worker*, and Jack English who was at that time the editor of their paper. He had served as a navigator on a plane during World War II. He had been shot down with his aircraft over Rumania, and severely wounded. His experience had affected him deeply. He was a sensitive, highly cultured and compassionate man and was soon to enter the Trappist Monastery of the Holy Ghost in Atlanta, Georgia. He received the tonsure and was ordained under the name of Father Charles. I last saw him in his Trappist habit when I visited his community in 1971. He had been a monk and a priest for eighteen years. Such were the "guardian angels" who escorted me to my doctor's office. Dr. Eichlin gave me a clean bill of health.

Soon after my return to work, our "commune" of 76th Street, came to an end. Dear old "Lady Seary" died, and the house was put up for sale. We were told we must clear the premises, without delay. George Flevitsky found an apartment and so did the Obolenskys. I began to study the classified ads for myself, and soon found a small apartment on East 91st Street. "What a strange and perhaps lucky omen," I said to myself, for it was on this street that I had first lived, upon arriving in America, at the home of Mrs. Kenneth Simpson. Now my old friend Kerensky was living there as a paying guest, for his wife had recently died.

I went to the address given in the ad, and found it had nothing like the glamour of Mrs. Simpson's elegant abode. The house was much further east, between First and Second Avenues. The place for rent was a so-called "railroad apartment" with its rooms *enfilade*, in a row, a good-sized kitchen in the middle, quite attractive, compared to my "hot plate," and quite surprisingly — a bathtub in the kitchen. This strange feature, I learned, was typical of the cheaper lodgings of New York's side streets.

They had been occupied mostly by blue-collar workers but were now often rented by less-affluent intellectuals and pensioners.

There was no elevator, of course, and my rooms were on the fourth floor. In spite of these drawbacks, I liked the place and signed a lease there and then. After twenty years, I was still there, though I moved to the second floor in the sixties. The rent was quite reasonable. Tall, steel and concrete buildings surround the old tenement and rents were skyrocketing in this neighborhood, near the popular Yorkville, or German section, with its many restaurants and bars. But the local parish church still stood firm, dedicated to Our Lady of Good Counsel with a large parochial school run by nuns next door.

I liked my new home, and the view of the East River, which I could catch at the further end of my street. There was a cool breeze in summer blowing in from the river and at times, I had a glimpse of a large ship or barge slowly moving along the channel, reminding me of some make-believe boat emerging from the wings of a stage in an opera. It has become a cliché to say that you "hate the city" but those who have lived for years on one of its East Side blocks, are still sentimental about their small-town atmosphere.

I did not regret my choice, especially because of my friend Kerensky, who had now become my neighbor. True, he lived on the more elegant part of 91st Street several blocks further west. But it was still only a fifteen-minute walk, and we visited each other quite often. As he grew older, Kerensky's eyesight began to fail; later, he suffered almost total blindness. But for some time, he could still walk down our street, climb my stairs and knock at my door with his cane. His words after our first meeting in Paris had now come true. He could hardly have been able to recognize me on the street. He dimly saw my features and could grope his way through my "railroad flat." As the years passed, I, too, realized my handicaps. It took me twenty-five minutes, instead of fifteen, to walk up the slope which led to Mrs. Simpson's house. She would invite me to her Sunday dinners, or a cocktail, served by her solemn Japanese butler and his gentle wife, Asahi, who were devoted to Kerensky and also became my friends. I linger over these memories, because they were pleasant ones, at least until my old friend's blindness became total. After that I used to read to him and visit him regularly, until a fatal illness carried him away in 1970. But I must return to my own story.

Soon after I had moved to my "railroad flat," I went back to teach at Fordham. It was still a pleasant and rewarding job. But gradually, changes took place and my work was less enjoyable. Richard Burgi, who had merely been "lent" to us from Yale, went back to his teaching there and the spirit that he had brought to our classes began to leave us. He was replaced, but unfortunately for only a short time, by the understanding and compassionate Father Ewing. But his successor, Father Walter

Jaskievich, was a man concerned with the strong political undercurrents which now penetrated academia. These were the years of the cold war and of Joseph McCarthy's anti-Red drive, which took a priority over all other preoccupations. The attempt to "understand" the Russian people was replaced by other programs intended to train Russian-speaking young men and women to serve their country "on the brink of war" with the Soviet Union. And the atmosphere grew to be that of a paramilitary school.

The boys returning from Korea were tougher, less idealistic than my former students. They were in a hurry to complete their education on the G.I. Bill of Rights, and to get a job, leaving the pursuit of scholarship far behind. The Russian programs on the Fordham radio station were taken out of my hands, my scripts on Russian literature, art, music and ecumenical activities, were cut or scrapped. They were replaced by political news and commentaries of a strictly anticommunist nature.

In my classes, however, I found responses, which were not negative. There was a freshman, Michael Minihan, who signed up for Russian language and literature and was almost immediately drawn by both subjects. He decided to major in Russian and later graduated from Princeton, writing a dissertation on Dostoevsky. He is now a full professor of Russian language and literature in a college in the New York area. He also translated for Princeton an important book on Dostoevsky by my late friend Constantine Mochulsky. Another of my former students, who got his degree from Harvard and was head of the Russian and Eastern European Center of Boston College, wrote several books on Russian religious thought. I was happy that I had recognized the exceptional talents and devotion to serious studies of these two young men and I had encouraged and stimulated their efforts in every way. They both admitted that I had awakened their interest in Russian spirituality and humanist culture, which each were to pursue in their own way. Both made considerable contributions to their fields.

I often used to tease Michael Minihan, reminding him how I taught him the Russian alphabet in those distant schooldays. Now the pupil-teacher relationship has turned into a warm and lasting friendship. Indeed, Michael has been one of my great consolations in later years, when, after retirement, I have sought to maintain *The Third Hour* and the spirit of later Russian literature and religion, which has been the passion of my life. His help and interest has never flagged.

A few Jesuit scholastics also took my advanced Russian courses. They were studying for the priesthood and were excellent students, as were several other religious who joined them. The Benedictine Father Vladimir Tarasevich became rector of the Byzantine-Catholic church in Chicago. Father Guthrie, a Franciscan, became superior of the Byzantine-rite Ukrainian monastery of New Canaan. Father Englert, a Redemptorist, is one of the most distinguished scholars in the field of Eastern Theology and church history. Father Bissonette, an Assumptionist, was for a time the chaplain of foreign diplomats in Moscow and later, president of Assumption College in Worcester, Massachusetts.

Perhaps the most remarkable of my students in clerical garb was Father Bernard Lambert, a Dominican scholar who was on leave from his community in Ottawa in order to make a study of the various Protestant churches of the United States. He has since published his monumental work entitled *Ecumenism*. I must say, however, that with the exception of Father Englert, Father Lambert and a few other scholars, clerics or laymen, there was still very little interest in the ecumenical dialogue. The "Irenic Movement," as it was sometimes called, was frowned upon by the Vatican. Catholics did not seek friendly contacts with Protestants and Orthodox, which true ecumenism needed as its first prerequisite. Instead, they demanded an immediate and unconditional conversion. This attitude seemed to me especially inopportune regarding the Russian people who had heroically defended their faith and preserved it, in spite of years of persecution. The Fatima apparition inferred that Russia was to be "converted" and this message, naively understood and hastily interpreted, meant this conversion literally, regardless of the fact that Russia had been Christian for some thousand years, ever since Saint Vladimir brought Christianity to Kiev in 900.

As the atmosphere in which I worked became more and more stifling, I sought refuge at the *Catholic Worker*, where Dorothy always made me welcome. In the past years, I had grown very close to her and her "little people." She had helped me face my brother's death and my own disability, after my fall. Now once more she gave me her strong moral and spiritual support. Though I was faraway from Dorothy and Peter Maurin's way of life, I had not forgotten the deep emotion that I had felt at the Maryfarm Angelus. I visited the community as often as I could. I often attended retreats and conferences held by the *Catholic Worker*, and one summer Dorothy let me arrange a *Third Hour* weekend at Maryfarm. This was one of our most successful meetings, reminding me of Mounier's gatherings and the atmosphere of *Esprit*.

Although Peter Maurin was no longer with us, his spirit was still alive at the farm and at the Mott Street House of Hospitality. But both these centers moved, as *Catholic Worker* houses often did. Mott Street had to be vacated and a new house was opened on Christie Street in the heart of the Bowery. Maryfarm was sold and a new rural community was acquired near Pleasant Plains on Staten Island. It was named Peter Maurin Farm. Since it was an easy trip from New York by ferry and a local train, I could get out to the farm more often, and got to know its inhabitants: Dorothy's poor, the staff workers and volunteers, and other young or old who had been broken or wounded by life.

This was the true hospitality as conceived by Peter Maurin, a home where people were free to recuperate and find their identity, where they were assured of bread in time of trouble, yet not bread alone, but clothing and warmth, not merely at the family hearth, but by love and friendship. A small chapel, installed in the barn, was a center of prayer and meditation. Mass was said daily by a resident priest who joined also in daily labor on the farm. Compline was sung and the rosary said every evening and by special permission of the New York diocese, the Blessed Sacrament was reserved in this poorest of all the chapels I had ever known, but radiating a strength and inspiration that I could not find elsewhere.

I was being more and more drawn to the *Worker's* way of life, though I was still not ready to participate in it fully. I had to continue my work as teacher and writer, but I felt I was already a member of the family.

Near the end of my fourth year as lecturer at Fordham, I was looking forward to my promotion to the title of assistant professor. Instead, I was advised, by official letter, that my assignment at the Institute was terminated. I was dumbfounded, since Father Jaskievich had never warned me of such a development. I appealed to him and to the president himself, for an explanation, but to no avail. Once more, I found myself without a job.

I do not wish to dwell on the reasons for my dismissal, except to say that the policy of the Russian Institute had changed. Nor was I *persona grata* with the Fordham authorities, because of my outspoken views concerning the simplistic plan to "convert Russia" as a solution to the complex rivalries of the great powers.

Whom could I call to share my problems, if not Dorothy Day? We met for lunch in a small Chinese restaurant where we would be able to talk quietly. As I walked to meet her, I found a tiny wooden cross on the pavement. I picked it up. Was it a symbol that I should give up my ambitions of teaching in a great cultural center, and be content with a humbler way of life?

Dorothy immediately invited me to come over to the farm. I still felt quite unworthy of joining such a dedicated community, but Dorothy had no doubt that this would be a good thing for me to do. She advised, however, that I keep my "railroad apartment," to have a pied-à-terre in the city, for *Third Hour* activities and literary contacts.

This was a simple and practical plan. Packing a few of my belongings and the manuscript I was working on, I took the Staten Island ferry on a bright sunny day. On the pier, I had bought the New York *Times*, and as I unfolded it before me, I was amazed to see the announcement officially sent to the *Times* by the *Catholic Worker*.

A civil defense drill had been ordered at noon that day, and at the sound of sirens, all people on the streets of New York were to take shelter, in special areas of office buildings or subways. Dorothy and other members of the *Catholic Worker* staff would be in the City Hall Park and refuse to take shelter.

I read their declaration of principle, which was later summarized in her book *Loaves and Fishes:* "We made our stand against the yearly *war game,* we are setting our faces against the terrible injustice our industrial system perpetuates by making profits out of war preparations."

I arrived at the farm in a state of anxiety. Dorothy was not there and later, a *Catholic Worker* volunteer called to tell us what had happened. Dorothy, Ammon Hennacy and others of the staff, as well as a group of Quakers, sat quietly on the benches of the small park, ignoring the sirens which screamed their warnings. Then police arrived. They arrested the demonstrators and hauled them into paddywagons. They were then held until arraignment at night court. Later, they were released on bail and their trial was set at the police court, as their act of civil disobedience was classified as a "misdemeanor."

We all went to the courthouse to assist at the trial, and I will never forget the scene. The defendants were aligned before the judge, very calm and self-possessed. The Quakers were defended by their lawyers, but the *Catholic Worker* group refused legal aid and undertook their own defense. Ammon Hennacy, one of Dorothy's ardent followers who said he was an anarchist and "leader of a one-man revolution," made an impassioned speech; other members of the group spoke very well, too, and Dorothy, in her usual, quiet manner, scarcely raising her voice, spoke with great clarity and circumspection.

The judge listened attentively to all the statements and then pronounced the sentences. The protestors all got five days in jail. When it was Dorothy's turn to be sentenced, the judge leaned over his desk and addressed her earnestly. He said that he considered her as a woman who had given more help to the poor than any other charitable person in New York City. But, she had broken the law and so he had to sentence her. She was led away with all the others and locked up in the New York Women's House of Detention, in Greenwich Village. As I saw the tall, dignified graying woman disappear behind the doors between two policemen, the words of the judge rang in my ears. As Dorothy often said herself, going to jail was also a work of mercy, since it gave her an opportunity of "visiting the prisoners," as the Gospel commanded and as she could not have done otherwise.

This was Dorothy's first civil defense protest and her first jail term for this offense. She participated in six demonstrations of this kind, and was six times in prison, the longest time being one month. Several other women had joined her in this protest, one being Deane Mowrer, a gifted writer of the *Catholic Worker* editorial board. She reported on the life of the rural community, with a Thoreau-like twist of thought. She was also an expert bird-watcher, until serious eye trouble caused her total blindness; still she kept on writing her column and corresponding with many friends of the movement.

Both Dorothy Day and Deane Mowrer wrote of their experiences in the Women's House of Detention. Its crowded conditions, and sordid circumstances under which the women lived, the lack of opportunity for the rehabilitation of prostitutes and drug-addicts, were presented in the harsh light of a criticism such as never before had appeared in the press. The inmates were described not by visitors, but by friends or sisters who wanted to help them. As a result of these reports, the House of Detention was inspected and improved in some respects. Finally, the prison was closed and transferred to Rikers Island. But as long as the prison was located in Greenwich Village, Dorothy and some of the staff members would go over on Christmas Eve and sing carols under its windows. Many faces would appear behind the bars to express their appreciation.

Year after year, demonstrations against the wargames grew in size and press coverage. More and more people began to join the Quakers and peace groups which were formed. By the end of the fifties so many young people from colleges and universities had joined in, that it was impossible to arrest them all. The air-raid drills began to slow down and were finally dropped. The wargames were suspended, saving the taxpayers considerable money.

During the summer months at the farm, Dorothy and Ammon would come and stay for a while, but they would always go back to Saint Joseph's House in the city, where the works of mercy went on from day to day. At the farm there were many retreats and conferences. During those days, I had time to study my companions. If I were an artist, I would paint a fresco of the different characters surrounding the central figures of Dorothy and Peter.

There was John Filliger, a former sailor now in charge of the farming operations. He was an expert in growing corn, vegetables and taking care of the animals. Strong, with broad shoulders, he had a stentorian voice and walked with the rolling gait of a seaman. There was another ex-sailor, Hans Tunnesen, born in Norway, who had sailed all over the world and had been a cook on the tug boats of New York. He became cook, carpenter and devoted handyman for the Catholic Worker Farms. Peter Maurin died in his arms and I believe he understood his and Dorothy's ideas better than many an intellectual who tried to explain them. He lived them with complete faith and simplicity. He received a small sailor's pension and gave most of it to the community. Later, when he died, Dorothy wrote a three-column obituary about Hans, telling, among other things, that the only earthly belongings he left, were a rosary, a suit of clothes to be buried in, and one dollar and ten cents in cash.

Stanley Vishnevsky was a character of Polish-Lithuanian origin who had joined the *Catholic Worker* at the age of sixteen, shortly after Dorothy and Peter founded the movement. He had never left the *Worker* except for short trips. Writer, storyteller for children and adults, humorist and philosopher, Stanley knew the secret of preserving his own balance and that of others in every crisis. Marge Hughes, also one of the earliest disciples who used to accompany Peter Maurin on his lecture tours at the age of eighteen. She got married, but came back to the *Worker*, a widow with five children. She participated fully with the community, in a life of work and prayer.

After staying a few months at the farm, I took a translator's job at the United Nations, during the General Assembly session, hired on a temporary basis.

I found the translations of documents, from French and English into Russian, extremely difficult. The political and technical terminology they used were completely new to me. True, we had supervisors whom we could consult and who checked our work, but they were cold, robot-like men who eyed me severely and looked down on me as an "extra," while they were firmly rooted in their offices where they had been for years. The entire building where I worked had something stiff and frozen about it. All the offices were air-conditioned, and I caught a cold in the icy atmosphere. Of course, no windows could be opened on the mild, fall days when the sessions opened. There were no stairs, only elevators and escalators, leading to endless halls and corridors. At the end of one was the office of my boss who was as cold and robot-like as the supervisors.

I was also depressed by the thorough investigation to which I was subjected, in spite of the fact that I had been screened by the F.B.I. and by the Office of War Information.

I do not wish to sound a hostile note concerning my UN experience. It was an encounter with an administrative machinery running a huge plant of hundreds of employees of various nationalities and cultural backgrounds. I was but a cog in this machinery, but I still believe that the United Nations is a very important step on the way to an international or supernational form of government which will finally emerge and for which many distinguished and humane men and women have made many sacrifices, including that of their lives. If you work even for a short time in the tall, blue and gray building on the East River, you breathe a peculiar air and feel the wind of a far-distant future blowing through the labyrinth of its halls and corridors. This great monument, reminding us of the spirit of Dag Hammarskjöld, is a landmark for us all.

We had a very tight office schedule and could leave our desks only for a short lunch hour and for a four o'clock tea or coffee break. So I could not observe the General Assembly proceedings, which are such an exciting feature of the international drama unfolding in the main building. But I did enjoy the four o'clock break which enabled me to meet and talk with various friends. It so happened that my cousin, Marguerite Langkjaer, was at that time, chief receptionist in the delegates' lounge. I could slip into the inner sanctum where many of the *dramatis personae* met for a drink or a cup of tea, made or received their telephone calls.

Anne Fremantle, who was also working as an extra in the English section of the UN, would come down to the lounge and join us. I was happy to meet Father Jerôme de Suza, a Jesuit who was a delegate from India. He had taken an interest in *The Third Hour* and contributed to our publication. Father de Suza was a member of the Indian Parliament and had been a friend of Ghandi's. A tall, stately man, with a friendly smile and courteous manner, he belonged to the Brahmin caste and was a link between the Christian and Hindu mystics and philosophers, a connection which Thomas Merton was seeking to revive on his last voyage. (He was attending a conference on contemplative religious in Bangkok, Thailand, when he met with a fatal accident.)

When the United Nations General Assembly session was over, I stayed on in my New York apartment. I wished to work on a project of a book in Russian, devoted to the lives of the American saints and other outstanding Catholics of the Americas. The stories of these men and women were very little known to Russian émigrés and even less, of course, to Soviet readers. I started it in a simple native style, that used by the average Russian writer, to tell a story. The book, entitled *American Saints and Heroes,* was to begin with the North American martyrs, and extend to the South American Saint Martin de Porres, Saint Rose of Lima and Saint Peter Claver. Concluding chapters would cover the lives of Mother Cabrini, Rose Hawthorne and Elizabeth Seton. There was also a chapter on two Russian Catholics in America: Father Dimitri Golitsyn (Prince Mitry) and Mother Elizabeth Golitsyn of the Sacred Heart Frontier Missions.

The Fordham Russian Center now had a new director, Father Paul Mailleux, a highly sensitive Belgian scholar and Russian specialist. He accepted my project and financed its publication, somewhat reluctantly, for he did not think such a book would be popular, nor purchased by many Russians.

Alas, Father Mailleux was right. *American Saints and Heroes* aroused little interest among émigrés and had little chance to get to Russia. Copies reached the office of the Catholic chaplain of the American Embassy in Moscow, but there they piled up without any chance of being distributed. My seed seemed to have been sown in the desert. Yet, I had felt so sure that it would grow and bear fruit.

I was finally rewarded fifteen years after its publication when I was informed that Archbishop John Wendland of the Moscow Patriarchate, who had just been sent to New York as Exarch, the Patriarch's representative for the Americas, wished to see me. He had read my book and wished to talk to me about it. Before being sent to America, he had been Exarch in Germany, and found the book there.

A mutual friend brought the Archbishop to tea at my apartment. He was a tall, dynamic man with a red beard, broad shoulders and a genial smile, although he was in his forties, there was something youthful about him. He loved nature and had studied geology before becoming a monk. He held a degree in science and taught in a Soviet university in Central Asia, even after his ordination to the priesthood. It was a new experience to meet this prelate who had chosen a religious vocation at the height of the persecution of the Church in Russia, at first, following his studies for the priesthood in secret and persevering, to become a Patriarchal envoy to foreign lands.

Archbishop John told me that he had been "thrilled" by my *Saints and Heroes*. He had especially enjoyed the chapters devoted to the American martyrs; the adventuresome and dramatic lives of the 17th century French Jesuits reminded him of the tales of Fenimore Cooper which have always been popular in Russia, and the missionary zeal of Isaac Jogues and his companions deeply moved him. His other favorite, he said, was Martin de Porres, and he asked me to get a picture of him who is the patron saint of the blacks. He wanted the picture to show Martin with all the mice following him when, according to the legend, he lead them all out of his monastery in Lima, Peru.

After this occasion, I had many opportunities of meeting with the Archbishop and always found him friendly and enthusiastic. He came to our *Third Hour* meetings and took part in our dialogues, having taken a crash program in English at the Berlitz School. I also took him to Dorothy's and he spoke at a Catholic Worker Forum. Of course, we avoided any discussion of politics or of the regime under which he served his Church. He appreciated the Catholic Worker atmosphere and when he was called back to Moscow, after six years in America, he said that Dorothy Day and her movement were among his most cherished memories of New York, and of America.

I regretted the Archbishop's departure. He had been appointed to the see of Yaroslavl and Rostov, an important archdiocese in the Volga region. Though I never saw him again, I felt that he did a great deal to make my book known in the Soviet Union. Somehow the ban which weighs heavily on most religious books in the country, seemed lifted for *Saints and Heroes*. Father Paul Mailleux, who had been transferred to the *Russicum* Institution in Rome, told me later that he had precise information that the book was circulated in Moscow and the priests and seminarians of the Patriarchal Church were reading it.

I must express my gratitude to Father Mailleux, whom I had first known when he came to the Fordham Russian Center, for his appreciation and help in the Third Hour movement. He was one of the first to recognize the importance of a dialogue between the Russian Orthodox clergy and hierarchy, behind the Iron Curtain. Thanks to him and the priests and laymen who share his views, there has been considerable progress in Catholic-Orthodox relations on the highest level.

Besides the writing I had undertaken after the end of the UN General Assembly, I was once more absorbed in developing the activities of the Third Hour. We were still a strictly private organization, working almost underground but there was a breakthrough in the mid-fifties when a small but select group of theologians and scholars began to acknowledge us. Dr. Reinhold Niebuhr, at that time head of the Union Theological Seminary, took an interest in our endeavor, as did his assistant, Dr. John Bennet. We held a meeting at the Niebuhr apartment on the campus and, though Niebuhr was incapacitated by a stroke and did not take part in the discussions, he followed them with great attention. His wife, Ursula, was a most gracious hostess. The speakers were Father Jean Danielou, S.J. (afterwards, a Cardinal), the distinguished English Jesuit and writer Martin d'Arcy and Father George Florovsky, a Russian Orthodox theologian whose works are basic for studies of the Eastern churches.

Our tenth anniversary issue came out that year (No. VII, 1956). It carried articles by Father Danielou, Reverend John Shakhovsky, Russian Orthodox bishop of San Francisco, Father George Tavard, Assumptionist theologian who led the dialogue with the Protestants, Abbé Pierre, worker for the *Sans-Foyers*, the homeless of Paris, Michael Scott, champion of the blacks of South Africa at the United Nations, Dorothy Day, Pastor von Schenk, Lutheran, Father Lambert, Dominican and Reverend Clement Lialine, a Russian-Benedictine scholar. The issue also carried articles by the *Third Hour* founders, Basil Yanovsky and Arthur Lourié. And there was a poem by Boris Pasternak, translated by Anne Fremantle and myself. Pasternak, still *persona grata* in the Soviet Union, had published this poem in the monthly review *Novy Mir*, but the American public at large had never heard of this great poet who became famous the world over when his book *Doctor Zhivago*, first published in Italy, came out in New York shortly after our little review.

As usual, our issue No. VII remained almost unnoticed, including Pasternak's beautiful poem. Unsold copies accumulated in my apartment. Nevertheless, we were now known and supported by a small but elite circle of priests and laymen of various denominations. A number of universities, including Harvard, Yale and Princeton, as well as seminaries and divinity schools, became our subscribers. So, in spite of my setback at Fordham, these were busy and exciting years.

But there was still in my mind and heart, an unsatisfied feeling when I thought of the Catholic Worker community and their simple way of life. Perhaps I should give up my too numerous and ambitious pursuits and be content to join the people at Peter Maurin's Farm? I had attended all of Dorothy's trials and each time, it was for me, a poignant and moving experience. "Yes," I said to myself, "this is the way one should think and live."

But this time, destiny decided for me. There had been considerable changes at Peter Maurin's. The health department visited the building and decided it must be classified as a family home and could not house so many people. There was no longer any room for me.

Feeling the need of a change, however, I accepted an invitation from my old friend, Catherine, now married to Eddie Doherty, to visit their new center for training lay apostles, in Combemere, Canada. She asked me to give a series of lectures on Russian history and culture, for she felt that her trainees should know every country and spirituality.

Madonna House is located near the small town of Combemere, between Ottawa and Toronto. A thick blanket of snow covered the ground. Since living quarters were limited, Catherine rented a room for me at a country inn, and I was driven daily to the center, to take my meals with the young men and women of the community. I attended daily Mass, readings and prayers in the large chapel, simple and noble in its design. I soon grew used to the arctic weather, the icy roads and deep woods surrounding us. They were like the Russian forests far away. I liked the young people who attended my lectures with much interest. It was an experience different from that of the Catholic Worker, for Madonna House was tightly structured and more intellectually oriented. It was not dedicated directly toward the peace movement nor to giving shelter to the poor. It did, however, provide medicines and clothing to the nearby lumberjacks' families, some of them suffering considerable destitution.

The three priests who served Madonna House in 1959 were not only expert liturgists, psychologists and counselors, but also did their share of manual labor in the workshops and on the farm. One of the priests was an experienced agronomist. Later, more priests and religious joined the community of Madonna House and all followed the way of life that I had observed during my visit. However much they may differ from the *Catholic Worker*, I found here the same spirit of dedication and poverty that was manifested by Dorothy Day and Peter Maurin. (Madonna House is a secular institute, approved by the Catholic Church with its own status. The young men and women who become its members, take the three religious vows of chastity, poverty and obedience.)

The quiet, recollected atmosphere was conducive to work, and I was able to finish several writing assignments. But I felt miles and miles away from the world whose voices I scarcely heard during those long, wintry days when everything was frozen and silent, and the Madonna House population led its own secluded life.

Then, on January 25th, came the great news over the radio — Pope John XXIII announced his decision to convoke a Council seeking a renewal of the Church and the reunion of Christendom. The last part of the announcement thrilled me in particular. I could not believe my ears, and listened to the radio again and again, until I was convinced, as I still am today, that this was one of the most important events that had taken place in Church history — at least in the ecumenical sphere. I was overjoyed by these perspectives, so long the ideal of our small group of *The Third Hour*. The Pope's inspiration now opened wide the road to Christian unity to which we aspired and for which we had worked. And now, almost immediately, I was given an opportunity to contribute, at least in a small way, to the ecumenical education so urgently needed.

The Bruce Publishing House in Milwaukee sent me a request for a book on the Russian Orthodox Church: her history, liturgical tradition, monasticism and spirituality. This was not to be a theological work, but rather a presentation for the public in general, of the Russian religious way of life. I was told that Bruce had made this request at the suggestion of a Benedictine priest who was not personally acquainted with me, but knew the type of work I had been doing. So back to New York I went, where Bruce had a branch office. I was given a contract and a deadline, spring, 1960, when preparations for the Council would start.

From then on, things moved quickly for me. Not only did I have the book on Russian Orthodoxy to write, but I received an almost simultaneous offer to teach Russian language and literature at Seton Hill, a college directed by the Sisters of Charity in Greensburg, Pennsylvania. This was due to another kind recommendation, this time by a friend and sympathizer of *The Third Hour*, who had known of my experience at Fordham. He was Czolt Arcadi, an author and journalist, exiled from Hungary, at that time teaching at Seton Hill. He had been looking for an opportunity to give me a job, and this chance came as the spirit of change and renewal began to spread through the American Catholic institutions. Father William Ryan, president of Seton Hill and his assistant, Sister Thecla Schmidt, were both highly cultured and liberal-minded educators who welcomed the *aggiornamento* with enthusiasm.

Sister Thecla had read my book *Light before Dusk* when she was a novice and graduate student at Columbia and later told me that the French Catholic renaissance and youth movement, which I had described, had influenced her thinking. I was introduced to Father Ryan at a small dinner party arranged by Dr. Arcadi. He approved of my nomination and our relations were most cordial. I was to start teaching in September, so I had the whole summer to do research for my book and hoped to have enough time between my teaching hours, to write and meet my deadline.

And so a whole, new chapter was opening for me, just when, according to age and a normal course of events, I should have been ready for retirement. I had had a premonition of these new horizons during my last days at Madonna House, as I walked from the country inn where I was staying, to the Easter midnight Mass to be celebrated in the chapel. It was early April and the river was still frozen asleep under its blanket of snow. As I walked along the road, the sky above was suddenly ablaze. The Northern Lights were spreading their gold and pale-green aura over the clouds, like the gigantic wings of "heavenly hosts." This was indeed the true sign of Resurrection. Would my life, too, like every snow-crystal glistening in the branches of the tall pines along the quiet, deserted road, reflect something of the dazzling light of these great wings?

I can say that the years that followed that Easter night were filled with the peculiar glow of the charisma of Pope John XXIII, and even with its afterglow after he died. The lights of the *aggiornamento* illumined my life which was nearing sunset, but was still an active and diversified one, with my teaching, writing and continuation of my ecumenical concern.

I enjoyed the teaching, which I could plan as I wished. It was a joy to work with Sister Thecla who proved to be one of the most intelligent, sensitive and gifted religious I have known in America. I also owe a tribute to Father Ryan, now a monsignor. After two years I received my promotion to assistant professor and chairman of the Russian department, which I had built up at Seton Hill. Our Saint Nicholas Russian Club gave performances of plays and folksongs.

During the first year of Seton Hill, I finished my book and it was published in 1960, under the title *Christ in Russia*. It was well-received by the Catholic press and was the choice of the Catholic Book Club. But what pleased me most was that it was favorably received by the Russian Orthodox circles in America. I was to learn later, that it was used as a Church history manual by Russian Orthodox teachers.

With the convocation of the first session of Vatican Council II, my ecumenical work, the *Third Hour* meetings and publications, became no more than an insignificant part of the new movement now taking shape. But the experience I had gained and the friendly contacts I had established with Christians of various denominations, as well as with Jews, now proved to be very useful. I was appointed by Bishop Connare of the Greensburg diocese to the newly founded Diocesan Ecumenical Commission, which originated private dialogues with Protestant ministers, rabbis, and Russian Orthodox priests. The Commission also held open sessions at Seton Hill and at other Catholic colleges.

But the most active and truly dynamic ecumenical center was at Pittsburgh, only thirty miles from Seton Hill. The initiator was Dr. Leonard Swidler of Duquesne University, who held a degree in theology from Marburg University in West Germany. This young scholar was an ardent ecumenist as well as a promoter of liturgical reform. With the support of Bishop Wright of Pittsburgh (later a Cardinal and member of the Roman *Curia*), and Dr. Alvyne Smith from the Presbyterian Theological Seminary of Pittsburgh, Dr. Swidler founded the center as a graduate ecumenical seminar of Duquesne.

Dr. Swidler invited me to join in the seminar's joint endeavors and I was most happy to learn that two distinguished scholars who had contributed to *The Third Hour*, were now residents of Pittsburgh and would lecture at the seminar. They were Father George Tavard, who had long conducted dialogues with Protestants, and Father Hans Rheinhold, well-known leader and pioneer in the liturgical movement. The hierarchy had frowned upon these two avant-garde priests, until Bishop Wright offered them assignments in his own diocese.

The seminar courses were inaugurated by the Bishop in person. His interest in the dialogue with non-Catholics was very great, though he observed a prudent view on experimentation. He was known to be on most cordial terms with the Jewish circles in Pittsburgh. It was said that he could be found at the lunch hour, not in his chancery, but in a nearby Jewish restaurant.

The first session of the seminar was followed by lectures and conferences given by Father Tavard, Father Rheinhold, Dr. Smith and Marcus Barth, the son of Karl Barth. I was happy to welcome the rector of Saint Vladimir's Russian Orthodox Seminary, Father Alexander Schmemann. This brilliant and charming scholar, a devoted priest and expert on the Byzantine liturgy, had always encouraged our little *Third Hour* group. He had now become a leading figure in the great, ecumenical symposiums which the renewal had stimulated in America and Europe.

From Germany came Hans Küng, the controversial theologian of Tubingen University who had just published a book on the Church which caused a stir in ecclesiastical circles. This tall, fair-haired, boyish-looking priest, without being aggressive, was as defiant in his writings as he was quiet and courteous in his personal relations. We had dinner with him and he impressed me, as in later years, with his combination of determination and calm, under a veiled humility.

Küng did not speak for the seminar but gave a public lecture in the main auditorium. It was packed with young people, priests, nuns and students.

Of all the remarkable theologians and scholars who contributed to the success of Pittsburgh's ecumenical development, the one I recall with the greatest admiration and warmth, is Father Hans Rheinhold. Feared by his colleagues as a harsh critic and inexorable defender of his own liturgical ideas, with me he was always considerate and gentle. Though I must have been a greenhorn in his eyes, he loved things Russian and had a deep understanding of the Byzantine liturgy. He was studying Russian from a text book I gave him and he always signed his letters to me Ivan, instead of John. Of many things we had in common was our love for Dorothy Day, indeed, Father Hans had been a friend of the *Worker* for many years.

Soon after the launching of the seminar, Leonard Swidler and Elwyn Smith started a theological review, or *Journal of Ecumenical Studies;* and I was invited to be one of the editors. There was a brilliant list of contributors of all Christian denominations, as well as Jews and agnostics. I must say humbly that I was not on a par with these eminent theologians, but I could at least serve as observer and interpreter of Russian Orthodox affairs, both in the Soviet Union and in the emigration. I owe a great deal to Seton Hill, for giving me a free hand to pursue outside interests, renewing in Pittsburgh, and even more fruitfully, the connections I had lost in leaving New York.

And there was another heartening development; because of my larger salary, I could now save enough to go back to Europe once more. I revisited Paris, where my former group of friends had dwindled to a few survivors; many like myself had come to America. I walked in the streets of Paris in a melancholy mood, but finally found comfort in an old colleague and friend of the Voice of America. Julien Green welcomed me at the apartment where he lived with his sister, Anne. It was on a street adjacent to the Russian Embassy. His windows opened out on the garden and terrace of our former residence, when my father was Ambassador to France. Together we leaned out to have a look at it. The new Soviet envoy now lived in the house. It had been freshly painted, an expenditure which, I remembered, the Tsarist government had not permitted!

Later, I read an entry in Julien Green's diary which referred to my visit. It was in June, 1960 and speaks very kindly of his *vraie affection*—his real affection for me—and recalls the topic of our conversation, the *rapprochement* between Catholics and Orthodox, and also Dorothy's civil disobedience. "The Catholic pacifist who gets herself put in prison at every repetition of the air-raid drill" (Julien Green, *Vers l'invisible*).

Continuing my journey into the past, another year I flew to Rome. Of course, I could not remember anything about living there, for I had been a baby in my mother's arms. But arriving on a beautiful, summer night and taking my first stroll in the narrow streets near my hotel, I distinctly had the feeling that I had been there before. Was that mere imagination or had the sights and sounds of the city awakened dim memories? They must have been happy memories, for I fell instantly in love with Rome.

The next morning I started exploring; I climbed up and down the Spanish Steps, looking at the houses which lined them, wondering in which one we had lived, but there was no one to tell me, since I had no idea of the exact address. But I could make some research into my father's diplomatic activities in Rome, when Signor Federico Alessandrini let me look into the files of the *Osservatore Romano* for the year 1894.

In Rome, I was fortunate to find Dimitri and Lydia Ivanov, son and daughter of Viachslav Ivanov, whose book I had translated with Charles du Bos in Paris. They remembered their father's appreciation of our work and immediately adopted me as an old member of the family. Dimitri and Lydia were both gifted. He was a journalist and author of several books. Lydia was a professor in the Academy of Music and a composer whose works were often performed. Their late father had become a Catholic and had known two popes who loved and admired him because of his work as a poet and scholar, and so his children, also Catholics, had close ties with the Vatican. They enjoyed the confidence of Pope John XXIII and of the ecclesiastical circles now preparing the Council. It was thanks to them that I had an introduction to the leaders of the ecumenical movement.

During this first visit to Rome and again in the years that followed, I met Cardinal Bea, the head of the Secretariat for Christian Unity, and his assistant, Bishop Willebrands, later a Cardinal, and also an active member, Monsignor Arrighi. I had an audience with Cardinal Tisserant, whom I had met at the inauguration of the Fordham Russian Institute. These men of the *aggiornamento,* or renewal, were most cordial to me, approved of my own small ecumenical work and encouraged me to continue it, giving me their blessing.

My greatest reward was to see with my own eyes, the man I had come to venerate. When I watched Pope John being carried in the *sedia* or appearing at the window of his apartment to speak to the crowds at Saint Peter's Square, or facing the pilgrims in the reception hall of Castel Gandolfo, I realized that this was not only a great Pope, but a prophet. It is hard to express the unforgettable impression he made on me on the Feast of Corpus Christi, 1963. Speaking on the steps of St. Peter's, he recalled the day when his decision to call the Council was made. His heavy, ailing body, his homely, peasant features, were transfigured and seemed to shine with a new light: "It was," he exclaimed, "the Holy Spirit (*il Spirito Sancto*) who struck me here" and he indicated his breast, covered with the wide, golden stole he wore for the procession.

The most important part of my "journey into the past," was my return to my homeland, now the Union of Soviet Socialist Republics, but for me still "Mother Russia." I went twice to the Soviet Union, once with my friend Marguerite Tjader in 1961. We motored from Leningrad to Moscow, and then to Kharkov and Kiev. The second time was in 1963, with a small group of American and European teachers, when we traveled as far as Central Asia. Of the two expeditions, the first was the most rewarding. Marguerite, who was an expert driver, holding an international license, rented a Soviet car, a four-seated Volga and together we followed the itinerary mapped out for us, with the help of the Intourist agency in New York. We had chosen our own places of interest, starting from Leningrad where we picked up the car. That first evening, we drove through the city and out to the Kamenny Ostrov. We did not need our lights; these were the white nights of June. Memories and emotions overwhelmed me; I have written of them elsewhere, but cannot linger over them here.

The next days, we went on to Novgorod, Kalinin, Moscow. In spite of the strictness of an official schedule, we were sufficiently independent to walk around and visit the sites that interested us most, especially the churches where we attended services and spoke to priests. We visited the Monastery of the Trinity and Saint Sergius at Zagorsk, heart of religious life today as it has been throughout the ages. At the Novodevichy Monastery in Moscow, I stood at the grave of my great master, Vladimir Soloviev, the pioneer of ecumenism.

In Zagorsk, in the cathedrals of Moscow and Leningrad as well as in many other churches, I saw the crowds of devout worshippers, praying, chanting, participating in the liturgy with a fervor I have never seen, except, perhaps, at Lourdes. During early morning Masses, I could observe dozens of babies being baptized in collective ceremonies. All these scenes of religious life in Soviet Russia have been reported by other tourists, but for me they were not only deeply moving, they were the confirmation of what I had written almost thirty years ago—that in spite of antireligious persecution, the faith of the Russian people had survived and would continue to live.

It is hard for me to recapitulate here, in these last pages of my life story, my impressions and emotions when revisiting my native land. I have recorded them elsewhere when they were still fresh and not yet outdated.[1] I can only sum up these impressions and emotions by saying that it was for me a unique and poignant experience. Of course, there was much that was new to me, some of it quite strange, a world in which I had no part, faces whose secrets I could not share. But there was so much that was familiar—the landscapes, the clouds in the vast Russian sky, the endless vistas of rivers and fields, the smile of a mother, the voices of children. And there were the cities — Moscow and the Kremlin cathedrals, Petersburg-Leningrad and the Palace Square, unforgotten during forty years of exile.

Will I ever return to Russia? I do not know, but I still long to do so. My feelings were best interpreted by a woman who sold newspapers, somewhere in the Caucasus. She asked me where I came from and I said I was Russian-born but now lived in America. "Are you ever homesick?" she asked and I said yes. "I know how you feel" she said, "I was away from home during the war, and it was hard to bear." Then she

---

1. I describe my trips to Russia in two articles published in *Jubilée* magazine, 1961 and 1963.

added gently: "I will bear your homesickness in my heart." I do not know if this Russian woman was a believer, but her words reminded me of Dostoevsky's Father Zosima when he said that we "must bear each other's burdens."

As the years at Seton Hill went by, I realized that my time of teaching was drawing to an end. I had "run my race" and at seventy, it was necessary for me to retire and make some plan for the remaining years of my life. Would I at last be able to fulfill my long-delayed wish to join the *Catholic Worker* community?[2] The possibility did present itself at that time. In 1964, Dorothy had sold Peter Maurin Farm, and since Staten Island real estate had risen in value because of the building of the Verazzano Bridge, she could buy a much larger property on the Hudson River. There were eighty acres of land and several buildings, enough to house some sixty people. When I called Dorothy to tell her of my retirement, she simply asked me: "When are you coming?" And so I packed my books and papers, put away my cap and gown, and drove down the long hill to my new home.

This, then, is the epilogue of my life in which there was much joy and sadness, many occasions for rejoicing, but no time to grieve, even when there was pain. Each time the years tore me away from something that I had thought important, there was more to be gained than what I had lost. But there is still a great deal to be learned, here, in my *Catholic Worker* family. The thing that really counts is not so much to be poor, as to be poor in spirit.

---

2. April, 1973. *Catholic Worker* Farm, Tivoli, N.Y. Revised in July, 1975. Cold Spring, N.Y.

Epilogue

THIS RATHER abrupt ending to Helene's long manuscript, giving the date and place of its finishing and also that of its revision, two years later, provides a clue to what actually happened to complete her remarkable life.

She did not remain at Tivoli, because, as so often in her career, circumstances changed: the peaceful and creative atmosphere she had hoped to find eluded her. Dorothy Day was constantly needed in the city and had little time to visit the farm. Helene felt isolated from her friends of *The Third Hour*. She had found joy and companionship at the tiny Benedictine monastery of Brother Victor-Antoine and Brother Patrick nearby and often went to share a simple meal with them, or sing Vespers.

The then Marist Novitiate of Cold Spring offered the monks a more adequate house with guest rooms, and the use of their larger chapel, until the monks built one of their own. It was located about sixty miles south of Tivoli. Every month, the young monks brought Helene down to spend a few days with them. She was able to take part in a series of lectures on the early Fathers of the Church, held in Cold Spring for the contemplative communities of the New York area. At the last lecture, Helene was asked to speak of the Russian saints. Brother Victor wrote: "With what depth, simplicity and love she explained to us the history and teachings and special qualities of Saint Sergius, Saint Seraphim and others . . ."

It was at this time that Helene asked Brother Victor-Antoine to help her look for a small place near Our Lady of the Resurrection Monastery where she could live and work and also create a center for Russian studies and *The Third Hour*. She had still kept her "railroad apartment" and had sometimes taken refuge there, but circumstances had also changed in the city. Thieves were constantly breaking in to take typewriters, radios, etc. (Fortunately, they did not recognize the value of her books!)

Finally, Helene was persuaded to take an attractive apartment in a building development in the village of Cold Spring. It had a large living-room, two bedrooms, bath and kitchen. With typical courage, she determined to write and translate, to make up for the extra expense. At last, she had a home of her own, in the peace of the country. She moved out of her "railroad flat" with its many meaningful memories, and once more was ready to begin again. Now she had room for her Russian library, her many icons and a meeting place for *The Third Hour*. She named it the Ben-Serg Center in honor of Saint Benedict and Saint Sergius.

It was not long before Helene attracted friends, old and new, to the Center. Many showed their loyalty by coming out to the first *Third Hour* meeting, by train and by car: Father Lyle Young, Dorothy Day, Father Gino Piovesana of the Fordham Russian department, Professor Alexander Obolensky, Eileen Egan, Michael Minihan, Helene's former pupil and, later, professor and writer on Dostoevsky and Mochulsky. Other visitors were the writer Basil Yanovsky and his wife, Isabella, Anne Fremantle, Father John Meyendorff, Russian theologian now dean of St. Vladimirs Seminary, Father Hopko, Sister Mary Louise from the Convent of St. Birgitta and others.

A local Episcopalian minister, John Mills, was eager to join in this ecumenical work. A young woman, Margaret Mudd, who worked with American Indians, had met Helene at the *Catholic Worker,* and came wishing to study Russian language and literature. Perceptive and eager, she stayed with Helene while settling in a place of her own nearby. She became an invaluable assistant; her youthful enthusiasm was both a help and a joy.

Helene's ability to arouse devotion and loyalty was beautifully illustrated by Brother Victor-Antoine and Brother Patrick, whose little monastery was now only twenty minutes away. Helene had always gone her way alone, without asking for help, but it was obvious that she was growing older, less able to cope with the details of daily living. They responded to her needs, both physical and emotional, becoming true sons to her. Brother Victor's own words can best convey her reliance on these young monks, and also the admiration and inspiration they felt as they observed her life of purpose and prayer:

> When Helene came to live near us, it was with the understanding and promise that the monks of this monastery would care for her and her needs. This was for us, a work of love. This brought us very close in daily life. Every morning at ten o'clock Helene used to call us and give us a report of her plans for the day, and the things she would need. She always asked our advice and consulted us about everything. It was very humbling for us that a woman of Helene's caliber and wisdom would consult poor, unexperienced monks like us. In the afternoon, one of us went regularly to see her, to help with the cleaning, do the marketing and other errands for her. She was always very grateful for this. She used to say: "I have many faults, but I have never lacked in gratitude."
>
> Another reason she moved to Cold Spring was, of course, to be near Our Lady of Resurrection Monastery. She wanted to share our monastic life as much as possible. She was very happy, knowing that our monastery

was consecrated to prayer and work for the unity of the Church and that in our work we had adapted many of the liturgical elements of the Christian East, especially the Russian chant of which she was so fond. When she came to see us, she loved to talk about the fine points of history, spirituality, culture, etc. and about the latest news of ecumenical encounters, or of the Russian Church, which she followed closely. She loved, especially, to attend the Liturgy and the Divine Office in our monastic chapel. The last time she joined us for Mass was, fittingly, on the Feast of the Transfiguration, dearly loved by all Russians and by all monks.

It is hard to describe what her own little Center meant to Helene and how much happiness it brought her in the last years of her life. There she lived a life of prayer, study, work and hospitality. We often came there to pray with her, to sing Compline in the icon corner of her bedroom. We realized that she was immersed in an intense life of union with Christ, a life hidden in Him. She often told us that Christ was always with her, her friend and companion, that she walked and talked with Him. This did not prevent her from caring for her other responsibilities.

Every day, for three or four hours, she worked on translations, to supplement her small income. She did this, up to the last day in her Center, when she had a fall and was taken to the hospital. When I had visited her that afternoon, she was working away on a life of Dom Prosper Guéranger, O.S.B., the founder of Solesmes.

Helene lived for about six weeks in the hospital. Her condition was complicated by several maladies of which she had never complained, not wishing to burden anyone. Many friends came to the hospital to see her. Bishop Pernicone from Poughkepsie often came to bring her Communion. Dorothy Day spent most of the last weeks at her bedside, as did Marguerite Tjader and Brother Victor or Brother Patrick. She was strengthened twice by the Sacrament of the Last Rites. The nuns of Regina Laudis, Mother Marie-Aline and Mother Assumpta, came to bid her farewell. They had brought a full Benedictine habit for her burial, for she was indeed, "Sister Olga," an oblate of St. Benedict. After her death, many remarked at the extraordinary serenity of her face, like that of a Russian icon.

The funeral Mass was sung in the large chapel of the Marist Brothers by three priests, according to the Byzantine liturgy. Many candles glowed. Outside it was a cold, wintry Russian day. But the chapel was crowded and many passed the simple casket, for the rite of the "Last Kiss."

A smaller number followed the hearse up to the Tivoli cemetery and the *Catholic Worker* plot. The soil, which we had taken from the grave of Soloviev in Moscow, was put on top of the casket — Russian soil.

Marguerite Tjader

Index

Affirmation (Utverzhdenie), 188-189, 191, 193, 194
Aistov, Mr., 55
Alexander Mikhailovich, Grand Duke, 86
Alexander I, Tsar, 97
Alexander II, Tsar, 44
Alexander III, Tsar, 3, 4, 27, 44
Alexandra Fedorovna, Tsarina, 73, 75, 77, 82, 86-88, 103, 123, 125, 161
Alexandra (wife of Edward VII), 3, 25
Arcadi, Czolt, 277
d'Arcy, Martin, 275
Argutinsky-Dolgoruky, Prince Vladimir Nikolaevich, 11, 70, 79, 98-99, 214
Artsymovich, Mademoiselle, 86
Assumpta, Mother, 287
Assumption College, 233
d'Astorg, Bertrand, 216
Auden, W.H., 250
Auric, George, 168
d'Avila, Brother Victor-Antoine, 260, 285, 286-287

Badnaev, Dr., 82
Bakunin, Mikhail, 12-13, 46-47;
  daughter's criticism of Helene's biography of, 170-17
  Kerensky's criticism of Helene's biography of, 193-194
Bainville, Jacques, 30
Bakhmetev, Mr., 214
Ballets Russes, 70-71, 90, 99
Banquet, Dom Romain, 154-156
Baring, Maurice, 78
Barney, Natalie, 199-200
Barth, Marcus, 279
de Bassiano, Marguerite (nee Chaplin), xi, 166-167, 168, 170

Bea, Cardinal, 281
Beloselsky, Princess, 79
Benkendorf, Count (ambassador to London), 34, 37, 40
Benkendorf, Grand Marshal, 84
Bennet, Dr. John, 251
Berckheim, Mousie, 105
Berdiaev, Nicholas, xi, xv, 223, 232, 249, 253;
  and circle of intellectuals meeting with, 185-192, 207, 208
  and *Dream and Reality*, 184
  and Helene's letters to and from, 250-251, 252-253
  and Helene's translation of, 192-193
  and Ilya Fondaminsky, 206
  and invasion of France, 210
  philosophy of, 183-184
  and philosophy of Mounier, 185-187
Berdiaev, Lydia, 184, 190
Bergson, Henri, 179
Bertillon, Suzanne, 171
Bibesco, Marthe, 92, Princess, 93-94, 97, 135
Bishop, Claire Huchet, 257
Blok, Alexander, 53, 56
Bloy, Leon, 146-147, 184
Blum, Léon, 247
Bolshevik Party, 70
Bonne Société Protestante, 95
Boris, Grand Duke (Tsar's cousin), 21-22
du Bos, Charles, 176-177, 178, 181, 185, 242, 281
du Bos, Madeleine, 176
Boxer Rebellion, 18
de Brantes, Colonel Count François, 216-217
Brémond, Henri Abbé, 160

Breton, André, 245-246, 250
Bulgakov, Father Sergius, 206
Bunin, Ivan, 171
Burgi, Richard, 253-256, 266

"Cadets" (Constitutional-Democratic Party), 38
Cantacuzene, Princess, 79
Carré, Fr., 212, 214, 257
Carroll, Lewis, 14
de Castellane, Marquis Boni, 96
de Castellane, Countess Jean, 139, 141
Catherine the Great, 57
Catherine, Princess (Aunt Kitty, sister of N. Kudashev), 17-18
Catholic University, 239-240
Catholic Worker (publication), 187, 241, 265, 280;
  and Catholic Worker Farm; *see* Maryfarm
  civil disobedience activity of, 270
  community of, 249, 260, 286-287
  Helene's activity with, 268-269
  Helene's first visit to, 234-235
Chandler, Mrs. Porter (Bebo), 250, 257-258
Chekov, 61, 120
de Chevigné, Countess Laure, 91-92
Christian IX of Denmark, 3, 25, 26
"Circle," 207-210
Cocteau, Jean, 179
Commerce, 165-168, 170
Commonweal, 186, 232, 243, 250
Couturier, Fr., 232, 246, 247
Cronier, Mother Abbess Marie, 150-154, 155, 156, 157
Council of State, 42, 48, 124

Danielou, Fr. Jean, xv, 187, 257, 275
Dantes, Baron, 141-142
Dantes, George, 141
Davies, Fr. Thurston, 254, 256
Day, Dorothy, 181, 187, 285, 286, 287;
  and anti-war activity, 248, 269-271
  and Brother Victor d'Avila, 260
  and Catholic Worker group, 271-272, 276
  and Christian community living, 249
  and Helene, 234-235, 264, 268, 280, 283, 285-286
  and *Third Hour*, 257, 268, 275

"Decembrists," 46, 47, 133
Demidov, Elim, 11, 15
Diaghilev, Serge, 70-71, 90, 99
Dillon, Dr. (journalist), 71
Dimitri (Helene's early friend), 56-59, 110
Dimitriev, Captain, 125
Dior, Christian, 171
Dostoevsky, Fedor, xi, 155, 170, 178, 184, 188, 191, 195, 235, 252, 255, 267, 283, 286
Doumic, René, 96
Dourgne, Abbey of, 149-157
Dufy, Raoul, 168
Duma, 29, 37, 39, 40, 57, 124, 125
Duncan, Isadora, 140
Düss, Mother Benedict, 258, 259

ecumenism, xvi, xviii, 2, 69, 185, 209, 223, 249-251, 257-258, 278-279
Ecumenism, 268
Ecumenical Center, Duquesne University, 279
Edward VII, King (of England), 3, 25
Efron, Sergei, 174, 197, 198, 200-202, 205
Egan, Eileen, 286
Eichlin, Dr., 265
Elapin, Madame, 46
Elena Vladimirovna, Grand Duchess (wife of Nicholas of Greece), 163
Eliot, T. S., 199
Englert, Fr. 268
English, Jack (later, Fr. Charles), 265
Esprit, 181, 186-187, 189, 193, 212, 216, 219, 245, 247, 250, 268
Essenin, Sergei, 140-141
d'Estaing, Valéry Giscard, 132, 217
Evreinov, Monsignor Alexander, 159
Eustochie, Mother, 149-157, 159
Ewing, Fr. J. Franklin, 256, 266

Fargue, Leon-Paul, 167, 168-169
de Faucigny-Lucinge, Aymone, 132, 216-217
de Faucigny-Lucinge, Charlotte, 132
de Faucigny-Lucinge, Jean-Louis, 132, 142, 217
de Faucigny-Lucinge, Princess Natividad (Natty), 132, 142, 216
Fedorov, George, 191, 207, 223, 226, 249;
  Treatise of Russian Spirituality, 249

Fedorov, Helen, 223, 225-226
Fernandez, Ramon, 142
Filliger, John, 271
Flevitsky, George, 257, 264
Florovsky, Fr. George, 275
Fondaminsky, Ilya Bunakov (Ilyusha), 206-209, 232, 251
Fordham University, 237, 239, 253
de Foucauld, Charles, 147
France, Anatole, 124
Fremantle, Anne, 250, 273, 275, 286
Friendship House, 237-238
Fumet, Stanislaus, 180, 212

de Gabriac, Count, 96
Gagarin, Prince, 18, 23, 79
Gagarin, Nina, 18, 79
Gerschenson, Michael, 177-178
Gheon, Henri, 180
Gide, André, 170, 177
Gillet, Fr., 185
Gilson, Etienne, 185
Golitsyn, Anne, 163
Golitsyn, Princess Mary (Aunt Masha), 50, 63, 91, 104, 107
Golitsyn, Olga, (Helene's cousin), 63-64
Golitsyn, Prince Serge, (Helene's uncle's father-in-law), 50, 63
Goll, Yvan, 141
Gordon, Helen, 243
Goremykin, Ivan Logginovich, 37-38, 39, 40
Greaves, Alexandra, 227
Green, Julien, xvii, 246-247, 280
Grigorievna, Eudoxie, (Helene's paternal grandmother), 46-47
Gulkevitch, Ambassador, 31-32, 37
Guthrie, Fr., 267

Haakon I, King (of Norway), 27
"Haias," 214, 215, 221-222, 223, 229
Hall, Alexander, 213, 219-220
Hall, Vera (mother), 213, 219-220
Hanotaux, Gabriel, 96
Harris, Natalie, 146
Hennacy, Ammon, 270-271
Herrick, Myron, 107, 111
Hitler, Adolf, 100, 133, 187, 205, 206, 208, 231, 232, 247
Hoguet, Robert, 232
Hopko, Fr., 286
Hôpital Russe, xi, 113-114, 115-121, 150, 199

House of Hospitality, 241, 249, 257
de Hueck, Catherine (Mrs. Eddie Doherty), 241-242, 276
Hughes, Marge, 272
Husserl, Edmund, 212

Ignatiev, Count, 114-115
"Irenic Movement," 268
Iswolsky, Alexander (Helene's father), as ambassador to France, xiii, 65-66, 68, 90
  and life in Paris, 93-94, 96-97
  and anti-Semitism, 214
  in Biarritz, xiv, 130-131
  as diplomat to Denmark, xiii, 3-5, 25-26
  early years, 2, 47
  death of, 134-135
  family life, 15, 19, 58-59, 62, 70, 72, 73
  as Foreign Minister, xiii, 29-34, 37-41, 54, 65
  liberal views and reform activity, 29, 32, 37-39, 40, 51, 67, 87
  as minister to Bavaria, xiii, 6
  as minister to Japan, xiii, 6, 9, 12, 16, 18, 21, 23, 25
  and Russo-Japanese conflict, 15, 18, 25, 27
  and Protestantism, 145-146
  and Russian Revolution, 124-126, 129-131
  as Vatican envoy, 2-3
Iswolsky, family, coat of arms of, xxii
Iswolsky, Gregory (Grisha, Helene's brother),
  in America, 137, 142, 229-230, 233, 235, 238
  in Biarritz, 134, 136
  in Copenhagen, 26-28
  death, 263-264
  early years, 6, 9, 15, 25, 40
  in the French Foreign Legion, 108, 110, 114, 118
  at Golum estate, 64
  in Hôpital Russe, 118-119
  marriage to Princess N. de Faucigny-Lucinge (Natty), xiii, 132, 134
  marriage to Mashenka, 137
  in Paris, 73, 80, 122, 211
  in Petersburg, 30, 54, 55, 56, 57, 59
  and Proust, 143-144

as student, 33, 34, 35, 41, 54, 66, 67,
in Tokyo, 17, 19, 20
trip to America, 214-215, 221-223, 225
trip to Germany, 103, 105
Iswolsky, Helene, xiii-xiv
  in Biarritz, 130-133, 139, 140
  with Benedictines, 149-157, 258-261
  and Berdiaev, 185-187
  and flight to Bordeaux, 111-112
  in Cold Spring, NY, 285-287
  in Copenhagen, 25-28
  and dancing school, 55-58
  death, 287
  and death of her brother, Grisha, 263-264
  as a debutant in Petersburg, 73, 74, 77-86
  at Dikana estate, 99-101, 103
  and Dimitri, 56-59
  and Dorothy Day, 234-235, 264, 268, 280, 283, 285-287
  early writing career, 140-142
  family origins and ancestors, 1-5
  and Father's estate, 138-139
  and Fordham University, 237, 267
  at the Russian Institute, 254-256, 266
  at Golum estate, 63-64, 65, 103-104
  and *Hôpital Russe*, xiii, 112, 120-121, 128
  interest in Catholicism, 117-118, 146-147
  interest and activity in ecumenism, xvi-xix, 2, 69, 209, 223
  in New York, 249-250, 278-279
  and Third Hour, 251, 257-258, 268, 275, 278-279
  and Orthodox-Catholic unity, xviii-xix, 157, 159, 237, 240
  injuries of, 58, 264-265
  and the invasion of France, 1939, 210-213
  journey to Tokyo, 9-16
  and Kerensky in Paris, 193-196
  at La Chère Villa, 29, 59
  on lecture tour in America, 239-242
  and Lieutenant B., 131-132
  and literary groups in Paris during 1920s, 164-172, 174-178, 180-181
  and Maria Tsvetaeva, 196-203

  in New York, 226-227, 229-230, 265
  and Orthodox liturgy, 68-69
  in Paris, 66, 70, 89-91, 93, 97-99
    during World War I, 105-107, 121-122
  and Paris circle of friends, 142-145
  in Pau, 145, 148
  in Petersburg, 30, 40, 42, 44-45, 53-55, 59
  and philosophical groups in Paris in 1930s, 183-184, 188-192
  and Russian emigres in Paris, 206
  at Saint Scholastica, 149-157
  at Seton Hill College, 277-278, 283
  as student, 67, 71, 133-134
  in Tokyo, 18-19
  and trip to America, 213-226
  and trips to Europe, 280-283
  and trip to Lipetzy estate, 59-61
  and Tsarina, 86-88
  as writer, 160-165
    American Saints and Heroes, 273-274
    Christ in Russia, xi, 278
    Life of Bakunin, 170-171, 193
    Light before Dusk, 232-233, 258, 277
    Soul of Russia, 239, 242
    Soviet Man, 181, 187, 233-234
    Three Blind Kings, 162-163, 193
  at the United Nations, 272-273
  and the Voice of America, 243, 245-248
Iswolsky, George (Helene's uncle), 5
Iswolsky, Marguerite (Helene's mother), xiii-xiv;
  in America, 227, 229, 233, 235
  in Biarritz, 130-131
  concern over Grisha, 137-138
  in Copenhagen, 25, 28, 29
  death, 235-236
  early years, 4, 5
  and *Hôpital Russe*, 112-113
  and husband's death, 135, 137
  journey to Tokyo, 9
  leaving France, 210-213
  marriage to Alexander Iswolsky, 3, 5
  in Paris, 65-66, 69, 90, 94-96, 98, 172
  in Pau, 145, 146, 148, 164, 172
  in Petersburg, 33, 42, 44, 58
  in Petersburg, 33, 42, 44, 58

for daughter's debut, 76-77, 81, 86-87
as a Protestant, 68, 95, 135
in Tokyo, 20
trip to America, 213-216, 218, 220-226
Iswolsky, Peter Alexandrovich (Helene's paternal grandfather), 1, 12, 46-47, 59
Iswolsky, Peter Petrovich (Helene's uncle), 48-51, 62, 63, 138, 139
Iswolsky, Peter (Helene's cousin) and family, 225
Iswolsky, Sergei and family, 212, 219, 225
Iswolsky, Vassily Dimitrievich, 1
Ivan III, Tsar, 1
Ivanov, Dimitri, 281
Ivanov, Venceslav, 177-178, 281

Jacobson, Dr. Roman, 255
Jaskievitch, Fr. Walter, 267, 269
Jews, 35, 44, 69, 100, 121, 208, 214
Jocists, 219
Jocist movement, 240
John XXIII (Pope), 155, 277, 278, 281
Joffre, Général, 115
Journal of Ecumenical Studies, 280
Joyce, James, 199

Kassatkin, Nicholas Vladyka, 21
Kerensky, Alexander Fedorovich, xv, 210, 213-214;
  and Helene in Paris, 193-196
  and Helene in New York, 226-227, 231, 238, 265, 266
  and Provisional Government, 38, 129
  and Theresa (wife), 238
Kernan, Julie, 232, 234, 236, 239
Kessel, Joseph, 160-162, 174
Klossovska, Maria, 165
Kochubey, Prince Victor, 99-101;
  and Princess Ella (wife of), 79, 100
  and Tatara (son of), 100
Komarov, Sasha, 149
Komarov, Mother Eustochie & M. Paule, 149-158
Konovalov, Alexander, 214, 219-220, 222-223, 225-226
Koriakov, Michail, 256
Korsakoff, Rimsky, 149
Kovarsky, Dr., 213

Knudson, Martha, 230
Kudashev, Prince Ivan, 184
Kudashev, Prince John (Uncle Vania), 3, 110, 138, 145, 147, 148, 164
Kudashev, Prince Nicholas, 17
Kulmann, Dr. Oscar, 251
Küng, Hans, 279
Kutepov, General P.A., 175
Kuprin, Alexander, 171
Kuzmich, Fedor, 97-98

La Chère Villa, 29, 59, 103
Lambert, Fr. Bernard, 268, 275
Lamsdorf, Count, 18, 29, 32
Landsberg (German philosopher), 212
Langkyaer, Marguerite, 227, 273
Lazareff, Pierre, 176, 243, 247
Le Bon, Gustave, 96-97
Leo XIV (Pope), 2, 6
Leontiev, Constantine, 193
Lenin, Vladimir Ilyich, 70, 109, 129, 130, 133, 193, 195, 207
Lialine, Clement, 275
Litvin, Felia, 128
Louise, Queen (of Denmark), 3, 25, 26
Lourié, Arthur, 210, 232, 265, 275
Lynch, Fr., 264

MacLeish, Archibald, 168
MacMahon, Monsignor, 233
Madeleva, Sr., 236, 241-242
Madonna House, 242, 276, 278
Magner, Fr. James, 240
Mailleux, Fr. Paul, 209, 273-275
Makinsky, Prince, 222, 223, 229
Maklakov, Basil, 130
Malraux, André, 177
Mandelstam, Ossip, 48, 53, 165, 166
de Manziarly, Irma, 223, 249
Marcel, Gabriel, 180, 185
Maria Fedorovna, Tsarina (dowager Empress), 3-4, 25, 26, 27, 29, 42, 83, 84, 85, 88, 97, 106, 112
Marie-Aline, Mother, 258, 287
Maritain, Jacques, xi, xv, 146, 147, 205, 210, 223, 246, 247;
  as author of *True Humanisn*, 180, 189
  and Berdiaev, 183-185
  and circle of, 180-182, 183, 185, 189

and Helene, 178, 232-233
and Jean Cocteau, 178-179
philosophy of, 180
and Raissa (wife of), 179, 180, 183, 210, 232
de Martel, Dr. Thierry, 116, 265
Maryfarm (later Peter Maurin Farm), 249, 268, 276, 283
Mashenka (also Princess Lieven; second wife of Grisha), 137, 211, 218
Massignon, Henri, 185
Masson, Frederich, 96, 97
Match, 176, 243
Mauriac, François, 180
Maurin, Peter, 182, 187, 234-235, 249, 268, 271-272, 276
Maximov, Sergei, 256
Maybury, Miss (governess), 54, 58, 59, 62, 67, 71-72
Meyendorf, Fr. John, 286
Meyer, Joseph, 116-117, 119
Mikhail Alexandrovich, Grand Duke, 125
Mills, John, 286
Milukov, Paul, 124, 129, 130
Minihan, Michael, 267, 286
Mirsky, Prince Dimitri Sviatopolk, 80-81, 166, 167, 174, 198, 200, 202
Mochulsky, Constantine, 191, 250, 251, 252, 253, 267, 286
Mounier, Emmanuel, xi, 180, 216, 223, 232, 249, 250;
and *Esprit*, 186-187, 189
philosophy of, 185-187
Mowrer, Deane, 270-271
Mudd, Margaret, 286
Mugnier, Abbé, 92, 93, 94, 132, 135, 136, 142
Mukhanova, Miss Nadezhda Vladimirovna, 10, 11, 15, 16, 19, 20, 21, 25, 26, 27, 28
Murphy, Josephine Ryan, 236, 239, 240

Nabokov, Vladimir, 207, 209
Nelidov, Mr. (ambassador), 34
Nesselrode, Count, 108
Nikolai Mikhailovich, Grand Duke, 68, 97-98
Nicholas Nicholaevich, Grand Duke, 123
Nicholas I, Tsar, 4, 25, 46, 133

Nicholas II, Tsar, 43, 68, 79, 86, 135, 161;
and Alexander Iswolsky, 26, 29, 33, 37, 42, 47;
reports to Tsar, 1905, 33, 37
meeting with Tsar, 1905, 38-39
meeting with Tsar and Poincare, 1914, 103-104
and Alexandra (Tsarina), 82, 161
appearance at Helene's debut, 83-85
coronation of, 46
and Count Pahlen, 44
and daughters (Olga and Tatiana), 83, 84, 85
and events of 1916-1917, xiv, 123-126
and sisters (Olga and Xenia), 84
and son (Alexis), 82, 86, 125, 126
as Tsarevitch, meeting with Marguerite Iswolsky, 4
Nicholson, Sir Arthur, 40
Nikolaevna, Elena, 227
Nikon, Fr. See Strandtmann, Nicholas
Niebuhr, Reinhold, 275
de Noailles, Comtesse Anne, 143
Nostitz, General Count, 77
Nouvelle Revue Française, 142, 170

O'Donnel, Jane, 265
Obolensky, Alexander, 257, 264, 286
Obolensky's, family of, 79
Octobrists, 38, 49
Oesterreicher, Monsignor John, 257
Orloff, Prince Vladimir and Princess Olga, 79
Osnobishin, Colonel, 115
Our Lady of Resurrection Monastery, 285, 286

Paléologue, Maurice, 83, 103, 125
Paléologos, Sophia, 1
Pahlen, Count Constantine Ivanovich (Uncle Constantine), 43-45, 46, 108
and Helena Karlovna (wife of), 45
Pahlen, Marussia, 44-45, 64
Pahlen, Count Peter, 31, 37, 46, 47
Paklevsky, Mr., 16
Paris society in 1920s, 89-101
Paris-Soir (later *France-Soir*), 243, 248
Pasternak, Boris, 11, 165, 166, 174, 196, 198, 201, 203, 275

Pastré, Countess, 139
Patrick, Br., 285-286, 287
Paul Alexandrovich, Grand Duke, 68
Paulding, Governor, 186, 232, 250
Péguy, Charles, 117-118, 147, 150, 251
Pernicone, Bishop Joseph, 287
Perse, Saint John, 166, 167, 168
personalism, 185-186
Peter (the Great of Russia), 39, 99
Petersburg University, 48-49, 66
Piovesana, Fr. Gino, 286
Pistolkors, Countess (later Princess Paley), 68
Pobedonostsev, 44, 48, 50
Poklevsky-Kozell, Mr., 17
de Polignac, Princess Winnie (Mrs. Singer), 143
Poincaré, Raymond (president of France), 103, 104, 118, 119, 125, 127, 130
Poplavsky, Boris, 206-207
Potemkin, Prince, 57
Poulenc, François, 168
Povolotsky, Jacob, 120, 141
de Pourtalès, Countess Mélanie, 95
Présence, 216
Prévost, Marcel, 141, 162
Prokofiev, Sergei, 168
Proust, Marcel, 91, 92, 97, 122, 143, 144, 145, 149, 170, 199
Provisional Government, 38, 126, 129, 133, 193, 195
Purishkevich Vladimir Mitrofanovich, 125
Pushkin, Alexander, 53, 99, 141
Put', 191, 192
Putz, Fr., 240

Quersaint, Marguerite, 164, 167, 175

Rasputin, Gregory, 51, 82-85, 88, 91, 95, 97, 123-124, 135, 161-162
Ravel, Maurice, 168
Reed Farm, 229-231, 232, 236, 238
Reinach, Joseph, 96, 132, 133
Regina Laudis, Abbey of, 259, 287
Religious-Philosophical Academy, 191
Renaud, Mr., 211
Revelstoke, Lord, 78
Revolution of 1905, 28-29, 37, 48-49
La Revue des Deux Mondes, 141

Revue de France, 141
Revue des Jeunes, 212
Rheinhold, Fr. Hans, 279, 280
Rilke, Rainer Maria, 18, 165, 167
Rivière, Jacques, 142
Rogosh, Fr. Andrew, 237
Rops, Daniel, 187
Rosary College, 240
de Rougement, Denis, 247, 249
Rubinstein, Ida, 113, 199
Rudnev, Vera, 213-214, 219, 222, 224-226, 229;
   and Vadim (husband of), 213
"Russian Brigades," 127-128
Russian Christian Student Movement, 191
Russian Institute, Fordham University (later Institute of Contemporary Russian Studies), 254, 255-256, 263, 269, 273, 275
"Russian Montparnasse" (later Paris School of Russian Authors), 206-207. See "Circle."
Russian Revolution, 125-130, 133
Russians in Paris, 172, 173
Russo-Japanese War, 27
Ryan, Fr. William, 277, 278

de Saint Chamant, Jean, 210-211
Saint Scholastica, 149-159, 177, 259, 260
Saint Mary's College, 236, 241
Sartre, Jean-Paul, 169, 250-251
Sasha, 149
Sava, Bishop, 230
de Sauvigny, Count Jean Bertier, 147-148
Saxe-Altenburg, Princess Helen (Helene's godmother), 9, 75-76
Sazonav, S. D., 31, 32, 95, 103, 124
Schmemann, Fr. Alexander, 258, 279
Schmidt, Sr. Thecla, 277, 278
Scott, Michael, 275
Seary, Miss, 236, 238-239, 242, 250, 257, 265
de Segonzac, Dunoyer, 168
Seton Hill College, 277-278
Shakhovsky, Rev. John, 250, 275
Sharpe, Ambassador, 107
Shavelsk, George, 123
Sheed, Frank, 233, 238, 248;
   and Maisie Ward (wife of), 233
Sheen, Bishop Fulton, 233

Sheil, Bishop, 241
Shestov, Leo, 191, 192
Sheremetev, Count, 86
Shimadzu, the Princes, 19
Shirinsky-Shikhmatov, Yuri, 188-189
Shuvalov, Countess Elizabeth, 78
Simonov, Constantine, 233, 234
Simpson, Helen, 227, 236, 265, 266
de Sinçay, Marie-Louise (*nee* Logan), 144-145
Sviatopolk-Mirsky, Dimitri, See Mirsky.
Skobtsova, Mother Mary, 191, 207, 208-209, 251
Socialist Revolutionary Party, 207
Sokolov, Fr., 128
Soloviev, Vladimir, 155, 178, 184, 191, 248, 282
Solzhenitsyn, Alexander, 110, 123
Smirnov, Fr. J., 126
Smith, Dr. Alvyne, 279
Stalin, Jozef, 187, 202, 203, 205, 231
Stein, Gertrude, 199
Stolypin, Peter Arkadevich, xiv, 38, 41, 48, 53
Strandtmann, Nicholas (Uncle Kodosha, later Father Nikon), 22-23
Stravinsky, Igor, 168
Stürmer, Borish Vladimirovich, 124
de Suza, Fr. Jerôme, 257, 273
Swidler, Dr. Leonard, 279, 280

Tannenberg, battle of, 59, 81, 110
Tarasevich, Fr. Chrysostom (Vladimir), 241, 267
Tavard, Fr. George, 257, 275, 279
Tchaikovsky, Modeste, 62
Teilhard de Chardin, Pierre, 164-165, 180
Temps Présent, 219
Tereshchenko, Mr., 129, 130
Terry, Emilio, 142
Third Hour, xvi-xvii, 251, 252, 257, 267, 268, 269, 273, 275, 277, 278, 279, 285, 286;
 and associates, 209, 251, 274, 275
Thomas Aquinas, Sr., 240
Timashev, Professor, 231
Tisserant, Eugene Cardinal, 256, 281
Tjader, Marguerite, 281-282, 287
Toll, Count (Helene's maternal grandfather), 3-4

Toll, Helen (*nee* Strandtmann), 3-4, 28, 47, 76
Toll, Marguerite. *See* Iswolsky, Marguerite
Toll, Olga, 3, 17, 139
Tolstoy, Alexis, 171
Tolstoy, Alexandra, 229-230, 233, 235, 238;
 and the Tolstoy Foundation, 229
Tolstoy, Leo, 1, 4, 40, 51, 59, 77, 79, 81, 105, 107, 171, 184, 188, 229, 230, 255;
 as author of *War and Peace*, 4, 40, 54, 77, 229
 as author of *Anna Karenina*, 105
Trubetzkoy, Prince, 68, 79
Trubetzkoy, Princess, 46, 79
Tsvetaeva, Marina, 172-174, 196-203, 205
 and Mur (son), 174, 197, 202, 203
 and Alya (daughter), 197-198, 201, 202, 203
Trubnikov, Alexander, 107
Tunnesen, Hans, 271
Turgenev, Ivan, 47, 59, 60, 155
Tyrrell, Lord, 160

Urusov, Prince, 34

Valéry, Paul, 160, 166-167, 168, 170, 199
Van der Meer, Pierre, 181
Vanetti, Dolores, 247
Vanovsky, Colonel, 18
Varshavsky, Vladimir, 210
Vasnetsov, 58
Vassar College, 252
Vatican, 268;
 and agreement with Russia, 6
Vatican II (council), 155, 258, 277, 278
Vigile, 178
Vishnevsky, Stanley, 272
Vitaly, Olga Petrovna, 59, 61, 62
Viviani, René, 103-104
Voice of America, xi, 243, 245-247, 249, 251, 280
Voillaume, Fr., 257
von Schenk, Pastor, 258, 275
Vtorov, 13, 25
Vyrubova, Mrs., 82

Waldemar, Prince, 4, 26
Wales, Arthur, 168

Wallace, Sir Donald McKensie, 40
Weiler, Lazare, 119, 133
Wendland, Archbishop John, 274
Wilhelm, Kaiser (of Germany), 15, 25
Willebrands, Bishop, 281
Winzen, Fr. Damasus, 259
Wolkonsky, Prince Serge, 46, 81
Wolkonsky, Catherine, 252
World Council of Churches, 258
World War I,
   outbreak of, 101, 104
   early war developments, 105, 109-111
   effects of war on Paris, 110
   Russian residents in Paris during, 106
   Russo-German conflict, 123
World War II,
   outbreak of, 210
   invasion of France, 211
   Vichy government in France, 211, 218
   Germany's invasion of Russia, 231, events of 1941, 235
   D-Day, 247
   Hiroshima and Nagasaki, 248
Wright, Bishop (of Pittsburgh), 279

Yanovsky, Basil, 208, 249, 275, 286
Young, Fr. Lyle, 286
youth in Paris in 1930s, 206-208
Yusupov, Prince Felix, 86, 125, 161
   and Irina Alexandrovna (wife of), 86, 161

Z., Count, 54-55
Z., Fr., 219
Zadkine, Ossip, 120-121